The Idaho
Political Field Guide
2014

Map: From U.S. Census

The IDAHO
POLITICAL
FIELD GUIDE

2014

Randy Stapilus
Marty Trillhaase

RIDENBAUGH PRESS
Carlton, Oregon

Composition and editing by Ridenbaugh Press, Carlton, Oregon.
Cover design by Randy Stapilus.
Cover photo by Jake Putnam.

Library of Congress Cataloging-in-Publication Data:

Stapilus, Randy; Trillhaase, Marty
      The Idaho Political Field Guide 2014
      Includes bibliographical references
      ISBN 978-0-945648-16-1
      1. Idaho. 2. Politics 3. Geography 4. Government-Public Policy. I. Title.

Printed in the United States of America.

February 2014

10 9 8 7 6 5 4 3 2 1

Contents

Acknowledging

Lots of people helped with putting all this together. Some of them helped with gathering the statistics, some helping with providing an understanding of what they mean, some with helping point to other useful directions.

As always, the Idaho Secretary of State's office was highly helpful (from individual assistance to its fine online resources), and county clerk's offices from one end of the state to the other helped a great deal in providing information and, within the limits of their professional responsibilities, helping me make sense of it.

Everyone who has helped me get a better grasp of Idaho politics over the years and especially recently – really, a list too long for this space – is hereby thanked.

And of course, Linda Watkins at Ridenbaugh Press.

Introduction

The first edition of the *Idaho Political Almanac*, from Ridenbaugh Press, came out in 1990 – now 22 years ago. It was intended then as an update and expansion on the Idaho history *Paradox Politics*, which had come out two years before. Almanacs continued for a while, every two years through 1996. In 1998 we tried a different approach, the Idaho Yearbook/Directory, intended to be an annual publication covering of the same material and more besides. We continued it through 1991, but it began to be a lot of work. After a couple subsidiary projects in early 2002, on influential Idaho people and organizations, we called a halt.

Two years ago we returned with the *Idaho Political Field Guide*, for a few reasons. One is that with the passage of a decade, the time seems right for a look back and a prospective look ahead. Another is technology: The availability of printing on demand, as opposed to printing in large quantities at once, makes it possible to keep these books precisely up to date without accumulating boxes of outdated editions.

In this edition I've gotten excellent help from Marty Trillhaase, the editorial page editor of the *Lewiston Tribune* and a journalist who has been observing and writing about Idaho politics for close to 40 years. His knowledge and understanding of the state and its politics are woven throughout the pages ahead.

Randy Stapilus
Carlton, Oregon
January 2014

Federal

President

Idaho's reputation as a solidly Republican state begins with its votes for president. Not only has no Democrat won the state's electoral votes for president since 1964, but it barely happened even in that national Democratic landslide, and it was the last time (to date) any Democrat for president has received even as much as 38% of the vote. Republicans have not always been of landslide levels in those years (see George H.W. Bush in 1992), but the usual reason for lower levels has been third-party candidacies.

Idaho, admitted to the union under presumption it would be a Republican state, in the administration of Republican Benjamin Harrison, ironically voted against him in its first presidential election, instead backing Populist James Weaver. (The Democrat, Grover Cleveland, who won nationally that year, wasn't on the Idaho ballot.) Idaho voted quirkily for president in its first half-century. On monetary/silver issues, Idaho went Democratic in the next two elections, then backed Republicans Theodore Roosevelt and William Taft in their 1904 and 1908 landslides, then supported Democrat Woodrow Wilson (over those two) in 1912, and again in 1916. After supporting Republicans Warren Harding, Calvin Coolidge and Herbert Hoover in the 20s, the state shifted decisively, supporting Democrat Franklin Roosevelt in his four elections and Democrat Harry Truman in in 1948. Since then, only Johnson has broken the string of Republican presidential wins in Idaho.

There were two closer Republican wins, in 1992 and 1996. That was not because the Democratic nominee, Bill Clinton, was popular in Idaho; he decidedly was not. (He pulled smaller vote percentages in Idaho than 1988 nominee Michael Dukakis had.) But independent Ross Perot did catch fire in Idaho, drawing conservative and centrist votes and diminishing totals from Republicans George Bush and Robert Dole. Absent a major third party, Republican percentages rose again to landslide levels in 2000, 2004 and 2008.

In 2012 Republicans as well as Democrats held caucuses in Idaho to select national convention delegates (who would vote directly on nominations), and both parties held them early in the nomination cycle. As a result several 2012 Republican presidential candidates campaigned in Idaho, including Mitt Romney and Ron Paul. Paul eventually did well in most of the northern Idaho counties, but Romney swept the southern counties (many of which have a strong LDS population).

	Democrat			Republican		
2012	**Barack Obama**	**212,787**	**32.62%**	**Mitt Romney**	**420,911**	**64.53%**
2008	Barack Obama	236,440	36.10%	John McCain	403,012	61.50%
2004	John Kerry	181,098	30.26%	George W Bush	409,235	68.38%
2000	Al Gore	138,637	27.64%	George W Bush	336,937	67.17%

1996	Bill Clinton	165,443	33.65%	Robert Dole	256,595	52.18%
1992	Bill Clinton	137,013	28.42%	George Bush	202,645	42.03%
1988	Michael Dukakis	147,272	36.01%	George Bush	253,881	62.08%
1984	Walter Mondale	108,510	26.39%	Ronald Reagan	297,523	72.36%
1980	Jimmy Carter	110,192	25.19%	Ronald Reagan	290,699	66.46%
1976	Jimmy Carter	126,549	37.12%	Gerald Ford	204,151	59.88%
1972	George McGovern	80,826	26.04%	Richard Nixon	199,384	64.24%
1968	Hubert Humphrey	89,273	30.66%	Richard Nixon	165,369	56.79%
1964	Lyndon Johnson	148,920	50.92%	Barry Goldwater	143,557	49.08%
1960	John Kennedy	138,853	46.22%	Richard Nixon	161,597	53.78%

Counties. A look at the split of counties won by the contenders best focuses on those won by Democrats – the shorter list.

■ 2012 – Blaine, Latah.

■ 2008 – Blaine, Latah, Teton.

■ 2004 – Blaine.

■ 2000 – Blaine.

■ 1996 – Blaine, Latah, Nez Perce, Shoshone.

■ 1992 – Benewah, Blaine, Bonner, Clearwater, Latah, Lewis, Nez Perce, Shoshone.

■ 1988 – Clearwater, Latah, Lewis, Nez Perce, Shoshone.

■ 1984 – none.

■ 1980 – none.

■ 1976 - Clearwater, Latah, Lewis, Nez Perce.

■ 1972 – none.

■ 1968 – Benewah, Clearwater, Lewis, Nez Perce, Shoshone.

■ 1964 – Adams, Bannock, Bear Lake, Benewah, Blaine, Boise, Bonner, Boundary, Butte, Caribou, Clearwater, Elmore, Fremont, Gem, Idaho, Kootenai, Latah, Lewis, Nez Perce, Power, Shoshone, Valley, Washington.

■ 1960 – Bannock, Benewah, Blaine, Bonner, Boundary, Butte, Camas, Clearwater, Custer, Elmore, Idaho, Kootenai, Lewis, Nez Perce, Shoshone.

In five of the last 10 presidential elections in Idaho, Republicans have won 43 or 44 of the state's 44 counties.

On the presidential level, the strongest Democratic/weakest Republican county in recent cycles has been Blaine, though only since the 90s.

Precincts (2012 presidential).

County	Precinct	Obama-D	Obama %	Romney-R	Romney %
Bingham	Fort Hall 20	565	88.70%	65	10.20%
Ada	1914	799	77.50%	174	16.88%
Nez Perce	Lapwai 26	501	76.49%	144	21.98%
Ada	1911	907	75.65%	244	20.35%
Ada	1912	760	74.95%	210	20.71%
Ada	1913	898	74.71%	261	21.71%
Blaine	009 SW Hailey	460	72.21%	161	25.27%
Ada	1915	771	69.77%	283	25.61%
Blaine	007 NW Hailey	511	69.71%	198	27.01%

Bannock	Chubbuck 60	393	69.68%	148	26.24%
Ada	1919	968	69.44%	371	26.61%
Ada	1908	603	68.99%	232	26.54%
Owyhee	11 Riddle	46	68.66%	20	29.85%
Ada	1606	701	67.15%	295	28.26%
Ada	1909	898	66.82%	397	29.54%
Blaine	008 NE Hailey	466	66.67%	213	30.47%
Ada	1917	563	66.31%	246	28.98%
Ada	1910	1,198	66.04%	537	29.60%
Blaine	004 S Ketchum	626	65.41%	311	32.50%
Blaine	003 N Ketchum	546	64.62%	274	32.43%
Latah	Moscow 11	336	64.62%	145	27.88%
Ada	1918	1,157	64.60%	576	32.16%
Ada	1709	725	63.32%	349	30.48%
Latah	Moscow 8	370	63.14%	180	30.72%
Latah	Moscow 6	352	62.97%	172	30.77%
Blaine	001 N Blaine County	624	62.78%	344	34.61%
Blaine	011 SE Woodside	397	62.62%	218	34.38%
Ada	1605	751	62.43%	392	32.59%
Blaine	010 NW Woodside	323	61.52%	185	35.24%
Ada	1707	572	61.44%	313	33.62%
Latah	Moscow 16	325	61.44%	143	27.03%
Custer	Stanley	73	61.34%	37	31.09%
Ada	1704	607	61.19%	318	32.06%
Latah	Moscow 13	226	60.75%	132	35.48%
Ada	1808	762	60.43%	435	34.50%
Ada	1916	515	60.30%	292	34.19%
Latah	Moscow 15	267	59.87%	156	34.98%
Ada	1711	526	59.57%	283	32.05%
Ada	1708	712	59.28%	435	36.22%
Latah	Moscow 14	272	59.26%	138	30.07%
Latah	Moscow 9	295	59.12%	188	37.68%
Ada	1920	420	58.74%	274	38.32%
Ada	1805	848	58.48%	537	37.03%
Ada	1905	607	58.42%	396	38.11%
Blaine	005 Quigley	502	58.10%	344	39.81%
Ada	1810	650	57.83%	448	39.86%
Ada	1604	705	57.65%	466	38.10%
Ada	1710	447	57.38%	284	36.46%
Ada	1603	1,064	57.05%	729	39.09%
Kootenai	59	187	57.01%	130	39.63%

Best precincts for Republican Romney, many of which are in rural areas. A variation: Many of his best precincts are in Madison County, very much a university as well as a farm area. But the difference in voting patterns shows the difference between the University of Idaho at Moscow and Brigham Young University-Idaho at Rexburg. Cassia and Franklin counties also were high performers for Romney.

Blaine	016 Yale	0	0.00%	9	100.00%
Caribou	Wayan	0	0.00%	30	100.00%
Caribou	Freedom	0	0.00%	51	100.00%
Lincoln	Kimama 6	0	0.00%	24	100.00%
Owyhee	05 Pleasant Valley	0	0.00%	56	100.00%
Cassia	112 Elba	1	1.04%	95	98.96%
Cassia	123 Sublett	1	2.56%	38	97.44%
Cassia	125 View	4	2.23%	173	96.65%
Franklin	Banida-Winder #6	3	2.56%	113	96.58%
Cassia	114 Heglar-Yale	3	3.45%	84	96.55%
Cassia	116 Malta	6	2.30%	251	96.17%

Butte	Howe	3	1.99%	145	96.03%
Franklin	Whitney #16	10	3.31%	290	96.03%
Franklin	Weston #15	13	3.25%	384	96.00%
Madison	1	7	2.49%	269	95.73%
Madison	15	25	3.69%	649	95.72%
Franklin	Mink Creek #12	6	4.55%	126	95.45%
Bear Lake	#5 Bennington	7	4.93%	135	95.07%
Madison	12	24	4.22%	540	94.90%
Franklin	Worm Creek #17	7	4.49%	148	94.87%
Madison	10	15	3.92%	363	94.78%
Oneida	Holbrook 6	3	5.36%	53	94.64%
Madison	9	52	4.78%	1,028	94.57%
Madison	17	11	4.98%	209	94.57%
Madison	13	25	4.30%	550	94.50%
Bannock	Swan Lake 68	3	5.56%	51	94.44%
Madison	4	17	5.01%	320	94.40%
Madison	3	45	5.28%	804	94.37%
Franklin	Dayton #8	12	3.77%	300	94.34%
Bear Lake	#10 Geneva/Pegram	4	4.71%	80	94.12%
Cassia	117 Oakley 1	11	5.39%	192	94.12%
Madison	8	40	5.17%	728	94.06%
Madison	11	23	4.85%	444	93.67%
Power	5	3	3.80%	74	93.67%
Franklin	Preston #2	19	4.48%	397	93.63%
Cassia	110 Bridge	1	2.13%	44	93.62%
Franklin	Clifton-Oxford #7	9	4.11%	205	93.61%
Bonneville	54	15	5.70%	246	93.54%
Fremont	2	22	5.05%	407	93.35%
Madison	6	47	5.82%	753	93.31%
Madison	14	32	5.43%	549	93.21%
Franklin	Preston #1	24	6.52%	343	93.21%
Madison	5	55	6.39%	802	93.15%
Jefferson	Lorenzo	15	6.88%	203	93.12%
Franklin	Preston #5	22	6.11%	335	93.06%
Madison	7	51	5.76%	824	93.00%
Franklin	Preston #3	20	5.62%	331	92.98%
Cassia	118 Oakley 2	17	5.21%	303	92.94%
Madison	18	42	6.54%	596	92.83%
Franklin	Fairview #9	23	6.65%	320	92.49%
Oneida	Malad 4	26	7.08%	339	92.37%
Caribou	Grace #2	18	6.64%	250	92.25%
Franklin	Thatcher-Cleveland #13	6	5.26%	105	92.11%
Jefferson	Hamer	18	7.63%	217	91.95%
Madison	Absentee	165	7.35%	2,062	91.85%
Madison	19	41	7.44%	506	91.83%
Bear Lake	#15 St. Charles	9	7.50%	110	91.67%
Oneida	Curlew 5	3	4.17%	66	91.67%
Franklin	Franklin #10	33	7.14%	423	91.56%
Bear Lake	#11 Georgetown	29	8.38%	316	91.33%
Bear Lake	#13 Paris	19	7.17%	242	91.32%
Latah	20 Farmington	2	8.70%	21	91.30%
Bear Lake	#7 Bloomington	9	7.14%	115	91.27%
Madison	2	50	6.34%	719	91.13%
Bingham	Rockford 12	39	7.29%	487	91.03%
Madison	16	65	8.10%	730	91.02%
Ada	2213	6	6.00%	91	91.00%
Adams	004 Bear	2	6.06%	30	90.91%
Franklin	Mapleton #11	14	6.11%	208	90.83%
Fremont	3	32	9.12%	318	90.60%
Jefferson	Labelle	45	8.49%	480	90.57%

Precincts (2008 presidential). Generally, as in many other cases, the best precincts for Democrats are among the most urban, the best for Republicans the most rural. The presidential contest requires some variation. Some of Democrat Obama's best precincts were in not only Boise but in the Wood River Valley, in the smaller-town (but urban-feeling) Ketchum and Hailey, and in the smallish Moscow (but in the university-influenced areas).

Note that Ada County completely overhauled its precinct list, changing many boundaries in the process, so strict comparison in that county between 2008 and 2012 is not possible.

Best precincts for Obama in 2008:

County	Precinct	McCain-R	Obama-D	McCain %	Obama %
Bingham	Fort Hall 20	90	464	16.13%	83.15%
Ada	39	210	1090	15.87%	82.39%
Ada	40	135	613	17.58%	79.82%
Blaine	001 NW Ketchum	83	338	19.26%	78.42%
Ada	77	219	859	19.87%	77.95%
Ada	37	248	924	20.70%	77.13%
Ada	59	323	1159	21.38%	76.70%
Blaine	006 Hailey #1	91	303	22.81%	75.94%
Blaine	002 SW Ketchum	127	438	21.97%	75.78%
Nez Perce	Lapwai 33	140	464	22.84%	75.69%
Blaine	004 S Ketchum	62	199	23.31%	74.81%
Ada	60	283	899	23.25%	73.87%
Ada	36	267	765	25.33%	72.58%
Blaine	007 Hailey #2	142	381	26.44%	70.95%
Ada	72	236	630	26.40%	70.47%
Ada	58	195	489	27.70%	69.46%
Ada	35	159	400	27.56%	69.32%
Blaine	Absentee	1346	3170	29.42%	69.29%
Ada	38	394	871	30.83%	68.15%
Owyhee	11 Riddle	16	36	30.19%	67.92%
Ada	41	463	1035	30.36%	67.87%
Ada	76	340	714	31.89%	66.98%
Latah	Moscow 16	165	371	29.78%	66.97%
Ada	73	380	769	32.65%	66.07%
Clearwater	7 Greer	12	25	31.58%	65.79%
Blaine	5 NE Blaine Co	94	186	32.87%	65.03%
Blaine	3 N&E Ketchum	52	102	33.12%	64.97%
Bannock	Chubbuck 60	180	352	33.21%	64.94%
Custer	011-Stanley	69	132	33.82%	64.71%
Latah	Moscow 1	128	251	32.82%	64.36%
Ada	70	237	456	33.38%	64.23%
Ada	85	454	870	33.21%	63.64%
Blaine	014 Hailey #4	261	474	34.94%	63.45%
Ada	86	330	624	33.47%	63.29%
Latah	Moscow 18	176	328	33.65%	62.72%
Latah	Moscow 6	175	337	32.47%	62.52%
Ada	75	324	621	32.30%	61.91%
Ada	84	315	546	35.71%	61.90%
Latah	Moscow 11	185	337	33.94%	61.83%
Ada	34	319	547	36.05%	61.81%
Ada	105	457	775	36.44%	61.80%
Blaine	008 Hailey #3	261	458	35.18%	61.73%
Latah	Absentee	1310	2168	37.03%	61.28%
Ada	87	588	983	36.43%	60.90%
Latah	Moscow 13	144	244	35.91%	60.85%
Latah	Moscow 15	230	389	35.94%	60.78%

Ada	33	536	893	36.31%	60.50%
Shoshone	2 Mullan	122	193	37.31%	59.02%
Latah	Moscow 14	193	310	35.87%	57.62%
Bonneville	57	3	0	25.00%	0.00%

Best precincts for Republican McCain, many in rural areas. A variation: Many of his best precincts are in Madison County, a university as well as a farm area. But that still shows the difference between the University of Idaho at Moscow and Brigham Young University-Idaho at Rexburg.

	County	Precinct	McCain-R	Obama-D	McCain %	Obama %
23	Owyhee	05 Pleasant Valley	63	1	98.44%	1.56%
27	Cassia	112 Elba	97	2	97.98%	2.02%
35	Butte	Howe	156	6	96.30%	3.70%
31	Caribou	Wayan	32	1	94.12%	2.94%
31	Caribou	Freedom	57	2	93.44%	3.28%
27	Cassia	125 View	149	7	93.13%	4.38%
27	Cassia	110 Bridge	38	2	92.68%	4.88%
31	Franklin	Banida-Winder #6	119	8	92.25%	6.20%
31	Bear Lake	#5 Bennington	145	10	91.77%	6.33%
27	Cassia	118 Oakley 2	282	20	90.97%	6.45%
34	Madison	11	178	16	90.82%	8.16%
34	Madison	19	478	44	90.70%	8.35%
27	Cassia	109 Almo	77	7	89.53%	8.14%
34	Madison	3	742	76	89.08%	9.12%
27	Power	5	88	11	88.89%	11.11%
34	Madison	15	811	82	88.83%	8.98%
35	Clark	#3	119	13	88.81%	9.70%
25	Lincoln	Kimama #6	23	2	88.46%	7.69%
27	Cassia	114 Heglar-Yale	69	6	88.46%	7.69%
27	Oneida	Holbrook 6	53	4	88.33%	6.67%
34	Madison	6	710	86	88.31%	10.70%
27	Cassia	116 Malta	211	12	88.28%	5.02%
23	Owyhee	12 Three Creek	15	2	88.24%	11.76%
34	Madison	13	127	15	88.19%	10.42%
21	Ada	125	44	4	88.00%	8.00%
31	Caribou	Bancroft	311	30	87.85%	8.47%
34	Fremont	4 Drummond/ Lamont/Squirrel	92	13	87.62%	12.38%
34	Madison	1	236	23	87.41%	8.52%
34	Madison	4	298	31	87.39%	9.09%
34	Fremont	7 Newdale	152	17	87.36%	9.77%
23	Owyhee	08 Oreana	103	10	87.29%	8.47%
27	Cassia	111 Declo	453	56	87.12%	10.77%
35	Jefferson	Annis	209	27	87.08%	11.25%
27	Oneida	Malad 4	314	38	86.98%	10.53%
22	Elmore	3-Chattin Flats	40	5	86.96%	10.87%
34	Madison	10	449	55	86.85%	10.64%
27	Cassia	123 Sublett	33	5	86.84%	13.16%
34	Madison	12	197	18	86.78%	7.93%
31	Bonneville	54	308	40	86.76%	11.27%
35	Jefferson	Hamer	188	24	86.64%	11.06%
27	Cassia	117 Oakley 1	206	26	86.55%	10.92%
31	Bear Lake	#11 Georgetown	293	38	86.18%	11.18%
34	Fremont	8 Parker	286	40	86.14%	12.05%
34	Fremont	5 Egin	397	52	86.12%	11.28%
27	Cassia	113 Grandview	254	37	86.10%	12.54%

31	Bonneville	59	396	49	86.09%	10.65%
27	Cassia	124 Unitv	377	52	86.07%	11.87%
31	Franklin	Clifton-Oxford #7	190	21	85.97%	9.50%
31	Franklin	Weston #15	336	37	85.93%	9.46%
31	Franklin	Preston #3	329	40	85.90%	10.44%

Senator Mike Crapo (right) at a tele-town hall. (photo/Office of Senator Crapo)

Senate-Senior: Mike Crapo (R)

Republican Mike Crapo set a benchmark in Idaho politics in 2004: He was the first U.S. Senator ever elected from the state unopposed on the ballot by another major party nominee. Nor was that on a technicality; he won more than 99% of the votes cast in the race.

This is more or less of a piece with Crapo's political history. He has never had anything resembling a close contest, and many of his elections, primary as well as general, have been unopposed.

The politics. An attorney from Idaho Falls whose brother Terry served in the Senate in the 70s, he was elected to the Idaho Senate in 1984 and re-elected twice – all three times without any ballot opposition. He was chosen assistant majority leader in 1986 and, with the defeat of then-Senate President pro tem Jim Risch in 1988, became pro tem for two terms.

When in 1992 Democrat Richard Stallings left his 2nd district U.S. House seat (to run for the Senate), Crapo filed for it, and faced opposition for the first time in both primary and general election. His primary opponent was Gary Glenn, a Republican right to work activist and later an Ada County commissioner; Crapo easily bested him with 67.9% of the vote. The general election, against Democratic state Auditor J.D. Williams, who had just been elected statewide, seemed more in doubt, but he won this too (in a very bad year for Idaho Democrats, the first of an eventual string) with 60.8%. His 1994 and 1996 re-elections were quiet landslides.

Crapo moved up again when in 1998 Republican Senator Dirk Kempthorne opted to run for governor instead. Unopposed in the primary, he faced in the general election Boise attorney (and former state Democratic Party leader) William Mauk. The campaign had some vigor, and the debates between the two could be called distinguished, but the outcome was not close. Crapo was the first Mormon elected to the U.S. Senate from Idaho, but no controversy surrounded that, and in-state he was not controversial on much else either. That and a large organizational and financial start, plus organizational weakness among Democrats, led to his unopposed record-set in 2004.

He did draw a Democratic opponent in 2010, in Teton County businessman Tom Sullivan. Sullivan waged one of the most energetic campaigns, and certainly the most sharp-tongued, that Crapo had faced. But he had little money or organization, and the sweeping Crapo win that fall did not surprise.

His seat is not up until 2016. He will be 65 at that general election.

The senator. Crapo is active in Banking and Finance issues, to the point that he has taken the unusual step (for an Idaho senator) of not seeking to join the appropriations committee, a move that has drawn editorial notice from his hometown newspaper, the Idaho Falls Post Register. He was an active figure in budget deficit reduction, working on the Simpson-Bowles negotiations and one of the members of the "Gang of Six." As such, he has drawn fire from Grover Norquist for at least flirting with the idea of additional tax revenues, although Crapo has been careful to avoid the phrase tax increase.

Crapo's most major Idaho-specific success story involves another area altogether. Drawing together elements from all sides of the natural resources debate, he helped push through the Owyhees Canyonland wilderness package and in north central Idaho, organized the Clearwater Basin Collaborative, which recently outlined a plan to both increase timber cut, wilderness acreage and wild and scenic river stream designations. At one point about 2009-2010, he suggested a similar move to resolve the stalemate over salmon recovery by suggesting regional talks with all options including dam breaching on the table.

Crapo is considered very conservative. National Journal rankings generally have placed him among the 10 most conservative U.S. senators. He has, however, reached across the aisle on a number of measures, so as co-sponsoring the Violence Against Women Act, a measure he had pushed for a number of years.

Controversy. Many years of avoiding controversy (other than on issue as such) ended in late 2012. The Lewiston *Tribune* said of him, "As a state senator, congressman and then senator, Crapo was Idaho's political Boy Scout, with a reputation so impeccably wholesome he was practically a nerd" But on Christmas Eve that year, he was stopped by police in Alexandria, Virginia, at 12:45 a.m., and ws booked for drunken driving." Crapo said that he had been unable to sleep. He pleased guilty on a charge of driving under the influence, and a court sentenced him to pay a $250 fine and undertake an alcohol safety program, a sentence normal in the area for first-time DUI offenders. The incident appeared to pass from general noticed after a few weeks.

In May 2013, the Associated Press reported that Crapo's campaign had submitted an amended finance report to reflect a $250,000 "investment loss" made in 2010 by campaign manager Jake Ball to an Idaho firm called Blueberry Guru LLC. The Crapo campaign said that "According to Gavin McCaleb, the managing member of the company that invested the loan, Blueberry Guru handed the funds over to a third-party venture that absconded with the money." Crapo was said not to have been personally involved.

The counties. Crapo won all 44 counties in 2010, in (of course) his unopposed election in 2004, and in his 1998 contest. Crapo lost two counties (Oneida and Power) in his 1992 U.S. House race, but those were the only county-level jurisdictions he has ever lost; he won all the 2nd district counties in 1994 and 1996.

The seat. The seat has some Idaho history attached: It was held for four terms by Democrat Frank Church, the only Democrat in Idaho history ever re-elected to the Senate. Before Kempthorne's one term starting in 1992, it was held for two terms by Republican Steve Symms, who had defeated Church. Before Church, it was held by Republican (and Joe McCarthy ally) Herman Welker, and the term before that by Democrat Glen Taylor. It's in considerable contrast to the other Senate seat, which has been in Republican hands continuously for much longer.

Sen	Democrat			Republican		
2010	Tom Sullivan	112,057	24.90%	Mike Crapo	319,953	71.20%
2004	-	-	-	Mike Crapo	499,796	99.20%
1998	Bill Mauk	107,375	28.40%	Mike Crapo	262,966	69.50%
1992	Richard Stallings	208,036	43.50%	Dirk Kempthorne	270,468	56.50%
1986	John Evans	185,066	48.40%	Steve Symms	196,958	51.60%
1980	Frank Church	214,439	48.78%	Steve Symms	218,701	49.74%

MICHAEL CRAPO, R-Idaho Falls

Office: http://crapo.senate.gov/
Campaign:
Background: Born, raised Idaho Falls. Attorney, Holden, Kidwell, Hahn & Crapo, 1979-1992. Attorney, Gibson, Dunn and Crutcher, 1978-1979. JD, Harvard University, 1977 BA, Political Science, Brigham Young University, 1973.
Political: Elected to Idaho Senate 1984, 1986, 1988, 1990. Elected Senate president pro tem, 1988, 1990. Elected to U.S. House 2nd district, 1992, 1994, 1996. Elected to U.S. Senate 1998, 2004, 2010.

Senator Risch, speaking on Syria policy. (image/video capture)

Senate-Junior: Jim Risch (R)

Jim Risch has been in electoral politics in Idaho longer than anyone else at a leading level, since 1972 as an Ada County county prosecutor and 1974 in the state senate. There have been a few losses along the way, but he has become one of the most successful political figures in Idaho history.

A forestry major from Wisconsin at the University of Idaho, he became an attorney. Moving to Boise, he went to work for the Ada County prosecutor's office, then learned that the prosecutor who had hired him was moving on; he won the prosecutor's job (amid considerable competition).

Political. Soon after, he founded a private law practice and won election to the Idaho Senate in 1974, rapidly moving up leadership – majority leader in 1978 (defeating future U.S. Senator Larry Craig), in 1982 president pro tem (unseating an incumbent, Reed Budge). A highly visible leader, he became a lightning rod and lost (in a heavily Republican legislative district) in 1988 to Democrat Mike Burkett. Risch was named by Batt to an open Senate seat in his old district. Opponents surfaced, but Risch won the next three sets of primary and general elections in landslides, and returned to Senate leadership, assistant majority leader leader in 1995 and majority leader in 1996. In 2000, after the death of President pro tem Jerry Twiggs, he ran for that office again, but lost to Robert Geddes, R-Soda Springs.

Risch had sought the office of lieutenant governor when the incumbent there, C.L. "Butch" Otter, left in early 2001 for the 1st District U.S. House seat. Governor Dirk Kempthorne instead appointed another senator, Jack Riggs, to the post. In 2002 Risch became one of four candidates (with Riggs, Celia Gould and Larry Eastland) in a close election, and emerged first, winning with 34.6%. That fall, against Democrat Bruce Perry, he won decisively with 58.3%.

When Kempthorne was named interior secretary in the Bush Administration in mid-2006, Risch served as governor for about seven months, even while filing for re-election as lieutenant governor. It could have been but was not a caretaker governorship; Risch's short tenure was widely regarded as notably energetic and impactful despite its brevity.

In 2007 Senator Larry Craig became embroiled in discussion about his arrest in a Minneapolis airport restroom, and said he would not run for re-election the next year. Risch did file; seven other Republicans competed, but all were unknowns and few ran visible campaigns; Risch won the primary with 65.3%. In the fall he faced a Democrat who had run against him before, Larry La Rocco, who from 1990 to 1994 was the 1st district U.S. Representative. La Rocco had run against Risch for the state Senate in 1986 and for lieutenant governor in 2006. As he had twice previously, Risch defeated La Rocco.

His seat is up in 2014. Risch has said he will run for re-election; he will be 71 on that election day. In January 2014 picked up a Democratic opponent, Boise attorney Nels Mitchell.

The senator. Risch's tenure as governor was brief but eventful. The Idaho roadless forest plan, which had enough agreement at the ground level to enable Idaho to craft its own plan for managing 9.3 million acres. Nearly 1.5 million acres of land received the "wild land recreation" designation, prohibiting roadbuilding, mining and timber harvest in those areas. Approximately 1.8 million acres were designated as "primitive," which allow some timber harvesting only for forest health or species habitat improvement. Not everyone was on board. But, the *Idaho Statesman's* Rocky Barker reported, "the 9th Circuit Court of Appeals upheld the Idaho roadless rule that protects 9.3 million acres of roadless national forest. The rule was developed by the state and negotiated by Republican Sen. Jim Risch — when he was governor — with local officials, conservation groups, the timber industry and recreation groups. The rule has varying levels of protections that set it apart from the national roadless rule put in place for 58 million acres in 2001 by President Bill Clinton. ..."

Risch also was responsible for a tax shift. In a one-day special legislative session, he pushed through a plan to pull the maintenance and operation property tax levy supporting a share of public education – about $260 million – and replace it with a penny increase in sales tax. A boon to large landowners, it increased taxes on low-income renters and most middle-class families. After the 2008 recession sales tax revenues plummeted, forcing a first-time ever cut in school budgets which, five years later, was not yet restored. The Twin Falls *Times-News*: "It's becoming increasingly clear that the 2006 experiment, while politically popular, has failed."

Risch is a member of the Intelligence and Foreign Relations committees; on the latter, he is the second ranking Republican, and given his rapid rise he could become the third Idahoan to chair that committee. Most recently, he opposed President Obama's bid (later pulled back) to retaliate against Syria for chemical warfare. His extensive report at a press conference in Boise describing in detail his rationale was widely praised as one of the comprehensive by any major office holder.

The assignment also allowed Risch and his chief of staff, former state Senator John Sandy, to engage in extensive travel. The Lewiston *Tribune* found Sandy had taken close to 20 trips in four years to 16 countries.

The *National Journal* rated him the Senate's most conservative member.

Controversy. Risch drew a great deal of attention for telling the *Idaho Statesman's* Dan Popkey how unproductive and undemanding his job was: "You know, I really enjoy this job. I really like this job," Risch said last week, saying it's a breeze compared to the seven months he served as governor in 2006. "Governor will wear you down. You can't do that job permanently. This you can do ad infinitum."

The seat. The Senate seat Risch holds has been in Republican control for a very long time. Republican Larry Craig held it three terms, winning landslides starting in 1990. Before that, Republican James McClure also held it three terms, winning the latter two in landslides. His predecessor was Republican (former Governor) Len Jordan, appointed in 1962, following Republican Henry Dworshak, who was appointed in 1949 (replacing the last Democrat to hold it, Bert Miller, who died in office). This seat has been in Republican hands for all but seven-plus years, most of that more than a century ago.

The counties. In 2008, Risch won 41 of 44 counties, missing only Blaine, Latah and Shoshone – a near-match for the presidential contest. In 2002, Craig lost only Blaine; in 1996 only Blaine, Latah and Shoshone. In his first Senate election, Craig lost those and Nez Perce County.

Sen	Democrat			Republican		
2008	Larry La Rocco	219,903	34.10%	Jim Risch	371,744	57.70%
2002	Alan Blinken	132,975	32.50%	Larry Craig	266,215	65.20%
1996	Walt Minnick	198,422	39.90%	Larry Craig	283,532	57.00%
1990	Ron Twilegar	122,248	61.00%	Larry Craig	193,541	39.00%
1984	Peter Busch	105,591	26.00%	James McClure	293,193	75.44%
1978	Dwight Jensen	89,635	31.56%	James McClure	194,412	68.44%

JIM RISCH, R-Boise

Office: risch.senate.gov/
Campaign: www.senatorrisch.com/
Background: Attorney, prosecuting attorney's office, later private practice. Ranch in rural Ada County. University of Idaho.
Political: Elected Ada County Prosecuting Attorney 1972. Elected Idaho Senate 1974, 1976, 1978, 1980, 1982, 1984, 1986, defeated for re-election 1988. Defeated for re-election 1992. Appointed to Senate 1995, re-elected 1996, 1998, 2000. Elected lieutenant governor 2002, 2006. Succeeded to the office of governor May 2006, served to end of term, January 2007. Re-elected lieutenant governor, 2006. Elected to U.S. Senate, 2008.

Representative Raul Laborador (right) on CNN.

U.S. House 1: Raul Labrador (R)

If many congressional districts are politically static and slow to change, that can't be said of Idaho's 1st District in recent elections. In the last four terms it has had four different representatives, both parties included in the mix, an unusual record nationally.

The politics. From its creation in 1918, the 1st was Republican for 14 years until the New Deal. It then shifted Democratic for all but two terms until reapportionment in 1966, when additional votes in Republican Ada County helped Republican James McClure win it. Of the 44 years since, it has been held by Republican for all but six. (Three successive representatives here, McClure, Steve Symms and Larry Craig, moved from it to the U.S. Senate, where they spent a combined total of 48 years.)

Four of those six Democratic years were accounted for by Larry La Rocco, winner in the last good years for Idaho Democrats (1990) but also one of the many Democrats tossed out in the Republican sweep of 1994. The winner then was Republican Helen Chenoweth, a highly quotable and controversial activist. In 2000, after two close re-election wins, she kept a campaign promise by opting out. The seat was then went, after a competitive primary, to Lieutenant Governor C.L. "Butch" Otter, who held it easily for three more terms before running for governor in 2006.

That opened up an intensely heated Republican primary among seven candidates including Robert Vasquez, whose primary issue was illegal immigration; state controller, Keith Johnson; attorney and future state Republican Chair Norm Semanko; former state Senator Sheila Sorensen who was widely described (though not by herself) as the lone moderate in the race. But the winner, with 25.8%, was Bill Sali, an eight-term state representative from Kuna, highly controversial and often at odds with his own party's leadership – but the recipient that year of large-scale help from the Club for Growth. He narrowly won the general election that year over

15

Democrat Larry Grant, but became the first Idaho Republican officeholder in the new millennium to take less than 50% of the vote.

After some jockeying, the Democratic nomination went to businessman Walt Minnick, who ran against Senator Larry Craig in 1996. Minnick ran a focused and well-funded campaign, while Sali, whose Club for Growth backing vanished in 2008, ran a slight campaign plagued by missteps. The result, in a year better than average for Democrats, was a slender Minnick win.

But could he keep the seat? Minnick's voting record in the House – he was one of the least caucus-loyal Democrats in the chamber – aggravated Democrats, while not diminishing Republican activism against him. State Representative Ken Roberts of Donnelly entered early, but dropped out in the fall of 2009. State Representative Raul Labrador then entered, but by that point much of the money and support in the field appeared to have been pre-empted by a newcomer in Idaho politics, Vaughn Ward (who drew on connections with former Senator and Governor Dirk Kempthorne, and elsewhere). Ward was a front runner until about two months before the May 2010 primary, when his campaign imploded spectacularly – a series of statements and actions, almost daily, wiping out his candidacy. Labrador, who ran steady and smooth, was the beneficiary, winning a plurality 47.6%.

Labrador was allied with the Tea Party movement, a subject of concern for a number of Idaho Republican leaders and organization workers. A number of organization Republicans sided with Minnick for the general election. Minnick ran an intensive campaign, the best-funded of any U.S. House campaign in Idaho history, raising more than $2 million; Labrador raised about a fifth as much. But Minnick made his own missteps (notably an ad linking Labrador, who as an attorney worked on immigration cases, with illegal immigration), and the year was Republican. The election was not close, Labrador winning by abut 24,000 votes.

Labrador was new to most people in the district, but not to Idaho politics. He had been active in Ada County Republican activities in the 90s, and ran for and won election to the Idaho House in 2006. His one significantly contested race pre-Congress was his primary in 2006 against other Republicans, but he won that with a 46.4% plurality. Running in a strongly Republican district based around Eagle, Star and Meridian, he won landslides in both general elections (65.55% in 2006, 69.1% in 2008).

The representative. Labrador may be the best-known – on a national level – of Idaho's four delegation members. As of late 2013, the two-term and relatively junior representative had made eight appearances on the Sunday morning program Meet the Press, not to mention numerous media appearances elsewhere, as on "This Week" and MSNBC's 'NOW.' He has an intriguing profile: Hispanic, raised poor, an up by the bootstraps rise from Puerto Rico to law school to Congress. And he has impeccable Tea Party credentials, to the point of twice voting to dramatically cut the research budget supplying the Idaho National Laboratory.

Columnist Martin Peterson said of him, "As a member of the Idaho Legislature he pretty much operated as an outsider, and that approach has continued since he was elected to Congress in 2010. Like Mourdock in Indiana, he has publicly stated that he did not come to Washington to be part of a team. He has been an articulate spokesman for the Tea Party element of the House Republicans."

Controversy, Labrador was among three ringleaders who sought to deny Speaker John Boehner a first-ballot victory, figuring another leader would emerge. When that did not happen, Labrador was among a dozen Republicans who either did not vote or supported someone else over Boehner. After that, Idaho's other representative Mike Simpson, ally of Boehner, told the *Idaho Statesman*: "I think there are 15 or 16 members of our conference that have substantially lost credibility... He just didn't vote ... which, as anyone who's ever been in a legislative body will tell you, you got one thing going for you and that's your credibility. And once you lose that credibility it's gone and it's gone forever."

Labrador fired back at Simpson as a "bully" and "an old-school legislator that went to Washington, D.C., to compromise. ... That's how you get to a $1 trillion deficit, by just tinkering around the edges." The Labrador-Simpson relationship reportedly has been periodically tense.

That was illustrated by Labrador's 2013 vote against the Energy and Water Development Appropriations bill, a measure Simpson had worked on heavily; Labrador voted for an unsuccessful amendment to unravel most of what Simpson had put in place.

He has been highly visible in immigration reform, for a time taking a role in the House Gang of Eight working on legislation; but he dropped out of that group soon after passage of a Senate bill.

He was among the hard-liners who pressed in the fall of 2013 Boehner not to agree to raise the federal debt ceiling without major changes in Obamacare, and voted against doing so (in contrast to Simpson) when the final vote occurred.

Right-leaning groups have scored Labrador highly; those include the Club for Growth (98%, tied for most conservative in the House), the American Conservative Union (96%), the John Birch Society (89%) and the Koch brothers' Americans for Prosperity (1005). Simpson's numbers were (respectively) 66%, 85%, 69% and 59%.

Rumors swirled that Labrador – a Club for Growth favorite – helped draw that group's support toward Simpson's GOP primary rival Bryan Smith. Labrador angrily denied it when columnist and former Cecil Andrus press secretary Chris Carlson published the accusation. But Labrador has withheld his endorsement of Simpson and concedes he's been in contact with Smith.

Unlike many members of Congress, Labrador is not wealthy. He has not rented a residence in DC, choosing instead to sleep at his office. His wife Becca is on the Labrador campaign payroll – a practice frowned upon and which would be illegal had the Senate not blocked a House-passed reform measure. She pulls down about $2,000 a month (after the campaign pays taxes on that income).

Labrador was long considered a prospect to run for governor in 2014; he ruled that out the year before. He has not cultivated, as Simpson has, the sense of a person who plans to stay in the House institution for a long stretch. But he said he does plan to run for a third term in 2014.

The seat. Labrador is not seriously opposed in the Republican primary (as of late 3013) and is widely considered a shoe-in against Democratic rival Shirley Ringo, an eight term Democratic House member from Moscow. But Ringo could provide some insights into Labrador's true appeal. She's the most experienced candidate to seek an Idaho congressional seat since Simpson ran in 1998. She's won and lost in a competitive district. And Ringo may benefit from an underground of establishment Republicans who first backed Ward, and then Minnick in 2010 – and who are incensed at his perceived efforts against Simpson now.

Although he got 63% against political novice Jimmy Farris in 2012, that was a lower percentage than Mitt Romney statewide (64.5%) and Simspon (65%) against a more credible challenger. In 2010, Labrador won the seat with just 51% of the vote.

The counties. In 2010, the incumbent Democrat won just four counties – Latah, Nez Perce, Shoshone and Valley – out of 19. Two years before, Minnick won seven – those four plus Ada (which appears to have provided much of the decisive edge), Benewah and Bonner. In 2006, Democrat Larry Grant won five – Clearwater, Latah, Nez Perce, Shoshone and Valley.

In 2012, Labrador won every county in the district except for Latah.

H1	Democrat			Republican		
2012	Jimmy Farris	97,450	30.77%	Raul Labrador	199,402	62.96%
2010	Walt Minnick	102,135	41.30%	Raul Labrador	126,231	51.00%
2008	Walt Minnick	175,898	50.60%	Bill Sali	171,687	49.40%
2006	Larry Grant	103,935	44.80%	Bill Sali	115,843	49.94%
2004	Naomi Preston	90,927	30.50%	C.L. Otter	207,662	69.50%
2002	Betty Richardson	80,269	38.90%	C.L. Otter	120,743	58.60%

RAUL R. LABRADOR, R-Eagle

Office: labrador.house.gov
Campaign: www.labrador4idaho.com
Background: Attorney.
Political: Elected to Idaho House 2006, 2008. Elected to U.S. House, 2010.

Representative Simpson (2nd from left) at the scene of a wildfire. (photo/office of Representative Simpson)

U.S. House 2: Mike Simpson (R)

Mike Simpson has had the opportunity to run for governor or senator, and would have been a top contender for either. He chose to stay in the U.S. House, and he already is one of Idaho's longest-timers there. With re-election in 2012 to an eighth term, he exceeds former Representative George Hansen (1964-68, 1974-84) and Addison Smith (1918-32) for length of service in the second district. Among all Idaho U.S. representatives, the longest-serving was Republican Burton French (13 terms starting in 1902 and ending in 1930). Simpson eventually could match or surpass that.

The politics. The 2nd district has always had a Republican tilt, though Democrats have occasionally broken in – mainly when a Republican incumbent was severely weakened. Democrats held the seat for three terms at the start of the New Deal, and for two when in 1960 Democrat Ralph Harding ousted veteran Hamer Budge. In 1984 Hansen, convicted of campaign finance-related felonies, narrowly lost to Democrat Richard Stallings, who held the seat four terms – its longest Democratic stretch. When Stallings ran for the Senate (unsuccessfully) in 1992, the seat went Republican, to Mike Crapo. When Crapo ran for the Senate (successfully) in 1998, it went to Simpson.

He was not an automatic or anointed choice. A dentist (in a family of dentists), Simpson's political career started with the Blackfoot City Council in 1979. In 1984, running for the Idaho House in a Republican district in a strongly Republican year, he won with just 53% of the vote, and was challenged seriously in coming years. But he kept winning re-election. He moved into House leadership, in 1990 running against incumbent House Speaker Tom Boyd (as a conservative against a more moderate leader) and lost. But when Boyd retired in 1992 Simpson became speaker, and held the job for three terms.

In 1998 Crapo's Senate run opened the 2nd district seat. Though House speaker, Simpson not an overwhelming favorite in the Republican primary. His opponents were fellow Representative Mark Stubbs of Twin Falls and Senators Dane Watkins (who had run for the 2nd district seat in 1988) and Ann Rydalch. Simpson won with a plurality 40.4%, not far ahead of Stubbs. In the general, he faced Democrat Richard Stallings, seeking a comeback. Simpson won with a modest 52.5%.

Since then, however, Simpson's percentages have been much stronger, and he has won in landslides throughout the last decade. (Those Democratic campaigns were lightly funded and organized, however, and just two of those candidates, Jim Hansen and Lin Whitworth, had substantial candidate experience or a personal base.) Simpson's big 2010 win against Democrat Mike Crawford was typical.

Tea Party activists in Idaho criticized him as insufficiently conservative, and three candidates against him emerged in the Republican primary. Simpson had no primary contests in his first four re-elections; a primary did emerge in 2008, but not seriously contested and he won with 85.2%. The challenge in 2008 was ramped up in energy and rhetoric. This time Simpson was held to 58.3% against three candidates (Chick Heileson 24.1%, Russell Mathews 9.6% and Katherine Burton 8%).

The representative. Simpson entered the U.S. House as part of the majority. In 2006, he returned to the minority; then in 2010, back in the majority, this time with enough seniority for subcommittee chairs and a strong role in the House Republican caucus. He has been close to House leadership while working on such long-running projects as a central Idaho wilderness proposal.

Simpson made a point after his first election to meet personally as many of the 435 members of the House as he could, in both parties. He developed some strong relationships; though not a member of House leadership, he is close to Speaker John Boehner. He has been described also as a practical legislator, which irritated some Republicans after 2008. In its October 2008 issue, *Esquire* magazine called Simpson one of the 10 best members of Congress: "More than any other representative, Simpson lives by the philosophy that democratic representation is a matter of finding not advantageous positions but common ground..."

He has become Idaho's only budget "appropriator," and one with some influence as one of the House Appropriations Committee "cardinals," chair of the Interior and Environment Appropriations Subcommittee.

At the same time and in his own way, Simpson has something of a maverick's history. In 1990, Simpson was the only GOP legislator from eastern Idaho to vote against that year's anti-abortion rights bill, doing so on constitutional grounds, saying the bill was contrary to Supreme Court rulings and to vote for it was a violation of his oath of office. Later that year, he was the conservative challenger to Speaker Tom Boyd, returning to the backbench until Boyd retired two years later and Simpson won the job. He was the last Republican Idaho House speaker to work with a Democratic governor, Cecil Andrus (93-94) before serving through the entire Phil Batt term.

When Simpson arrived in Washington, the Idaho National Laboratory was in serious trouble, with an unclear mission and uncertain support. By 2001-02, the George W. Bush Administration issued a budget that appeared to contemplate cleaning up the lab and then shutting it down. First with Craig, who also had an appropriations committee perch, and then continuing on his own, Simpson helped secure a lead nuclear research mission and then lined up the support for new infrastructure. Budgets for the Lab have been battered like most parts of the federal budget, but it might not have survived at all but for Simpson.

Simpson's other big footprint in Idaho concerns the environment. His appropriations chairmanship has allowed him to put pressure on EPA. Working with Senator Jon Tester, a Montana Democrat, he passed a rider to delist wolves from endangered species protection – a move supported by the Obama administration but blocked by a U.S. District court in Montana.

Simpson's signature legislation – and frustration – has been his decade-long effort to pass a wilderness package in the Boulder-White Clouds range. Not a wilderness bill in the traditional sense, the Central Idaho Economic Development and Recreation Act was a model of on-the-ground collaboration – 332,775 acres of wilderness, the opening of 130,453 acres toward multiple use, money for local services and trail maintenance, protection for ranchers and access for motorized recreation. Simpson came close to pulling it off in spite of opposition from Craig and then-Representative Butch Otter. In the lame duck 2006 Congress, CIERDA was attached to a must-pass $50 billion, 10-year tax and trade measure. He even went home believing the deal was done – only to see House Speaker Dennis Hastert pull CIEDRA at the last second.

"The fact that it got this far is nothing short of remarkable. Former Gov. Cecil Andrus, a Democrat, and then-Sen. Jim McClure, a Republican, tried and failed to broker a compromise wilderness bill in the early 1990s. Conventional wisdom was that if the two most influential Idaho politicians of the past 25 years couldn't get it done, nobody could," wrote the Twin Falls *Times-News* wrote.

At the opening of the 2009 session, Simpson seemed to be knocking on the door again. For the first time, he had a unanimous Idaho congressional delegation, including Walt Minnick, D-Idaho, lined up. Then Senator Jim Risch withdrew his support, putting a roadblock to passage in the Senate Energy and Natural Resources Committee, where he serves. In 2010 Raul Labrador, who opposes CIEDRA, bested Minnick. Governor C.L. (Butch) Otter has never supported CIEDRA. Since then former allies, such as Andrus and the Idaho Conservation League, are lobbying the Obama administration to resort to the Antiquities Act – used by Teddy Roosevelt to create Grand Canyon and Bill Clinton to designate the Grand Staircase Escalante – to create a Boulder White Clouds monument.

The seat. Idaho's second district House seat has emerged for 2014 as one of the hottest contests in the country – on the Republican side. Simpson once again has a challenger, newcomer Idaho Falls attorney Bryan Smith, who unlike his predecessors announced in the middle of the year prior to the election and began campaigning and fundraising early. He has prospectively emerged as Simpson's most serious primary challenge yet.

The *Idaho Statesman* has reported a mix of endorsements and support among Republican-leaning groups in the race. The Club for Growth and the Madison Project have backed Smith, but the Main Street Partnership, the American Chemistry Council, the Idaho Association of Commerce and Industry (through its federal PAC) have supported Simpson.

Historically, Republican incumbents here rarely lose a primary. It last happened in 1974 when Orval Hansen fell to George V. Hansen – but George Hansen held the seat previously. The closed GOP primary is a question mark, although it has not proven fatal for moderate Idaho legislators. This race is shaping up as a proxy for a Tea Party vs establishment GOP stand off.

The counties. In general elections, Simpson typically has won all 26 counties in his district, including often-Democratic Blaine and the part of Ada that includes most of its Democratic precincts. Those two counties did go to Democrat Nicole LeFavour in 2012, but Simpson won all the others. Simpson also won every county in 2010, 2008, 2004 and 2002, though he did lose Blaine and Ada in 2006.

He also won all the counties in his 2008 primary. In 2010, however, Jefferson County went to Heileson, while winning all the others.

There's no reason to think Simpson's track record against Democrats would change in 2012 from recent elections. The larger question is his primary challenge.

H1	Democrat			Republican		
2012	Nicole LeFavour	110,847	34.80%	Mike Simpson	207,412	65.12%
2010	Mike Crawford	48,749	24.40%	Mike Simpson	137,468	68.80%
2008	Deborah Holmes	83,878	29.00%	Mike Simpson	205,777	71.00%
2006	Jim Hansen	73,441	34.43%	Mike Simpson	58,821	62.00%
2004	Lin Whitworth	80,133	29.30%	Mike Simpson	193,704	70.70%
2002	Edward Kinghorn	57,769	29.00%	Mike Simpson	135,605	68.20%

MIKE SIMPSON, R-Blackfoot
Office: http://www.house.gov/simpson/
Campaign: www.simpsonforcongress.com
Background: Dentist, Simpson Dental Office, 1977-98. DDS, School of Dental Medicine, Washington University, 1977 Pre-Dentistry, Idaho State University, 1968-72. Utah State University, Logan.
Political: City council, Blackfoot. Elected to Idaho House 1982 through 1996. Elected Speaker, Idaho House, 1992, 1994, 1996. Elected to U.S. House 1998 to present.

State

Governor Otter at a bicycle race. (photo/Office of Governor Otter)

Governor C.L. "Butch" Otter (R)

C.L. (Clement Leroy) "Butch" Otter has campaigned as a critic of government for a very long time, even while spending many years in government at the state and federal levels. At the end of his current term his span in office will have run over a span of more than 40 years, since his first election to the Idaho House in 1972. That happened in a time and place of some philosophical ferment. A group of libertarian activists including Caldwell businessman Ralph Smeed launched that year the congressional campaign of Steve Symms, and other libertarian careers were started about the same time. Otter's has proven the most durable of them.

The governor. No governor in recent Idaho history has been so firmly identified with an ideological stance as Otter with small-L libertarianism: Limiting and reducing the taxes and the reach of government, especially the federal government. What has happened in the course of two terms has been a story more complex than any single sentence or two would suggest.

Otter may have been most consequential in cutting state spending. Whether by design or circumstance – the Idaho Legislature in this period would never have supported revenue bills even had Otter wanted them – he has presided over an actual diminution of state government. Spending for public schools and higher education remains well below pre-recession levels, while Otter and the legislature have approved income tax cuts for high-income families and corporations worth about $36 million and a $20 million cut in the personal property tax paid by companies.

In late 2012 at the Associated Taxpayers of Idaho conference, Otter's former chief economist, Mike Ferguson, pressed the governor on where the Legislature was meeting its constitutional obligation to "... establish and maintain a general, uniform and thorough system of public, free common schools." Otter conceded: "I would say that we're probably not (meeting the constitutional obligation), but we're doing the best job that we can and we're going to continue to do the best job we can."

Upon his election (and even before taking office) Otter entered his first conflict with the Legislature, and it was over a spending matter. The Legislature had proposed developing two underground floors as part of the Statehouse renovation and expansion. After some wrangling, a compromise emerged, as legislators got most though not all (they gave up a floor) of what they had wanted.

Otter might suggest as part of his low-budget argument that the state's economy, during much of his tenure, has been in poor shape, generating less tax revenue. That would be correct. Idaho fell harder and faster than just about any other state during the great recession, primarily because so much of its economy was predicated on an unsustainable building boom based largely in the Treasure Valley. The *Idaho Statesman* reported in 2011: "Idaho has set its own record, as the number of people receiving food stamps rose from about 87,000 in 2007 to about 229,000 in 2011, according to the U.S. Department of Agriculture. Now, 15 percent of Idahoans get food stamps." Since Otter became governor in 2007, the food stamp caseload has jumped 163%, putting Idaho behind only Nevada's 172% growth rate."

Idaho's per capita income ranking has slipped to 50th (including the state and District of Columbia); StateImpact Idaho reported in the spring of 2013: "More Idaho workers earned minimum wage in 2012 than in any year since the U.S. Bureau of Labor Statistics started keeping track a decade ago. The Idaho Department of Labor reports 7.7% of Idaho hourly workers earned $7.25 an hour or less last year. That's up from 5 percent in 2011. The new data show Idaho has the largest share of minimum-wage workers in the country."

In his first year in office, Otter proposed targeting sales tax relief to Idaho's needy, a response to predecessor Jim Risch's M&O tax levy tax shift. Instead, Otter gave in to legislators and approved a multi-year phased in expanded sales tax grocery tax credit that will be far more costly.

In other areas Otter has pushed for expanded spending, as in a strong push around 2008 and 2009 for highway expansion. He could have had a deal in 2008, when lawmakers offered him $68 million; but, holding out for $150 million, he said no. A year later, amid another highway spending battle, he came within an eyelash of matching former Governor Don Samuelson's record by vetoing 35 budget bills; he wound up with virtually nothing for transportation. He has not touched the issue since, even though the state falls about $262 million short of what's needed just to maintain transportation network each year.

His two other major initiatives followed developments initiated elsewhere.

In 2011 Otter followed Superintendent of Public Instruction Tom Luna's lead on the massive school overhaul package the school chief pushed through the Legislature, eliminating most school teacher collective bargaining rights, tying merit pay (bonuses) to testing results and diverting dollars from paying teachers to buying computers and online instruction.

After the "Luna laws" were reversed by voters in 2012 via referendum, Otter convened an education task force. The governor went on record supporting its recommendations, which included about $82.5 million in operational funds plus $250 million for a teacher career ladder. Even as a five-year project, it's unclear where he'll find the money – especially since Otter is on record supporting another business tax cut and/or total repeal of the personal property tax worth about $120 million.

More surprising was his role in national health care policy, as the Affordable Care Act was developed and passed in Congress in 2010. Otter was a relentless critic of it, even referring to nullification in a state of the state address. Otter then, however, took a back seat on the Legislature's ongoing debate whether to openly defy Obamacare – until he vetoed a nullification-lite measure, then implemented its terms through an executive order.

That was not the last twist. While Otter was among the first governors to campaign for challenging it in the courts – that issue was highly profiled in his 2010 re-election campaigns – he later emerged as an advocate for state action on one key part of it. He proposed passing, as the ACA contemplated, a state-based health insurance exchange through which individuals and small businesses can shop for policies and, critically, moderate income individuals can obtain federal subsidies. Passed with some difficulty in the Legislature, it made Idaho the only GOP-dominated state (where Republicans control both the governor's office and the Legislature) to do so. Many of Otter's business supporters (including the key business organization Idaho Association of Commerce and Industry) were supportive, but much of the Republican base was not. Otter's role on the exchange was a central lever leading to his 2014 Republican primary challenge from state Senator Russ Fulcher, who voted against it.

Nevertheless, the exchange is, ironically, the one major legislative victory Otter can claim. Hence, friend and foe alike have christened it "Ottercare."

Controversy. Otter's tenure also has been marked by intances of cronyism and irregularities.

Otter has championed privatization and only a skeptical Legislature has restrained his desire to expand the practice. However, in 2012 Corrections Corporation of American (which contributed $19,000 to Otter's campaign and which counts among its lobbyists Otter's former chief of staff, Jason Kreizenbeck), effectively was shown the door as manager of the Idaho Correctional Center. The ICC was so known for inmate violence it was dubbed the "gladiator school." CCA scrimped on staff and got a federal contempt of court citation in the process.

Otter's State Tax Commission Chairman – and former campaign treasurer – Royce Chigbrow was accused of displaying favoritism, and left the commission.

The Idaho Transportation Board so mishandled the firing of Idaho's first female transportation chief, Pam Lowe, that the state ended up settling her wrongful termination lawsuit by writing a check for $750,000.

Closer to home, Otter's closest friend, Mike Gwartney, was at the center of a a lawsuit involving a broadband network among schools, higher education and business. One of the bidders for the $25 million project, Syringa Networks, accused Gwartney of steering business to Qwest, although Syringa had the lower bid. When Syringa complained, CEO Greg Lowe quoted, Gwartney: "I'd sure hate to see the rest of your (state) business go away."

The politics. Otter served two terms in the House, opted out in 1976 and then ran for governor in 1978, emerging third in the Republican primary (of six candidates). Toward the end of that race he conflicted with House Speaker Allan Larsen, the eventual primary winner, and for years afterward hard feelings persisted among parts of Larsen's core constituency (eastern Idaho Mormon conservatives). For the next eight years Otter stayed out of electoral politics, sticking to business, working for his then-father-in-law J.R. Simplot at the Simplot Company, and later at the Farmer & Merchants Bank. In 1986 he re-emerged as the Republican candidate for lieutenant governor, winning his primary with a modest 58% against a relative unknown, and only barely (by about 1,000 votes) defeating Democratic state Treasurer Marjorie Ruth Moon.

Otter would serve as lieutenant governor longer than anyone in Idaho history, most of that time as second to Democrat Cecil Andrus. (The two seem to have had an amicable relationship.) After a series of bad headlines in the early 90s (a DUI arrest, a tight jeans contest, a divorce), Otter had a close call in 1994, winning his primary with just 39.7% over two challengers, and (in a sweep Republican year) the general over Democrat John Peavey, with just 53.2%. He recovered with a landslide win in 1998.

That set a pattern, evidently, for when he ran for the U.S. House in 2000. He easily won that primary and general election, and did well in 2002 (at 58.6%, a relatively modest win) and 2004 (another landslide).

After that, he early entered the race for governor in 2006, pre-empting serious Republican competition. (Then Lieutenant Governor Jim Risch considered the race but eventually decided against it.) His general election that year, however, was relatively close, well short of a landslide, against a Democrat (Jerry Brady) who had run for governor four years before. Otter became the third of Idaho's five most recent governors to have sought the office unsuccessfully before winning it.

Otter drew some criticism as governor for his sometimes rocky relations with the legislature and some of his management approaches; grumbling could be heard from other Republican officials. Speculation that he might be vulnerable grew as 2010 approached.

Democrats, beaten repeatedly for major office by this point, recruited intensively. Their eventual choice was Keith Allred, a mediator who had taught at Harvard who for most of the recent decade had lived at Eagle (and grew up in the Twin Falls area). He was also an avowed political independent and had run an organization (the Common Interest) which had support from both Republicans and Democrats. A number of moderate Republicans, including some former legislators, signed up with his campaign. In a strong Republican year, however, Allred wound up with the smallest Democratic percentage for a gubernatorial candidate in a dozen years, and Otter only barely missed a landslide win.

Spokesman-Review reporter Betsy Russell famously told the Boise City Club that the voters of Idaho will forgive Butch Otter anything. Evidence for that was hardly lacking.

He has benefited enormously from no serious opposition from the Democrats. His two opponents, Jerry Brady and Keith Allred, were highly accomplished men in their fields but neither had so much as run or run for a county commission seat, much less a statewide office.

Counties. In the 2010 general election, Otter won all but three counties – Blaine, Latah and Teton. That was a considerable improvement over 2006, when he lost Ada, Bannock, Blaine, Latah, Nez Perce, Shoshone, Teton and Valley. That was his weakest recent performance in a general election. In 2004, running for U.S. House, he won all the counties in the 1st district (that is, including Ada, Latah, Nez Perce, Shoshone and Valley). In 2002, he lost only Latah and Nez Perce.

H1	Democrat			Republican		
2010	Keith Allred	148,680	32.90%	C.L."Butch" Otter	267,483	59.10%
2006	Jerry Brady	198,845	44.11%	C.L."Butch" Otter	237,437	52.67%
2002	Jerry Brady	171,711	41.70%	Dirk Kempthorne	231,566	56.30%
1998	Robert Huntley	110,815	29.10%	Dirk Kempthorne	258,095	67.70%
1994	Larry EchoHawk	181,363	43.90%	Phil Batt	216,123	52.30%
1990	Cecil Andrus	218,673	68.20%	Roger Fairchild	101,937	31.30%
1986	Cecil Andrus	193,429	50.20%	David Leroy	189,794	49.80%
1982	John Evans			Phil Batt		

CLEMENT LEROY "BUTCH" OTTER

Office: http://gov.idaho.gov/
Campaign: (former) otter4.idaho.com
Background: Business executive. Residence at Star. Wife Lori Easley; 4 Children: John, Carolyn, Kimberly Dawn, Corrine. Professional: President/Vice President/Food Products Division Director/Board of Directors, J.R. Simplot Company, 1965-1993. Enlisted, Idaho Army National Guard, 1967-1973. Albertson College of Idaho (BA, Political Science, 1967). Elks Lodge, 1967-present; Maple Grove State Grange, 1958-present; National Rifle Association, 1958-present; National Cowboy Hall of Fame, 1991-1992; American Legion; Chair, Canyon County Republican Party.
Political: Elected to Idaho House 1972, 1974. Unsuccessful run for governor, 1978 (finished 3rd in Republican primary). Elected lieutenant governor 1986, 1990, 1994, 1998. Elected to U. S. House 2000, 2002, 2004. Elected governor 2006, 2010.

Lieutenant Governor Brad Little (R)

For years, Brad Little was the "tough get" for Idaho Republicans.

He was a member of one of Idaho's major ranching families, with headquarters at Emmett. He was an obvious prospect: His father had been a veteran state senator and leader in the party, another relatively had served a couple of decades in the Idaho House and was majority leader there. And Brad Little was plenty involved in public affairs and business organizations (a chairmanship in the Idaho Association of Commerce & Industry, for example), and even became something of a policy wonk (a term he probably would not accept for himself). But his work on the family business was at least one factor in keeping him off the ballot over a number of years when the idea was widely floated.

The politics. In May 2001, state Senator Judi Danielson was named to the Northwest Power Planning Council, and Little was appointed to replace her. Little quickly became a leader in the Senate, in 2003 becoming caucus chair and holding that job through his Senate years. He was also the subject of concern on the right for his initial opposition to a constitutional ban on same-sex marriage, but he appears to have been politically impervious. In 2002 he won his first primary contest with 72.1% of the vote; in 2004 won another against two opponents with 65%; and was unopposed in the primary in 2006 and 2008. He has easily won his general elections.

In January 2009, Lieutenant Governor Jim Risch left the Idaho for the U.S. Senate, opening a second appointment for lieutenant governor within a decade. Governor C.L. "Butch" Otter quickly chose Little, who emerged as an active lieutenant both in working with the governor and independently on some projects. In 2010 Little faced light opposition in both the primary and the general. He won the former (over two little-known candidates) with 67.6%, and the latter (against a little-known Democrat and a minor party candidate) with 67.8%.

The lieutenant governor's office has been in Republican control since Republican Phil Batt won it in 1978 over appointed Democrat William Murphy. That means Republicans have held the top two offices in state government, governor and lieutenant governor, since they were first won by Batt.

The last lieutenant governor to move up to governor, by the way, was Risch in 2006, when Governor Dirk Kempthorne left to become secretary of the interior. Symmetry: The last before that (in 1977) was Democrat John Evans, who became governor when Cecil Andrus became interior secretary. Before that, the last was Arnold Williams in 1945, who became governor after his predecessor, Charles Gossett, appointed himself to the U.S. Senate. (Gossett and Williams both lost election in 1946)

After Otter made clear his plans to seek a third term in 2014, Little staged a marketing coup with his two-week, 19-city announcement tour, the kind of event exceeding even most senatorial and gubernatorial announcements, and seemingly a rebuttal to the long-running discussion about his plans (such as the headline in the Moscow-Pullman *Daily News*: "Rumors rife that Little to reveal a run for governor").

The Idaho Falls *Post Register* commented, "Although Idaho's political insiders saw this nonstory for what it was – a way to draw attention to Little's announcement that he wants a part-time job with a staff of one and salary barely above that of a beginning teacher – they could not stop talking about it. ... Little is regarded as one of the GOP's bright lights, articulate, pragmatic and intelligent. Otter is well-liked, but after seven years on this job and more than three decades in public office, fatigue is setting in. ... Give Otter credit for getting a crowd to Little's announcement in Emmett."

Counties. In his first statewide elections, Little just barely missed a clean sweep. He won all 44 counties in his 2010 primary, but missed Blaine County in the general election.

H1	Democrat			Republican		
2010	Eldon Wallace	120,174	27.20%	Brad Little	299,979	67.80%
2006	Larry La Rocco	175,312	39.36%	Jim Risch	259,648	58.29%
2002	Bruce Perry	160,438	39.90%	Jim Risch	226,017	56.20%
1998	Sue Reents	133,688	35.60%	C.L."Butch" Otter	225,704	60.20%
1994	John Peavey	191,625	47.40%	C.L."Butch" Otter	213,009	52.60%
1990	-	-	-	C.L."Butch" Otter	246,132	100.00%

BRAD LITTLE, R-Emmett

Office: http://lgo.idaho.gov/
Campaign: www.bradlittleforidaho.com
Background: P.O. Box 488, Emmett, 83617-0488. Home (208) 365-6566. Bus (208) 365-4611. Rancher
Political: Elected to the Senate 2002, 2004, 2006. Appointed lieutenant governor January 2007. Elected lieutenant governor, 2008.

Secretary of State Ben Ysursa (R)

You could say that the Secretary of State's office in Idaho has been in the hands of Cenarrusa/Ysursa for a very long stretch – since 1967. The names connect. Just seven years after Pete Cenarrusa, a former Idaho House speaker, was appointed, Ben Ysursa came to work there, soon after named chief deputy (1976). From then to Cenarrusa's retirement in 2002, Ysursa was the day to day manager of the office, and when Ysursa succeeded Cenarrusa in 2002, hardly a ripple surfaced. An office with potential for trouble and scandal (as it handles election law, among other things) has operated without significant complaint more than 40 years.

The secretary. Probably no major Idaho officeholder in Idaho has generated broader respect than Ysursa. He has, to begin, deep personal expertise in Idaho election law and other work done by the office; he often has been regarded as the most authoritative person in the state on those subjects. Ysursa spent decades as a deputy directly managing the office.

Ysursa has been compared with such figures as former Washington Secretary of State Sam Reed as an "old school" official: conscientious, an advocate of the voter (and of voting), a guardian of the state's campaign finance and sunshine laws.

Controversy. That does not mean he has shied away from conflict. In 2012, Ysursa went to court to compel Education Voters of Idaho – allies of fellow Republican state school Superintendent Tom Luna – to comply with Idaho's Sunshine Law and disclose the source of its money. Before that, it was Ysursa – with Attorney General Lawrence Wasden – who blew the whistle on fellow Republican Governor Dirk Kempthorne's use of campaign accounts for personal business, and then passed laws to curb the practice.

He opposed Republican leaders in their move (ultimately successful) toward closing the Republican primary election to only registered Republicans. Working with the county clerks, Ysrusa supported more flexible absentee voting rules – a measure legislators from his own party blocked. He went to court against Denney and former Idaho GOP Chairman Norm Semanko when they sought to fire their appointees to the legislative redistricting commission.

The politics. Ysursa's long tenure in the office was a key point when Ysursa, seeking the top job for the first time, faced state Senator Evan Frasure in the 2002 Republican primary: The office had not been changed or really shaken up in a long time. But Ysursa's 66.3% win underscored approval. In 2010, Democratic challenger Mack Sermon (the only Democratic opponent Ysursa has faced) acknowledged as much in their debate: The office was well-run, and he offered mainly a shaking-up.

The office is the scene of a major 2014 Republican primary battle, involving Frasure, former House Speaker Lawerence Denney, former state Senator Mitch Toryanski and Ada County deputy clerk Phil McGrane.

H1	Democrat			Republican		
2010	Mack Sermon	113,164	25.70%	Ben Ysursa	326,453	74.30%
2006	-	-	-	Ben Ysursa	364,871	100.00%
2002	-	-	-	Ben Ysursa	297,189	77.50%
1998	Jerry Seiffert	103,423	27.80%	Pete Cenarrusa	256,594	68.90%
1994	Edith Stanger	131,475	33.00%	Pete Cenarrusa	267,039	67.00%
1990	-	-	-	Pete Cenarrusa	247,908	100.00%

BEN YSURSA, R-Boise

Office: http://www.sos.idaho.gov/

Campaign: not running in 2014

Background: Attorney; for most of his career prior to election as secretary of state, he was chief deputy secretary of state. Gonzaga University, St. Louis University (law).

Political: Elected secretary of state 2002, 2006, 2010.

State Controller Brandon Woolf (R)

State controller may be the least-understood of Idaho's major elective offices. Its job functions have varied, and changed somewhat with the job title change in 1994 (from state auditor, which it had been since statehood). At present, you could loosely say the office functions mainly as the state's bookkeeper and manager of most of its financial records. There are also some side responsibilities, however, the most visible of those being a seat on the state land board.

The controller. Brandon Woolf is the second controller in the last decade to rise to the elective job from the ranks of the office's staff – and also the second Republican to do so after having been hired into the office originally by Democrat D.J. Williams. He also is one of three former chief deputies now serving as statewide elective office holders (with Secretary of State Ben Ysusa and Attorney General Lawrence Wasden).

Woolf was appointed to the position by Governor C.L. "Butch" Otter after a May 2012 motor vehicle accident incapacitated the elected controller, Donna Jones, Woolf was appointed first on an interim and then on a permanent basis. He has been a quiet manager of the office, making no very visible waves. Raised in southeast Idaho in the farm community of Whitney, Woolf started at the controller's office in 1997 as an intern, and worked his way up the ranks.

The politics. No state-level office in Idaho was in Democratic hands in a single stretch longer than that of state auditor, renamed controller by the voters in 1994. After a short period of Republican control, it was taken over by Democrat Joe Williams (for whom a large Capital Mall building is named) in 1958, and held by him and then his Democratic relative J.D. Williams until the latter Williams' resignation (to take a corporate executive position) in September 2002. Since that stretch of almost 44 years, it has been in Republican hands.

It went first, by appointment, to Williams' chief deputy, Keith Johnson, who was Republican. Johnson easily won it outright in 2002, after a close primary (winning with 39.6%) against two former state legislators, Donna Jones and Gene Winchester. He probably would have held it in 2006 but decided instead to run for Congress, in the newly-opened 1st U.S. House district. Jones, who was executive director of the Board of Realtors, filed again for the office, and this time won decisively (59.4%) over accountant (and future Tax Commission member) Royce Chigbrow. She did about as well in the general election, and better in a low-key 2010 race.

In 2010 she was held to about 56% of the vote in the Republican primary against Todd Hatfield, who has been a state Republican Party official.

Woolf has said he plans to seek election as controller in 2014. Hatfield said in June 2013 that he planned to run again for the office as well.

H1	Democrat			Republican		
2010	Bruce Robinett	125,571	28.90%	Donna Jones	308,207	71.10%

2006	Jackie Twilegar	179,811	41.47%	Donna Jones	253,780	58.53%
2002	Bob Sonnichsen	129,542	33.20%	Keith Johnson	242,161	62.00%
1998	J.D. Williams	211,286	56.80%	Ron Pollock	160,569	43.20%
1994	J.D. Williams	201,002	50.40%	Ralph J. Gines	197,742	49.60%
1990	J.D. Williams	177,367	58.00%	Richard Williams	127,233	42.00%

BRANDON WOOLF, R-Boise

Office: http://www.sco.idaho.gov/
Campaign: www.reelectdonnajones.com/wordpress/
Background: Staffer, starting as an intern and rising to chief deputy, in the state controller's office. Boise.
Political: Not yet elected to office.

State Treasurer Ron Crane (R)

Ron Crane is the second Idaho treasurer in a row to jump there from the Idaho House without an especially high profile. Hehas maintained a mostly low profile in the treasurer's job since.

After Democrat Marjorie Ruth Moon held the office for 24 years in 1986, she ran instead for lieutenant governor (losing to Republican C.L. "Butch" Otter), and the office went to Republican state Representative Lydia Justice Edwards of Donnelly. After 12 years, she said she would retire (and left for her native Kentucky), opening the office again in 1998.

Three Republicans filed for the job, including Trudy Jackson and Barbara Bauer, both familiar from extensive Republican Party work, but the edge from the start seemed to be with Ron Crane, who had been a state representative for 14 years and had a substantial base of support. He won the primary with 45%, then defeated a Reform Party candidate (no Democrat filed) in the fall with 75.5%. He has had no strong challenge since, and was unchallenged in 2010. Crane has been mentioned as a prospect for some higher office, but has made no active moves in that direction.

In 2012, he was the one major Idaho official to break from the wave of Republican primary support for former Massachusetts Governor Mitt Romney, and instead support first Texas Governor Rick Perry, then former Pennsylvania Governor Rick Santorum.

Crane drew some praise for development of programs to help women with personal finances, and for helping maintain high ratings on state bonds.

The normally low-key Crane got into hot water in 2011 and 2012 when aspects of his bookkeeping came to light. As one news story summarized, legislative auditors found that "Crane's New York trips weren't adequately documented; he didn't properly account for a taxpayer-provided Chevron card used to gas up his private vehicle; and he exceeded his office's authority with several programs." Crane later said his office has changed some of its accounting procedures.

H1	Democrat			Republican		
2010	-	-		- Ron Crane	367,460	100.00%
2006	Howard Faux	153,293	35.64%	Ron Crane	276,779	64.36%
2002	Sally Beitia	136,796	35.00%	Ron Crane	239,431	61.20%
1998	-	-		- Ron Crane	258,755	75.50%
1994	-	-		- Lydia Edwards	341,509	99.50%
1990	Marjorie Moon	135,224	43.60%	Lydia Edwards	175,080	56.40%

RON CRANE, R-Caldwell

Office: sto.idaho.gov

Campaign:

Background: Founder and owner, Crane Alarm Service, Caldwell. Idaho National Guard 1971-77. Wife Cheryl, six children.

Political: Elected state House 1982, 1984, 1986, 1988, 1990, 1992, 1994, 1996. Elected treasurer 1998, 2002, 2006, 2010.

Attorney General
Lawrence Wasden (R)

Republicans have held this office since Democrat Larry EchoHawk left it to run for governor in 1994.

2002 was the year of promotions for chief deputies in Idaho constitutional offices – three of them were elected to the top job: Ben Ysursa at secretary state, Keith Johnson at controller, and Lawrence Wasden for attorney general. Of them, Wasden probably had the toughest go at first.

The attorney general's office handles a wide range of territory, providing legal services across state government, periodically helping out local governments and providing consumer assistance as well.

Seeking to replace Republican Al Lance, who had decided to opt out after two terms, Wasden had an immediately difficult primary against three other candidates – governor's attorney Michael Bogert, Todd Lakey of Canyon County and Myron Dan Gabbert of New Meadows – known about as well statewide as he was, which not very. In that close contest, Wasden won with 32.2% of the vote, but tracked along with other Republicans in the fall against Keith Roark (who would become state Democrat chair later). Having survived a crowded 2002 GOP primary, to compete against a self-funded Keith Roark, Wasden drew deeply from Melaleuca CEO Frank VanderSloot's bank account; contributions tied to him come to at least $35,000, plus another $16,500 made to a group called Concerned Citizens for Family Values, whose radio ads blasted Roark.

Wasden has had an easier road then, though he has periodically issued rulings and guidelines counter to the desires of some Republican legislators and others. He considered but did not undertake a run for the U.S. Senate during the period when Senator Larry Craig considered resigning in 2007.

Wasden's office has developed a procession of local officials – mostly Republicans – doing the perp walk on public corruption charges. Wasden's office has been called in (he has jurisdiction on local criminal matters when a prosecutor declares a conflict and invites him in) on major profile cases:

■ Boise Mayor Brent Coles (2003), was convicted and served six months for misusing public funds, including an instance of using public funds to attend a Broadway play during a New York trip to attend U.S Conference of Mayors. Also convicted was Coles' chief of staff Chief Of Staff Gary Lyman.

■ Twin Falls County Clerk Bob Fort (2003) was charged with embezzling more than $60,000. He served a year behind bars; restitution was ordered.

■ Wasden's office investigated and prosecuted former Bonneville County Prosecutor Kimball Mason in two cases (2006, 2007) linked to Mason's theft of firearms from the Idaho Falls Police evidence locker. Mason wen to prison.

■ Minidoka County Sheriff Kevin Halverson, who resigned and was facing charges for misappropriating gas charges.

Lawmakers voted in 2013 to extend the attorney general's authority over public corruption cases. A bill giving him autonomy to launch investigations – while leaving local prosecutors in charge about who files charges – reached Governor Otter's desk, but was vetoed (at Wasden's request) because a companion bill to fund the operation failed. Wasden's office has has an 8% budget cut since 2009.

Wasden has characterized himself as the state's lawyer first, a politician second. He defended the independence of the citizen redistricting commission against GOP Chairman Norm Semanko and House Speaker Lawerence Denney, who wanted to fire their appointees. He defended Idaho's open primary system against Republicans who sought to close it to none other than registered Republicans. When lawmakers in 2011 got infatuated with the idea of nullifying Obamacare, Wasden's office labeled it unconstitutional. One of his deputies, Brian Kane, went so far as to suggest such actions were contrary to the legislators' oath of office. No surprise, then, that lawmakers such as Rep Vito Barbieri, R-Dalton Gardens, thought it would be a swell idea if lawmakers hired their legislative counsel to tell them what they wanted to hear. The idea died in committee.

Wasden's singular act of independence may have been on the land board, where he serves with Otter, Secretary of State Ben Ysurusa, Controller Brandon Woolf and Superintendent of Public Instruction Tom Luna. That board has a constitutional duty to manage assets owned the state endowment for the maximum long term benefit of the students and others who rely upon it. In deciding terms for 521 endowment-owned cottage sites at Priest and Payette lakes, the board sided with the lease holders. Rents had fallen so far below market rates that, analysts said, the state was losing about $3 million a year. In 2010, Wasden took his fellow Republican board members to court, arguing they were violating the state constitution. In 2012, the Idaho Supreme Court sided with Wasden. The result has been a steady drive toward rising rents and appraisals.

Wasden was awarded the "Courage in Public Service Award" from the Conference of Western Attorneys General in 2010. It's been presented only four times in all, most previously in 2004. Karen White, the group's executive director, said Wasden was recognized for "placing himself in a position of political peril with his peers, in order to better the state of affairs for the people of Idaho and throughout the country," and that he "is an effective leader because he consistently does what he thinks follows his legal obligations and responsibilities of office and lets the chips fall where they may."

H1	Democrat			Republican		
2010	-		-	- Lawrence Wasden	367,737	100.00%
2006	Robert Wallace	165,857	38.25%	Lawrence Wasden	267,700	61.75%
2002	Keith Roark	167,353	41.90%	Lawrence Wasden	231,851	58.10%
1998	Brit Groom	118,116	32.20%	Alan Lance	248,813	67.80%
1994	Mike Burkett	174,290	43.90%	Alan Lance	222,765	56.10%
1990	Larry EchoHawk	175,000	55.70%	Pat Kole	138,822	44.30%

LAWRENCE WASDEN, R-Boise

Office: http://www.ag.idaho.gov
Campaign: www.lawrencewasden.com
Background: Attorney. Chief deputy attorney general when elected. Deputy prosecutor in Canyon and Owyhee counties. University of Idaho. Wife Tracey, four children.
Political: Elected attorney general 2002, 2006, 2010.

Superintendent of Public Instruction Tom Luna (R)

Of all the statewide offices apart from governor, probably more controversy and vote shifting has attached to the superintendent of instruction than any other. Superintendent Tom Luna has become one of Idaho's most visible public officials, and one of its most consequential as a promoter of change.

The superintendent. It was not always so. For the 12 years Republican Jerry Evans held the job, and for decades before, it was a usually uncontroversial office. That changed after Evans retired in 1994 and, after sharp primary and general elections both, the office went to Republican Anne Fox. She wound up generating intensive controversy, to the point that in 1998 voters did what they had not done with any Republican statewide office holder since 1970: They ousted her from office and replaced her with a Democrat. That was Marilyn Howard, a Moscow school principal, who in

2002 became the last Democrat (to date) to win an Idaho statewide constitutional office.

In 2006 she retired, and her 2002 Republican opponent, former Nampa school board member Tom Luna, filed and quickly became the favorite.

The superintendent. Luna was the first person who was not an educator by profession, at least in recent decades, to become superintendent; he had served on the Nampa School Board and thinly met statutory requirements for the job by obtaining an online degree from Thomas Edison State College in 2002. His relations with professional educators (in general) was rugged from early on.

Nonetheless, his first term was not marked by controversy. He sought a merit pay program which generated only muted criticism. For the first two years of his term, money for schools was not a major issue and in the next two, as the economy flattened, the state had strategic reserves and federal stimulus. Luna presided over some cuts, but said he was drawing a line – and challenged fellow Republicans to come up with more money, including digging into state endowment fund reserves and calling for a sales tax on Internet sales.

In early 2011, newly re-elected Luna switched gears. Saying Idaho could not afford more money for schools, he proposed "Students Come First":

■ Eliminating the continuing contract that offered veteran teachers due process – but not tenure – before they can be fired. Contract talks would be limited to salaries and benefits.

■ Pulling teacher pay, diverting it into a $38 million merit pay plan based on standardized testing results. Rewards flowed to the school – which critics argued meant teachers were paid based largely on the socio-economic status of the schools where they worked. Luna's plan amounted to a one-year bonus.

■ Equipping every Idaho high school student with a laptop computer and require each student to complete two online classes to graduate.

Since Luna did not offer this vision during in re-election campaign, he was accused of blindsiding teachers and the public.

The *Idaho Statesman* chronicled how Luna's allies in the for-profit education industry, some of whom might benefit from some of Luna's proposed changes, had nurtured his career. Of the $255,000 Luna raised in 2010, $72,581 came from the for-profit industry – among them K-12 ($25,000), the Apollo Group ($5,500) and Education Networks of America $8,000). With support from Governor C.L. "Butch" Otter, Luna's package sailed through the legislature. But it triggered a referendum (in response, he engineered an emergency clause for his package, thereby putting it into effect before the referendum campaign could be certified).

What ensued was a legislative voter reversal unlike any Idaho seen since 1936's sales tax act ("A penny for Benny"). Here too the laws were personalized, dubbed the Luna laws. Luna allies Education Voters of Idaho refused to say where they got nearly $700,000 until Secretary of State Ben Ysursa sued under Idaho's Sunshine Law and District Court Judge Mike Wetherell insisted. (One answer: New York City Mayor Mike Bloomberg). Luna signed a contract with Hewlett-Packard to deliver the laptops. That became a controversial deal. The *Spokesman-Review*'s Betsy Russell, researching the $182 million contract, found the units were overpriced – possibly 25% more than what they would cost at retail – and the state wasn't buying the computers, merely leasing them. The state was on the hook for $14 million if it canceled the eight-year contract early, while H-P would be reimbursed if a student lost or damaged a unit. Prop 1 (collective bargaining) failed 57.3%; Prop 2 (merit pay) died by 58% and Prop 3 (laptops) was rejected by 66.7%.

As the *Idaho Statesman* reported, Luna told his first post-election press conference the defeat was "a bump in the road." Luna spent much of 2013 taking a back seat to Otter's education reform task force, which emerged in the summer with a $350 million package – $82.5 million to restore the operational funding schools had lost during the budget cuts of the Great Recession and a $250 million career ladder program for teachers. Luna embraced both.

Summer brought new problems when Russell reported Luna signed a long-term contract with Education Networks of America to deliver Wi-Fi to Idaho high schools though key legislative budget writers such as Senator Dean Cameron, R-Rupert, questioned his authority to do so. The contract could run 15 years and run $30 million, which lawmakers did not authorize. The process also favored ENA's profile over two Idaho-based competitors, Ednetics of Post Falls and Tek-Hut Inc., of Twin Falls. ENA was a Luna campaign contributor and its Idaho director, Garry Lough, was Idaho Republican Party executive director 2004-06; and was Luna's deputy of legislative affairs in 2007.

The politics. After losing for superintendent against Democratic incumbent Marilyn Howard in 2002, Luna won narrowly in 2006. Howard was retiring, and Luna's service in the George W. Bush Education department had provided him with allies. Even so, he claimed the GOP nomination over state Rep. Steve Smylie by a mere 893 votes. That fall he faced Democrat Jana Jones, Howard's deputy, who had won the primary over state Senator Bert Marley. In the general election, Jones found herself maneuvered into serving as an apologist for the status quo. Even so, Luna's margin that year was the smallest of any major-office GOP candidate.

In 2010 he won strongly against retired Boise School Superintendent Stan Olson. Relative moderation from Luna, and the lack of a case from Olson for firing him, gave him a 60.5% margin.

Luna's political strength after his second-term problems has become a subject of much debate. He is expected to seek re-election in 2014 (his statements suggest as much, at least). Democrat Jana Jones (who lost to Luna in 2006) has announced for the office.

H1	Democrat			Republican		
2010	Stan Olson	175,541	39.50%	Tom Luna	268,852	60.50%
2006	Jane Jones	216,013	48.74%	Tom Luna	227,171	51.26%
2002	Marilyn Howard	211,566	52.20%	Tom Luna	184,018	45.40%
1998	Marilyn Howard	202,978	54.10%	Anne Fox	171,976	45.90%
1994	Will Sullivan	170,938	42.90%	Anne Fox	227,257	57.10%
1990	-	-		Jerry Evans	244,864	100.00%

TOM LUNA, R-Boise

Office: www.sde.idaho.gov/
Campaign: www.lunaforidaho.com
Background: Official in federal Department of Education.
Political: Nampa school board. Unsuccessful race for superintendent of public instruction 2002 (45.4% losing to Democratic incumbent Marilyn Howard). Elected 2006 (51.3% over Jana Jones-D), 2010 (60.5% over Stan Olsen).

Legislature

Senate: Republicans: 28, Democrats: 7. Men: 31, Women: 4

Analogue districts

Districts from the 00s on the left, new districts for the 10s on the right. Analogues are district not exactly the same as but roughly similar to their predecessors.

New districts are noted on the left, old (predecessor) districts on the right .

1	1		19	19
2	3		20	20
3	5		21	21
4	4		22	no clear analogue
5	6		23	22, 23
6	7		24	24
7	2		25	26
8	no clear analogue, part 8		26	25
9	9		27	27
10	10		28	29
11	11		29	30
12	12		30	32
13	13		31	28
14	14		32	31
15	15		33	33
16	16		34	34
17	17		35	35
18	18			

Legislative control

As of 2010, Republicans had held control of the Idaho Legislature for a half century – 50 years, since winning it back (after losing both chambers for one term) in 1960.

Democrats did reach a 21-21 Senate tie in 1990, but Republican Lieutenant Governor C.L. "Butch" Otter was able to vote to organize the session so that Republicans retained control.

The number of members in the chambers changed over the years, though little in recent decades.

Until reapportionment in 1966, the Senate had one member for each county (so, 44 from 1958 to 1964), and the House a varying number based on county population (59 in 1958 and 1960, then 63 in 1962, and 79 in 1964). Since then, the Senate has had 35 member and the House 70, except for period in the 80s when a "floterial" apportionment system was used, and expanded the Senate (for 1984 through 1990) to 42 members, and the House to 84.

Here is how the numbers have varied in the cycles since (beginning in 1958); years are in reference to election years, changes refer to changes from previous cycle, and aren't noted when the number of members in the body changed:

	Senate R	Senate D	Change	House R	House D	Change
1958	17	27	+2D	24	35	+8D
1960	23	21	+6R	31	28	+7R
1962	23	21	0	34	29	
1964	25	19	+2R	42	37	
1966	22	13		38	32	
1968	20	15	+2D	38	32	0
1970	19	16	+1D	41	29	+3R
1972	23	12	+4R	51	19	+10R
1974	21	14	+2D	43	27	+8D
1976	20	15	+1D	48	22	+5R
1978	19	16	+1D	50	20	+2R
1980	23	12	+4R	56	14	+6R
1982	21	14	+2D	51	19	+5D
1984	28	14		67	17	
1986	26	16	+2D	64	20	+3D
1988	23	19	+3D	64	20	0
1990	21	21	+2D	56	28	+8D
1992	23	12		50	20	
1994	27	8	+4R	57	13	+7R
1996	30	5	+3R	59	11	+2R
1998	31	4	+1R	58	12	+1D
2000	32	3	+1R	61	9	+3R
2002	28	7	+4D	54	16	+7D
2004	28	7	0	57	13	+3R
2006	28	7	0	51	19	+6D
2008	28	7	0	52	18	+1R
2010	28	7	0	57	13	+5R
2012	28	7	0	57	13	0

2012 primaries

In many cases, the major legislative races of 2012 were held in the Republican primaries. Since 2012 was the first election following redistricting, that contributed to some contests. The rise of the Tea Party and similar groups in 2010 contributed to a number of others.

One primary featured two incumbent legislators, thrown into one district: In new District 23, Republican Senator Bert Brackett (57.4%) defeated fellow Republican incumbent Tim Corder (42.6%). Other primaries involving an incumbent (all Republican except District 17 House B, incumbents listed first):

1	Senate	Shawn Keough (70.3%), Danielle Ahrens
1	House A	Eric Anderson (63.9%), Donna Capurso, Louis Kins
1	House B	George Eskridge (66.9%), Pam Stout
2	Senate	Steve Vick (61.8%), Mike Jorgenson
2	House A	Vito Barbieri (57.0%), Mark Fisher
2	House B	Phil Hart (31.2%), Ed Morse (35.4%), Ron Vieselmeyer, Fritz Wiedenhoff
3	House B	Frank Henderson (55.6%), Jack Schroeder
6	Senate	Dan Johnson (59.6%), Jeff Nesset
7	Senate	Sheryl Nuxoll (73.2%), Mary Wade Heston
7	House A	Shannon McMillan (47.8%), Rex Rammell, Ed Galloway
8	House A	Ken Roberts (44.9%), John Blattler, Dan Davis
8	House B	Lenore Barrett (37.1%), Merrill Beyeler, K. Keene, L. Dresen
9	Senate	Monty Pearce (56.0%), Matthew Faulks
9	House B	Judy Boyle (56.2%), Jeri Soulier, Daniel Weston, Kendall Nelson-Jeffs
10	Senate	Jim Rice (68.6%), Kent Marmon
11	Senate	Patti Anne Lodge (59.8%), Maurice Clements
11	House A	Gayle Batt (66.0%), Greg Collett
11	House B	Christy Perry (50.1%), Matt Dorsey, Ronalee Linsenmann, John Gough
13	Senate	Curt McKenzie (54.3%), Hubert Osborne
14	House B	Reed DeMordaunt (72.5%), Michael Greenway
17	House B	**Democratic primary.** Sue Chew (88.9%), Greg Nielson
20	House A	Joe Palmer (65.9%), Chris MacCloud, Richard Dees
23	House B	Pete Nielsen (45.7%), Matthew Bundy, Steve Millington
27	Senate	Dean Cameron (56.5%), Douglas Pickett
28	Senate	Jim Guthrie (65.3%), Rusty Barlow (34.7%)
30	House A	Jeff Thompson (86.8%), Trimelda Concepcion McDaniels
31	House B	Jim Marriott (37.6%), Julie Van Orden (62.4%)
32	House B	Tom Loertscher (54.4%), Kelton Larsen, Franklyn Vilt
33	Senate	Bart Davis (74.7%), Brian Schad
33	House B	Linden Bateman (75.6%), David Lyon
34	House B	Dell Raybould (58.6%), Dan Roberts
35	House A	Jo An Wood (44.4%), Joshua Anderson, Dale Mortimer

Presidential voting

The vote for president by legislative district, listing in rank order from best vote for Republican Mitt Romney.

District	Legislators	Obama	Obama%	Romney	Romney%	Total
34	3 R	1,240	6.92%	16,485	92.00%	17,919
35	3 R	2,437	12.96%	16,038	85.32%	18,797
27	3 R	2,488	16.19%	12,596	81.96%	15,369
32	3 R	3,467	17.05%	16,490	81.10%	20,333
30	3 R	3,755	19.06%	15,545	78.92%	19,696
31	3 R	3,822	21.71%	13,440	76.35%	17,603
11	3 R	4,184	23.55%	13,116	73.82%	17,767
25	3 R	3,833	23.52%	12,033	73.82%	16,300
9	3 R	4,636	25.68%	12,944	71.70%	18,053
2	3 R	6,033	26.93%	15,823	70.62%	22,406
23	3 R	3,881	27.41%	9,858	69.63%	14,157
14	3 R	6,637	28.40%	16,209	69.37%	23,367
22	3 R	4,549	28.40%	10,999	68.66%	16,019
3	3 R	5,339	29.14%	12,486	68.14%	18,324
8	3 R	6,595	29.55%	15,032	67.36%	22,316
7	3 R	5,802	30.10%	12,893	66.90%	19,273
13	3 R	5,051	30.45%	11,087	66.85%	16,586
24	3 R	4,872	30.28%	10,707	66.54%	16,091
33	3 R	5,429	30.56%	11,789	66.37%	17,763
28	3 R	6,411	31.76%	13,333	66.06%	20,183
20	3 R	6,073	31.96%	12,475	65.66%	18,999
12	3 R	4,885	31.70%	10,086	65.46%	15,409
21	3 R	7,053	33.56%	13,390	63.72%	21,015
1	3 R	6,940	33.87%	12,773	62.34%	20,488
6	2 R 1 D	6,847	37.09%	11,140	60.34%	18,462
10	3 R	5,062	38.47%	7,681	58.37%	13,160
4	3 R	7,479	39.16%	11,072	57.97%	19,098
15	3 R	7,684	40.27%	10,756	56.38%	19,079
29	3 D	7,785	43.30%	9,547	53.10%	17,980
26	2 D 1 R	7,907	45.05%	9,178	52.29%	17,552
5	2 D 1 R	9,470	45.88%	10,185	49.34%	20,643
18	3 D	11,138	50.74%	10,041	45.74%	21,952
16	3 D	10,207	51.36%	8,948	45.03%	19,872
17	3 D	9,197	54.87%	6,747	40.25%	16,762
19	3 D	14,599	62.17%	7,989	34.02%	23,481

Health insurance exchange

A few items about one of the major issues in Idaho in 2014, the state's adoption of a state-run health insurance exchange, a component of the Affordable Care Act. The bill which passed, setting up the system, was House Bill 248. From legislative records:

H0248   by HEALTH AND WELFARE COMMITTEE
HEALTH INSURANCE EXCHANGE - Adds to law relating to the Health Insurance Exchange to provide a short title, to state legislative purpose and intent, to define terms, to establish the exchange and the board, to provide for powers and authority of the exchange, to provide for reporting, to authorize reliance by the exchange on other agencies, to provide that the exchange shall not preempt the duties of the Department of Insurance and to provide for the preference for Idaho contractors in a health insurance exchange.
     Read Third Time in Full - Motion to send to GO, motion failed
03/13

PASSED - 41-29-0 (House)
AYES -- Anderson(01), Anderson(31), Anderst, Bell, Bolz, Burgoyne, Chew, Clow, Collins, Erpelding, Eskridge, Gannon, Gibbs, Hancey, Hartgen, Henderson, Hixon, Horman, Kauffman, King, Kloc, Malek, Meline, Miller, Morse, Packer, Pence, Perry, Raybould, Ringo, Romrell, Rusche, Smith, Thompson, VanOrden, Ward-Engelking, Wills, Wood(27), Woodings, Youngblood, Mr. Speaker
NAYS -- Agidius, Andrus, Barbieri, Barrett, Bateman, Batt, Boyle, Crane, Dayley, DeMordaunt, Denney, Gestrin, Harris, Holtzclaw, Loertscher, Luker, McMillan, Mendive, Monks, Moyle, Nielsen, Palmer, Patterson, Shepherd, Sims, Stevenson, Trujillo, Vander Woude, Wood(35)
Absent and excused -- None
Floor Sponsor - Wood(27)
03/21   Read third time in full - **PASSED - 23-12-0 (Senate)**
AYES -- Bair, Bock, Brackett, Buckner-Webb, Cameron, Davis, Goedde, Guthrie, Hagedorn, Heider, Hill, Keough, Lacey, Lakey, Lodge, Martin, Patrick, Rice, Schmidt, Siddoway, Stennett, Tippets, Werk
NAYS -- Bayer, Durst, Fulcher, Johnson, McKenzie, Mortimer, Nonini, Nuxoll, Pearce, Thayn, Vick, Winder
Absent and excused -- None
Floor Sponsor - Tippets

Gang of 16. In February 2013 a group of freshman Republican legislators said they would support Governor C.L. ""Butch" Otter in his push to enact a state exchange (with some conditions attached). Their support for the plan may have made the difference in the House vote.

The original 16 (there was some decline in membership later), all Republicans, included: Luke Malek of Coeur d'Aene (lead negotiator), Cindy Agidius of Moscow, Neil Anderson of Blackfoot, Robert Anderst of Nampa, Lance Clow of of Twin Falls, Tom Dayley of Boise, Brandon Hixon of Caldwell, Wendy Horman of Idaho Falls, Clark Kauffman of Filer, Doug Hancey of Rexburg, Steven Miller of Fairfield, Ed Morse of Hayden, Kelley Packer of McCammon, Paul Romrell of St. Anthony, Julie VanOrden of Pingree and Rick Youngblood of Nampa.

District 1

District 1 (Boundary County and Bonner County (part)). Separately, neither Boundary County nor Bonner County have sufficiently large populations to constitute one ideal district of 44,788 persons. When combined, they exceed 44,788 people, the population of an ideal district, by more than allowable deviation. The Commission therefore finds that it is necessary to divide the population of Bonner County to create District 1 because it is the only Idaho county contiguous to Boundary County and the division is necessary to satisfy the one person, one vote requirement of the 14 th Amendment to the United States Constitution. Bonner County was divided along major highways and roads in an effort to keep communities of interest together. District 1 contains 46,712 people, a deviation of +4.30% from the ideal district.

District 1 gains territory in southwestern Bonner County but gives up some land in the south-center area (around Sagle).

Its delegation is all-Republican, and stable for a full decade.

In the Senate, Shawn Keough has become vice-chair of the Joint Finance-Appropriations Committee, and with the Senate chair, Dean Cameron, both moderating and cooling influences with the chamber, but also something of a target for activists. All three voted in 2013 for the state health insurance exchange proposed by Governor Otter.

All three members of this delegation – the House members are Eric Anderson and George Eskridge – were targeted by Tea Party activists in 2012. All three incumbents defeated those candidates with landslides. Still, at least one and possibly more of those candidates will be back with renewed challenges in 2014. One indicator of some of that is in the libertarian Idaho Freedom Foundation's 2013 index of legislators. On it, Keough ranked sixth from the bottom (and second to last among Republicans). Eskridge and Anderson also came up with negative scores from that group.

ELECTIONS The district's delegation remained stable in 2012, but not for lack of challenges.

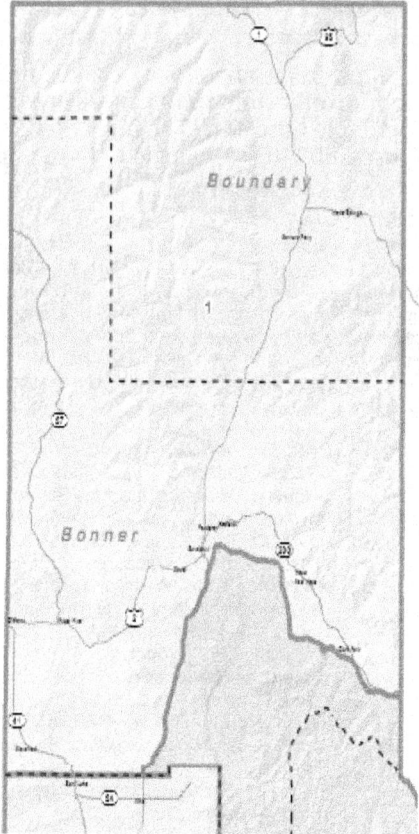

44

Anderson was closely challenged by Democrat Steve Elgar in 2004 and 2006; the closest of these brought Elgar, who was well-financed and regarded as running an unusually strong campaign, to within 235 votes of beating Anderson. But those have been the only really close general election races here in more than a decade.

Predecessor district 1

ELECTIONS Traditionally timber and sometimes mining country, the far north of Idaho still has some timber economic base but has increasingly become a tourist and retirement center, especially around Sandpoint.

For decades the northernmost Idaho legislative district (which has been number 1 since numbering began) was Democratic territory. With occasional exceptions (three-term Republican Senator Don Samuelson, from Bonner, being the most prominent), the long-timers here were for many years Democrats – Jim Stoicheff, Marion Davidson, Kermit Kiebert, Tim Tucker among them.

In the 90s, the district turned Republican. Tucker, seeking a fifth term in the Senate, was upset by Sandpoint Republican Shawn Keough, winning with a strong 59.1%. Keough has not had a close election since, winning in landslides when she challenged at all in the general (as she wasn't in 2008 or 2010). She has won occasional primaries easily as well.

Also in 1996, the House A seat was vacated by Democrat Carol Pietsch, and Republican outdoor writer John Campbell defeated Democrat Monica Beaudoin, who had been a president of the Idaho Education Association. Campbell was steadily re-elected, sometimes (as in 2002) against serious opposition, before retiring in 2004. That year the seat went to Republican Eric Anderson, who three times faced serious challenges from Democrat Steve Elgar, one of the best Democratic legislative fundraisers in the state in his elections, and well-organized and hard-campaigning. Anderson was unopposed for re-election in 2010.

The other House seat was held for many years by Democrat Stoicheff, who died in office in 2000. His wife was appointed to replace him, but she was defeated that year by Republican George Eskridge, who has held the seat since.

In 2012, all were challenged most energetically by Tea Party-backed candidates, though one came close to defeating the incumbents.

Presdt	Democrat			Republican		
2012	Barack Obama	6,940	33.87%	Mitt Romney	12,773	62.34%
Sen	Democrat			Republican		
2012	-	-	-	Shawn Keough	17,217	100.00%
2010	-	-	-	Shawn Keough	11,593	100.00%
2008	-	-	-	Shawn Keough	15,322	100.00%
2006	Jim Ramsey	4,265	31.42%	Shawn Keough	9,308	68.58%
2004	Patty Palmer	4,177	24.90%	Shawn Keough	12,630	75.10%
2002	Gary Pietsch	3,133	28.40%	Shawn Keough	7,904	71.60%
H1	Democrat			Republican		

	Democrat			Republican		
2012	**Andrew C. Sorg**	**5,567**	**29.05%**	**Eric Anderson**	**13,599**	**70.95%**
2010	-		-	- Eric Anderson	10,978	100.00%
2008	Steve Elgar	8,404	45.60%	Eric Anderson	10,030	54.40%
2006	Steve Elgar	6,634	49.13%	Eric Anderson	6,869	50.87%
2004	Steve Elgar	7,538	45.00%	Eric Anderson	8,399	50.20%
2002	Dale Van Stone	4,860	44.60%	John Campbell	6,033	55.40%
H2	**Democrat**			**Republican**		
2012	-		-	**- George Eskridge**	**16,412**	**100.00%**
2010	-		-	- George Eskridge	11,191	100.00%
2008	Tom Hollingsworth	6,494	35.80%	George Eskridge	11,651	64.20%
2006	Bob Wynhausen	4,973	37.24%	George Eskridge	8,382	62.76%
2004	-		-	- George Eskridge	13,233	100.00%
2002	Sandra Lamson	3,786	35.00%	George Eskridge	7,019	65.00%

PRIMARIES Keough has been primaried three times in the last decade, in 2008, 2010 and 2012 (Donald Heckel, Steve Tanner and Danielle Ahrens, respectively) but the results were closely similar in each case, Keough taking about three-fourths of the vote (70.3% in 2012). Ahrens has launched another challenge for 2014.

Anderson was primaried by Daniel Lawrence in 2008, but won with 70.9%; in 2012, he defeated Donna Capurso and Luis Kins with 63.9%. Eskridge won a 2012 primary over Pam Stout with 66.9%.

Senator SHAWN KEOUGH, R-Sandpoint

Web: www.shawnkeough.com
Background: Public relations. North Idaho College, Lewis Clark State College.
Political: Elected to Senate 1996, 1998, 2000, 2002, 2004, 2006, 2008, 2010, 2012.

Representative ERIC ANDERSON, R-Priest Lake

Web:
Background: General Contracting and real estate Development. Board member, Northwest Public Power Association.
Political: Elected to House 2004, 2006, 2008, 2010, 2012.

Representative GEORGE ESKRIDGE, R-Dover

Web: www.sandpoint.com/geskridge/
Background: Real estate (Four Seasons Real Estate). Pacific State Marine Fisheries Commission (2002-06). University of Montana.
Political: Elected to House 2000, 2002, 2004, 2006, 2008, 2010, 2012.

District 2

District 2 (Kootenai County (part)). Consists primarily of the northern and eastern rural areas of Kootenai County. Includes the communities of Hayden, Dalton Gardens. Runs South to the Benewah County line, east to Shoshone County Line, and West to the Washington Border. District 2 contains 45,894 people with a deviation of +2.47 % from the ideal district.

The new district 2 covers most of the northern Kootenai County area in the old district 3 (though not some of the Rathdrum area), along with a lot of the forested and lightly-populated area east and southeast of Lake Coeur d'Alene. Partisan difference: Little or none.

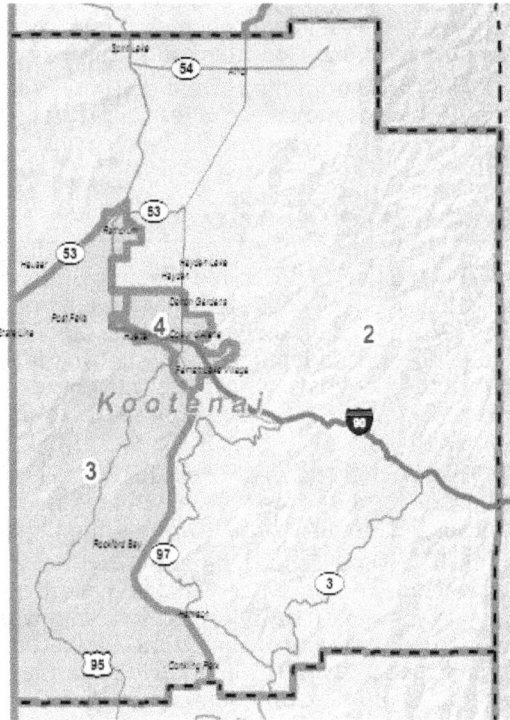

This is a growth area, though much of the turf in eastern Kootenai has a very different feel than the area north of Coeur d'Alene: Much more rural, not just ex-urban.

As a matter of ideology, this could be considered the land of nullification, where Tea Party sentiment and ideas run especially strong even in the context of a state that often sympathizes with them. Only on unuual occasions have candidates other than the most "conservative" (as locally defined among activist Republicans) on the ballot won elections.

That did happen in 2012, however, when veteran Representative Phil Hart lost a four-way Republican primary. Hart was one of the Idaho Legislature's harshest critics of taxes, and had personally been involved in long-running battles with the Internal Revenue Service and the state of Idaho. For some years he retained support but finally lost it in 2012, falling in an intense primary contest to Ed Morse, who had been backed by a mainstream coalition.

Hart was unusual his personal legal troubles, but other delegation members here have had similar policy views.

Primary contests are not unusual here, and often are dispositive; there's not been a closely contested general election here in a couple of decades. Senator Steve Vick was a close ally of Hart, and proposed a rule requiring two-thirds of the legislature raise taxes and fees; the libertarian Idaho Freedom Foundation ranked him second most favorably (with 137 points) among all 105 Idaho legislators. Representative Vito Barbieri was the backer of a bill attempting to nullifiy the provisions of the Affordable Care Act in the state, and was quoted on public schools, "If you accept Jesus Christ as Lord and God, then pull your kids out of that Godless institution."

There's a split in the current delegation, evidenced by the vote on the state health insurance exchange proposed by Governor Otter: Morse voted in favor of it, and Vick and Barbieri against.

Predecessor district 3

The population growth in the area of Kootenai County north of Coeur d'Alene has beern such that what couldn't have been a legislative district in the 80s had made it inevitable by the 00s. Though located in the prtty Panhandle, this is suburb country not so different from Meridian or Eagle to the south, though drawing for its new residents maybe a little more sharply on conservative expatriates from southern California and western Washington.

The key political figure here for some years was Phil Hart, known statewide for anti-tax activism and for running afoul of federal and state tax officials, leading to legal difficulties and inquiries by a House committee.

ELECTIONS The retirement in 2010 of veteran Republican Representative Jim Clark (who had ben unopposed for many cycles) opened the way for a Hart ally, Vito Barbieri, who won a contested primary but was unopposed in the general election. Barbieri moved quickly into statewide prominence in the 2011 legislative session as a prime sponsor of a federal health care nullification bill.

The Senate seat here is another matter, turning over twice turning the decade, but both times in Republican primaries; Democrats did not even challenge for it from 2004 to 2010.

Presdt	Democrat			Republican		
2012	Barack Obama	6,033	26.93%	Mitt Romney	15,823	70.62%
Sen	Democrat			Republican		
2012	Shirley McFaddan	6,688	31.00%	Steve Vick	14,871	65.70%
2010	-	-	-	Steve Vick	12,309	100.00%
2008	-	-	-	Mike Jorgenson	17,007	100.00%
2006	-	-	-	Mike Jorgenson	9,825	100.00%
2004	-	-	-	Mike Jorgenson	14,309	100.00%
2002	JoAnn Harvey	4,634	44.40%	Kent Bailey	5,813	55.60%
H1	Democrat			Republican		
2012	Cheryl Stransky	7,371	34.30%	Vito Barbieri	14,142	65.70%
2010	-	-	-	Vito Barbieri	12,168	100.00%
2008	-	-	-	Jim Clark	16,724	100.00%
2006	-	-	-	Jim Clark	9,825	100.00%
2004	-	-	-	Jim Clark	13,945	100.00%
2002	-	-	-	Jim Clark	8,524	100.00%
H2	Democrat			Republican		
2012	Dan English	7,868	36.70%	Ed Morse	13,555	63.30%

2010	-	-	- Phil Hart	9,170	80.10%
2008	-	-	- Phil Hart	16,762	100.00%
2006	-	-	- Phil Hart	9,751	100.00%
2004	-	-	- Phil Hart	13,315	91.00%
2002	-	-	- Wayne Meyer	6,705	68.30%

PRIMARIES District 3 has had a full filling of primaries, in all five cycles of the last decade. Three successive senators were ousted in Republican primaries here. First, in 2002, incumbent Clyde Boatright (46.5%) lost to challenger Kent Bailey (53.5%). In 2004, incumbent Bailey came in third (27.64%) behind a comeback try from Boatright (32.94%) but both lost to Mike Jorgenson (39.42%). In 2006, Jorgenson (67.4%) survived a Bailey comeback attempt, and two years later (60.9%) a challenge from Jim Connell (39.1%). But in 2010 he lost (40.5%) to challenger Steve Vick (59.5%), and again – challenging the new incumbent – in 2012. This has been a challenging district for Senate incumbents.

Republican Wayne Meyer turned back in 2002 a minor-party challenge from Phil Hart, but when Hart challenged him in the Republican primary in 2004, he ousted the incumbent (60.25% to 39.75%). Hart was challenged in primaries in 2006 (beating a Meyer comeback attempt, 57%-43%) and 2008 (beating David Rawls 70.1% to 29.9%). However, after a series of negative headlines, Hart in 2012 became one of only two Idaho House member to lose his primary re-election, taking only 31.2% of the vote, losing to Ed Morse by 238 votes.

Jim Clark turned back two primary challenges in 2004 (62.32% over Jeri DeLange) and 2006 (59.8% over DeLange again). In 2012 Vito Barbieri turned back (57.0%) a challenge from Mark Fisher.

Senator STEVE VICK, R-Dalton Gardens

Web: www.stevevickusa.com
Background: Owner, Vick Homes. Farmer. Utility Division, Montana Public Service Commission. Montana State University.
Political: Montana House, 1994-2001. Elected to Senate 2010, 2012.

Representative VITO BARBIERI, R-Dalton Gardens

Web: www.vitobarbieri.com
Background: Attorney. Moved from California, 2004. Board member, Open Arms Crisis Pregnancy Center, Coeur d'Alene. Western State University College of Law, Fullerton, California.
Political: Elected to House 2010, 2012.

Representative ED MORSE, R-Hayden

Web: www.votemorse.com/
Background: Real estate appraiser and consultant. University of Idaho; Gonzaga University College of Law (JD).
Political: Elected to House 2012.

District 3

District 3 (Kootenai County (part)).
District 3 is contained wholly within
Kootenai County. It includes the
remainder of Kootenai County that is
west of the city of Coeur d'Alene and
Highway 95 to the Idaho border.
Consistent with public testimony
received at the June 22, 2011 hearings
in Coeur d'Alene and Sandpoint, and
the October 6, 2011 hearing in Coeur
d'Alene, District 3 includes the majority
of the cities of Post Falls and
Rathdrum, keeping traditional
communities of interest intact. Further,
the district was divided along major
highways providing an easily
distinguished boundary. District 3
contains 46,278 people with a deviation
of +3.32% from the ideal district.

The Post Falls area was
considered for a time, up to the
early 90s, a Democratic-competitive
area; and in that period, thrugh the
80s, a number of Democrats were
elected from the general area.
There's little evidence for that now,
with an influx of more conservative
voters. This area west and
southwest of Coeur d'Alene has
drawn lots of exurban and
suburban voters.

It reaches down as well into part
of the Coeur d'Alene Indian
Reservation. Some of these areas
are quite different from the Post
Falls-Ranthdrum area, and could
affect the way people campaign for votes. This area is similar in many
respects to District 2 – almost a west-side version of that north-east side
district – but has a somewhat less activist base on the Tea Party front. Post
Falls, while oriented to Republicans, may be a little less Tea Party receptive
than some other parts of the district, as indicated by the 2013 city election
results there.

The senator, Bob Nonini, has been notably active on the education front.
He was a House member from 2002-12, and as chair of the education
committee there helped in 2011 shepherd through the "Luna laws" on
public schools, and backed them on the House floor. He also has supported
a proposed tax break for donors to private, but not to public, schools. In

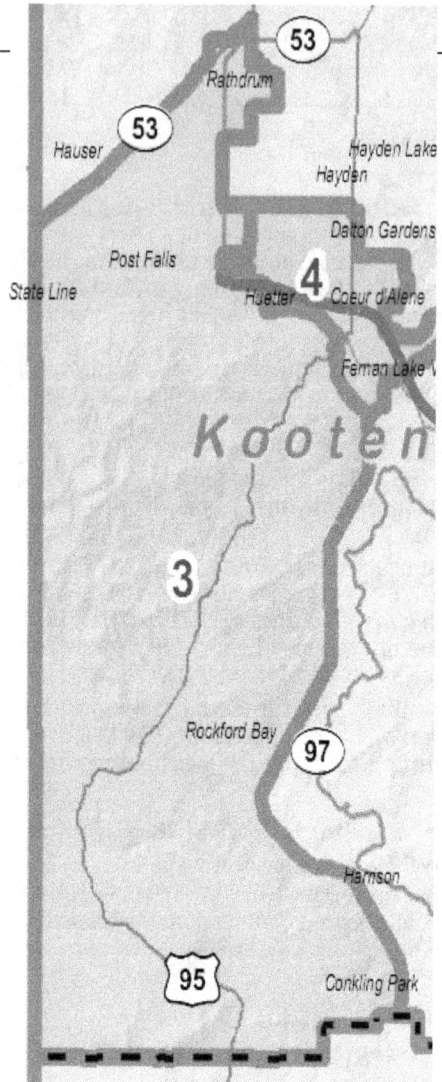

2013 he ranked very high (third place among 105 legislators, with 136 points) by the libertarian Idaho Freedom Foundation.

Within the legislature, he became well known for taking an active role in campaigning against fellow Republican incumbents (among them, Senate budget panel chair Dean Cameron), in favor of replacing them with challengers deemed more conservative. He has had tense relations with the press, reportedly talking to no reporters except those from the Coeur d'Alene *Press*.

The Republican who replaced Nonini in the House, Ron Mendive, who went viral on the Internet when he adked, at an American Civil Liberties Union presentation, whether the group supported prostitution as well as abortion access on grounds that it too was "a woman's choice." The Idaho Freedom Foundation ranked him 10th most favorably on its list of 105 (118 points).

Representative Frank Henderson, a city and county official for years before reaching the legislature, and now the legislature's most senior member in age, has been regarded as a more moderate vote. He voted in favor of the governor's health insurance exchange proposal, while Nonini and Mendive voted against.

Predecessor district 5

ELECTIONS In 2002, when the district was created, it saw a streuous Senate contest between Democrat Wally Wright, a former legislator with some populist appeal, and Republican Dick Compton, a Kootenai County commissioner. Compton held the seat for two terms until he retired, at which point it went to Republican Jim Hammond, who had been administrator at the city of Post Falls. Hammond was lightly opposed in 2006 and unopposed in the two elections since.

The House A seat was held, after the 2002 election, by Hilde Kellogg, a veteran Post Falls civic activist whose long run in the Idaho House went back to 1982. When she retired in 2004, the seat was won (after a contested primary and a lightly contested general) by Bob Nonini, who had been active in the Kootenai County Republican organization.

The third seat has been since held, without much struggle, since 2004 by Frank Henderson, a former county commissioner who had run unsuccessfully for the legislature before.

Presdt	Democrat			Republican		
2012	Barack Obama	5,339	29.14%	Mitt Romney	12,486	68.14%
Sen	Democrat			Republican		
2012	Kristy Johnson	5,641	31.7%	Bob Nonini	12,132	68.30%
2010	-	-	-	Jim Hammond	11,739	100.00%
2008	-	-	-	Jim Hammond	16,301	100.00%
2006	Chuck Thomas	3,929	33.36%	Jim Hammond	7,848	66.64%
2004	Ian Stenseng	4,826	29.10%	Dick Compton	11,750	70.90%
2002	Wally Wright	4,797	47.90%	Dick Compton	5,222	52.10%
H1	Democrat			Republican		

2012	David Larsen	5,609	32.10%	Ron Mendive	11,855	67.90%
2010	David Larsen	3,674	26.90%	Bob Nonini	9,973	73.10%
2008	-	-	-	Bob Nonini	15,850	96.90%
2006	David Larsen	4,278	36.06%	Bob Nonini	7,562	63.74%
2004	David Larsen	5,217	31.00%	Bob Nonini	10,804	64.30%
2002	Kristy Johnson	3,933	39.30%	Hilde Kellogg	5,603	56.00%
H2	**Democrat**			**Republican**		
2012	**Ronald K. Johnson**	**5,227**	**29.90%**	**Frank Henderson**	**12,270**	**70.10%**
2010	-	-	-	Frank Henderson	11,707	100.00%
2008	-	-	-	Frank Henderson	16,057	100.00%
2006	Lyndon Harriman	4,054	34.46%	Frank Henderson	7,710	65.54%
2004	Lyndon Harriman	5,005	30.50%	Frank Henderson	11,381	69.50%
2002	Lyndon Harriman	3,474	35.30%	Charles Eberle	5,285	53.70%

PRIMARIES The district's previous two senators, Dick Compton and Jim Hammond, each were challenged as incumbents (in 2002 and 2010 respectively) to little effect (61.5% over Joyce Nowacki and 50.6% over John Green and Jack Schroeder, respectively).

Two representatives, in seat B, were taken out in primaries: Don Pischner by Charles Eberle (52.5%) in 2002, then Eberle in 2004 by Frank Henderson (51.57%). When the A seat was opened with the retirement of Hilde Kellogg, a primary developed between Bob Nonini (51.88%) and former legislator Ron Vieselmeyer (48.12%). There was also in 2002 a rare Democratic primary for the B seat, won by Lyndon Harriman (50.9%), who would go on to run twice more for the seat. The open House A seat in 2012 was the subject of a Republican primary between Ron Mendive, who won (50.1%), and Jeff Tyler.

Senator BOB NONINI, R-Coeur d'Alene
Web: www.bobnoniniforidaho.com
Background: Financial consultant, investments. Former Kootenai County Republican chair, 1998-2004. North Idaho College.
Political: Elected to House 2002, 2004, 2006, 2008, 2010. Elected to Senate 2012.

Representative RON MENDIVE, R-Coeur d'Alene
Web: mendive4idaho.com/
Background: Construction, land services, semi-retired. North Idaho College.
Political: Elected to House 2012.

Representative FRANK HENDERSON, R-Post Falls
Web: www.facebook.com/frank.henderson.1023
Background: Retired, newspaper publisher and marketing executive. Publisher, Post Falls *Tribune*, 1976-80. U.S. Army. University of Idaho.
Political: Mayor, Post Falls, 1980-83. Commissioner, Kootenai County, 1983-91. Elected to House 2004, 1006, 2008, 2010, 2012.

District 4

District 4 (Kootenai County (part)).
District 4 is contained entirely within
Kootenai County and includes the
majority of the city of Coeur d'Alene, a
traditional community of interest unto
itself. The district line follows well
known and clearly identifiable streets
and highways. District 4 contains
46,324 people with a deviation of
+3.43% from the ideal district.

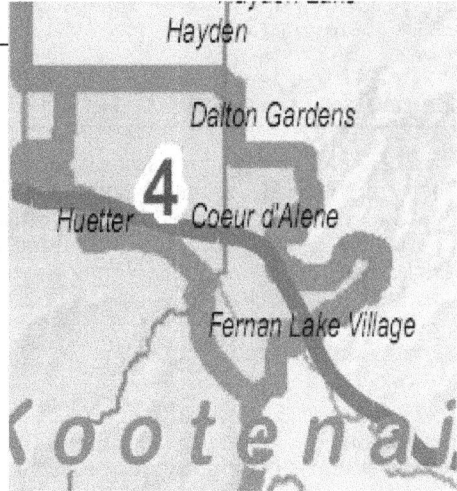

Until the 70s, Kootenai County, then a timber-based county with a significant tourism component, was largely Democratic, owig partly to union influence at the time and partly to a collection of other smaller interests. The county has become much more suburban since, and began electing Republicans periodically in the 70s and 80s and almost completely since then. District 4, which consists generally of the city of Coeur d'Alene, has retained much of what is left of the old Democratic influences, and that district has remained generally intact through the 2011 redistricting process.

That is enough to make this the most competitive district in the Panhandle, though not enough to keep Republicans from winning here more often than they lose.

The senator here, John Goedde, was a member on the Coeur d'Alene School Board when he entered the Senate in 2000, and education has been a prime subject for him since – he is chair of the Senate Education Committee. In that role he's been a little difficult to pin down, sometimes allying with more moderate members of his committee.

He also, however, supported the "Luna laws" in 2011, backing their passage through his committee. And in 2013 he proposed legislation (which he said was intended only as a gesture aimed at the state Board of Education, and not seriously intended for passage) to require that every high school student read the Ayn Rand book *Atlas Shrugged*, and pass a test on it before graduating.

Representative Kathleen Sims, who also has served in the Senate (from 2002 to 2002), once lost a primary contest to Goedde when redistricting threw them into the same district. She has been active in conservative groups in Kootenai County's local political battles. The libertarian Idaho Freedom Foundation ranked her fourth most positively (134 points) among the 105 legislators in 2013.

New House member Luke Malek was one of the leaders of the "Gang of 16" freshmen supporting (with some adjustments) passage of the governor's health insurance exchange. He also got some national attention, ranking second among the "Worst State Legislators of 2013" released by the Marijuana Policy Project. Malek was placed on the list of nine of his backing of a resolution opposing the legalization of marijuana "for any purpose," and a quote describing medical marijuana is a "farcical predatory scheme."

Predecessor district 4

ELECTIONS The consistent figure here through the last decade has been John Goedde, a businessman and former Coeur d'Alene School District board member first elected in 2000 (after a contentious primary). It may be partly a measure of the district, and partly some newspaper reports, that his electoral record has been less than a series of landslides or unopposeds. He was held to very close re-elections in 2006 and 2008, and might have been again in 2010 except that no Democrat filed against him. As chair of the Senate Education committee, he has been in the middle of controversial issues.

House seat B was held for most of the decade by Democrat George Sayler, a retired educator and one of the few Democrats elected from northern Idaho during the decade. He won often narrowly but steadily through 2008, then retired in 2010. In that Republican tide year, the seat went to Republican Kathleen Sims, who had been a state senator and had worked in Kootenai Republican politics for many years.

In the first election (2002) after the new district was created, Democrat Bonnie Douglas won the A seat. But that lasted only one term. In 2004 she lost her primary and Republican Marge Chadderdon defeated the Democratic nominee and has held it, with modest margins, since. Those margins have remained close enough, however, to suggest that this is reasonably thought of as a competitive island in a Republican sea.

Presdt	Democrat			Republican		
2012	Barack Obama	7,479	39.16%	Mitt Romney	11,072	57.97%

Sen	Democrat			Republican		
2012	Warren Ducote	6,499	35.40%	John Goedde	10,468	56.90%
2010	-	-	-	John Goedde	8,263	70.80%
2008	Ken Howard	8,036	43.00%	John Goedde	9,525	50.90%
2006	Steven Foxx	5,536	46.96%	John Goedde	5,728	48.58%
2004	-	-	-	John Goedde	13,155	100.00%
2002	David Hunt	3,443	33.80%	John Goedde	6,022	59.20%

H1	Democrat			Republican		
2012	Janet Callen	7,016	38.70%	Luke Malek	10,417	57.50%
2010	Mike Bullard	4,739	38.10%	Marge Chadderdon	7,685	61.90%
2008	Tamara Poelstra	7,778	42.00%	Marge Chadderdon	10,720	58.00%
2006	Bonnie Douglas	5,463	46.49%	Marge Chadderdon	6,287	53.51%
2004	Mike Gridley	7,850	46.30%	Marge Chadderdon	9,121	53.70%
2002	Bonnie Douglas	4,879	48.10%	Jim Hollingsworth	4,852	47.80%

H2	Democrat			Republican		
2012	Anne L. Nesse	7,903	43.20%	Kathleen Sims	10,373	56.80%
2010	Paula Marano	5,230	41.90%	Kathleen Sims	7,242	58.10%
2008	George Sayler	9,809	52.80%	Jim Hollingsworth	8,779	47.20%

2006	George Sayler	6,757	57.15%	Sharon Culbreth	5,066	42.85%
2004	George Sayler	8,612	50.80%	Dan Yake	8,351	49.20%
2002	George Sayler	5,034	48.70%	Kris Ellis	4,965	48.10%

PRIMARIES Less primary action in the last decade in Coeur d'Alene than in most of northern Idaho. Redistricting in 2002 pitted Republican incumbents John Goedde (50.4%) against Kathy Sims (49.6%). In 2004, both parties primaried for the House A seat. Democratic incumbent Bonnie Douglas (43.95%) was ousted in her primary by Mike Gridley (56.05%), and Republican Marge Chadderdon (55.87%) defeated 2002 Republican nominee Jim Hollingsworth (44.13%).

In 2012 the open House A seat was the subject of a Republican primary between Luke Malek, who won (65.5%), and Jeff Ames.

Senator JOHN GOEDDE, R-Coeur d'Alene

Web: www.johngoedde.com
Background: Property/casualty insurance sales. Independent insurance agent. Former president, North Idaho Chamber of Commerce. Washington State University.
Political: Former, Coeur d'Alene School Board. Elected to Senate 2000, 2002, 2004, 2006, 2008, 2010, 2012.

Representative LUKE MALEK, R-Coeur d'Alene

Web: http://www.lukemalek.com/
Background: Attorney, business consultant. Former county deputy prosecutor. College of Idaho; University of Idaho College of Law.
Political: Elected to House 2012.

Representative KATHLEEN SIMS, R-Coeur d'Alene

Web: twitter.com/votekathysims
Background: Auto/motorcycle dealer. Former Kootenai County Republican chair, former state Republican vice chair. North Idaho College.
Political: Appointed to Senate, 2001. Unsuccessful run for Senate, 2002 (losing in primary to John Goedde). Elected to House 2010, 2012.

District 5

District 5 (Benewah County and Latah County). District 5 is comprised of the entirety of Benewah County and Latah County. Separately, Benewah County and Latah County do not have a large enough population to constitute an entire legislative district. Therefore, combining Benewah County and Latah County is necessary to meet the one person one vote requirement. Further, combining these counties keeps communities of interest intact. Idaho's major state highway, Highway 95 runs the entire length of the District 5. District 5 contains 46,529 people with a deviation of +3.89% from the ideal district.

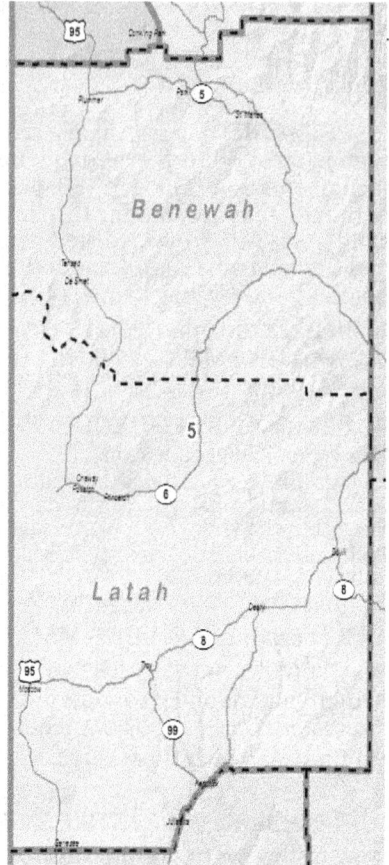

The University of Idaho is the centerpiece of District 6, which consists of Latah County. The county as a whole still is much involved in agricture and to some extent (in the east) timber, as anyone driving through can see. But the University of Idaho is a key influencer on the whole of the city of Moscow (which has more than half the county's population). In its votes Moscow leans Democratic, and in places very strongly; many of the outlying rural precincts, however, are as strongly Republican. The addition to Benewah County to Latah has made this a tightly competitive district.

This area has made an accommodation of sorts. It has elected Republicans more often than Democrats, but the Republicans are among the most moderate in their (majority) caucuses. So this county with the strong Democratic base has had committee chairs in the Senate (for most of the decade up to 2010) and in the House (until the current term).

That accommodation showed up in the terms of Gary Schroeder, one of the most moderate Senate Republicans in recent times and for many years chair of Senate Education. In 2010 he lost his primary election to Gresham Bouma, who had Tea Party and other activist support. But then Bouma lost the general election to Dan Schmidt, a former Latah County coroner. Gresham lost to Schmidt again in 2012.

The area's long-serving Democratic legislator, Shirley Ringo, was first elected in 1998, lost in 2000, and won each term since; she has said she is running for the U.S. House rather than re-election for 2014. Her wins have been steady but modest in winning margins, reflecting the district. She may have been among the least compromising among Democrats with conservatives. The libertarian Idaho Freedom Foundation index in 2013 rated her at the bottom of its favorability list (-96 points).

Her long-serving Republican fellow representative, Tom Trail, probably was for some years the closest among Republican House members to voting like a Democrat among the members of his caucus. He retired from the House to make a run (unsuccessful) for the county commission in 2012. The contest for his seat could reasonably have gone either way, but Republican Cindy Agidius won it partly on the strength on deep Moscow community roots (she was highly active in the community, and her husband had been mayor) and personal support there. She was one of the original Gang of 16 freshman supporters of a state health insurance exchange, but voted against it on the House floor. Ringo and Schmidt, like most other Democrats, voted in favor.

Predecessor district 6

ELECTIONS Republican Gary Schroeder, first elected to the Senate in 1992, steered a moderate course for 18 years in the chamber as he rose to the chair of education and of natural resources. As time went on his critics became more vociferous on the right than on the left, and in 2010 that caught up with him when a Tea Party activist, Gresham Bouma, defeated him in the Republican primary. In most other Idaho districts that would have been tantamount to election for Bouma, but he was too far from the centrist line preferred here. Democrat Dan Schmidt, a former county coroner, defeated him in the fall, becoming the only Democrat to pick up a Republican legislative seat in Idaho that year.

The lesson was taught by the voters here as well in House seat B, where in 2000 Republican Gary Young, running as a Schroeder-type moderate, unseated Democrat Shirley Ringo. In office, Young ran harder to the right, and in 2002 Ringo ousted him. She has held the seat, with varying margins, since.

The other House member here, Tom Trail, may have been the most moderate Republican in the Idaho House. And as such he has been a fit for this district, though he was held to moderate-sized wins in 2008 and 2010.

A note: 2010 marked the first time since 1990 that Latah County has elected a majority-Democratic delegation.

Presdt	Democrat			Republican		
2012	Barack Obama	9,470	45.88%	Mitt Romney	10,185	49.34%
Sen	Democrat			Republican		
2012	Dan Schmidt	10,340	51.00%	Gresham Bouma	9,936	49.00%
2010	Dan Schmidt	6,551	53.30%	Gresham Bouma	5,741	46.70%
2008	Sheldon Vincenti	7,264	42.90%	Gary Schroeder	9,685	57.10%
2006	-	-	-	Gary Schroeder	9,138	100.00%
2004	-	-	-	Gary Schroeder	13,026	100.00%
2002	Duncan Palmatier	4,641	40.40%	Gary Schroeder	6,856	59.60%
H1	Democrat			Republican		
2012	Paulette Jordan	9,960	49.70%	Cindy Agidius	10,083	50.30%
2010	Judith Brown	5,180	42.60%	Tom Trail	6,985	57.40%
2008	Judith Brown	7,981	46.60%	Tom Trail	9,146	53.40%

	Democrat			Republican		
2006	-	-	-	Tom Trail	9,258	100.00%
2004	Mark Solomon	6,569	39.20%	Tom Trail	10,198	60.80%
2002	-	-	-	Tom Trail	9,285	100.00%
H2	**Democrat**			**Republican**		
2012	**Shirley Ringo**	**10,739**	**53.60%**	**Kenneth De Vries**	**9,293**	**46.40%**
2010	Shirley Ringo	6,748	55.40%	Isaac Young	5,424	44.60%
2008	Shirley Ringo	9,773	57.60%	Bob Hassoldt	7,187	42.40%
2006	Shirley Ringo	7,329	61.56%	Roger Falen	4,576	38.44%
2004	Shirley Ringo	9,272	55.30%	Earl Bennett	7,480	44.70%
2002	Shirley Ringo	6,179	53.20%	Gary Young	5,443	46.80%

PRIMARIES Just three primary contests in the last decade. In 2004, Republican Senator Gary Schroeder easily dispatched (69.03%) challenger Gregg Vance. But in 2010 he fell in the primary (42.5%) to challenger Gresham Dale Bouma (57.5%), who would go on to lose the general. The closest primary here was for the House B seat in 2010, when Isaac "Ike" Young narrowly defeated (51.9%) David Klingenberg.

In 2012 each of the three seats had one contested primary – by the party that went on to lose the general election for that seat. For the Senate, Republican Gresham Bouma won his second primary in a row, only to lose again in the general. Democrat Paulette Jordon (68.5%) defeated Jim Stivers in the House A primary, and Republican Kenneth De Vries defeated (58.7%) two other contenders for House B, but both lost their general election contests.

Senator DAN SCHMIDT, D-Moscow
Web: www.danschmidtforsenate.com
Background: Physician; family practice. University of Washington.
Political: Coroner, Latah County, 15 years. Elected to Senate, 2010, 2012.

Representative CINDY AGIDIUS, R-Moscow
Web: cindyagidius.com/
Background: Realtor. Staffer for former Senators Larry Craig and Dirk Kempthonr. Latah County Planning Commission. University of Idaho.
Political: Elected to House 2012.

Representative SHIRLEY RINGO, D-Moscow
Web: www.shirleyringo.com
Background: Retired, teacher. Human Rights Task Force. Washington State University.
Political: Elected to House, 10098. Unsuccessful run for re-election, 2000. Elected to House 2002, 2004, 2006, 2008, 2010, 2012.

District 6

District 6 (Lewis County and Nez Perce County). District 6 contains all of Lewis County and Nez Perce County. Separately, Lewis County and Nez Perce County do not have enough population to constitute an entire legislative district. As Nez Perce County is bounded by Oregon and Washington on the west, the only contiguous county that could be combined with Nez Perce County to make compact legislative district is Lewis County. District 6 contains 43,086 people with a deviation of -3.80% from the ideal district.

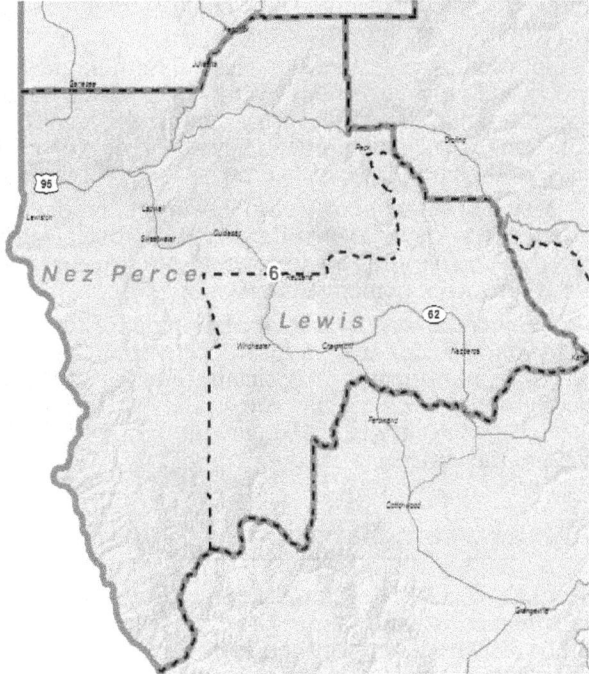

The single most visible landmark in Nez Perce County may be the big Clearwater (formerly Potlatch) paper mill on the Clearwater River. For decades it has been a major employer – often the major employer – in the area, and it is important still. Lewiston remains mainly a manufacturing city (it is a significant national producer of firarm ammunition) and a farm center. It has not grown much in recent decades, but neither has it fallen into decline.

Once solidly Democratic, then seemingly on the verge of moving into the Republican column, Nez Perce County now is better described as closely competitive, probably with a small Republican tilt – not too distant in partisan results from Latah County, and one of the few such in the state. Its traditionally Democratic legislative delegation has in the last couple of decades become closely split between the parties.

One speculation from local political observers: The one Democrat left in the delegtion, John Rusche, who often has won with strong percentages, might have lost his seat in 2010 had he been challenged that year.

Some of the history shows up in the story of Dan Johnson, the area's state senator who seemed to come out of nowhere. When long-time Senator Joe Stegner resigned early in 2012 to take a job with the University of Idaho, House member Jeff Nesset was thought liked to be appointed to replace him. He wasn't; the appointment went to Johnson, the city of Lewiston's solid waste manager and a Port of Lewiston commissioner.

Nessett filed for the Senate seat in the primary, but Johnson won there too. In the fall he faced a Democratic candidate, former district judge John Bradbury, who was well-known in the area and had a substantial base of support – and opposition, since he has sometimes been a polarizing figure too. Johnson again prevailed.

Johnson became a key vote on a $35 million corporate tax cut measure proposed by the governor in 2012. He was not chained to the governor who appointed him, however, voting against the health insurance exchange. Johnson's votes and approach have been described as moving well to the right of the mark Stegner had set.

Nesset's seat went to Thyra Stevenson, a member of the Lewiston City Council who stayed there after her legislative election. She often was on the more activist Tea Party side of the House caucus, and voted against the Otter insurance exchange proposal.

Rusche, the lone Democrat remaining for several terms the House Democratic leader, was an insurance exchange supporter (with a professional history as a physician). First elected in 2004, he was unopposed three times in a row in the last decade. On the two occasions when Republicans did challenge him, however, he was held to less than 53% of the vote.

Predecessor district 7

ELECTIONS The Republican mainstay, since 1998, was businessman Joe Stegner, who lost a race the cycle before that against veteran Democrat Bruce Sweeney, then won the seat when Sweeney retired. As a senator Stegner has been enough of a Republican caucus loyalist to serve in leadership for most of the last decade, but moderate enough to draw a denouncing call of "Democrat!" at the 2010 Republican state convention. The combination of that and his thoughtful, even-tempered demeanor has been enough for re-election in Lewiston. He nearly lost on two occasions (2002 and 2006), but was unopposed by a Democrat in 2010.

The House seats here, after a run of Republican control in the 90s, returned to the Democrats in the 00s. Former Senator Mike Mitchell came out of retirement and took Seat A in 2002 from House Majority Leader Frank Bruneel. With Mitchell's retirement, it went to Democrat Liz Chavez in 2006. But in the Republican tide of 2010, Chevez lost to Republican Jeff Nessett, a former Lewiston mayor.

The other seat remains in Democratic hands, those of the House Democratic leader, John Rusche. Rusche ran in 2004 when the seat was opened by Democrat Mike Naccarato's (unsuccessful) decision to run against Stegner. Rusche barely won the first time.

Presdt	Democrat			Republican		
2012	Barack Obama	6,847	37.09%	Mitt Romney	11.140	60.34%

Sen	Democrat			Republican		
2012	John Bradbury	8,197	44.60%	Dan Johnson	10,168	55.40%
2010	-	-	-	Joe Stegner	10,708	100.00%
2008	Barb Kramer	6,842	38.50%	Joe Stegner	10,920	61.50%

Year	Democrat			Republican		
2006	Mike Naccarato	5,912	48.78%	Joe Stegner	6,207	51.22%
2004	Mike Naccarato	7,923	39.20%	Joe Stegner	10,198	60.80%
2002	Dick Riggs	5,885	47.30%	Joe Stegner	6,569	52.70%
H1	**Democrat**			**Republican**		
2012	**Pete Gertonson**	**8,294**	**45.80%**	**Thyra Stevenson**	**9,814**	**54.20%**
2010	Liz Chavez	5,688	45.40%	Jeff Nesset	6,835	54.60%
2008	Liz Chavez	13,430	100.00%	-	-	-
2006	Liz Chavez	6,667	55.25%	Tony Snodderly	5,400	44.75%
2004	Mike Mitchell	9,877	57.20%	Jason Hollibaugh	7,389	42.80%
2002	Mike Mitchell	6,492	51.70%	Frank Bruneel	5,800	46.20%
H2	**Democrat**			**Republican**		
2012	**John Rusche**	**9,531**	**52.30%**	**Daniel Santiago**	**8,705**	**47.70%**
2010	John Rusche	9,499	100.00%	-	-	-
2008	John Rusche	13,608	100.00%	-	-	-
2006	John Rusche	9,824	100.00%	-	-	-
2004	John Rusche	8,850	50.90%	Charlie Pottenger	8,535	49.10%
2002	Mike Naccarato	7,398	59.70%	Earl Ferguson	4,985	40.30%

PRIMARIES Remarkably, just two primary contests here in the last decade. One was in 2002 when Republican for House B, in which former County Commissioner Earl Ferguson beat (50.6%) Ray Sanders (49.4%). There were no more until a hot 2012 Republican contest for the Senate, in which incumbent Dan Johnson (59.6%) beat House member Jeff Nesset.

Senator DAN JOHNSON, R-Lewiston

Web: www.idaho4johnson.com
Background: Manager, solid waste, city of Lewiston. University of Idaho, Virginia Tech.
Political: Commissioner, Port of Lewiston. Appointed to Senate 2011. Elected to Senate, 2012.

Representative THYRA STEVENSON, R-Lewiston

Web: thyrastevensonidahohouse.com
Background: Pilot, teacher. Chief information officer, Coast Guard Auxilliary Association. Boston University; New York University (Madrid, Spain), University of Washington.
Political: City Council, Lewiston. Elected to House 2012.

Representative JOHN RUSCHE, D-Lewiston

Web: www.johnrusche.us
Background: Retired, physician (Valley Medical Center). Medical director, Blue Shield of Idaho.
Political: Elected to House, 2004, 2006, 2008, 2010. Elected Democratic leader, 2008, 2010, 2012.

District 7

District 7 (Bonner County (part), Shoshone County, Clearwater County, and Idaho County). District 7 includes a portion of Bonner County, the entirety of Shoshone County, the entirety of Clearwater County and the entirety of Idaho County. In order to meet the one person one vote requirement, the Commission combined this portion of Bonner County with Shoshone County because of the requirements of Article III sec. 5 and the geography of the panhandle. Any alternative configuration would result in an additional split of a county elsewhere. This district is evidence of the great difficulty in creating legislative districts in a state the size and shape of Idaho with its diverse landscape and comparatively sparse population density. The Commission recognizes that this district is large and not ideal; however, it is necessary to meet the one person one vote requirement and preserve county boundaries whenever possible. It is particularly revealing that this district comprised of a massive geographical area is still population light, which clearly reflects the disparity between population and county land size evident throughout Idaho. District 7 includes 42,930 people with a deviation of -4.15% from the ideal district.

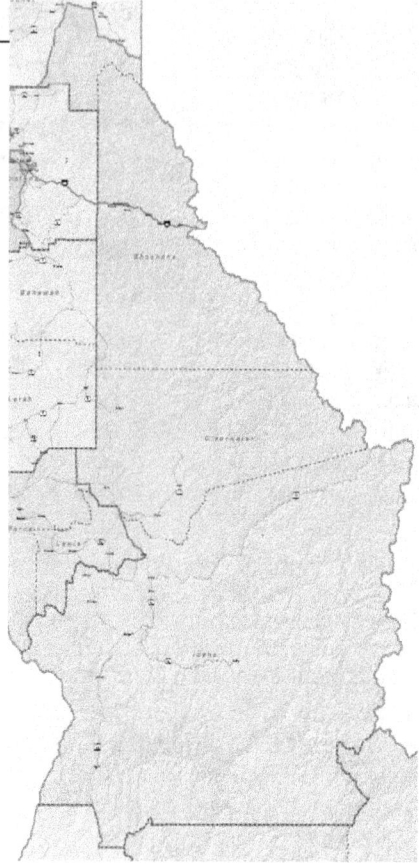

A lot of woods, mountains and backcountry form the scenery of this massive district, much of which isn't directly linked by paved road. There are three population centers. One is the Silver Valley, in Shoshone County along I-90, the old silver mining district anchored by Kellogg and Wallace. 100 miles or more to the south is the Clearwater River communities along Highway 12 anchored by Orofino. And south of that, up on the Camas Prairie, are farming communities including Grangeville and Cottonwood. Further to the south, across White Bird Pass, is lightly-populated recreation country around Riggins.

As a matter of access and transportation, it is an unusually difficult district to represent, running nearly from Sandpoint to McCall. There are points of commonality, however. The communities are all rural, small and similarly-sized, and the typical world view, economic interests (resource industries are important) and politics do not vary massively from one end to the end other.

As a part of the state that has, over the decades, been accounting for smaller and smaller percentages of its overall population, the districts in

62

this area have been pulled like taffy to ever-growing geographic areas. The land mass in this district is so large as to amount to almost half of the size of the first congressional district.

Senator Sheryl Nuxoll is the best known of the delegation, widely quoted for her 2012 request to the electoral college to not give its votes to Barack Obama for president; she has also compared Obamacare to the holocaust. As might be expected, she was also a vote against setting up the state health insurance exchange.

She also, however, has been among a handful of Republican legislators in favor of considering state takeover of the private prison near Boise; the location of two state prison facilities in her district could have been a factor in her thinking.

Representative Paul Shepherd, who has been in the House since 2004, has been focused more on helping resource industries. He and new Representative Shannon McMillan (who in 2010 defeated the one remaining Democrat from a rural northern district) both were, like Nuxoll, votes against the governor's health insurance exchange proposal.

The libertarian Idaho Freedom Foundation thought highly of this delegation, in 2013 ranking Nuxoll sixth highest (131 points) and McMillan sevenths (130 points) among the 105 legislators. Shepherd ranked highly too, placing 19th (90 points).

Former District 2

In 1900 Shoshone County had more people than Ada County, fourth-largest in the state. It housed only slightly fewer people in 2000. Mining, for silver and other precious metals, was the base; the Silver Valley was once a major Idaho population center. No longer. With closure of most of the mines, it is turning more reliant on tourism and timber, and becoming more like eastern Benewah County, where St. Maries has been a timber production center.

The union base long meant this area elected Democrats, and to some extent it still does. The courthouses of Shoshone and Benewah counties are still mainly Democratic, but they are mostly very conservative Democrats with deep community roots.

Democratic roots still existed at the start of the new millenium, and in the 2002 election three Democrats with legislative experience, all women, were on the ballot. Senator Marti Calabretta, with a base in the Silver Valley, had served from 1984-92 (in a district more centered on Shoshone County), and won the seat in 2002. But she was ousted in 2004 by Republican Joyce Broadsword, who held it until 2012.

Since 2002 District 2 has elected just one Democrat, Mary Lou Shepherd. She had been appointed in 1999 to replace fellow Democrat Larry Watson, who was appointed to the state Tax Commission. She was unopposed three elections in a row until 2010, when the Republican tide finally caught up with her (and suggested the GOP had been missing an opportunity for another seat). Republican Shannon McMillan, of Silverton, beat her that year.

The battle over the third seat was between two candidates who had each won and lost. Democrat June Judd had represented a district reaching south into Idaho County; Republican Dick Harwood unseated her in 2000, and barely fended off a challenge from her in 2002. Harwood retired in 2012.

Presdt	Democrat				Republican		
2012	Barack Obama	5,802	30.10%		Mitt Romney	12,893	66.90%

Sen	Democrat				Republican		
2012	-*	-		-	Sheryl Nuxoll	11,583	64.00%
2010	-	-		-	Joyce Broadsword	9,671	100.00%
2008	Rand Lewis	4,919	32.00%		Joyce Broadsword	10,475	68.00%
2006	Steve Johnson	4,426	41.49%		Joyce Broadsword	6,241	58.51%
2004	Marti Calabretta	6,705	46.70%		Joyce Broadsword	7,650	53.30%
2002	Marti Calabretta	5,415	51.00%		Russell Lowry	4,422	41.70%

H1	Democrat				Republican		
2012	Casey Drews	6,263	35.10%		Shannon McMillan	11,561	64.90%
2010	Mary Lou Shepherd	5,126	45.10%		Shannon McMillan	6,244	54.90%
2008	Mary Lou Shepherd	11,093	100.00%		-	-	-
2006	Mary Lou Shepherd	8,021	100.00%		-	-	-
2004	Mary Lou Shepherd	9,569	74.00%		-	-	-
2002	Mary Lou Shepherd	6,097	57.10%		Michael Stevenson	3,405	31.90%

H2	Democrat				Republican		
2012	Nancy Lerandeau	5,882	32.70%		Paul Shepherd	12,095	67.30%
2010	Jon Ruggles	3,404	29.80%		RJ Harwood	8,006	70.20%
2008	C.J. Rose	5,495	36.30%		RJ Harwood	9,624	63.70%
2006	Richard Taniguchi	4,625	43.62%		RJ Harwood	5,978	56.38%
2004	George Currier	6,030	41.90%		RJ Harwood	8,345	58.10%
2002	June Judd	5,271	49.20%		RJ Harwood	5,434	50.80%

*Jon Cantamessa of Shoshone County, who has in the past run as a Democrat, ran for this seat as an independent, receiving 6,522 votes (36%).

PRIMARIES Sheryl Nuxoll was challenged in the new 2012 district by Mary Wade Heston, but won with 73.2%.

The hottest primary here may have involved Shannon McMillan, who was opposed by two challengers, one little-known (Ed Galloway) both the other a former statewide candidate for governor and U.S. senator, Rex Rammell. McMillan won with 47.8%.

Former Senator Joyce Broadsword was twice challenged and held to around half of the primary vote, but helped by having two challengers. In 2008, she defeated (55.3%) Bill Largen and James Stives; in 2010, (49%) Stivers and Dennis Engelhardt. In 2002, there was a Democratic House primary between former Representative June Judd (66.2%) and Steve Johnson (33.8%).

Senator SHERYL NUXOLL, R-Cottonwood

Web: www.sherylnuxoll.com
Background: Accountant (CPA). Teacher. Bookkeeper, Hoene Implement (Cottonwood). Co-owner, farm and ranch. Gonzaga University.
Political: Elected 2010, 2012.

Representative SHANNON McMILLAN, R-Silverton

Web:
Background: Tax preparer, H&R Block. M.L. Guenther Associates. Apollo College.
Political: Elected to House, 2010, 2012.

Representative PAUL SHEPHERD, R-Riggins

Web: twitter.com/PaulShepherdUSA
Background: Partner and manager, Shepherd Sawmill & Log Homes Inc.
Political: Board, Garden Valley School District. Council, Crouch. Council, Riggins. Elected to House 2004, 2006, 2008, 2010, 2012.

District 8

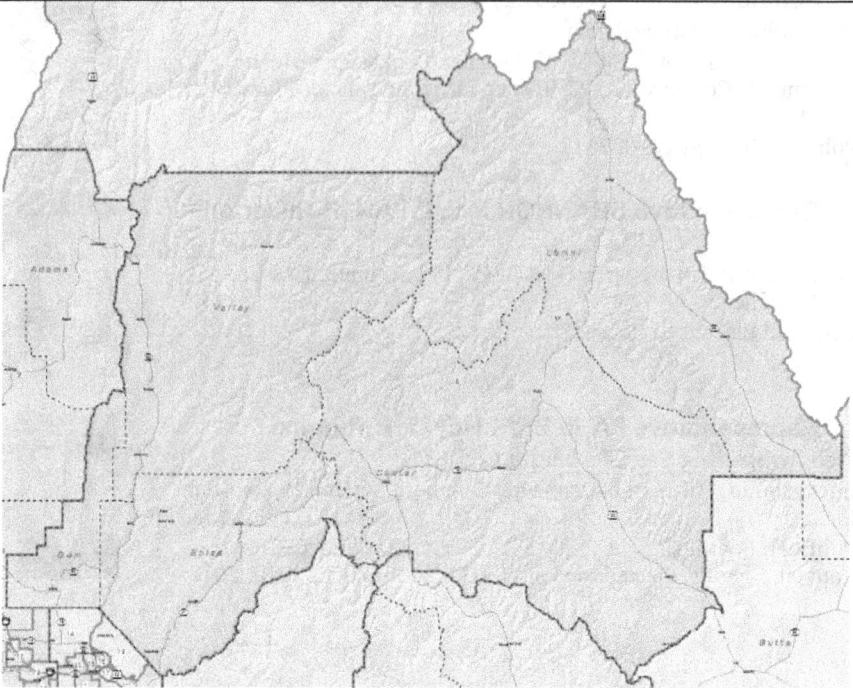

District 8 (Gem, Valley, Boise, Custer, Lemhi). District 8 consists of the entirety of Gem, Boise, Valley and Custer and Lemhi Counties. Separately, none of these counties have sufficient population to form independent legislative districts. More compact configurations were rejected because they would have required the splitting of counties .. District 8 has 45,913 people, a deviation of +2.51% from the ideal district.

The new District 8 looks reasonably compact and coherent on a map, but it will seem much less so to anyone who has driven its expanse. It is also a clearly new district (none quite like it has existed before), putting together two pieces – Lemhi and Custer counties to the east with Valley, Gem and Boise in the west – which never previously shared a legislative district. Politically, all of these counties are Republican, but Lemhi and Custer traditionally more than Valley, Boise and Gem, each of which historically has had some Democratic base (and in Valley's case has seen some Democratic resurgence).

Two of the member of this delegation have been among the more raw-edged conservatives in the legislature. The *Idaho Statesman* noted that Steven Thayn, formerly a House member from a Gem County-based district and since 2012 senator in District 8, "sees the breakdown of the traditional family structure as the root of societal ills such as drug abuse, crime and domestic violence." (That made the April 2007 arrest of his 28-year old son on domestic battery charges somewhat larger news.) He was a rare southern Idaho participant in a September 2013 "Liberty Expo" at Coeur d'Alene on nullification of federal laws. He also has been spokesman for a group called MP Squared, which he said among other things argues government program "just not working any more, especially entitlement programs." But Thayn has been especially highly interested in education, and is highly supportive of home and charter schools. He has proposed legislation to eliminate kindergarten in Idaho and compressed the number of years needed for a college degree.

Representative Lenore Hardy Barrett of Challis also has been a fierce opponent of governmental regulation and taxes generally. She is one of the veterans of the House, first elected there in 1992.

The other House member here, Terry Gestrin, was appointed to the House in August 2012 to replace Ken Roberts, who had been appointed to the State Tax Commission.

All three members of the delegation opposed the governor's health insurance exchange proposal.

Predecessor district 8

ELECTIONS Traditionally, Valley County has been linked in legislative districts with Idaho County to the north, and Gem and Boise counties often have been as well. Now, nearly half of the new district's population will come from east of the wilderness, from Challis and Custer and their environs.

All of this area is lightly populated and geared heavily around natural resources economies and recreation. (The major exception would be the irrigation, orchard and Boise-oriented suburban country of southern Gem County.) The major economic shakeup in the area has been the Tamarack development near Donnelly, initially a massive and well-heeled development which fell on hard economic times. In the last few decades, this district's territory all has been definably Republican, though the southwestern parts of this territory have elected a few Democrats to the legislature in recent years.

The last of the legislative Democrats from this region was Chuck Cuddy (from Orofino, but representing an area including Valley County) first elected in 1990 and considered the most conservative Democrat in his caucus by the end of his time here. He narrowly survived in his new district in 2002 but narrowly lost two years later (by 64 votes) to Republican Paul Shepherd. Shepherd has been re-elected with generally strong margins since.

The other House seat in District 8 was held through the decade by Ken Roberts, a member of House leadership who for some months campaigned for the 1ˢᵗ District U.S. House seat. Robert's percentages in his last three contested elected all were under 60%. He was unopposed in 2010.

The Senate seat has been Republican throughout the decade, but gone through significant changes regardless. It started the decade with Skip Brandt, a mayor of Kooskia; he departed to run (unsuccessfully) for the U.S. House in 2006. (That seems to be a legislator's graveyard in this district; Brandt did go on to election to the Idaho County commission.) The seat went to Valley County Clerk Lee Heinrich, who only narrowly won it in 2006 but finished stronger in 2008. In an upset, he lost his primary election in 2010 to Cottonwood bookkeeper Sheryl Nuxoll, who appeared to be aligned with the Tea Party (she said she isn't a member) and during the campaign supported toll roads over a gas tax.

The big change of this district's territory from its previous cast make it logically about as Republican as it was before, but relatively unpredictable in terms which Republican options (west-side or east-side; or will it matter?) the district chooses to embrace.

Lemhi and Custer, which for decades were part of a District 35 united with area reaching over to Rigby, Arco and Dubois, have been very strongly Republican since the days of conservative Democratic ranchers in the 50s and 60s. The legislator who in recent decades who has lived in that area (at Challis) and now represents the new district, is Lenore Hardy Barrett. *See the section on the old district 35 for a look at Custer and Lemhi politics.*

Presdt	Democrat			Republican		
2012	Barack Obama	6,595	29.55%	Mitt Romney	15,032	67.36%

Sen	Democrat			Republican		
2012	Joanna Clausen	6,656	31.00%	Steven Thayn	13,068	61.00%
2010	Leta Strauss	4,331	30.10%	Sheryl Nuxoll	10,051	69.90%
2008	Randy Doman	7,111	38.30%	Lee Heinrich	11,434	61.70%
2006	Scott McLeod	6,958	48.45%	Lee Heinrich	7,403	51.55%
2004	-	-	-	Skip Brandt	14,140	100.00%
2002	Dave Holland	5,523	39.20%	Skip Brandt	8,558	60.80%
H1	Democrat			Republican		
2012	Karla J. Miller	7,405	34.80%	Terry F. Gestrin	13,894	65.20%
2010	-	-	0.00%	Ken Roberts	11,486	100.00%
2008	Richard Adams	7,455	40.30%	Ken Roberts	11,043	59.70%
2006	Darcy James	6,789	47.00%	Ken Roberts	7,655	53.00%
2004	Darcy James	7,471	42.60%	Ken Roberts	10,058	57.40%
2002	Jerry Lockhart	5,439	39.50%	Ken Roberts	8,314	60.50%
H2	Democrat			Republican		
2012	Cindy Phelps	7,672	36.20%	Lenore Barrett	13,515	63.80%
2010	Jerry Lockhart	4,259	29.80%	Paul Shepherd	10,016	70.20%
2008	Jim Rehder	7,649	41.10%	Paul Shepherd	10,979	58.90%
2006	Charlene Douglas	5,411	38.61%	Paul Shepherd	8,603	61.39%
2004	Charles Cuddy	8,698	49.80%	Paul Shepherd	8,762	50.20%
2002	Charles Cuddy	7,355	52.40%	Twila Hornbeck	6,688	47.60%

PRIMARIES 2002 was big for primaries here. Incumbent Senator Skip Brandt was challenged by Almon Manes but won easily (69.6%). Democratic Representative Charles Cuddy was also challenged, by George Stockton, but also won easily (70.1%). The most interesting contest that year may have been for the Republican nomination to challenge Cuddy; four candidates filed, with Twila Hornbeck (37%) emerging to defeat Lot Smith (31.4%), Dan Proskine (18.8%) and Michael Fischer (12.8%).

Brandt's 2006 departure from the Senate occasioned a pair of primaries, won on the Republican side by Lee Heinrich (59%) over Ronn Julian, and on the Democratic by Scott McLeod (56.1%) over Dave Holland. In 2010, however, Heinrich lost (43.1%) to challenger Sheryl Nuxoll (56.9%). Also that year, Representative Ken Roberts (who had been running for Congress early in the cycle) easily dispatched (69.6%) a challenge from Gordon Conrad.

In 2012 the heavy redistricting in this part of Idaho led to populous Republican primaries, with a least three candidates for each of the three seats. Incumbent House member Steve Thayn (44.6%) took the Senate seat over Alan Ward (27.8%) and Terry Gestrin (27.6%). In House A, incumbent Ken Roberts won (44.9%) the primary over John Blattler and Dan Davis, but soon after opted out, and was replaced on the ballot for November by Gestriin. The B seat was won by incumbent Lenore Barrett (37.1%) in a hard-to-predict four-way contest.

Senator STEVEN THAYN, R-Emmett

Web: www.steventhayn.com/
Background: Farmer. Teacher. Treasure Valley Community College, Boise State University.
Political: Unsuccessful run for Senate, 2004. Elected to House 2006, 2008, 2010. Elected to Senate, 2012.

Representative TERRY GESTRIN, R-Donnelly

Web: terry-gestrin.blogspot.com/
Background: Long Valley farm Service, Donnelly. Idaho State University.
Political: Valley County Commission. Appointed to House, August 2012. Elected to House, 2012.

Representative LENORE HARDY BARRETT, R-Challis

Web: www.facebook.com/pages/Lenore-Barrett-for-Idaho/270974432283
Background: Mining, investments. Oklahoma Baptist University.
Political: Former member, city council, Challis. Elected to House 1992, 1994, 1996, 1998, 2000, 2002, 2004, 2006, 2008, 2010, 2012.

District 9

District 9 (Canyon County (part), Washington, Adams, and Payette County). District 9 contains a portion of Canyon County, Washington County, Adams County, and Payette County. Payette County is bounded on the west by the state of Oregon and does not have sufficient population to constitute one district. Payette County is bordered by both Canyon and Washington Counties. Adams, Washington, and Payette counties lack sufficient population to satisfy the one person one vote requirement requiring that a portion of Canyon County, the only remaining county that is contiguous to Payette County, be combined to create District 9. In dividing Canyon County, the Commission kept communities of interest intact by keeping the cities of Parma whole and including them in this district. Further, Payette County is connected to this portion of Canyon County by two major roadways, Highway 95 and Interstate 84, both major routes of commerce that create communities of interest and commonality throughout the region. District 9 includes 44,559 people with a deviation of -.51% from the ideal district.

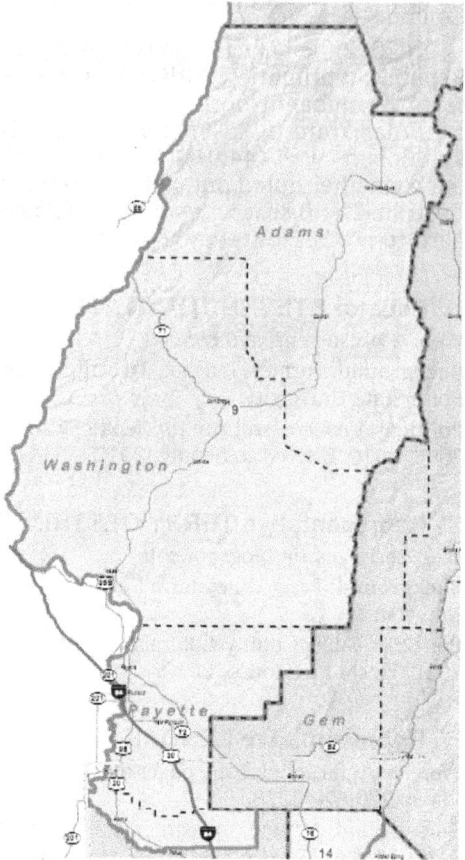

The side of Idaho facing across to Oregon – the edge of it being Hells Canyon country, the inlands being mostly mountainous agricultural and ranch territory – has not changed enormously in recent decades. Its population growth has been slow enough to expand the size of its legislative districts, but the area is consistent in its economy and demographics: Older-line agriculture, some food processing. And small town stressed by urban pulls and, in the case of Payette especially, by the lack of a sales tax in neighboring Oregon.

This is consistent Republican country.

Monty Pearce, the senator here since 2002, has from time to time been a controversial figure, but in general elections he has fallen below a landslide win only once, when his opponent was a popular county sheriff. More recently, Pearce has been a key figure in the discussion of oil and gas leases. In March 2012 Senate Democrats asked for an ethics inquiry into Pearce, who for weeks chaired a committee which considered oil and gas rules but disclosed that he has leased such rights on his own property to a company when the measure came to a final floor vote.

The libertarian Idaho Freedom Foundation ranked him fifth most positively (132 points) among the 105 legislators in 2013.

Representative Judy Boyle has been highly interested in resource issues since long before she joined the legislature; she worked on the subject for former U.S. Representative Helen Chenoweth.

The most prominent member of this delegation, however, and its most senior as well, is Lawerence Denney, who served as House speaker from 2006-12, when he lost a caucus vote for re-election to Scott Bedke. Denney since has been chair of the House Resource committee. In 2013 he said he would leave the House the next year to run for secretary of state.

Predecessor district 9

ELECTIONS In only one legislative election in the last decade did a Republican candidate fall short of a landslide: In 2004, when long-time Payette County Sheriff Bob Barowsky held Republican Monty Pearce to 59.2%. Pearce, who has been opposed each cycle in the decade, otherwise won in landslides each time out.

This is also the home district of Lawerence Denney of Midvale. Denney's legislative electoral history goes back to 1988, when he ran against Republican incumbent Wayne Sutton and lost. In 1990, Denney did win in a race for another seat, but won and lost in succession in the next few cycles. He has been in the House steadily since the 1996 election, however, and was only lightly challenged in the last decade.

The other House seat was held for most of the decade by Clete Edmunson, a former teacher, who was unopposed from 202 to 2006. In August 2007, he resigned to take a job in the governor's office, and the seat went to activist Judy Boyle of Midvale. She was challenged in 2008 but not in 2010.

Presdt	Democrat			Republican		
2012	Barack Obama	4,636	25.68%	Mitt Romney	12,944	71.70%

Sen	Democrat			Republican		
2012	Alma Hasse	5,013	28.90%	Monty Pearce	12,356	71.10%
2010	Wayne Fuller	2,952	25.80%	Monty Pearce	8,487	74.20%
2008	Wayne Fuller	4,987	32.20%	Monty Pearce	10,492	67.80%
2006	Tony Edmondson	4,338	38.93%	Monty Pearce	6,805	61.07%
2004	Bob Barowsky	5,995	40.80%	Monty Pearce	8,685	59.20%
2002	Barbara Wilson	3,309	32.00%	Monty Pearce	7,036	68.00%

H1	Democrat			Republican		
2012	Steve Worthley	5,013	28.90%	Lawerence Denney	12,234	70.90%
2010	Lynn Webster	2,660	23.30%	Lawerence Denney	6,076	76.70%
2008	Fritz Hallberg	4,286	28.10%	Lawerence Denney	10,968	71.90%
2006	-	-	-	Lawerence Denney	9,189	100.00%
2004	-	-	-	Lawerence Denney	11,541	100.00%

2002	Lori Steiniker	3,952	38.00%	Lawerence Denney	6,449	62.00%
H2	**Democrat**			**Republican**		
2012	-	-		**- Judy Boyle**	**11,066**	**65.20%**
2010	-	-		- Judy Boyle	9,798	100.00%
2008	Jennifer Morgan	5,034	33.20%	Judy Boyle	10,133	66.80%
2006	-	-		- Clete Edmunson	9,088	100.00%
2004	-	-		- Clete Edmunson	11,349	100.00%
2002	-	-		- Clete Edmunson	7,974	79.80%

PRIMARIES The only Senate primary in the last decade came in 2012, when Matthew Faulks challenged but lost to incumbent Monty Pearce (56.0%). Pearce was last primaried in 2002 when he won (38.8%) narrowly over former Senator Roger Fairchild (36.8%) and James Grunke (24.4%).

Former House Speaker Lawerence Denney has not had a primary in the last decade, but several primaries emerged for the other House seat. In 2002, Clete Edmunson prevailed (53.2%) over Kent Banner for the open seat, then in 2004 fended off (57.97%) a challenge from Duane Youngberg. In 2008, appointed Representative Judy Boyle was challenged but won (53.4%) over Diana Thomas. In 2012, Boyle defeated (56.2%) three challengers, the major vote-getter among them being Jeri Soulier (31.4%).

Senator MONTY PEARCE, R-New Plymouth
Web: senatormontypearce.com
Background: Rancher. Ricks College; Brigham Young University.
Political: Elected to House, 2000. Elected to Senate 2002, 2004, 2006, 2008, 2010, 2012.

Representative LAWERENCE DENNEY, R-Midvale
Web: www.denneyforidaho.com
Background: Farmer. Army. University of Idaho.
Political: Unsuccessful run for House, 1988. Elected to House (floterial district), 1990. Unsuccessful run for House, 1992. Elected to House 1996, 1998, 2000, 2002, 2004, 2006, 2008, 2010, 2012. Elected speaker 2006, 2008, 2010; unsuccessful run for speaker, 2012.

Representative JUDY BOYLE, R-Midvale
Web: www.judyboyle.net
Background: Rancher. Former staff, U.S. Representative Helen Chenoweth. Lassen Community College, Boise State University, University of Idaho.
Political: Elected to House 2008, 2010, 2012.

District 10

District 10 (Canyon County (part)) is compact, follows major roads and highways and consists of the majority of the city of Caldwell, a traditional community of interest located entirely in Canyon County. District 10 contains 45,422 people, a deviation of +1.42% from the ideal district.

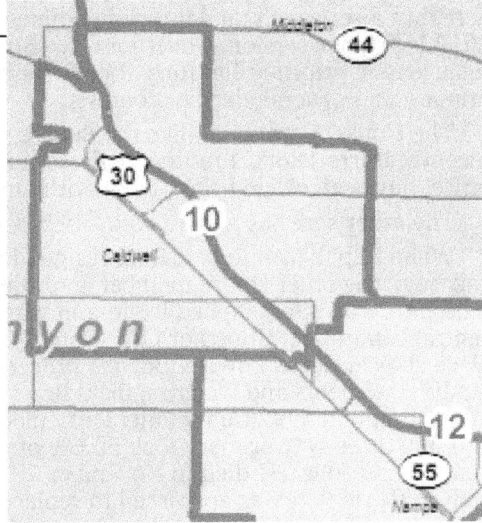

Caldwell, which has been growing apace with subdivisions (or was until the great recession hit), makes up most of District 10, along with some farm country around its perimeter. The political base here has been solidly Republican, probably the most consistently so in Canyon County. There is some line of thought, however, that the substantial Hispanic base here plus the small college at Caldwell (the College of Idaho) may make a dent. It hasn't yet, at least: No Republican has fallen below landslide levels in this area for a very long time.

The senator here, Jim Rice, has taken a measured and cool tone, fitting int to ward the middle of the Senate Republican caucus (and the Senate overall) in several rankings. He was among the caucus supporters of the governor's health insurance exchange. Rice did make the Huffington Post in February 2013, however, for his proposal to amend the Idaho constitution to make all adults eligible for service in militias. He was quoted as saying, "It gives the state standing to defend [gun rights] if the federal government were to ban weapons."

Freshman Representative Brandon Hixon scored an unusually low 54% win in 2012 after reports about a string of scrapes with the law several years previous, including five misdemeanors and 15 infractions (mainly for traffic and alcohol-related offenses). There were more headlines in December 2013, however, when newspapers reported that he had fallen behind on mortgage payments to the point that his house was slated for foreclosure sale in the spring of 2014.

On the legislative front, Hixon was one of the Gang of 16, freshman Republicans who said they supported passage of the governor's health insurance exchange proposal.

Darrell Bolz is one of the senior members of the House, and located in a position of some influence as House vice chair of the budget committee.

Predecessor district 10

ELECTIONS The Senate seat has been held since 2004 by John McGee, who had been a policy advisory for Governor Dirk Kempthorne. McGee was been mentioned as a prospect for higher office and has no close elections here, but a series of scandal-type headlines led to his resignation during the 2012 legislative session. Governor C.L. "Butch" Otter appointed as his replacement attorney Jim Rice. Rice is running for the seat, and has both primary and general election contests.

The House A seat here, like the Senate seat, has not seen contests recently. Darrell Bolz, a retired professor at a University of Idaho extension office, has been elected since 2000 with almost no opposition.

The other seat has a more complex history.

When Republican Robert Ring resigned from the House in 2007, Pat Takasugi, the other House member, a former state Department of Agriculture director, applied for it, and was the top choice of the local GOP central committee. Governor C.L. "Butch" Otter instead picked the third-place choice, Curtis Bowers. Bowers proceeded to make a series of ridiculed public statements and writings, including what he said was an account of infiltration of a 1992 Community Party meeting. Takasugi filed against him, and in a three-way primary took 56.6% of the vote, and easily won two general elections. He died in November 2011 after an extended illness; civic activist Gayle Batt was appointed to replace him.

Presdt	Democrat			Republican		
2012	Barack Obama	5,062	38.47%	Mitt Romney	7,681	58.37%

Sen	Democrat			Republican		
2012	Leif Skyving	4,885	38.80%	Jim Rice	7,706	61.20%
2010	Leif Skyving	2,672	27.40%	John McGee	7,068	72.60%
2008	Harold Stiles	3,728	27.10%	John McGee	10,011	72.90%
2006	-	-	-	John McGee	7,550	100.00%
2004	-	-	-	John McGee	10,153	100.00%
2002	-	-	-	Ron McWilliams	7,253	100.00%

H1	Democrat			Republican		
2012	Travis Manning	5,685	46.00%	Brandon Hixon	6,677	54.00%
2010	Judy Ferro	2,371	24.40%	Pat Takasugi	7,342	75.60%
2008	Mike Warwick	4,480	32.70%	Pat Takasugi	9,235	67.30%
2006	-	-	-	Robert Ring	7,521	100.00%
2004	-	-	-	Robert Ring	9,803	100.00%
2002	Loren Dale Kenyon	2,589	30.20%	Robert Ring	5,970	69.80%

H2	Democrat			Republican		
2012	Angel Zeimantz	4,127	33.70%	Darrell Bolz	8,123	66.30%
2010	-	-	-	Darrell Bolz	8,280	100.00%
2008	-	-	-	Darrell Bolz	11,382	100.00%
2006	Darlene Madsen	3,054	33.73%	Darrell Bolz	6,001	66.27%
2004	-	-	-	Darrell Bolz	9,298	100.00%
2002	-	-	-	Darrell Bolz	7,276	100.00%

PRIMARIES Lots of primaries here, all Republican.

Since 2002 the Senate seat has seen four primaries, and incumbents lost two of those: In 2002 Darrell Deide (44.2%) lost to Ron McWilliams

(55.8%), then two years later McWilliams (40.99%) lost to John McGee (59.01%). In 2010, McGee was challenged but easily won (75.2%) over Greg Collett. After McGee resigned and Jim Rice was appointed to replace him, Rice was challenged from the right in 2012 by Kent Marmon, but easily won (68.8%).

In the House A seat, Robert Ring was challenged but won primaries three times in a row: In 2002 (60%) over Thomas Tingey (23.8% and John H. Lee (16.1%); in 2002 (62.94%) over Gilbert Nelson; and in 2006 (59.8%) over Rob Oates. In 2008 Curt Bowers, appointed to replace Ring, lost in the primary (43.4%) to Pat Takasugi (56.6%). The seat opened in 2012, when Brandon Hixon narrowly (51.5%) beat Jaromm Wagoner. The B seat saw one primary in the last decade, in 2010 when incumbent Darrell Bolz (74%) beat Kent Marmon (26%). In 2012 incumbent Gayle Batt defeated (66.0%) Greg Collett.

Senator JIM RICE, R-Caldwell

Web: jimriceidaho.com
Background: Attorney. Brigham Young University; William Howard Taft University (California).
Political: Appointed to Senate March 2012. Elected to Senate 2012.

Representative BRANDON HIXON, R-Caldwell

Web: hixoninthehouse.com
Background: Insurance agent. Native, Salmon. Boise State University.
Political: Elected to House 2012.

Representative DARRELL BOLZ, R-Caldwell

Web: www.facebook.com/pages/Darrell-Bolz-Idaho-House-of-Representatives/317971911648676
Background: Professor emeritus, University of Idaho Agricultural Extension. Navy. University of Idaho.
Political: Elected to House 2000, 2002, 2004, 2006, 2008, 2010.

District 11

District 11 (Canyon County (part)). District 11 consists of all of rural Canyon County including Wilder, Notus, Greenleaf, and Middleton. This portion of Canyon County is tied together by Highways 44, 45, 55, and 95 that runs throughout the district as well as several other roads which creates a corridor for commerce and a commonality of interest between the two counties. District 11 contains 43,430 people, a deviation of -3.03% from the ideal district.

Not so long ago it would have been fair to call this sprawling area, which includes most of Canyon County outside Nampa and Caldwell, to be farm country – and leave it at that. Much of it still is farm country, but a lot of the population is accounted for by the many subdivisions and other developments bringing people to the exurbs. It's overwhelmingly Republican.

Redistricting has changed the mapping of this district considerably. It has added much of southern Canyon County (down to the Snake River) but removes Gem County to the north, which changes legislative politics here. It makes the district a little more Republican, though not by a lot, but more importantly changes the personnel.

Patti Ann Lodge, who served in the Senate from Canyon County since 2000, was seriously contested in the 2012 primary (by former legislator Maurice Clements), but won strongly. An educator by profession, she has focused more on health and legal areas in the Senate, and supported the governor's health insurance exchange proposal.

The two representatives here are newer. Both usually are considered closer than not to the Tea Party wing of the caucus, but on the health insurance exchange Christy Perry voted in favor, and Batt against.

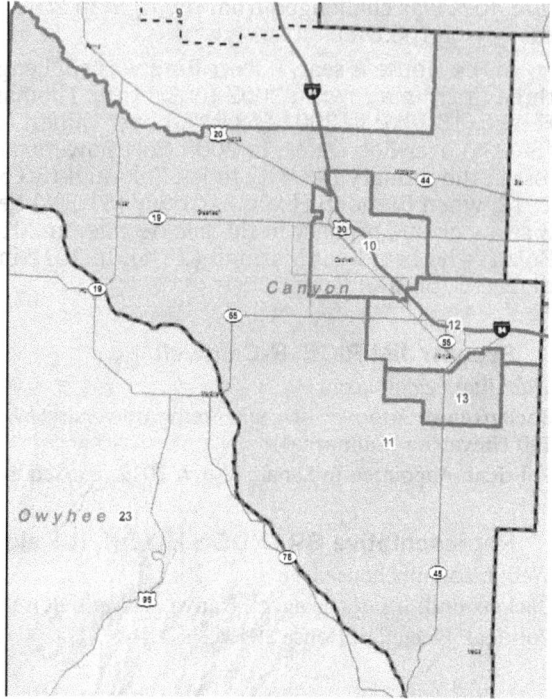

Predecessor district 11

ELECTIONS Two large parts to District 11: Gem County, centered on Emmett, and the fast-growth distant-from-Boise suburbs around Middleton, and beyond out to Parma. Gem was politically competitive years back, in the days when timber operations at Emmett were locally dominant alongside farming and ranching. With the collapse of timber, and the arrival of bedroom community developments at Emmett, the climate has changed. Gem County has been solidly Republican for at least a couple of decades. The northwest region of Canyon County has been so longer, and is more conservative.

The Little family, based at Emmett, has for three or four generations been a major presence through its large ranching operations. Brad, long active in business and ranching circles around the region, was appointed to a vacancy in the Senate in 2001, and won easy election four times before his appointment as lieutenant governor in 2009. His appointed replacement, Melinda Smyser, had Senate connections of her own: Husband C.A. "Skip" Smyser had been a senator before an (unsuccessful) run for the U.S. House in 1990.

Redistricting changed the representatives from District 11 from mostly Gem to Canyon County. Smyser opted out, and veteran Senator Patti Anne Lodge, from the Nampa area, ran for this seat. She was challenged in the primary by former Canyon County legislator Maurice Clements, but won (59.8%).

The two established Gem County House members were gone from here after 2012, Carlos Bilbao opting out of the legislature and Steven Thayn moving to the Senate in district 8. They were replaced by two incumbent Canyon County Republicans, Gayle Batt and Christy Perry.

Presdt	Democrat			Republican		
2012	Barack Obama	4,181	23.55%	Mitt Romney	13,116	73.82%

Sen	Democrat			Republican		
2012	Victoria Brown	4,092	24.10%	Patti Anne Lodge	12,872	75.90%
2010	Shannon Forrester	2,822	19.90%	Melinda Smyser	10,386	73.30%
2008	-	-	-	Brad Little	14,870	77.50%
2006	-	-	-	Brad Little	10,090	77.05%
2004	-	-	-	Brad Little	13,533	100.00%
2002	-	-	-	Brad Little	8,478	76.20%

H1	Democrat			Republican		
2012	-	-	-	Gayle L. Batt	14,609	100.00%
2010	-	-	-	Steven Thayn	11,687	100.00%
2008	Bob Solomon	7,724	40.10%	Steven Thayn	11,538	59.90%
2006	-	-	-	Steven Thayn	9,294	75.44%
2004	-	-	-	Kathy Skippen	11,216	77.90%
2002	-	-	-	Kathy Skippen	8,423	100.00%

H2	Democrat			Republican		
2012	-	-	-	Christy Perry	14,475	100.00%
2010	-	-	-	Carlos Bilbao	11,260	84.20%
2008	-	-	-	Carlos Bilbao	14,056	77.10%
2006	-	-	-	Carlos Bilbao	11,446	100.00%
2004	Tom Gatfield	4,524	29.80%	Carlos Bilbao	10,645	70.20%
2002	-	-	-	Gary Bauer	9,072	100.00%

PRIMARIES One of the most primary-packed districts in Idaho, in the last decade at least, and all Republican.

The Senate seat was challenged twice when (now-Lieutenant Governor) Brad Little held it, in 2002 (his first election) by Mike Pullin; Little won with 72.1%. In 2004 he took 65% against periodic gubernatorial candidate Walter Bayes (8.29%) and Steven Thayn (26.71%). The essentially new Senate seat was won (59.8% in 2012 by Patti Anne Lodge, who was challenged in the Republican primary by former Canyon County legislator Maurice Clements.

Both House seats were challenged in every primary election in the last decade – one of the few places in Idaho where that has happened. In 2002 Kathy Skippen won the open seat A (28.2%) narrowly, over Jonna Weber (27%), Terry Jones (26.8%) and Ed Falkenstien (18%); her winning margin was 66 votes. She expanded that in 2004 (50.7%), defeating Jones (39.29%) and Dale Salyers (10.02%). But in 2006 she lost (47.7%) to Steve Thayn (52.3%). Thayn was challenged in 2008 but won thinly (38.3%) over former Representative Gary Bauer (30.8%) and Matt Beebe (30.9%). In 2010, he easily beat (65.1%) Mike Pullin. In 2012 the tradition continued, as incumbent Gayle Batt defeated (66.0%) Greg Collett.

In the B seat, Bauer won in 2002 (59.8%) over Roger Reynoldson, but in 2004 narrowly lost (49.57%) to Carlos Bilbao (50.43%). Bilbao has been challenged three times since, in 2006 by Bauer (Bilbao took 55.7%), in 2008 winning (64.1%) over Bayes (12.6%), Steve Coyle (13.9%) and Jeff Justus (9.4%); and in 2010 (58.5%) over Thomas Munds (41.5%). In the shakeup of 2012, legislator Christy Perry (50.1%) defeated three challengers.

Senator PATTI ANNE LODGE, R-Huston

Web: pattiannelodge.net
Background: Retired, educator. Owner, agri-business. Marylhurst University, University of Idaho, Idaho State University, Albertson College of Idaho.
Political: Elected to Senate, 2000, 2002, 2004, 2006, 2008, 2010, 2012.

Representative GAYLE BATT, R-Wilder

Web:
Background: Homemaker. Nampa native. Oregon State University.
Political: Appointed to House, November 2011. Elected to House 2012.

Representative CHRISTY PERRY, R-Nampa

Web: www.christyperryforidaho.com
Background: Network marketing, "Home & Garden Party." Co-owner, operator, Buckhorn Gun & Pawn, Boise. Boise State University.
Political: Elected to House 2010.

District 12

District 12 (Canyon County (part)) is compact and consists of a portion of the city of Nampa, which had to be split due to its size. Nampa was divided along major roads and highways and in accordance with traditional communities of interest. This district is located entirely in Canyon County. District 12 contains 45,525 people, a deviation of +1.65% from the ideal district.

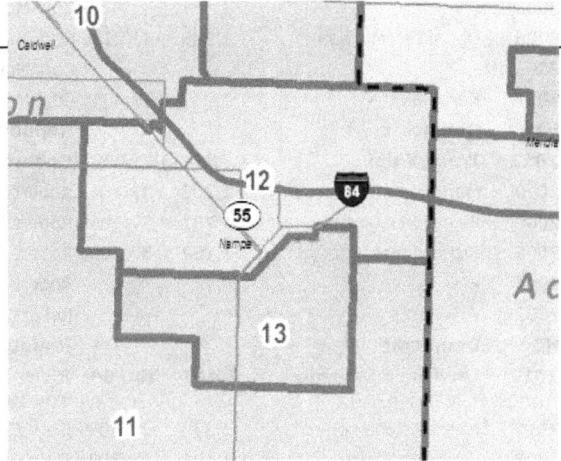

District 12 takes in much of northern Nampa and the industrial and commercial areas around it, many of the area's large agribusinesses, shopping centers and the new Mercy Medical centers, as well as (generally) the downtown area.

In theory, District 12 should be politically competitive. It takes up much of central Nampa, which is becoming a more urban area (increasingly similar to Democratic bases around Boise, Moscow, Coeur d'Alene, Idaho Falls) and has been working on urban redevelopment. It also has a potentially significant Hispanic voting base. So far, however, it has remained steadily Republican.

The senator is Todd Lakey, a former member of the Canyon County commission. New Representatives Robert Anderst and Rick Youngblood both were members of the Gang of 16, freshmen supportive of a state health insurance exchange proposal, and both voted in favor of it on the House floor. Senator Lakey voted in favor as well.

Former District 12

ELECTIONS None of this has made a dent, yet at least, on actual voting patterns in the area. Three Republican legislators have held the seats here in the last decade, and they collectively won all 15 elections during that time by more than 60% of the vote every time out. And contests were staged; Democrats forfeited only four of those 15 elections.

Presdt	Democrat			Republican		
2012	Barack Obama	4,885	31.70%	Mitt Romney	10,086	65.46%

Sen	Democrat			Republican		
2012	Melissa Sue Robinson	4,752	32.30%	Todd Lakey	9,976	67.70%
2010	Leta Neustaedter	2,235	27.20%	Curt McKenzie	5,985	72.80%

	Democrat			Republican		
2008	-	-	-	Curt McKenzie	10,644	100.00%
2006	Donald McMurrian	2,909	34.21%	Curt McKenzie	5,594	65.79%
2004	-	-	-	Curt McKenzie	10,417	100.00%
2002	Karl Malott	2,942	35.40%	Curt McKenzie	5,074	61.00%
H1	**Democrat**			**Republican**		
2012	**Tracy Volpi**	**4,759**	**32.90%**	**Robert Anderst**	**9,693**	**67.10%**
2010	Maria Mabbutt	2,709	32.80%	Robert Schaefer	5,559	67.20%
2008	Richard Mabbutt	4,781	37.50%	Robert Schaefer	7,973	62.50%
2006	Richard Mabbutt	3,152	37.28%	Robert Schaefer	5,303	62.72%
2004	-	-	-	Robert Schaefer	10,245	100.00%
2002	-	-	-	Robert Schaefer	5,997	76.70%
H2	**Democrat**			**Republican**		
2012	**Lawrence Dawson**	**4,447**	**30.70%**	**Rick Youngblood**	**10,032**	**69.30%**
2010	Melissa Robinson	2,300	27.80%	Gary Collins	5,970	72.20%
2008	Sunny Freeman	4,401	34.50%	Gary Collins	8,352	65.50%
2006	Sunny Freeman-Genz	2,672	31.61%	Gary Collins	5,781	68.39%
2004	Ralph L. Smith	3,778	30.50%	Gary Collins	8,614	69.50%
2002	Amanda Brown	2,858	34.90%	Gary Collins	5,331	65.10%

PRIMARIES Three of the four contests were came in 2002.

In 2012 Lakey defeated (61.4%) House member Robert Schaefer in the primary. The two House seats that year were open and drew three Republican candidates each. The close contest was for seat A, with Robert Anderst (44.5%) defeating Roger Hunt and Steve Nible. In B, Rick Youngblood easily (68.7%) dispatched Sherri Nible and Aaron Gonzalez.

Senator TODD LAKEY, R-Nampa

Web: toddlakey.us
Background: Attorney; former county deputy prosecutor. U.S. Army reserves. Brigham Young University. Lewis and Clark Northwestern School of Law.
Political: Canyon County Commission. Unsuccessful candidate for attorney general, 2002. Elected to Senate, 2012.

Representative ROBERT ANDERST, R-Nampa

Web: anderstforidaho.com
Background: Commercial real estate broker. Idaho State University.
Political: Elected to House, 2012.

Representative RICK YOUNGBLOOD, R-Nampa

Web: youngbloodforidaho.com
Background: Banker. North Idaho College, College of Idaho. Pacific Coast Banking School-University of Washington.
Political: Canyon County Highway Commission. Elected to House, 2012.

District 13

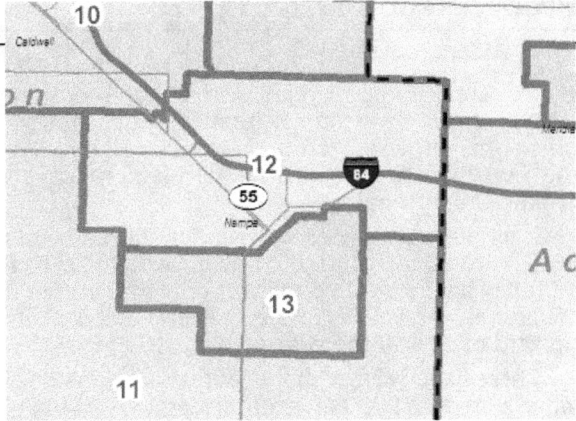

District 13 (Canyon County (part)) is compact and includes the remainder of the city of Nampa, which had to be split due to its size. Nampa was divided along major roads and highways and in accordance with traditional communities of interest. This district is located entirely in Canyon County and contains 46,784 people, a deviation of +4.46% from the ideal district.

This relatively compact district (one of the smallest in the state outside Boise) takes in southern Nampa, much of which is relatively newly developed – consisting of new subdivisions and other developments, many dating from the 90s and early 00s. The growth has slowed since the 2008 recession, but as it regains steam this area may add population again.

This might logically have been an area featuring freshman legislators, but instead three relative veterans represent it: Curt McKenzie, a senator since 2004, Gary Collins, a representative since 2000 and Brent Crane, a House member since 2006. Crane's personal informal political experience could be said to have gone back further, since his father is State Treasurer Ron Crane, who first was elected to the House in 1982. McKenzie chairs the Senate State Affairs Committee.

In October 2011, the Associated Press reported that he had received payments of about $6,400 as legislative per diem to compensate him for keeping a second home in Boise during the legislative session, though he had been staying on a couch in his law office in Boise. (The AP reported that then-Senator John McGee had been filing for similar payments.)

Brent Crane has been mentioned as a prospect for higher office, including the 1st district U.S. House seat if incumbent Raul Laborador departs from it.

The delegation split in the governor's health insurance exchange proposal. McKenzie and Crane voted no, but Collins voted yes, in floor votes. In March 2013, debating on the insurance exchange proposal, Crane (in a quite that went viral) tried to invoke civil rights protester Rosa Parks in his states-rights argument: "One little lady got tired of the federal government telling her what to do." Parks, in her bus seating protest, protested state and local law.

Predecessor district 13

ELECTIONS The area around Nampa has been one of Idaho's major growth areas in recent years, with subdivisions growing rapidly ever further from Nampa's city center. But much of this area's original feel remains. Much of it (especially around Lake Lowell and Melba and points south, to the Snake River) still are rural, farm and ranch land. Food processing remains important here.

It has long been conservative Republican country, and its votes for the legislature do not contradict. As in District 12, its Republican legislators – and they have been Republicans only in this area for a quarter-century – collectively won all 15 of their general elections in the last decade by upward of 60% of the vote.

There have been primary contests, however. Senator Patti Anne Lodge won the seat in 2000 after prevailing (57.7%) in one of them, a four-way battle. She has had much less challenge since.

The House delegation here had included two true long-timers in the Canyon delegation, members of very different stripes. The departure in 2006 of long-time moderate Representative Bill Deal in 2007 (to become state director of insurance) led to shifts in the seat. Nampa City Council member Steve Kren won the seat in 2008, but he was ousted two years later by newcomer Christy Perry. The other seat was held for many years by Dolores Crow, who became a statewide figure as chair of the House tax committee. Her retirement opened a door for Brent Crane, son of the state treasurer, who was unopposed in either 2008 or 2010.

Presdt	Democrat			Republican		
2012	Barack Obama	5,051	30.45%	Mitt Romney	11,087	66.85%

Sen	Democrat			Republican		
2012	Matthew Green	4,896	31.10%	Curt McKenzie	10,834	68.90%
2010	Chris Breshears	3,487	21.50%	Patti Anne Lodge	12,711	78.50%
2008	Dan Romero	6,028	27.00%	Patti Anne Lodge	16,269	73.00%
2006	Rohn Webb	3,807	24.42%	Patti Anne Lodge	11,101	71.22%
2004	-		-	Patti Anne Lodge	15,734	100.00%
2002	Corrine Fisher	3,803	30.00%	Patti Anne Lodge	8,886	70.00%
H1	**Democrat**			**Republican**		
2012	Clayton Trehal	5,170	32.60%	Brent Crane	10,706	67.40%
2010	-		-	Brent Crane	14,122	100.00%
2008	-		-	Brent Crane	18,759	100.00%
2006	Douglas Yarbrough	4,231	27.35%	Brent Crane	10,361	68.72%
2004	-		-	Dolores Crow	15,173	100.00%
2002	Robbie Allen	3,625	28.70%	Dolores Crow	8,394	66.60%
H2	**Democrat**			**Republican**		
2012	-		-	Gary Collins	13,051	100.00%
2010	-		-	Christy Perry	14,016	100.00%
2008	Byron Yankey	6,514	29.80%	Steve Kren	15,353	70.20%
2006	-		-	Bill Deal	13,188	100.00%

2004	-		-	- Bill Deal	13,747	81.20%
2002	-		-	- Bill Deal	9,738	79.80%

PRIMARIES Senator Patti Ann Lodge was primaried in 2002 (a 66.5% win over Wendell Cass) and 2004 (70.61% over Ronald Harriman) but not since; her large wins may have discouraged challenges since. In House A, veteran Representative Dolores Crow was challenged in 2002 and only barely defeated (50.4%) Scott McDonald (49.6%, by just 40 votes. She won again in 2004, but in the five-way primary she prevailed (33.82%) with only a third of the total, over Jim Barnes (27.55%), McDonald (21.44%), Steve Kren (11.55%), and Matt Wissel (5.65%). Her 2006 opt-out led to a primary between Brent Crane (57.5%) and Barnes (42.5%). The B seat, long held by Bill Deal, was primaried the election (2008) after he resigned and Steve Kren was named to replace him. Kren won that primary (64.8% over Russ Johnson. But he lost in 2010 (43.4% to Christy Perry (56.6%).

In 2012, incumbent Curt McKenzie ran for the district seat which had been held by Lodge; he defeated (54.3%) Hubert Osborne.

Senator CURT McKENZIE, R-Nampa

Web: www.curtmckenzieidaho.com
Background: Attorney (McKenzie Law Offices), private law practice, Nampa and Boise. Northwest Nazarene University. Georgetown University.
Political: Elected to Senate 2004, 2006, 2008, 2010, 2012.

Representative BRENT CRANE, R-Nampa

Web: www.brentcrane.com
Background: Vice president, Crane Alarm Service. Boise State University.
Political: Elected to House 2006, 2008, 2010, 2012.

Representative GARY COLLINS, R-Nampa

Web:
Background: Owner, insurance agency.
Political: Elected to House 2000, 2002, 2004, 2006, 2008, 2010, 2012.

District 14

District 14 (Ada County (part)). Ada County has sufficient population for nine total districts. This plan keeps Ada County intact, uses major roads and highways as easily identifiable boundaries and divides the districts based on city lines which constitute traditional communities of interest. The majority of the districts in Ada County have a population deviation of less than the ideal district in order to accommodate for future growth in these areas. District 14 consists of the cities of Eagle and Star, traditional communities of interest unto themselves. District 14 contains 44,919 people, a deviation of .29% from the ideal district.

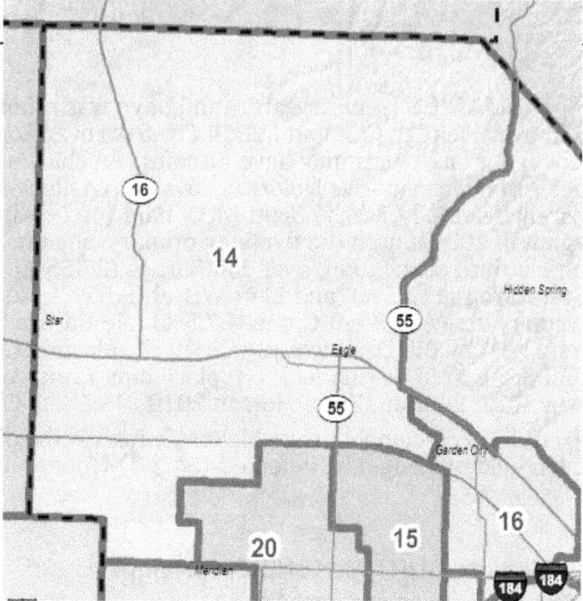

District 14 centers on the area around Eagle and Star, and the short distance between them and north to the Ada County line. It has been a fast-developing area; for a while in the 90s and the 00s new subdivisions seemed to be popping up weekly. (An exaggeration, but not by a lot.) The population of Eagle alone came close to doubling in the decade of the 00s; it shot up from 3,327 in 1990 to 19,908 in 2010; in legislative terms, from a small sliver of a district in 1990 to the dominant factor in one by 2010. District 14's land area is small than it was in the 00s, which was smaller than it was in the 90s, a function of the rapid growth here. The population of the old district had topped 75,000, approaching enough for legislative district mitosis.

Growth has slowed since the 2008 recession, but it has continued.

Nearly all of this area has been voting heavily Republican; many can be considered ex-urban voters in mindset at least.

The senator, Marv Hagedorn, was a two-term house member and considered, but abandoned, running for secretary of state in 2014. He is a popular figure among conservative Republican activists and in Tea Party circles. He did, however, vote in favor of the governor's health insurance exchange proposal.

In December 2013 he attended a "planning event" toward calling a federal constitutional convention, which if called could results in an overhaul of the national constitution.

Mike Moyle, the veteran from this area (a House member since 1998) and House majority leader, is one of the most influential members of the legislature and a key figure in the House, though he has had conflicts with others in leadership. He had open conflicts with Ken Roberts when both were in leadership.

And he and new Speaker Scott Bedke have had issues, notably over their different stances on the governor's proposal for a state health insurance exchange. Bedke helped push the measure through the House; Moyle vigorously debated against it.

The other House member here, Reed DeMordaunt, also voted against the exchange. DeMordaunt won an early chairmanship of the House Education Committee, and has focused most of his efforts in that area. He supported the three big law changes proposed in 2011 by Superintendent of Public Instruction Tom Luna. His interest in charter schools is personal: He was one of the founders of North Star Charter School in Eagle.

Predecessor district

ELECTIONS A curiosity indicating just how significant the Boise suburbs are becoming: Both the Democratic and Republican nominees for governor and for the hard-fought 1st district U.S. House seat in 2010 came from District 14, and none of them were natives of it.

Though not large geographically, it has distinct regions. The area toward its northeast is relatively remote, including some farmers but more occupants of subdivisions, at least one (Hidden Springs) seems designed to mirror a more urban living space. This area is relatively competitive politically. But it is outnumbered by the larger population bases around Eagle, some of which are high-income, and in northern Meridian. Overall, this has been a very conservative area.

Count this as another district where Democrats simply have not gotten close. The closest legislative race here in the last decade was in 2002 for seat B, when controversial Representative Henry Kulczyk was held to 59.3% - by far the weakest of the 15 Republican runs for seats here in the decade. The most determined Democratic contest may have come in 2010 for an open House seat (the same one), run by Steve Berch against a little-known Republican, Reed DeMordaunt. The end results did not much differ from various other Democratic challenges: A big Republican win.

The major figure from here in the Idaho House has been, for more than a decade, Mike Moyle, who early on became a leader of the House members most vociferously opposed to taxes; in recent years, he has been House majority leader. In his district, he has had no close calls either in the primary or general election.

The most interesting contest was a write-in challenge from former Eagle Mayor Nancy Merrill; the contest was energetic, but it easily went to Moyle. Merrill was later named state parks director.

Presdt	Democrat		Republican		
2012	Barack Obama	6,637	28.40%	Mitt Romney	16,209	69.37%

Sen	Democrat		Republican		
2012	-	-	- Marv Hagedorn	14,284	66.40%
2010	-	-	- Chuck Winder	20,674	100.00%

	Democrat			Republican		
2008	-	-	-	Chuck Winder	27,253	100.00%
2006	Glida Bothwell	6,591	32.41%	Stan Bastian	13,746	67.59%
2004	Daniel Weston	6,521	27.20%	Hal Bunderson	16,806	70.20%
2002	-	-	-	Hal Bunderson	11,281	78.80%
H1	**Democrat**			**Republican**		
2012	-	-	-	**Mike Moyle**	**18,045**	**100.00%**
2010	William Young	6,666	27.40%	Mike Moyle	17,678	72.60%
2008	Michelle Waddell	11,124	34.20%	Mike Moyle	21,405	65.80%
2006	-	-	-	Mike Moyle	16,949	100.00%
2004	-	-	-	Mike Moyle	19,842	100.00%
2002	Claude Shubert	5,111	34.60%	Mike Moyle	9,674	65.40%
H2	**Democrat**			**Republican**		
2012	**Glida Bothwell**	**6,349**	**29.60%**	**Reed DeMordaunt**	**15,091**	**70.40%**
2010	Steve Berch	7,891	32.20%	Reed DeMordaunt	16,624	67.80%
2008	Glida Bothwell	9,869	30.90%	Raul Labrador	22,093	69.10%
2006	Daniel Weston	6,943	34.45%	Raul Labrador	13,208	65.55%
2004	Del Bunce	7,150	30.50%	Stan Bastian	16,320	69.50%
2002	Sue Stadler	5,728	38.50%	Henry Kulczyk	8,817	59.30%

PRIMARIES Primary contests here every cycle of the decade, and all among Republicans.

The first three cycles featured the same close challenger each time. In 2002 incumbent Hal Bunderson (44.7%) finished just 125 votes ahead of former Senator Rod Beck (42.4%), and third-place Daniel Weston (12.8%). In 2004, in a two-way, Bunderson again defeated (54.49%) Beck (45.51%), a little more broadly. In 2006, with Bunderson opting out, Beck ran again but narrowly lost (47.2%) to Stan Bastian (52.8%). In 2008, Bastian was challenged by three opponents, and lost (32.6%) to one of them, Chuck Winder (42.7%); the others were former Representative Henry Kulczyk 3.9%) and Saundra McDavid (20.8%). In 2012 Bastian was challenged again, this time losing (29.6%) to House member Marv Hagedorn (55.5%); a third candidate, Gary Bauer, took 15%.

Representative Mike Moyle, in the A seat, was challenged twice, once in 2002 by former legislator Dean Van Engelen (Moyle won with 57.7%), and once in 2008 in a write-in primary challenge from former Eagle Mayor Nancy Merrill (Moyle took 69.3%).

The B seat went, after a competitive five-way 2002 primary, to Kulczyk (28.2%) over Kimm Rhoades (24.1%), Corey Christensen (22.1%), Morgan Masner (16%) and Stanley Swanson (9.6%). He lost the seat in 2004 primary to Bastian (51.64%). When Bastian ran for the Senate, the open seat went, in a three-way primary, to Raul Labrador (46.4%) over John Tomkinson (29.1%) and Jim Borton (24.5%).

When Labrador left in 2010 to run for Congress, Reed DeMordaunt (54.1%) won the three-way primary for the open seat over Nathan Mitchell (32.4%) and Christopher MacCloud (13.5%). In 2012 DeMordaunt was challenged but won (72.5%) over Michael Greenway.

Senator MARV HAGEDORN, R-Meridian

Web: www.marvhagedorn.com
Background: Navy (20 years, intelligence). Business manager. Co-founder, Wyakin Warrior Foundartion. Native of Omak, Washington. University of Maryland, Pensacola Junior College.
Political: Appointed to House, January 2007. Elected to House 2008, 2010. Elected to Senate, 2012.

Representative MIKE MOYLE, R-Star

Web: votemikemoyle.com
Background: Agribusiness. Commissioner, Star Fire District. Brigham Young University.
Political: Elected to House 1998, 2000, 2002, 2004, 2006, 2008, 2010, 2012. House majority leader.

Representative REED DEMORDAUNT, R-Eagle

Web: www.reed4idaho.com
Background: CEO, Med Management Technology. University of South Carolina, American University (Cairo), Brigham Young University.
Political: Elected 2010.

District 15

District 15 (Ada County (part)) is made up of a community of interest located wholly within the city of Boise and Ada County. District 15 contains 42,799 people, a deviation of -4.44% from the ideal district.

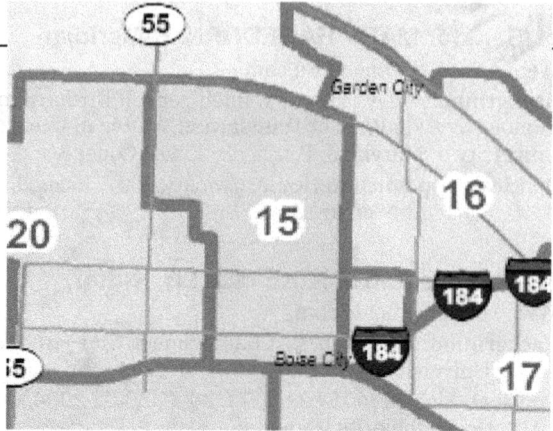

This is western Boise – the whole district is within Boise, but this area has voted a good deal differently from the areas closer to downtown. It never has elected a Democrat to the legislature, but demographically it is not a distant remove from District 16 or District 17, the districts to its east where Democrats recently have done well, or in some cases even become dominant.

District 15 was somewhat re-formed as well, however, moving a bit to the east, rendering it a little less Republican than it had been previously, but with a clear Republican edge.

This was home in 2012 to one of the premier legislative races in the state, between Republican Fred Martin, a businessman and former state official, and Betty Richardson, a former U.S attorney and Industrial Commission member and a top state Democratic organizers. Both campaigns were highly active and raised substantial funds, and the race was closely watched.

One of the House races in this new 15 got some attention too. Democrat Steve Berch, who had run an intensive but unsuccessful campaign in the old District 14, ran again for the House in this new 15 (without moving his residence). His opponent was a relatively unknown Republican, Mark Patterson, who for some years had run a business in Meridian. That seat was open due to redistricting; the race for the other House seat, where incumbent Lynn Luke was on the ballot was more low-key.

The Republicans won both races, but by modest margins: 52.1% in Martin's case, and 53.1% in Patterson's. That suggests that while Democrats have a hard haul to win in District 15, it could be possible in coming cycles. (Some Democrats said the presence of Mitt Romney on the presidential ballot may have damaged their chances in 2012 in this district with a substantial Mormon population.)

Patterson because the unexpected center of statewide political attention late in 2013 after his application for a concealed weapons permit was denied by the Ada County sheriff's office. The explanation for that was Patterson's legal history: He had pleaded guilty in 1974 to a Florida charge of assault with intent to commit rape, and was tried for rape (but not convicted) in Ohio two years later. The uproar that followed led to Martin, among other Republicans, calling for his district colleague to resign; and Patterson finally did so, effective at the start of the 2014 session.

The well-known name among the three nominees to replace him was Rod Beck, a former state senator and in recent years an activist in the Republican Party, who sometimes has conflicted with Governor C.L. "Butch" Otter. Otter chose elsewhere: Former U.S. Marshal Patrick McDonald, a candidate nearly certain to emerge clean after even a thorough vetting (which he also would have gotten before becoming marshal). McDonald was sworn in January 2014.

Martin voted in favor of the governor's proposal for a state-run health insurance exchange. Luker and Patterson voted against. Martin's vote may have been a large factor in his scorig by the libertarian Idaho Freedom Foundation group in its 2013 legislative index: Fourth from last overall, and last (with a -83 points) among all legislative Republicans.

Predecessor district 15

ELECTIONS If Democrats in Idaho are ever to become competitive again, they will need support in the Boise suburbs. Their best shot in that area seems to be District 15. It has a lot in common with the more Republican and more completely suburban district 14 and 15 to the west. But parts of it also have some of the attributes of a Boise city district. And Republican wins in general elections have not been quite so automatic or overwhelming here.

Representative Lynn Luker, for example, was held to 56% in 2010 (a strong Republican year) and 55.2% in 2006. Long-time Representative Max Black got a bye from Democrats in three of his elections in the last decade, but was held to 54.3% and 53.2% in the other two.

The senator, John Andreason (holding the seat since 1994, plus a term in the Senate in the late 60s), has had a slightly easier time in general elections, but has had primary contests, including a serious one in 2006 from former congressional candidate Dennis Mansfield.

Presdt	Democrat			Republican		
2012	Barack Obama	7,684	40.27%	Mitt Romney	10,756	56.38%

Sen	Democrat			Republican		
2012	Betty Richardson	8,783	47.90%	Fred Martin	9,545	52.10%
2010	Warren Bean	3,760	33.40%	John Andreason	7,493	66.60%
2008	-	-	-	John Andreason	13,198	100.00%
2006	Phyllis Hower	4,721	38.11%	John Andreason	7,667	61.89%
2004	Jerry Brown	5,616	34.50%	John Andreason	10,667	65.50%
2002	Jerry Peterson	4,382	36.70%	John Andreason	7,020	58.80%
H1	**Democrat**			**Republican**		
2012	Richard Keller	7,379	41.00%	Lynn Luker	10,602	59.00%
2010	Brenda Lovell	4,280	37.50%	Lynn Luker	6,401	56.00%
2008	-	-	-	Lynn Luker	12,857	100.00%
2006	Jerry Peterson	5,524	44.78%	Lynn Luker	6,811	55.22%
2004	-	-	-	Steve Smylie	12,428	80.40%
2002	Sue Sharp	3,998	33.50%	Steve Smylie	7,496	62.80%
H2	**Democrat**			**Republican**		

2012	Steve Berch	8,481	46.90%	Mark Patterson	9,618	53.10%
-			-	- Max Black	8,188	78.70%
2008	Greg Funk	6,747	40.90%	Max Black	8,963	54.30%
2006	-		-	- Max Black	8,622	73.51%
2004	-		-	- Max Black	11,764	77.10%
2002	Kathy Waddell	5,178	43.40%	Max Black	6,353	53.20%

PRIMARIES Another heavy-Republican, heavy-primary district, and again all Republican. Senator John Andreason was primary challenged twice, in 2002 and 2006, by the same challenger, Dennis Mansfield (and winning with 58% and 63% respectively). Representative Steve Smylie in the A seat prevailed in 2002 (74.7%) over Tom LeClaire and in 2004 (73.1%) over Kathryn Mooney. His departure to run for state school superintendent led to a three way primary decisively won by Lynn Luker (53.2%) over Bob Jacobson (27.1%) and Jeremy Olson (19.7%). Luker was challenged in 2010 but easily won (68.9%) over Jen Stanko. Max Black, who held the B seat throughout the decade, was challenged and won three times. In 2002 he beat (53.5%) Jack Friesz; in 2004 he beat (51.61%) Luker, who would go on to join him in the House; in 2010 he defeated (58.3%) Mark Patterson.

In 2012 the open B seat was challenged by two Republicans, with Mark Patterson defeating (60.1%) Curtis Ellis. In seat A, two Democrats competed for the nomination, which went to Richard Keller (58.0%) over John Hart.

Senator FRED MARTIN, R-Boise
Web: fredsmartinforsenate.com
Background: Retired. Executive Director, Citizens for Progressive Government. Ricks College, Idaho State University.
Political: Elected to Senate 2012.

Representative LYNN LUKER, R-Boise
Web: www.lynnmluker.com
Background: Attorney. University of California, Berkley. University of Idaho.
Political: Unsuccessful run for House, 2004. Elected to House 2006, 2008, 2010, 2012.

Representative PATRICK McDONALD, R-Boise
Web:
Background: Former U.S. marshal (Bush Administration). Idaho State Police (33 years). Idaho State University.
Political: Appointed to House January 2014.

District 16

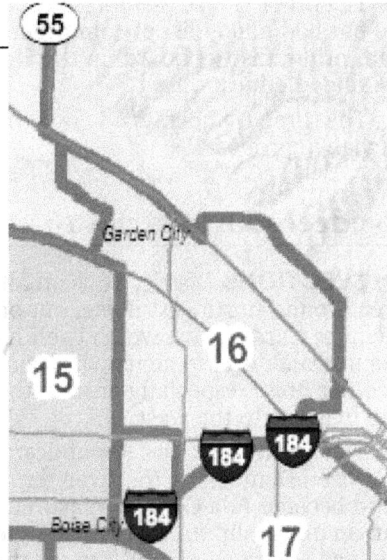

District 16 (Ada County (part)) consists of the entirety of Garden City as well as traditional communities of interest in the city of Boise. Portions of the city of Boise were included in order to satisfy the one person one vote requirement. District 16 includes 44,383 people, a deviation of -.90% from the ideal district.

Roughly similar to the old District 16, but with several changes in territory (mainly shifts with the old District 15), the new 16 is probably less friendly to Democrats than the old, but not by a great degree. It continues to include a sizable chunk of northwest Boise, and as well Garden City.

This is an urban area, much of it with a suburban feel. A good deal of the area around Garden City (and its main street, Chinden Boulevard) has an industrial/retail feel, and parts of this district are lower income and ethnically diverse demographically. There are also many older Boise neighborhoods and some new high-end developments as well.

This is an area that transitioned from a clear Republican lean in the 80s to a clear Democratic lean by the 00s – a pattern it shares with the central Boise district 17. It is not strongly Democratic, however: Although Democrats have been winning recent elections, they have not reached a landslide level whenever opposed by Republicans, and usually have polled in the mid-50s.

Through the 90s moderate Republicans like Cecil Ingram and Hod Pomeroy held two of the seats here, frequently turning back challenges both from Democrats and more conservative Republicans. The third seat was held for much of that time by Democrat Margaret Henbest. In 2002 she was joined by Democrat David Langhorst when he defeated Pomeroy, and two years later won the Senate seat when Ingram retired. Then in 2006 Democratic attorney Les Bock defeated Republican Jana Kemp (now an independent, and in 2010 as such a candidate for governor), and the three seats have stayed in Democratic hands since.

Bock moved to the Senate in 2008, and emerged in the Senate as a critic of the state Tax Commission. He has said he would not run again in 2014, and might resign before the term is up.

One of the representatives, Democrat Grant Burgoyne, has announced for the seat. (He also took the seat Bock had held in the House.) Burgoyne has been active in a variety of areas, from the "add the words" effort to include sexual orientation to the list of discriminatory practices, to criticism (teaming on this with Republican John Vander Woude) of the state land board's handling of private property management as a money-making approach.

The other House member here, Hy Kloc, is a freshman elected in 2012. He has had a long list of community activities including work on the Boise auditorium district board. In the House he has been active pushing for early childhood education.

The three Democrats all voted for Governor Otter's health insurance exchange proposal.

Predecessor district 16

ELECTIONS District 16 is an all-urban district, taking in roughly the area around northwest Boise, but one with a good deal of variety. It includes Garden City, which itself has two distinct areas (the old city and the upscale developments which have been annexed in). It has some parts of older Boise, especially around the Collister area, and also some newer subdivisions to the west.

The Senate seat was Republican, held by Cecil Ingram, from 1992 (it had been Democratic for three terms before that) until 2004, when he left (and became Ada County treasurer). In 2004, Democrat David Langhorst ran an unusually strong campaign to win it, and was unopposed in 2006. He made an unsuccessful run for the Ada County commission at that point, but Democrats had a House member to take his place, and Les Bock held the seat in 2008 and (more narrowly) in 2010 and 2012.

The House seats changed hands several times in the late 80s and early 90s. Margaret Henbest held on the longest, from 1996 to 2008, when he retired from the House. The Democratic nomination went to attorney Grant Burgoyne, who has held the seat. His percentages closely tracked Bock's.

A similar pattern held with the other House seat, which Bock held for a term (after defeating Republican incumbent Jana Kemp, later a candidate for governor) before his Senate run.

Since 2006, this has been one of the few all-Democratic legislative districts in Idaho.

Presdt	Democrat			Republican		
2012	**Barack Obama**	**10,207**	**51.36%**	**Mitt Romney**	**8,948**	**45.03%**
Sen	Democrat			Republican		
2012	**Les Bock**	**10,897**	**57.30%**	**Joan Cloonan**	**8,135**	**42.70%**
2010	Les Bock	6,081	53.70%	Bill Eisenbarth	5,238	46.30%
2008	Les Bock	9,615	57.60%	Christ Troupis	7,066	42.40%
2006	David Langhorst	9,816	100.00%	-	-	-
2004	David Langhorst	8,702	53.70%	Graham Patterson	7,513	46.30%
2002	Gino White	5,547	46.40%	Cecil Ingram	6,405	53.60%
H1	Democrat			Republican		
2012	**Grant Burgoyne**	**10,158**	**54.00%**	**Lee-Mark Ruff**	**7,230**	**38.40%**
2010	Grant Burgoyne	5,934	52.70%	Ralph Perez	5,319	47.30%
2008	Grant Burgoyne	9,096	55.70%	Joan Cloonan	7,225	44.30%
2006	Margaret Henbest	9,663	100.00%	-	-	-
2004	Margaret Henbest	9,242	57.40%	Tom LeClaire	6,868	42.60%

2002	Margaret Henbest	8,785	79.40%	-	-	-

H2	Democrat			Republican		
2012	**Hy Kloc**	**10,258**	**54.20%**	**Graham Paterson**	**8,673**	**45.80%**
2010	Elfreda Higgins	6,385	56.60%	Lee-Mark Ruff	4,898	43.40%
2008	Elfreda Higgins	9,017	55.00%	Elizabeth Hodge	7,376	45.00%
2006	Les Bock	6,458	52.68%	Jana Kemp	5,802	47.32%
2004	Gino White	7,823	48.70%	Jana Kemp	8,237	51.30%
2002	David Langhorst	6,404	54.00%	Hod Pomeroy	5,055	42.60%

PRIMARIES Though a Democratic-leaning district in the last decade, 16 has seen in that time only Republican primaries. There were Senate contests in 2004 won by Clinton Miner (58.73%) over Charles M. Roberts; and in 2008, by Christ Troupis (50.4%) narrowly over Dennis Warren. Also in 2004, Tom LeClaire (62.53%) defeated Adam Graham for the House A seat; and in the B, Jana Kemp (42.98%) defeated Graham Paterson (39.59%) and Mike Gollaher (17.43%). In 2008, running for the open House B seat vacated by Democrat Les Bock, who was running for the Senate, the Republican nomination was won by former legislator Elizabeth Allan Hodge (54.1%) over Ralph Perez (29.4%) and Ormond Howell (16.5%).

In 2012, when the B seat came open, primaries appeared in both parties. On the Democratic side, veteran local official Hy Kloc defeated (73.3%) perennial local candidate David Honey. On the Republican, Graham Patterson defeated (85.4%) Fairy Hitchcock.

Senator LES BOCK, D-Boise

Web: www.lesbock.org
Background: Attorney. Executive Director, Idaho Human Rights Education Center. University of California, Davis. Hastings College of Law.
Political: Elected to House 2006. Elected to Senate, 2008, 2010, 2012.

Representative GRANT BURGOYNE, D-Boise

Web: www.burgoyneforhouse.com
Background: Attorney (Mauk & Burgoyne). Staff, Idaho Secretary of State. Hearing officer, Idaho Department of Employment, 1980-95. Former chair, Ada County Democrats. University of Idaho. University of Kansas.
Political: Elected to House, 2008, 2010, 2012.

Representative HY KLOC, D-Boise

Web: hykloc.org
Background: Retired. Boise State Public Radio. Idaho Humane Society; Gene Harris Jazz Festival. New York City Community College; Western Michigan University.
Political: Great Boise Auditorium District board. Elected to House, 2012.

District 17

District 17 (Ada County (part)) is made up of communities of interest located wholly within the city of Boise in Ada County. District 17 includes 43,778 people, a deviation of -2.26% from the ideal district.

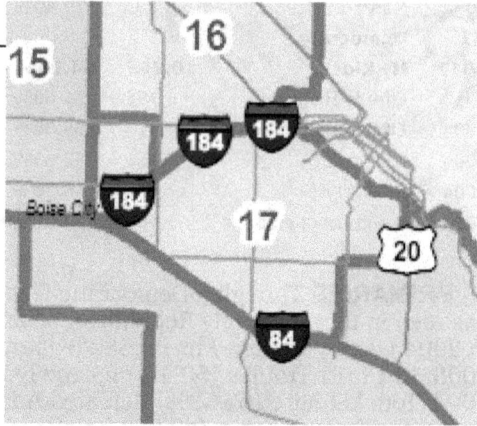

District 17 looks much the same as it did in the 00s, centered and mostly occupied by the central Boise bench, in the area between the jaws bordered by I-84 and the I-184 connector. It is mostly an older section of Boise (in many areas its population apparently skews a little older than most of Boise as well), some of it once (pre-60s) including several small communities absorbed into Boise.

The bench district has evolved into the second-most reliable district in the state for Democrats; contested Democratic candidates often win in landslides here, and they have won reliably. Senator Elliot Werk, who defeated a veteran Republican incumbent to win the seat, has notched four landslides in a row, and Representative Sue Chew has done nearly as well.

Three-term Democratic Representative Bill Killen retired from the House I 2012, and was replaced by Democratic attorney John Gannon, who had a rare distinction: A Democrat who had been elected to the House from this area in the pre-Werk period. (Gannon was elected in the strong Democratic year of 1990, then lost the seat in 1992.)

The representatives here have been among the most active in development during-sessions town hall events, interacting with constituents. That may be one reason this district, like District 16, has stayed all-Democratic since 2006, one of the few such in Idaho.

The three Democrats here all voted for Governor Otter's health insurance exchange proposal. None of the three were favorites of the Idaho Freedom Foundation's 2013 index. Werk was second last (-88 points) among the 105, and Chew scored -70 and Gannon -66.

Predecessor district 17

ELECTIONS The Boise bench was for years one of the most frustrating areas of Idaho politically for Democrats. An urban and long-settled area, a Democratic base existed; the district includes most of the Boise State University area and houses many government workers. For many years seemed just about ready to vote for Democrats.

But it resisted, coming very close on a number of occasions. It actually happened once in 1990, when attorney John Gannon won a House seat, but not again for another dozen years.

That occurred in 2002 when a very hard-working Democrat, Elliot Werk, defeated five-term Republican Senator Grant Ipsen. Werk dug in. He is the first Democratic senator elected from the Boise bench, and the first Democratic legislator there to be re-elected. By 2006, the demographics and strong Democratic organizing were making a difference. In that year, two Democrats – Bill Killen and Sue Chew – defeated two incumbent Republicans – Kathie Garrett and Janet Miller, respectively. (The signs of change had been visible; Miller won her last term with just 52% of the vote, and Garrett by a margin of nine votes.)

By the new decade, all three were winning steadily.

Presdt	Democrat			Republican		
2012	Barack Obama	9,197	54.87%	Mitt Romney	6,747	40.25%

Sen	Democrat			Republican		
2012	Elliot Werk	10,150	62.90%	Judy Peavey-Derr	5,980	37.10%
2010	Elliot Werk	5,665	60.60%	Lucas Baumbach	3,689	39.40%
2008	Elliot Werk	10,120	66.10%	T Allen Hoover	5,183	33.90%
2006	Elliot Werk	7,680	67.06%	Tim Flaherty	3,772	32.94%
2004	Elliot Werk	8,275	55.70%	Heather Cunningham	6,573	44.30%
2002	Elliot Werk	5,873	53.90%	Grant Ipsen	4,630	42.50%
H1	Democrat			Republican		
2012	John Gannon	8,959	56.60%	Kreed Kleinkopf	4,988	31.50%
2010	Bill Killen	5,276	56.70%	Craig Thomas	3,529	37.90%
2008	Bill Killen	10875	76.70%	-	-	-
2006	Bill Killen	6,489	56.72%	Kathie Garrett	4,537	39.66%
2004	Sean Spence	7,370	50.00%	Kathie Garrett	7,379	50.00%
2002	Bryan Goold	4,721	44.60%	Kathie Garrett	5,358	50.70%
H2	Democrat			Republican		
2012	Sue Chew	10,188	62.70%	Chad Inman	5,076	31.3%
2010	Sue Chew	5,591	59.40%	Dan Loughrey	3,814	40.60%
2008	Sue Chew	9,940	64.70%	Dan Loughrey	5,414	35.30%
2006	Sue Chew	6,735	58.38%	Janet Miller	4,426	38.37%
2004	Deborah Spindler	7,038	48.00%	Janet Miller	7,634	52.00%
2002	Linda Emery	4,880	46.00%	Janet Miller	5,064	47.70%

PRIMARIES Most of the primaries here in the last decade came in 2002, the most recent time when Republicans still held all three seats here. The then-Republican senator, Grant Ipsen, was primaried by T. Allen Hoover but easily won (66%), though he would lost to Elliot Werk later in the year. In 2010, Hoover ran again for the Senate and won the Republicans primary (55%) over activist Lucas Baumbach, but lost the general.

The House A seat was not primaried during the decade, but the House B was, when it was open in 2002. Janet Miller (38.5% won that year on the Republican side over former legislator Jesse Berain (30.4% and Heather Cunningham (31.1%); on the Democratic, Linda Emery (50.7%) narrowly beat former legislator John Gannon (49.3%). In 2004, Miller was primaried by Hoover, but defeated him (64.48%).

A rare Democratic primary cropped up in 2012, when Sue Chew was challenged but won (88.9%) over Greg Nielson.

Senator ELLIOT WERK, D-Boise

Web: www.elliotwerk.com
Background: Environmental consultant. Engineering geologist. Sonoma State University. University of Arizona.
Political: Elected to Senate 2002, 2004, 2006, 2008, 2010, 2012.

Representative JOHN GANNON, D-Boise

Web: johngannon.org
Background: Attorney. Director, New York Irrigation District. University of California Davis, Hastings College of Law, USAR JAG school.
Political: Elected to House 1990, defeated for re-election 1992, re-elected to House 2012.

Representative SUE CHEW, D-Boise

Web: www.suechew.com
Background: Licensed pharmacist. Adjunct professor, Boise State University.
Political: Elected to House 2006, 2008, 2010, 2012.

District 18

District 18 (Ada County (part)) includes traditional communities of interest in the city of Boise and continues to Ada County's boundary. District 18 includes 43,586 people, a deviation of -2.68% from the ideal district.

Most of the population of District 18 can be found in what might be reasonably called southeastern Boise, even if much of the district's new and added-on land area runs well into the mountains and desert southeast of Boise. Most of that new area, however, is populated lightly or not at all, though it does include some development in areas around Highway 21 (and some other areas which may yet be developed). The district overall is the closest Idaho has to evenly-balanced between the parties, and both have won and lost tight contests here in recent years. Since 2006, no candidate here has won with as much as 60% of the vote; in 2012, the top vote-getter won with 56.2%.

Democrats have been winning here more since 2000 (all but two of the last 15 contests), but neither party can take this district for granted.

Branden Durst, the young Democrat who was elected to both House and Senate, would be a good case study. An intense campaigner (with a strong interest in legislative redistricting). He ran for the House in 2006 and defeated the kind of relatively moderate Republican (Debbie Field) who had been highly popular here. After a narrow re-election, he ran for the then-open Senate seat, losing by 103 votes to Republican Mitch Toryanski; two years later he beat Toryanski by 1,496. Durst turned out to be one of the more unpredictable members of the Democratic caucus, even becoming the lone Democratic legislator to vote against the governor's health insurance exchange proposal in 2013.

Midway through the term he moved to western Washington state. Governor C.L. "Butch" Otter appointed freshman Representative Janie Ward-Engelking (who had narrowly lost in 2010 before winning in 2012) to replace him.

Her House seat in turn went by appointment, in January 2014, to Boise attorney Ilana Rubel.

The third member of the delegation, Phyllis King, has had a steadier and quieter electoral run here since her first election in 2006.

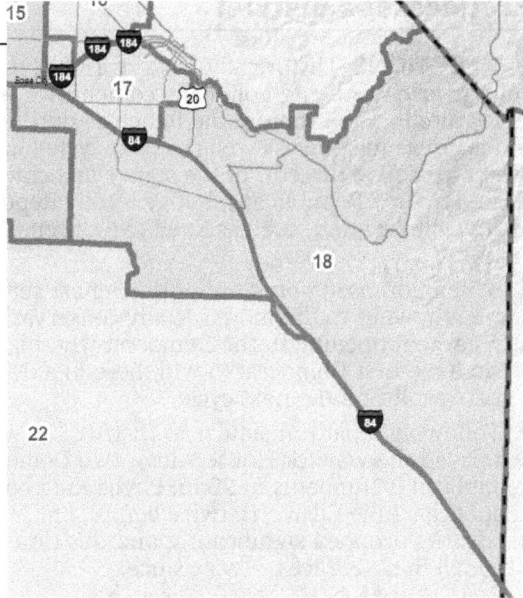

Predecessor district

ELECTIONS Historically, District 18 has the longest tradition of the Boise districts of being politically competitive, electing a Democrat to the legislature in 1986 (before the Bench or northwest Boise did consistently) and a House member as well the next cycle (Jim Hansen, an attorney and recent executive director of the state Democratic Party). In the 90s it elected mainly Republicans, but generally Republicans with a reputaton for relative moderation, such as Sheila Sorensen, Pamela Ahrens and Debbie Field.

When Sorensen opted out of the Senate seat in 2004, the Republican nominatin went to the more socially conservative Dave Baumann, which in turn gave an opening to the Democrat who filed, attorney Kate Kelly. She became the first Democrat to win there in a decade, and paved the way for a near-revolution the next cycle.

Following a pattern similar to District 17 (where a Democratic Senate win paved the way for House wins), two Democrats ousted veteran Republican incumbents in 2006. Phylis King had run losing races against Republican Julie Ellsworth twice before, but in 2006 the Republican vote in the district dropped significantly, and this time she won. She has won again – though in close races – twice since.

Debbie Field fit the pattern of moderate-appealing Republicans who had done well in the southeast for a decade, but in 2006 she was also working hard on the Otter campaign for governor. She in-district vote slipped, even more than Ellsworth's, and she too lost, to Democrat Branden Durst.

The district flipped, however, in 2010. Kelly opted out of the Senate (she would move to Seattle to work for a federal agency), and Durst ran for her seat. The opening allowed Republicans to win back both – narrowly. Attorney Mitch Toryanski beat Durst for the Senate by 103 votes, and Ellsworth staged a comeback over Democrat Jamie Ward-Engelking by just nine votes. (King's margin of almost 1,000 votes loomed large by comparison.)

Presdt	Democrat			Republican		
2012	Barack Obama	11,138	50.74%	Mitt Romney	10,041	45.74%

Sen	Democrat			Republican		
2012	Branden Durst	11,292	53.50%	Mitch Toryanski	9,796	46.50%
2010	Branden Durst	6,352	49.60%	Mitch Toryanski	6,455	50.40%
2008	Kate Kelly	11,432	59.50%	Dean Sorensen	7,797	40.50%
2006	Kate Kelly	8,945	63.01%	Brad Bolicek	5,252	36.99%
2004	Kate Kelly	9,913	54.90%	Dave Baumann	8,144	45.10%
2002	-		-	Sheila Sorensen	8,618	67.90%

H1	Democrat			Republican		
2012	Janie Ward-Engelking	11,693	55.30%	Julie Ellsworth	9,434	44.70%
2010	Janie Ward-Engelking	6,420	50.00%	Julie Ellsworth	6,429	50.00%
2008	Branden Durst	9,653	51.10%	Julie Ellsworth	9,222	48.90%
2006	Branden Durst	6,664	48.63%	Debbie Field	6,489	47.35%
2004	Earl Cook	7,153	40.80%	Debbie Field	10,37	59.20%

					8	
2002	-		-	- Debbie Field	7,386	59.60%
H2	**Democrat**			**Republican**		
2012	**Phylis King**	**11,748**	**56.20%**	**Brad Bolicek**	**9,145**	**54.80%**
2010	Phylis King	6,886	53.80%	Trevor Grigg	5,909	46.20%
2008	Phylis King	9,564	50.90%	Becky Young	8,404	44.70%
2006	Phylis King	7,240	52.53%	Julie Ellsworth	6,543	47.47%
2004	Phylis King	8,006	45.10%	Julie Ellsworth	9,571	54.90%
2002	Phylis King	5,676	44.20%	Julie Ellsworth	7,178	55.80%

PRIMARIES A Senate seat opening in 2004 drew three Republicans to the primary that year, former legislator Dave Baumann (47.27%) winning over Cheryl Miller (44.3%) and Harry Lear (8.43%). In 2010, another Senate opening (by departing Democrat Kate Kelly) drew three more Republicans; this contest was won by Mitch Toryanski (46.6%) over former legislator Dean Sorensen (41.7%) and Robert Lauritson (11.7%). House B was challenged when the seat was still Republican, on the GOP side in 2002 when incumbent Julie Ellsworth (65.4%) was challenged by Cheryl Miller (22.5) and Michael Law (12.1%), and in 2004 on the Democratic between Phylis King (53.82%) over Cara Walker. In 2010, as a challenger, Republican Ellsworth first had to win (64.5%) a primary over Gregory Ferch for the B seat.

In 2012, Durst won a primary contest (77.1%) over Matthew Duncan en route to winning the Senate seat. In House B, Republicans Brad Bolicek (50.5%) and John Hruby had a close contest in the primary.

Senator JANIE WARD-ENGELKING, D-Boise
Web: ward-engelking.com
Background: Teacher. Whittier College, Idaho State University, Boise State University.
Political: Unsuccessful race for House, 2010. Elected to House 2012.

Representative ILANA S. RUBEL, D-Boise
Web:
Background: Attorney. Georgetown University, Harvard Law School.
Political: Appointed to House, January 2014.

Representative PHYLIS KING, D-Boise
Web: www.king4idaho.com
Background: Commercial photographer. Medical technologist; St. Alphonsus Medical Center (11 years). Colorado State University.
Political: Elected to House 2006, 2008, 2010, 2012.

District 19

District 19 (Ada County (part)) includes traditional communities of interest in the city of Boise and continues to Ada County's northern boundary and Highway 55. District 19 includes 42,921 people, a deviation of -4.17% from the ideal district.

A high irony: The legislative district that includes the Idaho statehouse is the most Democratic in the state. And it is the most Democratic, in that there are strong Democratic bases throughout and no really strong Republican base at all – the only district of Idaho's 35 where that is true. It is the one district that, politically, bears some resemblance to most of Seattle or Portland. The biggest difference is that Republicans do almost always contest legislative elections here.

It includes most of Boise's east end, downtown and north end, and its residents include many government workers, professionals, students and a significant number of retirees. The new district does extend a little further in the northwest toward the foothills, and lost some territory toward the southeast near Highway 21, but its core is largely unchanged.

Its senator for two terms was Nicole LaFavour, probably most widely known as Idaho's first openly gay legislator; she was an advocate then and continued since for the "add the words" campaign for legal protections on sexual orientation. In 2012 she ran (unsuccessfully) for the U.S. House, and after an energetic Democratic primary the seat went to Cherie Buckner-Webb, who had served a term in the House. Founder of Sojourner Coaching, she has been active on a long list of community organizations and even has been a recording vocalist (with, among others, long-time Boisean Gene Harris).

Representative Holli High Woodings, first elected in 2012, was reported as interested in a run for secretary of state in 2014.

Like the few other districts where Democrats are elected, this one drew little favor with the libertarian Idaho Freedom Foundation's 2012 legislative index – and depending on how you count, this may be its least favorite delegation. Buckner-Webb scored second from last among all legislators (-88), Erpelding ninth from last (-76) and Woodings 21st from last (-68).

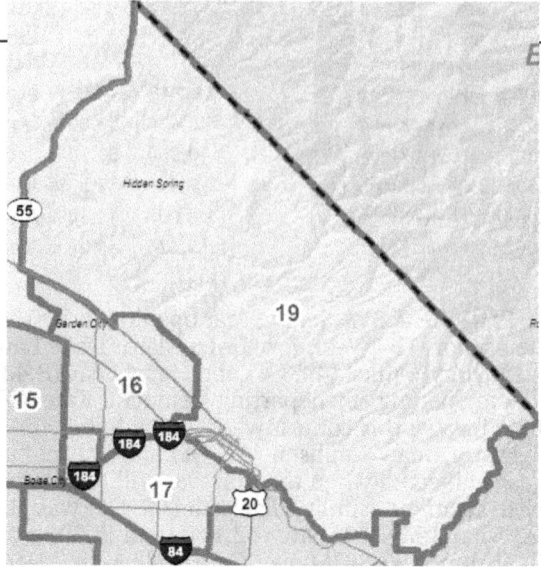

Predecessor district 19

ELECTIONS The last Republican elected here was Kitty Gurnsey in 1994; she had served 20 years in the House and rose to co-chair of the Joint Finance Appropriations Committee. Before 1974 northern Boise, like the rest of Ada County, was solidly Republican, but in that same election Democrat Ron Twilegar, an attorney with a strong skill for campaign organizing, won a House seat, and the next election the Senate. From there, a Democrats gradually won ever-larger percentages as the demographics of the district changed in their favor.

Gurnsey's Democratic successor was Pat Bieter, a retired Boise State professor and prominent North End figure. After unopposed re-election in 1998, he was killed in a car crash in 1999. His son David Bieter was appointed to replace him, and easily held the seat until his 2003 run for mayor of Boise, a position he still holds. Democratic activist Anne Pasley-Stuart held the seat for three terms after that, until she opted out in 2010. That led to a crisply contested primary, won by Cherie Buckner-Webb, who easily won the seat in November.

The Senate seat was held for much of the decade by Democrat Mike Burkett, who earlier had had a different Senate seat from 1988-92. Burkett's opt-out in 2008 also led to a primary, won by freshman Representative Nicole LeFavour. LeFavour drew attention as Idaho's first opely gay legislator. LeFavour's seat went to Democratic businessman Brian Cronin.

Both House members left their seats in 2012, Cronin and Pasley-Stuart both departing the legislature. Both were easily won by Democrats who had won strongly-contested three-way primaries, Mathew Erpelding in seat A and Holli Woodings in seat B.

Presdt	Democrat			Republican		
2012	Barack Obama	14,599	62.17%	Mitt Romney	7,989	34.02%

Sen	Democrat			Republican		
2012	Cherie Buckner-Webb	15,778	70.00%	Paul O'Leary	6,755	30.00%
2010	Nicole LeFavour	10,246	68.80%	Debra Miller	4,655	31.20%
2008	Nicole LeFavour	15,163	71.30%	Chuck Meissner	6,111	28.70%
2006	Mike Burkett	12,657	75.26%	Charles Seldon	4,160	24.74%
2004	Mike Burkett	14,305	70.80%	Charles Seldon	5,911	29.20%
2002	Mike Burkett	10,789	71.20%	Joan Cloonan	4,362	28.80%
H1	Democrat			Republican		
2012	Mathew Erpelding	14,695	66.70%	Mike Washburn	7,345	33.30%
2010	Cherie Buckner-Webb	10,196	68.40%	Jim Morland	4,716	31.60%
2008	Anne Pasley-Stuart	17,211	99.90%	-	-	-
2006	Anne Pasley-Stuart	14,418	100.00%	-	-	-
2004	Anne Pasley-Stuart	14,047	70.50%	Kevin Wink	5,874	29.50%
2002	David Bieter	12,213	85.60%	-	-	-
H2	Democrat			Republican		
2012	Holli Woodings	14,378	65.70%	Don Howard	7,509	34.30%
2010	Brian Cronin	9,974	68.10%	John Magnan	4,677	31.90%

2008	Brian Cronin	14,004	66.60%	Kevin McGowan	7,008	33.40%
2006	Nicole LeFavour	14,217	100.00%	-	-	-
2004	Nicole LeFavour	13,350	67.20%	Alicia Cassarino	6,523	32.80%
2002	Ken Robison	11,742	83.40%	-	-	-

PRIMARIES A rare Democratic district, with mostly Democratic primaries. An open Senate seat in 2002 led to a close primary won by Mike Burkett (51.9%) over Anne-Pasley Stuart. (Republicans contested internally for this seat then too, with Joan Cloonan winning 59.3% over Myrtle Mae Christensen. That same year, incumbent Democrat Ken Robison won easily (85.9%) over Gordon Conrad. When Robison opted out in 2004, a primary resulted, won by Nicole LeFavour (54.55%) over future legislator Brian Cronin (36.32%) and former legislator Steve Scanlin (9.13%). Finally, in 2010, when the holder of the A seat opted out, the primary was won by Cherie Buckner-Webb (78.4%) over David Cadwell (20.5%) and Dallas Gudgell (1.1%).

When both House seats opened in 2012, three Democrats filed for each. Mathew Erpelding (48.0%) defeated Troy Rohn and Dallas Gudgell in what appeared to be the hotter of the two races. In seat B, Holli Woodings (56.4%) beat Brad Goodsell and Andy Edstrom. The A seat also drew a quiet Republican primary, won by Mike Washburn (60.1%) over Geoffrey Talmon.

Senator CHERIE BUCKNER-WEBB, D-Boise
Web: www.votecheriebuckner-webb.org
Background: Coach, business consulting (Sojourning Consulting). George Fox University. Northwest Nazarene University.
Political: Elected to House, 2010. Elected to Senate, 2012.

Representative MAT ERPELDING, D-Boise
Web: erpforidaho.com
Background: President, Association of Outdoor Recreation and Education. Idaho State University; University of Idaho.
Political: Elected to House, 2012.

Representative HOLLI HIGH WOODINGS, D-Boise
Web: woodingsforidaho.com
Background: Energy industry, public relations. Boise State University.
Political: Elected to House, 2012.

District 20

District 20 (Ada County (part)) includes the majority of the city of Meridian, a traditional community of interest wholly contained in Ada County. Significant public testimony supported keeping the city of Meridian whole. District 20 includes 42,610 people, a deviation of -4.86% from the ideal district.

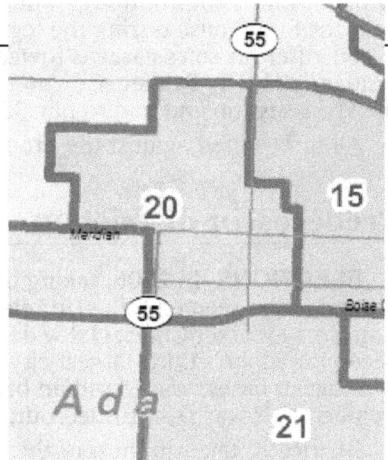

The larger share of the city of Meridian is in district 20, not that you could easily use that description on the ground to discern its limits: Meridian sprawls, and development in the area extends well beyond city limits. District 20 does include the center of Meridian – the older downtown area, the area where some remnants of the old dairy town (which Meridian still was up to the late 70s). Its new iteration is contracted inward, toward Meridian's downtown, from the old boundaries; that means this district leans toward some of the older suburban developments here, which means most of them are at least 20 years or so old.

The senator here is one of the best-known – for three decades or so – political figures in the Boise area, Chuck Winder. For many years he was best known for his work on transportation (especially on the board of the Ada County Highway District). He ran for governor in 1994 and mayor of Boise in 2003, falling short in both. Then in 2008 he won election to the Senate from a district based around Eagle, and became identified (in a surprise to some who had watched his earlier brick-and-mortar public career) with social issues. In 2012 he made national headlines after he proposed a bill to require women seeking an abortion first obtain an ultrasound examination. He also said, in testimony, that "Rape and incest was used as a reason to oppose this. I would hope that when a woman goes into a physician, with a rape issue, that that physician will indeed ask her about perhaps her marriage, was this pregnancy caused by normal relations in a marriage, or was it truly caused by a rape. I assume that's part of the counseling that goes on." The comments led to a political firestorm, and fellow Senator Cherie Buckner-Webb described them as "so disrespectful." Winder, who had been unopposed for election that year, drew an active write-in challenge, but he easily was re-elected.

Winder also has been a central figure on resource issues, co-chairing a federal lands task force.

The House members here have been less visible. James Holtzclaw, elected in 2012, is a real estate broker active in a number of community organizations. Joe Palmer, now in his third term, got a boost early in his House tenure with appointed to head the chamber's transportation committee. He has been outdone for news reports by his son, Ty Palmer, a candidate for Meridian city council in 2013 (he lost) and a political campaign worker who has been sharply outspoken on a number of political figures, not least other Republicans. The *Idaho Statesman* reported in 2012 "when his father introduced a bill to disable 259 Boise city parking meters near the Statehouse during the legislative session. Rep. Palmer introduced his bill after his son's car was towed from a Capitol Mall parking spot in January 2012. Ty Palmer had run up $186 in unpaid parking tickets during the 2011 session and had to pay $343 to get his car out of impoundment."

All three voted against the proposed health insurance exchange.

Predecessor district 20

ELECTIONS In 2006, taking note of how a number of urban areas around Idaho seemed to be (in relative terms) the most Democratic, former state party worker Chuck Oxley decided to test the idea in Meridian, then becoming Idaho's third-largest city – and for many years a strong Republican bases. Was Meridian becoming urban enough to elect a Democrat? It wasn't, it turned out; Oxley took 30.6% of the vote.

District 20 takes in most of the city of Meridian, which may at its center turn more urban over time, but which in the last decade has been definitely suburban, and in temperament maybe even exurban. Much of the development here is new, and there are a lot of newcomers, and people who are here because they're rather not live in "the city" (Boise).

During the 00s the most consistent political figure here has been Shirley McKague, first elected to the Idaho House in 1996. In January 2007, when then-Senator Gerry Sweet left to take a staff job with new U.S. Representative Bill Sali, McKague was appointed to replace him. She has not had any close calls in her general election races.

Snodgrass was replaced by Joe Palmer. McKague's House seat went to Republican retired naval officer Marv Hagedorn.

Presdt	Democrat			Republican		
2012	Barack Obama	6,073	31.96%	Mitt Romney	12,475	65.66%
Sen	Democrat			Republican		
2012	James Mace	5,695	31.60%	Chuck Winder	12,303	68.40%
2010	-	-		Shirley McKague	11,731	100.00%
2008	Ryndy Williams	6,435	31.30%	Shirley McKague	14,153	68.70%
2006	Ryndy Williams	5,001	36.09%	Gerry Sweet	8,855	63.91%
2004	Samuel McEvoy	5,637	29.80%	Gerry Sweet	13,310	70.20%
2002	Samuel McEvoy	3,850	31.90%	Gerry Sweet	7,788	64.50%
H1	Democrat			Republican		
2012	Caitlin Lister	5,958	33.50%	Joe Palmer	11,848	66.50%
2010	-	-		Joe Palmer	11,829	100.00%
2008	-	-		Joe Palmer	14,732	77.30%
2006	-	-		Mark Snodgrass	10,813	81.22%
2004	-	-		Mark Snodgrass	15,176	84.70%
2002	Wayne Foster	3,092	25.80%	Mark Snodgrass	8,166	68.10%
H2	Democrat			Republican		
2012	-	-		James Holtzclaw	14,706	100.00%

2010	-		-	-	Marv Hagedorn	11,851	100.00%
2008	-		-	-	Marv Hagedorn	17,035	100.00%
2006	Chuck Oxley	4,181	30.56%	Shirley McKague	8,975	65.59%
2004	Kenton Travis	6,447	34.40%	Shirley McKague	12,316	65.60%
2002	Eileen Thornburgh	5,042	38.60%	Shirley McKague	7,712	64.00%

PRIMARIES The House B seat here was not primaried at all in the last decade, but the Senate seat was primaried four times and the House A seat in all five cycles. Senator Gerry Sweet won primaries both in his first winning Senate race in 2002 (53.1%) over Bob Haley (35.3%) and Darrel McRoberts (11.6%), and in his first re-election in 2004 (53.09% over Joe Borton). When he resigned to work for new U.S. Representative Bill Sali, Shirley McKague was appointed to replace him. She won her first election for the seat (53.4%) over Representative Mark Snodgrass, and another 2010 challenge (60.1%) over Mike Vuittonet. In his three House races before the Senate run, Snodgrass was challenged and won each time: in 2002 (55%) over Sean Moorhouse, in 2004 (54.1%) over Dan Hollowell, and in 2006 (59.2%) over Marv Hagedorn, who would later win McKague's House seat. Snodgrass's Seat A replacement, Joe Palmer, was primaried in 2008 for the open seat (winning narrowly, 50.7%, over Keith Bird) and in 2010 (winning 54% over Shaun Wardle).

Both House seats had three-way Republican primaries in 2012. Incumbent Palmer (65.9%) was lightly challenged by Richard Dees and Chris MacCloud. In the open seat B, James Holtzclaw (41.8%) defeated Patrick Malloy and Tom LeClaire.

Senator CHUCK WINDER, R-Boise

Web: chuckwinder.wordpress.com
Background: Businessman. Former member and chair, Idaho Transportation Board.
Political: Ada County Highway District. Unsuccessful run for governor, 1994. Unsuccessful run for Boise mayor, 2003. Elected to Senate, 2008, 2010, 2012.

Representative JOE PALMER, R-Meridian

Web: www.palmerfor20.com
Background: Owner, furniture store (Cherry's Consignment). Idaho Army National Guard. Ricks College. Boise State University.
Political: Elected to House, 2008, 2010, 2012.

Representative JAMES HOLTZCLAW, R-Meridian

Web: holtzclawfor20.com
Background: Real estate broker. U.S. Air Force. Veterans of Foreign Wars, American Legion. George Fox Univresity.
Political: Elected to House, 2012.

District 21

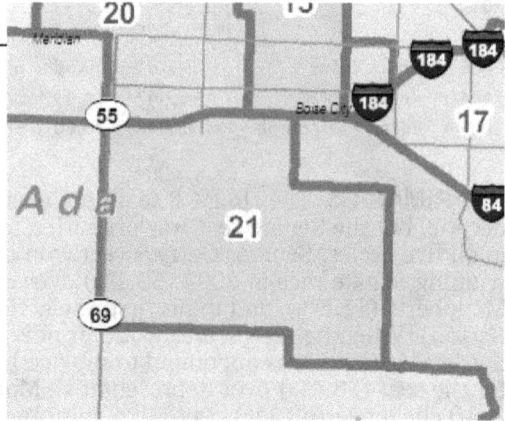

District 21 (Ada County (part)) includes traditional communities of interest south of Interstate 84 that are wholly included in Ada County. District 21 includes 43,541 people, a deviation of -2.78% from the ideal district.

The new District 21 includes part of what used to be District 21, but only a small geographic slide of it – the bulk of the land area, along with much of its population, has been exported to District 22. In effect, the new District 22 as well as 21 are the children of the parent old District 21.

This portion is the Meridian area south of Interstate 84, an area rapidly and heavily developed in the late 90s and early 00s.

The senator, Clifford Bayer, who was a close ally of now-U.S. Representative Raul Labrador when both were in the Idaho House, made some waves in House internal politics. In 2010 he moved to challenge veteran House Majority Leader Mike Moyle for that spot, but Moyle prevailed.

Both House members, Steven Harris and Tom Dayley, are freshmen, first elected in 2012 (Dayley had run for the House in 2012 but lost in a primary to Bayer), and all three members of the delegation are alumni of Brigham Young University. Harris and Dayley have split on some significant matters, however. Harris, like Bayer, voted against the governor's proposed health insurance exchange bill, while Dayley was one of the Gang of 16 supporting and voting for its passage.

Predecessor district 21

ELECTIONS Which of Ada County's suburban districts could be considered the most Republican, and most "conservative"? Districts 14 and 20 could certainly pitch a case, but the winner during the 00s decade probably was District 21, the area farthest physically, socially, and politically from central Boise in that decade. The mileage between this and District 19 could be traversed in a half hour, but their politics are night and day. District 21 includes part of the Meridian area, but its main city is Kuna and it includes a piece of the Southwest community (most of it has been exported to the new District 22), a sprawl of unincorporated development whose people are very determined not to be in a city, and want little to do with urban life. They also want little to do with Democrats, who rarely have reached 40% of the vote here in legislative races – ever.

This was the district sometimes-controversial Republican Bill Sali represented for 16 years before winning a U.S. House seat (for one term) in

2006. That House A seat went to John Vander Woude, who won a four-way primary with 38.9%. The next cycle, he lost his seat in the primary to Rich Jarvis, by 65 votes; then in 2010, he beat Jarvis by a little larger margin, with 47.7%. One key to some of the switches may have been the city of Kuna. The Kuna Melba News noted in a June 2010 report that Vander Woude's percentage in Kuna rose from 55% in 2008 to 65% in 2010, closing tracking the margin of win, or loss. Kuna is becoming a de facto urban center for this district.

The Senate seat here was held by Jack Noble as the decade opened. But ethical issues led to hearings in the Senate over whether to expel him, and he resigned in 2005 ahead of the vote. Governor C.L. "Butch" Otter named real estate agent Russ Fulcher to replace him. Fulcher had a tight primary contest in 2008 against Steven Ricks (winning with 51.5%), but defeated him more decisively in 2010 (70.2%). Fulcher was an unsuccessful candidate for president pro tem in 2010.

Presdt	Democrat			Republican		
2012	Barack Obama	7,053	33.56%	Mitt Romney	13,390	63.72%

Sen	Democrat			Republican		
2012	Kirsten Hooker	6,978	35.20%	Cliff Bayer	12,858	64.80%
2010	Kelly Victorine	4,740	25.20%	Russell Fulcher	14,063	74.80%
2008	-	-	-	Russell Fulcher	21,842	100.00%
2006	-	-	-	Russell Fulcher	13,845	100.00%
2004	-	-	-	Jack Noble	16,687	100.00%
2002	Eileen Thornburgh	5,042	38.60%	Jack Noble	7,637	58.40%

H1	Democrat			Republican		
2012	Craig Kreiser	6,942	35.40%	Steven Harris	12,675	64.60%
2010	Sharon Fisher	5,418	28.90%	John VanderWoude	13,361	71.10%
2008	Sharon Fisher	9,468	36.00%	Rich Jarvis	16,798	64.00%
2006	-	-	-	John VanderWoude	13,635	100.00%
2004	Scott Erskine	5,945	30.20%	Bill Sali	13,735	69.80%
2002	Scott Erskine	4,370	33.70%	Bill Sali	8,016	61.80%

H2	Democrat			Republican		
2012	Erin Zaleski	6,729	34.30%	Tom Dayley	12,871	65.70%
2010	Sean Carrick	4,985	26.70%	Cliff Bayer	13,661	73.30%
2008	Steven Dillehay	8,732	33.80%	Cliff Bayer	17,097	66.20%
2006	-	-	-	Cliff Bayer	13,536	100.00%
2004	-	-	-	Cliff Bayer	15,593	100.00%
2002	Jay Gooden	3,953	30.70%	Fred Tilman	8,415	65.40%

PRIMARIES District 21 is plenty Republican, but it has generated some close primaries and – in-party – seat turnovers. That was less true on the Senate level, where Senator Jack Noble was primaried in 2002 but won decisively (58.4%) over Greg Nelson (31.8%) and David Owen (9.8%). His appointed replacement, Russell Fulcher, has been primaried ever time out. He won in 2006 narrowly (45.9%) over Steven Ricks (43.1%) and Patrick Avella; in 2008 narrowly again, 51.5% over Ricks; then in 2010 in a landslide (70.2%) in his third contest in a row with Ricks. In his last two pre-Congressional state House races, Bill Sali was challenged in the primary once, in 2002, winning (59%) over Stephen Bright. After he left, though, the seat was hotly contested within the Republican primary. In 2006, John Vander Woude won (38.9%) a closely-contested four-way, defeating Don W. Johnson (31.1%), Michael Law (19.3%) and Daniel Dunham (10.7%). In 2008, Vander Woude lost (49.3%) a very tight race against Rich Jarvis (50.7%), a 65-vote margin. In 2010 they rematched, with the addition of Michael Roy, and this time Vander Woude took 47.7%, Jarvis 38.3% and Roy 14.1%. Seat B has been less contested, though there was a Democratic primary in 2002, where Jay Gooden took 67.3% to Joe Tawney's 32.7%. Also that year, Cliff Bayer lose to long-time incumbent Fred Tilman (60%). But the next election Tilman opted out for the Ada County Commission, and Bayer took the seat. He was primaried in 2008 and 2010 but defeated Jefferson Hunt West with 58.4% and Thomas Dayley with 62.8%, respectively.

In 2012, both House seat were open. The A seat went, after a three-way primary, to Steven Harris (49.3% in the primary); he defeated Robert Simison and Parrish Miller. In 2013 Harris ranked at the top (scoring a positive 142 points) of all 105 legislators ranked by the libertarian Idaho Freedom Foundation.

The open seat B was won in a competitive four-way primary by Tom Dayley (34.3%), defeating Mike Vuittonet, Lori Shewmaker and Charles Hoffman.

Senator CLIFFORD BAYER, R-Boise

Web: www.cliffbayer.com
Background: Medical research (infectious disease). Brigham Young University-Hawaii. Boise State University.
Political: Appointed to House 2003. Elected to House 2004, 2006, 2008, 2010. Elected to Senate, 2012.

Representative STEVEN HARRIS, R-Meridian

Web:
Background: Brigham Young University.
Political: Elected to House, 2012.

Representative THOMAS DAYLEY, R-Boise

Web: dayleyforrepresentative.com
Background: Retired. U.S. Air Force. Brigham Young University, University of Southern California (England).
Political: Unsuccessful candidate for House, 2010 (losing to Clifford Bayer). Elected to House, 2012.

District 22

District 22 (Ada County (part)) keeps the majority of the city of Kuna intact and continues to the Ada County boundary. District 22 includes 43,828 people, a deviation of -2.14% from the ideal district.

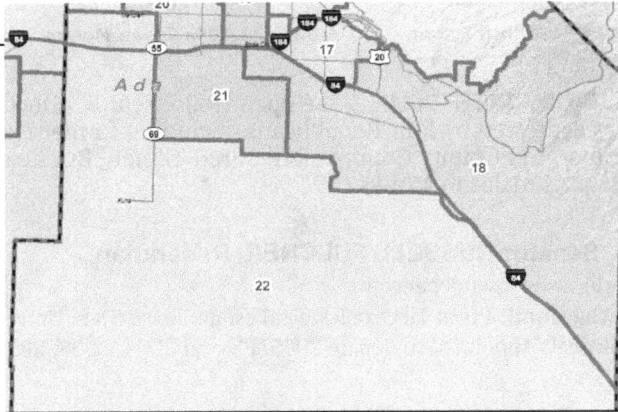

The brand new District 21 is an original creation, carved out of part of what used to be District 21, but only part of it. It may be, however, the more Republican part of that older district (though we're not talking about massive distinctions). This is overwhelming Republican territory; Mitt Romney won more than two-thirds of the presidential vote here, and Barack Obama little more than a fourth.

In the first general election here in 2012, two of the legislative Republican candidates – the returning legislators – were unopposed. Newcomer Jason Monks was opposed by Democrat Sharon Fisher, whose slightly under a third of the vote here may be indicator of things to come. Representative John Vander Woude, who was reapportioned into this district, was visible in 2013 in his critique (with Democratic Representative Grant Burgoyne) of the state land board's obtaining and managing various type of private property for state benefit, not simply endowment lands or other resources lands swapped for them, as was more traditionally the case.

The most visible legislator by far from this area, however, is Senator Russell Fulcher, a Meridian Republican who in 2013, while serving as Senate Republican caucus chair, said he would oppose Governor C.L. "Butch" Otter in the Republican primary in 2014. Late in the year he said he would retain his spot in leadership in the coming session, even as the campaign against a governor of his own party took form.

Predecessor district – no clear analogue

See old district 21.

Presdt	Democrat			Republican		
2012	Barack Obama	4,549	28.40%	Mitt Romney	10,999	68.66%
Sen	Democrat			Republican		
2012	-	-	-	Russell Fulcher	12,602	100.00%
H1	Democrat			Republican		
2012	-	-	-	John Vander Woude	12,454	100.00%

H2	Democrat			Republican		
2012	Sharon Fisher	4,821	32.40%	Jason Monks	10,080	67.60%

PRIMARIES In 2012, the open House seat B, effectively vacated by was contested by four Republicans, including former House member and former Ada County Commissioner Fred Tilman, But he came in second (35.3%) to Jason Monks (39.7%).

Senator RUSSELL FULCHER, R-Meridian

Web: www.russfulcher.com
Background: Preco Electronics. Real estate. Boise State University.
Political: Appointed to Senate 2005. Elected 2006, 2008, 2010.

Representative JOHN VANDER WOUDE, R-Nampa

Web: www.vanderwoudeforidaho.com
Background: Dairyman, farmer. Retail store owner. Army.
Political: Elected to House 2006. Unsuccessful run fore House 2008. Elected to House, 2010, 2012.

Representative JASON MONKS, R-Meridian

Web: monksforidaho.com
Background: Brigham Young University.
Political: Elected to House, 2012.

District 23

District 23 (Owyhee County, Elmore County, and Twin Falls County (part)). District 23 includes all of Elmore and Owyhee Counties. Elmore County does not have a large enough population to constitute a district by itself and therefore in order to meet the one vote requirement, it was combined with Owyhee County and a small portion of Twin Falls County. Due to Owyhee County's geographic location this combination was necessary as Elmore and Twin Falls Counties are its only two remaining neighboring counties that could be combined to form a complete legislative district. Elmore and Owyhee Counties are connected by Highway 51 which runs north to south, creating a commercial zone and linking the communities within those counties together. Combined, these two counties did not have sufficient population to form a complete legislative district, and in the interest of forming compact districts, a portion of Twin Falls County which is contiguous to both Elmore and Owyhee Counties, had to be included. District 23 contains 44,458 people, a deviation of -0.74% from the ideal district.

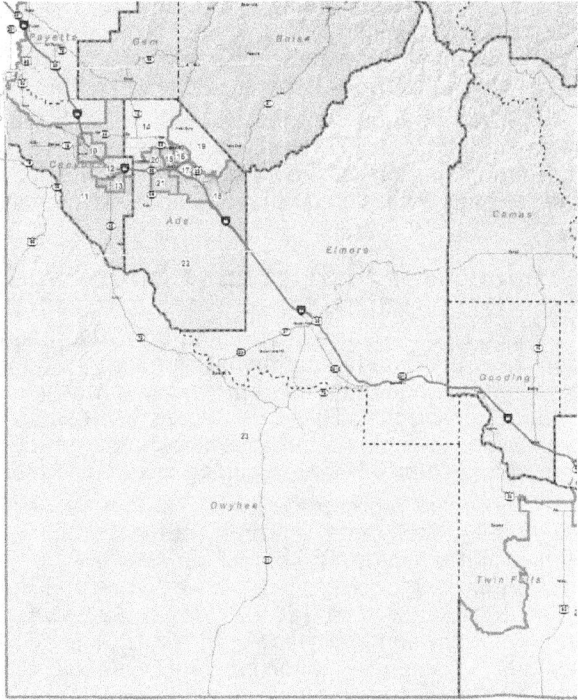

This is one of the most-deeply changed, from the previous decade, districts in the state. Here, we assign two predecessor districts – 22 and 23. In the last decade, Elmore County was the dominant part of one district (the old 22), and Owyhee County and western Twin Falls County made up another (the old 23). In this new configuration, those two districts are effectively joined together (with some land territory, mainly Boise County, thrown off to other districts).

The dominant piece is Elmore County, and the main population center – the city of Mountain Home with its nearby air force base – is the political axle. Elmore was traditionally a competitive county, and sometimes leaning a bit Democratic, but that has not been the case for at least 20 years.

Still, the senator here, Bert Brackett, was the winner in 2012 of a primary against another Republican senator, Tim Corder; redistricting threw them into the same district together. Brackett was from the far removed and thinly-populated eastern edge of the district, while Corder was from Mountain Home. But Brackett, a rancher, was more deeply connected to the ranching and business community, and Corder had been campaigned against as moderate. A family note: Brackett's daughter, Jani Revier, has been since December 2012 administrator of the state Division of Financial Management (an appointee of Governor C.L. "Butch" Otter) and is married to the chief of staff for Representative Mike Simpson.

Brackett and the two House members, Rich Wills and Pete Nielsen (both from Elmore County), have been regularly re-elected with landslides. The delegation split on the governor's proposed health insurance exchange; Brackett and Wills voted in favor, and Nielsen against.

Predecessor district 22 (Elmore and Boise counties)

ELECTIONS Once, Elmore and Boise counties connected fairly directly; now, the only road linking them (running through the small mining outpost of Atlanta) is one only a well-provisioned four-wheel drive should attempt even in midsummer. These are two distinct counties nowadays with little on the surface in common but leading to some similarity in politics. Boise, the old mining county, is now occupied more by exurbanites from Boise city.

Elmore was represented for 12 years in the Senate by Democrat Claire Wetherell, a member of a prominent local family (her husband served earlier in the Senate, and one of her sons is a former state Democratic chair and presently a district judge). After she retired in 1996, the seat went to Robbi King (later Barrutia), a Republican who was defeated in her primary in 2002. That nominee was Sher Sellman, a state representative and former Mountain Home City Council member who had run as a Democrat, lost, then (in 1998) as a Republican and won. That history may have been enough to cost her in the 2002 general election, and in a slightly less Republican district, against Democrat Fred Kennedy, an attorney, who narrowly defeated her.

Kennedy opted out after a single term, however, and the seat reverted to form with a win by Republican trucking company owner Tim Corder of Mountain Home. His 2008 primary was unusual and contentious. A more conservative candidate named Clayton Cramer filed against him, and received (evidently unsolicited) help from Boise political activists including the Idaho Association of Commerce & Industry, whose contractor was the source of a misleading flyer widely distributed. Corder won with 62%.

The House seats have been held decade-long by Richard Wills and Pete Nielsen, who did have a series of tight contests through 2006, but not since.

Presdt	Democrat			Republican		
2012	Barack Obama	3,881	27.41%	Mitt Romney	9,858	69.63%
Sen	Democrat			Republican		
2012	-	-	-	Bert Brackett	9,177	68.80%
2010	Henry Hibbert	1,905	24.10%	Tim Corder	6,009	75.90%
2008	Rustyn Casiano	3,086	26.70%	Tim Corder	8,479	73.30%
2006	Henry Hibbert	2,651	32.09%	Tim Corder	5,611	67.91%
2004	James Alexander	5,031	45.00%	Tim Corder	6,144	55.00%
2002	Fred Kennedy	3,834	48.90%	Sher Sellman	3,701	47.20%
H1	Democrat			Republican		

2012	Jody Bickle	3,926	28.90%	Richard Wills	9,641	71.10%
2010	-	-	-	Richard Wills	6,791	100.00%
2008	-	-	-	Richard Wills	9,550	100.00%
2006	Karen Schindele	3,163	38.53%	Richard Wills	5,047	61.47%
2004	Bob M. Works	2,972	28.00%	Richard Wills	7,627	72.00%
2002	-	-	-	Richard Wills	6,281	100.00%
H2	**Democrat**			**Republican**		
2012	**Pam Chiarella**	**4,556**	**33.50%**	**Pete Nielsen**	**9,037**	**66.50%**
2010	-	-	-	Pete Nielsen	6,550	100.00%
2008	Rosemary Ardinger	4,133	36.10%	Pete Nielsen	7,310	63.90%
2006	Dawn Best	3,638	43.80%	Pete Nielsen	4,667	56.20%
2004	Wayne Lasuen	4,947	45.00%	Pete Nielsen	6,057	55.00%
2002	David Phillips	3,476	45.70%	Pete Nielsen	4,124	54.30%

PRIMARIES All but one of the legislative primaries here in the last decade were for the Senate seat, and all the contests were Republican. In 2002, incumbent Robbi Barrutia was upset by Representative Sher Sellman (60.1%), who lost the general to Democrat Fred Kennedy. When Kennedy opted out in 2004, two Republicans filed; in the contest, Tim Corder (53.5%) defeated Marla Lawson (46.5%). Corder was challenged in 2008, defeating Clayton Cramer with 62% and Lawson in 2010 with 58.3%.

In 2012, in the one primary contest pitting Senate incumbents lumped together in redistricting, Bert Brackett defeated (57.4%) Corder.

In the one House contest, Peter Nielsen in 2002 beat Tish O'Donnell-Bageman with 60.1%. Nielsen was held to under half the primary vote in 2012, getting 45.7% against Matthew Bundy and Steven Millington.

Senator BERT BRACKETT, R-Rogerson
Web: brackettforsenate.com
Background: Rancher, Flat Creek Ranch. Former president, Idaho Cattle Association. Idaho National Guard. University of Idaho.
Political: Appointed to House, 2005. Elected to House, 2006. Elected to Senate, 2008, 2010, 2012.

Representative RICHARD WILLS, R-Glenns Ferry
Web:
Background: Retired, Idaho State Police. Part-time Elmore County deputy. Business owner, Opera Theatre. Three Island Crossing Committee.
Political: Elected to House 2002, 2004, 2006, 2008, 2010, 2012.

Representative PETE NIELSEN, R-Mountain Home
Web:
Background: Insurance agent. Part-time farmer. Former Elmore County Republican chair. Brigham Young University. Utah State University.
Political: Elected to House 2002, 2004, 2006, 2008, 2010, 2012.

Former District 23 (Owyhee, west Twin Falls counties)

The eastern part of this ungainly district, running from the city of Twin Falls west to the Oregon state line, is in the Magic Valley. But much of it is desert country a lot like much of Nevada. (Jackpot is across the state line to the south.) Owyhee County retains its rustic feel. But much of the population does come from the area to the west side of the city of Twin Falls. This area elects Republicans exclusively. So its most remarkable political figure could be Bill Chisholm, an iconoclastic Buhl Democrat (sometimes running as an independent) who probably holds the Idaho record for running most times for the legislature without winning. He ran in each election in District 23 of the 00s (four times for the Senate, once for the House), and reportedly was a candidate in every cycle since 1978 – which would mean 17 runs.

Twin Falls farmer Jim Patrick won races in 2006 and 2008 and was unopposed in 2010. Jones was replaced by rancher Bert Brackett (of a very prominent ranching family in Twin Falls County); when Senator Tom Gannon died in 2009, he was appointed to replace him there. Brackett's seat went (through appointment and then election) to former Twin Falls *Times News* publisher Stephen Hartgen.

Sen	Democrat			Republican		
2010	-	-		- Bert Brackett	9,689	100.00%
2008	Bill Chisholm	5,312	33.50%	Bert Brackett	10,550	66.50%
2006	Bill Chisholm	4,139	37.23%	Tom Gannon	6,977	62.77%
2004	Bill Chisholm	4,920	35.10%	Tom Gannon	9,116	64.90%
2002	Bill Chisholm	4,382	44.20%	Tom Gannon	5,534	55.80%
H1	**Democrat**			**Republican**		
2010	-	-		- Jim Patrick	9,629	100.00%
2008	Peter Rickards	4,365	27.90%	Jim Patrick	11,257	72.10%
2006	Peter Rickards	3,499	31.84%	Jim Patrick	7,492	68.16%
2004	Howard Meiers	3,935	29.10%	Frances Field	9,574	70.90%
2002	Mike Ihler	3,900	39.80%	Frances Field	5,890	60.20%
H2	**Democrat**			**Republican**		
2010	Bill Chisholm	3,465	31.60%	Stephen Hartgen	7,496	68.40%
2008	Mike Ihler	5,413	35.20%	Stephen Hartgen	9,951	64.80%
2006	-	-		- Bert Brackett	9,357	100.00%
2004	-	-		- Doug Jones	11,246	100.00%
2002	Grant Atkinson	3,240	33.30%	Doug Jones	6,500	66.70%

PRIMARIES In his first run for the Senate, Tom Gannon won a three-way primary (45.2%) over future House member Jim Patrick (39.2%) and Rex W. Reed (15.5%). In his last, in 2008, he won (66.4%) over Doran Parkins. In the House B 2002 primary, veteran House member Douglas Jones won (53.1%) somewhat narrowly over John Wiggins (46.9%). In her last contest, Representative Frances Field (54.51%) was challenged by Jim Conder (34.22%) and James Morrison (11.27%). Her opt-out in 2006 led to a primary won by Patrick (63.7%) over Tim Conder.

District 24

District 24 (Twin Falls County (part)). District 24 consists of the majority of the city of Twin Falls, a traditional community of interest entirely contained within Twin Falls County. District 24 includes 46,915 people, a deviation of 4.75% from the ideal district.

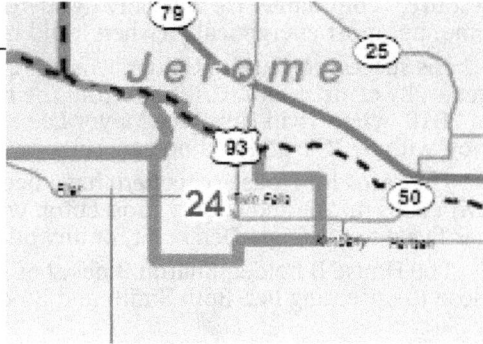

The new District 24 is the only essentially urban legislative district between the Boise and Pocatello areas. Its feel is suburban apart from the scattered industrial and retail sectors; in redistricting in 2011 it lost an extension south of the city of Twin Falls, which ran halfway down to Jackpot; the new district does reach out through some farm country eastward toward Kimberly.

The senator, Lee Heider, got to the legislature by breaking a chain of relatively moderate Republican senators from Twin Falls stretching back several decades: Richard High, Laird Noh and then Chuck Coiner, all taking a generally centrist tack. Criticism from the right mounted and overtook him in 2010, when Twin Falls Vice Mayor Heider challenged him in the primary, saying flatly, "He is not a conservative."

Heider demonstrated his philosphical credentials on a number of occasions (his key role in blocking nomination of the first female member of the Fish & Game Commission may be part of that). But he also has worked in recent years on regulation of payday loan businesses.

The delegation here is considered strongly conservative. Representative Steve Hartgen, whose strictly conservative editorials from his days as editor and publisher of the Twin Falls *Times News* were much remarked around the region (the remarks varied depending on one's point of view), was very much a loyal caucus vote in Boise. (First appointed to the House to replace Bert Brackett, he has been highly active on the Statehouse redevelopment and on economic growth, among other subjects.)

Representative Lance Clow was a veteran Twin Falls city council member. On the Idaho Freedom Foundation index for 2013, he came closer to that group's center than any other legislator, scoring a -4 points.

But this is one of the unusual all-Republican delegations in which all three members voted in favor of Governor Otter's health insurance exchange proposal in 2013.

ELECTIONS Of the two Twin Falls-based districts, both centered on farming and food processing, 24 is centrally based on the city, while 23 includes only some of its west side. The new 24 likely is the more moderate, though elections have yet to provide a clear demonstration of that idea.

It was the core of the area that sent Laird Noh to the Senate for 24 years, until he retired in 2004. Noh, one of the most studious of senators, was often regarded as a moderate, and for many years chaired the Senate resources committee. He was only lightly challenged during most of that time, but most energetically (when it did happen) from the right.

His successor, Charles Coiner, was a fairly close match for Noh, taking a generally centrist tack. Criticism from the right mounted and overtook him in 2010, when Twin Falls Vice Mayor Lee Heider challenged him; Heider won with 57.2%, and had no general election opposition.

The races for House seats here have been quieter. Leon Smith, a former Twin Falls mayor and county prosecutor, was elected to seat A in 1998 and has faced not a single Democrat, or any other serious opposition, since.

The House B holder, Sharon Block, has had opposition but none coming close to unseating her. Both Smith and Block retired in 2012.

Presdt	Democrat			Republican		
2012	Barack Obama	4,872	30.28%	Mitt Romney	10,707	66.54%
Sen	Democrat			Republican		
2012	Pat Marcantonio	5,545	35.70%	Lee Heider	10,003	64.30%
2010	-	-	-	Lee Heider	8,566	100.00%
2008	-	-	-	Charles Coiner	13,341	100.00%
2006	-	-	-	Charles Coiner	9,537	100.00%
2004	Gary Baty	3,369	22.50%	Charles Coiner	11,602	77.50%
2002	-	-	-	Laird Noh	8,595	100.00%
H1	Democrat			Republican		
	-	-	-	Lance Clow	13,001	100.00%
2010	-	-	-	Leon Smith	8,960	100.00%
2008	-	-	-	Leon Smith	13,216	100.00%
2006	-	-	-	Leon Smith	9,644	100.00%
2004	-	-	-	Leon Smith	12,259	100.00%
2002	-	-	-	Leon Smith	8,596	100.00%
H2	Democrat			Republican		
2012	Rosemary Fornshell	6,164	40.10%	Stephen Hartgen	9,202	59.90%
2010	-	-	-	Sharon Block	8,818	100.00%
2008	Carolyn Elexpuru	4,035	26.30%	Sharon Block	11,331	73.70%
2006	-	-	-	Sharon Block	9,449	100.00%
2004	Maggi Fortner	5,062	33.90%	Sharon Block	9,859	66.10%
2002	Will Buhler	3,284	32.50%	Sharon Block	6,817	67.50%

PRIMARIES When veteran Laird Noh departed in 2004, a three-way primary ensued, won by Charles Coiner (52.35%) over former Representative Randy Hansen (34.81%) and Kenneth Edmunds (12.84%). Coiner wasn't challenged in the next two cycles, but in 2010 he lost (42.8%) to challenger Lee Heider (57.2%).

House A, long held by Leon Smith, was challenged in 2010; he won less than a majority (48.4%) against two challengers, Rusty Satterwhite (29.3%) and Mark Goodman (22.3%). Incumbent Sharon Block was challenged but prevailed (69.2%) in 2002 in a comeback attempt by former legislator Ron Black.

Senator LEE HEIDER, R-Twin Falls

Web: www.leeheider.com
Background: Contractor, broker. Brigham Young University. Ball State University.
Political: Member, council, Twin Falls city. Elected to Senate, 2010, 2012.

Representative LANCE CLOW, R-Twin Falls

Web:
Background: Retired. California Lutheran University.
Political: Mayor, Twin Falls (six years). Member, city council, Twin Falls. Elected to House 2012.

Representative STEPHEN HARTGEN, R-Twin Falls

Web: www.stephenhartgen.com
Background: Retired, newspaper publisher (Twin Falls *Times News*, Hailey *Wood River Journal*). Idaho Capitol Commission. Amherst College. University of Minnesota.
Political: Appointed to House, July 2008. Elected to House, 2008, 2010, 2012.

District 25

District 25 (Jerome County and Twin Falls County). District 25 includes the entirety of Jerome County and Twin Falls County. Separately, these counties do not have a large enough population to constitute an entire legislative district. They are contiguous counties connected by Interstate 84 and Highways 30 and 93. This district keeps Buhl and Filer as well as Kimberly, Hansen and Murtaugh together. District 25 includes 46,795 people, a deviation of +4.48% from the ideal district.

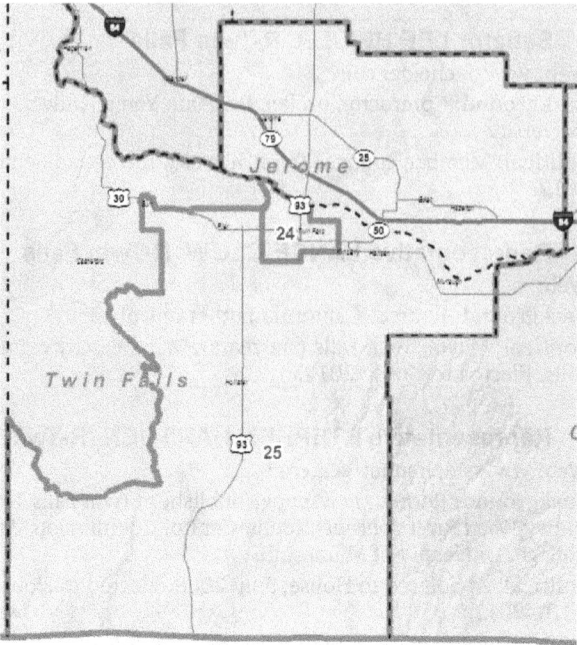

In the creation of this district, and the reapportionment of Twin Falls County in particular, Districts 23, 24 and 25 reflect the difficulty of reapportionment in Idaho. A single plan was advanced (out of 8 possibilities) that split Twin Falls only once (apportioning it among two districts instead of three). The Commission considered that alternative but rejected it because it required the bisection of the City of Twin Falls, a combination of Minidoka and Jerome Counties (which are connected by a sliver of land constituting the Snake River Canyon, and breaks up the natural combination of Minidoka and Cassia Counties, an area that is commonly referred to based upon the combination as "MiniCassia." Based upon the Idaho Supreme Court's express recognition of the advisory nature of Idaho Code § 72-1506(5), the Commission after careful consideration determined that the configuration of Plan L 93 best served the citizens of the State of Idaho, as well as, Twin Falls, Minidoka, Jerome, and Cassia Counties. This configuration represents the Commission's adherence to the mandatory requirements of Idaho Code § 72-1506, including ¶ (2) that "to the maximum extent possible, districts shall preserve traditional neighborhoods and local communities of interest" over the advisory requirement of Idaho Code § 72-1506(5) that "In the event that a county must be divided, the number of such divisions, per county, should be kept to a minimum.

This is another one of those legislative areas heavily altered, politically, by redistricting; the two incumbents filing for re-election here served in different districts in the last term. The new district takes in most of the area to the north, east and south of the city of Twin Falls, including all of Jerome County and most of the cities of Twin Falls County other than the county seat (that is, Buhl, Filer, Kimberly, Hansen, Murtaugh). All are agricultural and food-processing communities.

The old district 26 included all of two counties – Jerome and Minidoka. In the new scheme, Minidoka is thrown off for unification with Cassia County; that means the state senator from the old 26, Republican Dean Cameron, in 2012 filed to represent the new district 27.

The most prominent member of this delegation is Maxine Bell, who for many years has co-chaired the Joint Finance-Appropriations Committee, which drafts the state budget. She for many years represented the same district as her co-chair, Cameron; after the 2011 redistricting they were placed in separate districts. Bell has been known to be sharply outspoken from her position as co-chair, but she seldom ventures very far from the overall stance of the House Republican caucus.

Predecessor district 26

ELECTIONS Irrigation farming and food processing – especially, for sheer job and economic impact, food processing – made up the core of 26, which lies on the north side of the Snake River (often locally called the "Northside") across from Twin Falls. Minidoka has sometimes, though uncommonly, shown some indications of Democratic activism (the significant Hispanic population here could eventually affect that), but Jerome almost never has.

And its legislative delegation has been as stable as any in Idaho, to the point that its senator and one of its representatives have built up enough seniority to co-chair the legislature's budget committee (Joint Finance-Appropriations).

Senator Dean Cameron (who lives and whose base is on the Minidoka side) was appointed in August 1991, a young and relatively unknown insurance agent active in Republican politics. He faced a serious primary contest in 1992 from a former mayor of Jerome, but since winning that has faced no major challenges since; his low percentage in the last decade was 70.8%.

Representative B Maxine Bell (who lives and whose base is on the Jerome side) has served even longer, since 1988, and has only seldom been challenged (one in 2010 drew her down to 79.3%).

The relative newcomer, John "Bert" Stevenson, a Rupert farmer, has drawn a few more challenges but not real threats.

Presdt	Democrat			Republican		
2012	Barack Obama	3,833	23.52%	Mitt Romney	12,033	73.82%

Sen	Democrat			Republican		
2012	Scott McClure	5,214	32.90%	Jim Patrick	10,650	67.10%
2010	-	-	-	Dean Cameron	8,560	100.00%
2008	Scott McClure	3,998	29.20%	Dean Cameron	9,704	70.80%
2006	-	-	-	Dean Cameron	8,678	100.00%
2004	-	-	-	Dean Cameron	11,788	100.00%
2002	Douglas Jones	2,806	28.80%	Dean Cameron	6,943	71.20%
H1	Democrat			Republican		
2012	-	-	-	Maxine Bell	14,035	100.00

			%			%
2010	Scott McClure	2,270	24.30%	John Stevenson	7,079	75.70%
2008	-	-	-	John Stevenson	11,767	100.00%
2006	Scott McClure	3,258	32.95%	John Stevenson	6,631	67.05%
2004	Lee Halper	2,745	22.10%	John Stevenson	9,662	77.90%
2002	-	-	-	John Stevenson	8,498	100.00%
H2	**Democrat**			**Republican**		
2012	**Cindy Shotswell**	**4,503**	**28.80%**	**Clark Kauffman**	**11,148**	**71.20%**
2010	Cindy Shotswell	1,950	20.70%	Maxine Bell	7,465	79.30%
2008	-	-	-	Maxine Bell	11,741	100.00%
2006	-	-	-	Maxine Bell	8,714	100.00%
2004	-	-	-	Maxine Bell	11,640	100.00%
2002	-	-	-	Maxine Bell	8,653	100.00%

PRIMARIES Just three primary contests here in the last decade, both easily beaten back by incumbents. In 2012, the open House B seat drew two Republicans, Clark Kauffman (who won, 53.4%) and David Funk. Senator Dean Cameron (who also had a primary contest in 2012, in district 27) won in 2010 (78%) over Harold Mohlman. And in 2006 John Stevenson won (76.2%) over Lee J. Halper.

Senator JIM PATRICK, R-Twin Falls
Web: www.votejimpatrick.com
Background: Retired, teacher. Retired, clerk, business manager, farm operation. Board, Salmon River Canal Company. University of Idaho.
Political: Elected to House 2006, 2008, 2010. Elected to Senate 2012.

Representative MAXINE BELL, R-Jerome
Web:
Background: Farmer. College of Southern Idaho. Idaho State University.
Political: Elected to House 1988, 1990, 1992, 1994, 1996, 1998, 2000, 2002, 2004, 2006, 2008, 2010.

Representative CLARK KAUFFMAN, R-Filer
Web: clarkkauffman.com
Background: Farmer. U.S. Air Force. Board member, Filer Mutual Telephone Co-op.
Political: Filer Highway District commission. Elected to House 2012.

District 26

District 26 (Blaine County, Lincoln County, Gooding County, and Camas County). Consistent with the Idaho Constitutional requirement to keep counties whole to the maximum extent possible, District 26 combines the entirety of Blaine, Lincoln, Gooding, and Camas counties. These counties are contiguous, connected by several different roads and highways and share common watersheds creating communities of interest. District 26 has 43,165 people, a deviation of -3.62% from the ideal district.

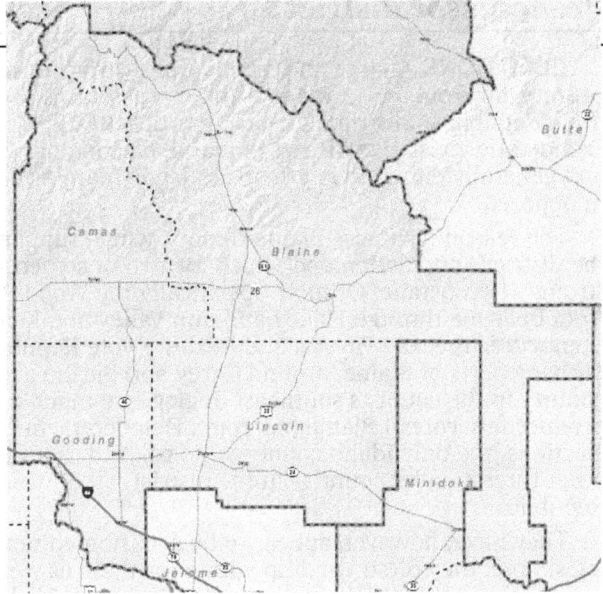

Considering its geographic size, inclusion of four counties and its central spot in the state, District 26 is a marvel in how closely it matches the old (of the 00s) District 25. It includes the same four counties as the old district.

And while two of those counties (Gooding and Camas) ordinarily are clearly Republican, and another (Lincoln) leans that way, the new district is likely to remain, as the old one was, strongly favorable for Democratic legislative candidates. That owes, as for the last couple of decades, to the strongly Democratic edge in Blaine County, the largest of the four.

A Stennett has held the Senate seat in this area since 1994, and Clint Stennett was a representative here for four years before that. When he died in October 2010, his wife Michelle was appointed to replace him, and she has held the seat since. Currently minority leader in the Senate, she has been mentioned from time to time as a prospect for higher office.

Democrat Donna Pence is relatively veteran here as well, a House member since 2004. But a change came in 2012 with the inclusion, for the first time since Pence defeated incumbent Tim Ridinger in 2004, of a Republican: Steve Miller, a rancher. Miller won by a thin 306 votes.

This is a currently-rare case in Idaho of a Republican representing a mostly Democratic district, and Miller may be Idaho Democrats' top target for 2014 among Republican incumbents. He may recognize his tight situation; in 2013 he was among the Gang of 16 Republican freshmen supporting Governor Otter's proposed health insurance exchange, which he and both Democrats in the district voted for.

Predecessor district 25

ELECTIONS A large and spread-out district consisting mainly of farm country, far from any of Idaho's urban areas – this sounds like another slam dunk Republican district. It isn't: After district 19, it is the second most Democratic legislative district in Idaho, electing only Democrats since 2004 and generally either giving them landslide margins or leaving them unopposed.

The reason for this is Blaine County, which supplies more than half of the district's population and which for two or so decades has been very strongly Democratic. Or more specifically the Wood River Valley, the area from Bellevue through Hailey and Sun Valley and Ketchum, which vote Democratic the way Payette and Rexburg vote Republican. (The more outlying parts of Blaine, around Carey and Picabo and in the remote Yale country in the county's southeast dogleg, are much more Republican, but produce few votes.) Blaine has voted Democratic in the last five presidential elections, the only Idaho county to do so. And that's in sharp contrast to the other three smaller counties in the district, all of which vote more generally Republican.

They have, however, appear to be accustomed now to the Democratic legislators; they often wind up voting for them as well, or giving them solid losing margins. In 2010, for example, Democrat Michelle Stennett won Blaine, Camas and Lincoln, and lost Gooding only narrowly. That same year Democrat Donna Pence won only Blaine, but lost the other three only narrowly.

The launcher of the Democratic edge in Blaine may have been John Peavey, a Carey rancher who entered the Idaho Senate as a Republican but became a Democrat, winning narrowly at first but by the end of the 80s strongly. One of the House members he helped bring along was Clint Stennett, a local radio and cable television owner, first in the House then into the Senate when Peavey retired in 1994 (to run, unsuccessfully, for lieutenant governor). Stennett held the Senate seat until his death in 2010, when his wife Michelle was first appointed and then elected to it.

The other long-timer here has been Wendy Jaquet, for many years leader of the Idaho House Democrats, elected in 1994 to the House seat Stennett left. She had an energetic first race but has been unopposed more often than not since. She has said she will not run for re-election in 2012.

The third legislator here, Donna Pence, won her House seat in 2002 after defeating (in a rerun race) the last Republican from this area, Tim Ridinger. She was unopposed in the 2006 and 2008 cycles, but was held to a modest 54.90% win in 2010.

Presdt	Democrat			Republican		
2012	Barack Obama	7,907	45.05%	Mitt Romney	9,178	52.29%

Sen	Democrat			Republican		
2012	Michelle Stennett	13,799	100.00%	-	-	-
2010	Michelle Stennett	7,113	57.90%	Jim Donoval	4,390	35.80%
2008	Clint Stennett	14,878	100.00%	-	-	-
2006	Clint Stennett	10,760	100.00%	-	-	-

	Democrat			Republican		
2004	Clint Stennett	13,745	100.00%	-	-	-
2002	Clint Stennett	7,782	64.00%	Tom Faulkner	4,376	36.00%
H1	**Democrat**			**Republican**		
2012	**John Remington**	**8,229**	**49.10%**	**Steve Miller**	**8,535**	**50.90%**
2010	Wendy Jaquet	9,356	100.00%	-	-	-
2008	Wendy Jaquet	11,440	63.40%	Jeff Faulkner	6,608	36.60%
2006	Wendy Jaquet	10,702	100.00%	-	-	-
2004	Wendy Jaquet	13,201	100.00%	-	-	-
2002	Wendy Jaquet	9,814	100.00%	-	-	-
H2	**Democrat**			**Republican**		
2012	**Donna Pence**	**9,999**	**58.90%**	**Lee Barron**	**6,987**	**41.10%**
2010	Donna Pence	6,706	54.90%	Alex Sutter	5,509	45.10%
2008	Donna Pence	13,960	100.00%	-	-	-
2006	Donna Pence	10,380	100.00%	-	-	-
2004	Donna Pence	8,790	51.00%	Tim Ridinger	8,446	49.00%
2002	Donna Pence	5,903	49.40%	Tim Ridinger	6,047	50.60%

PRIMARIES The only primary here in the last decade came after Michelle Stennett was appointed to replace her deceased husband in the Senate, and ran for the seat in 2010. She won easily (86.3%) over David Maestas (9.7%) and Robert John Blakely (4%).

Senator MICHELLE STENNETT, D-Ketchum

Web: www.michellestennett.com
Background: Advertising sales. Flight operations (Horizon Air, Sun Valley Aviation). University of Oregon.
Political: Elected to Senate, 2010, 2012.

Representative STEVEN MILLER, D-Fairfield

Web: www.MillerforHouse.org
Background: Farmer, rancher. Former president, Idaho Association of Conservation Districts. University of Idaho.
Political: Elected to House 2012.

Representative DONNA PENCE, D-Gooding

Web: www.donnapence.com
Background: Retired, teacher. Tree farmer. University of Idaho.
Political: Elected to House 2004, 2006, 2008, 2010, 2012.

District 27

District 27 (Cassia County and Minidoka County). Cassia and Minidoka counties are combined to create a district. This combination reflects a common community of interest as it is commonly referred to as the Mini-Cassia area. This keeps the cities of Rupert, Paul, Heyburn, Burley and Declo together. Geographically, the Snake River and Snake River Canyon create a natural divide between District 27 and District 25. District 27 includes 43,021 people, a deviation of -3.95% from the ideal population district.

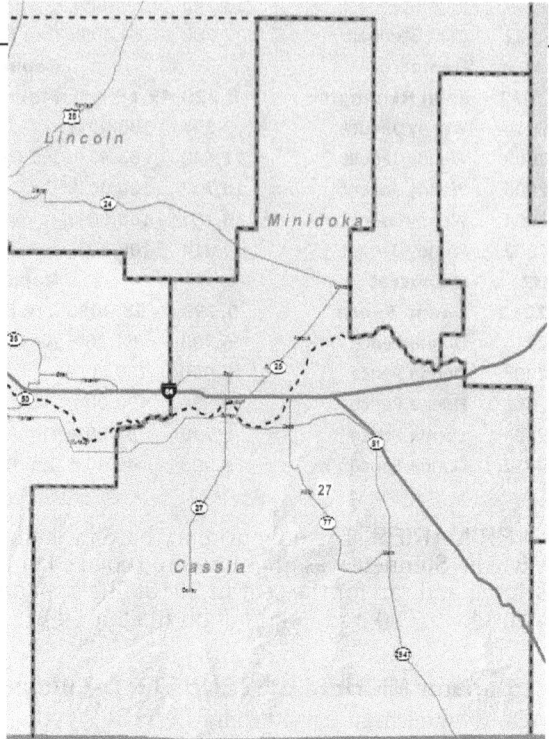

The eastern Magic Valley was rocked in the 2002 redistricting, and was rocked again in 2012, not least because the generally logical merging of Cassia and Minidoka Counties into one district threw the Senate's two most senior Republican members into the same district. (The two counties have some clear community of interest, however. They are often groups together in economic and other ways, share a chamber of commerce and other services, they have similar population types and economic bases, and their population centers are located, both near the Snake River, only a few miles apart.)

The new – as of December 2012 – House speaker, Scott Bedke, comes from a prominent Oakley ranching family, and moved up quickly after his first election to the House. In running for speaker in 2012 against incumbent Lawerence Denney, he was trying to do what no one had done at least half a century and maybe much longer: Topple an incumbent Idaho House speaker. He succeeding (though the vote was said to have been close), and the House changed as a result. Exactly how and how much depends on point of view, but it's fair to say that Governor Otter's proposed health insurance exchange bill would have failed in a Denney House, but passed with Bedke's help.

Not only that, it passed with the help of this district – all three Republicans here voted in favor and played important roles. Representative Fred Wood, a physician in private life and also the new chair of the House Health & Welfare Committee, was a floor sponsor of the measure. And Senator Dean Cameron added critical Senate support.

All three have been among the legislators targeted on billboards backed in October 2013 by the Idaho Freedom Foundation, mentioning them by name and criticizing them over the exchange.

Cameron, long described as a conservative more or less in the middle of the Senate Republican caucus, has fielded complaints in recent years that he's a "RINO" (Republican in Name Only), and a primary challenge to him in 2012 was fielded on that basis. Cameron was strongly opposed to the 2011 "Luna laws" on public school changes.

Predecessor district 27

ELECTIONS District 27 as it existed up to 2012 took in Cassia, Power and Oneida counties. Farming and food processing have been central as long as there have been people in this oddly-configured district from the 00s – odd in part because sprawls over two distinct regions of Idaho, the Magic Valley (Cassia County, where the largest population base is located) and Southeast Idaho (Power, Oneida and Bingham). Many of Idaho's legislative districts fairly closely resemble their predecessors; this one closely resembled nothing before 2002. The political weight resided with Cassia; its legislators came from there.

Cassia has been almost unilaterally Republican for a very long time; the last Democrat it elected to the legislature, Robert Saxvik, lost that seat in 1976 to retailer Dean Van Engelen. When Van Engelen left to run for state auditor, Declo teacher and farmer Denton Darrington won it, in 1982. And he has held it for almost three decades since, and is now the senior member of the Idaho Senate. He has had no close challenges, either in primary or general, since. He was unopposed entirely in the last decade, except for the first primary, when he defeated fellow senator Ralph "Moon" Wheeler (of Power County) for the seat they both were reapportioned into.

Bruce Newcomb was first elected from the Cassia-area district in 1986 and served 20 years; physician Fred Wood won a four-way contested primary (with 46%) to replace him, and has been unopposed since.

Presdt	Democrat		Republican		
2012	Barack Obama	2,488	16.19%	Mitt Romney	12,596	81.96%

Sen	Democrat		Republican		
2012	-	-	- Dean Cameron	13,642	100.00%
2010	-	-	- Denton Darrington	8,705	100.00%
2008	-	-	- Denton Darrington	11,667	100.00%
2006	-	-	- Denton Darrington	8,786	100.00%
2004	-	-	- Denton Darrington	11,273	100.00%
2002	-	-	- Denton Darrington	8,758	100.00%

H1	Democrat		Republican		
2012	-	-	-	Scott Bedke	13,197	100.00%
2010	-	-	- Scott Bedke	8,801	100.00%
2008	-	-	- Scott Bedke	11,736	100.00%
2006	-	-	- Scott Bedke	8,801	100.00%
2004	-	-	- Scott Bedke	11,215	100.00%

2002	Dan Ralphs	3,521	34.20%	Scott Bedke	6,768	65.80%
H2	**Democrat**			**Republican**		
2012	-	-	-	**- Fred Wood**	**13,232**	**100.00%**
2010	-	-	-	- Fred Wood	8,864	100.00%
2008	-	-	-	- Fred Wood	11,470	100.00%
2006	-	-	-	- Fred Wood	8,729	100.00%
2004	-	-	-	- Bruce Newcomb	10,179	83.10%
2002	-	-	-	- Bruce Newcomb	8,920	100.00%

PRIMARIES Not a lot of primary action here. The big contest came after reapportionment in 2002, when two Republican veterans, Denton Darrington and Ralph "Moon" Wheeler, squared off in the district they were both thrown into; Darrington won (59.6%). A decade later, redistricting placed Darrington in the same district with fellow Republican Senator Dean Cameron; this time, the veteran Darrington bowed out. Cameron still had a primary contest, however, winning with just 56.5% over Douglas Pickett.

One of the 2002 redistricted House members, Scott Bedke, also won (73.2%) a primary, though against non-legislator Tim Willie. Bedke again easily won a primary in 2004 (67.36%), against Wayne Bagwell.

In House B, the departure of long-time House Speaker Bruce Newcomb in 2006 led to a four-way primary decisively won by Fred Wood (46%) over Timothy Deeg (36.6%), Jim Paskett (13.3%) and Ben Maggart (4.1%).

Senator DEAN CAMERON, R-Rupert

Web: www.vote4cameron.com
Background: Owner, insurance and investment agency, at Rupert. Ricks College.
Political: Appointed to Senate, 1991. Elected to Senate 1992, 1994, 1996, 1998, 2000, 2002, 2004, 2006, 2008, 2010, 2012.

Representative SCOTT BEDKE, R-Oakley

Web: www.scottbedke.com
Background: Farmer, rancher. Former president, Idaho Cattle Association. Brigham Young University.
Political: Elected to House 2000, 2002, 2004, 2006, 2008, 2010, 2012.

Representative FRED WOOD, R-Burley

Web:
Background: Physician, medical director. Air Force. Tulane University.
Political: Elected to House, 2006, 2008, 2010, 2012.

District 28

District 28 (Bannock County(part) and Power County)). District 28 includes all of Power County and part of Bannock County.

This district includes the airport shared by these two counties and is tied together by a major interstate highway. District 28 includes 46,955 people, a deviation of -4.84% from the ideal district.

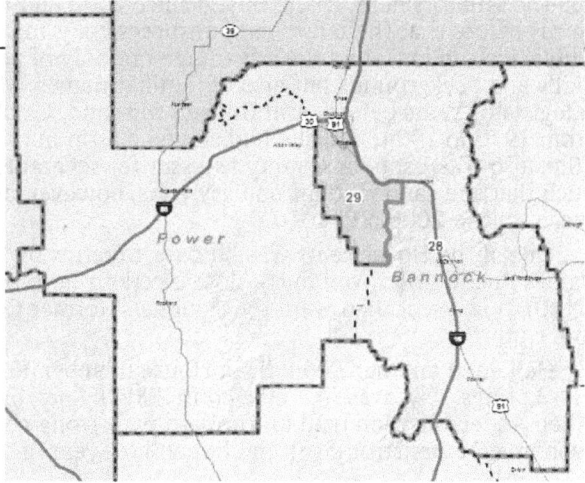

The new district 28 looks on the surface a lot like last decade's district 29 with a few exceptions. The most obvious on a map is that the new version tacks on, in addition to the Bannock County portion that provides most of the population, all of Power County as well. That more or less makes the new district 29, a successor to the central-Pocatello district 30, an island. Power County could be a significant factor in this politically competitive district; that smaller county alone is competitive, sometimes leaning, in local and regional races, gently Democratic. But it does not include the Democratic parts of Pocatello, which kicks the district over to the Republican side.

So, after the 2011 redistricting, the district went from a 2-1 Democratic delegation, to a 3-0 Republican delegation – and all three of those Republicans elected in landslides.

The delegation split on the question of the governor's health insurance exchange proposal: Senator Jim Guthrie and Representative Kelley Packer voted in favor, and the veteran of the three, Ken Andrus, voted against. Packer was one of the Gang of 16 Republican freshmen who argued in favor of the exchange and helped push it through the House.

Predecessor district 29

ELECTIONS This is the more competitive of the two 00s Bannock County districts, covering nearly all of the county's geographical area but only a piece of its main city, Pocatello. The split in the city is a significant matter; district 29 included the part of the city to the east of Interstate 15 and north of Interstate 86 (they converge at the northeast edge of the city); 29 also includes Chubbuck. That means that while a significant Pocatello Democratic vote was included in 29, it also takes in the agricultural and much more Republican "down-county" – McCammon, Arimo, Lava Hot Springs, Downey – as well as (generally) the large suburb of Chubbuck, which mostly votes Republican. The result is one of Idaho's more competitive districts.

The senators here, Diane Bilyeu since 2006 and Bert Marley for several terms before that (he left to run, unsuccessfully, for superintendent of public instruction), had the advantage not only of personal campaigning skills and backgrounds but also of familiar names. Marley's father had been a legislator years before. And Bilyeu's husband, Chick, had been a senator from 1970 to 1994; and she had served a term in the Senate *before* him. (She also was Bannock County assessor for several terms.) The district is such that she cannot count on easy wins, however, and has been held to close calls in 2006 and 2010.

One of the House seats was held for to terms by Democratic attorney James Ruchti (who won fairly close elections both times), but he opted out in 2010. The seat then went to Republican former County Commissioner Jim Guthrie.

He joined another Republican House member, Ken Andrus from Lava Hot Springs, who was first elected in 2004 by narrowly ousting Democrat Allen Anderson, then held on through two strong comeback attempts. He won much more strongly in the Republican year of 2010.

Presdt	Democrat			Republican		
2012	Barack Obama	6,411	31.76%	Mitt Romney	13,333	66.06%

Sen	Democrat			Republican		
2012	Dave Finkelnburg	6,707	33.90%	Jim Guthrie	13,087	66.10%
2010	Diane Bilyeu	7,222	51.40%	Lance Kolbet	6,831	48.60%
2008	Diane Bilyeu	11,579	58.60%	Ralph Lillig	8,191	41.40%
2006	Diane Bilyeu	7,444	51.27%	Jim Guthrie	7,074	48.73%
2004	Bert Marley	9,526	51.50%	Evan Frasure	8,987	48.50%
2002	Bert Marley	7,006	52.50%	Kent Kunz	6,334	47.50%
H1	**Democrat**			**Republican**		
2012	Sam McKee	7,333	37.30%	Ken Andrus	12,344	62.70%
2010	Jim Allen	5,492	39.00%	Ken Andrus	8,591	61.00%
2008	Allen Andersen	8,623	43.80%	Ken Andrus	11,044	56.20%
2006	Allen Andersen	6,997	48.59%	Ken Andrus	7,404	51.41%
2004	Allen Andersen	8,806	48.10%	Ken Andrus	9,504	51.90%
2002	Allen Anderson	6,565	50.10%	Tari Jensen	6,538	49.90%
H2	**Democrat**			**Republican**		
2012	Kemren Koompin	7,212	37.00%	Kelley Packer	12,299	63.00%
2010	Greg Anderson	5,668	40.20%	Jim Guthrie	8,424	59.80%
2008	James Ruchti	10,520	54.40%	James Dorman	8,823	45.60%
2006	James Ruchti	7,266	50.61%	Richard Kirkham	7,092	49.39%
2004	Elmer Martinez	9,358	51.20%	Kent Hansen	8,907	48.80%
2002	Elmer Martinez	6,900	52.70%	Vern Tilton	6,184	47.30%

PRIMARIES A 2012 Republican Senate primary pitted two locally well-known names against each other, House member Jim Guthrie (65.3%), who won, against former legislator Rusty Barlow.

Just two House primaries here, both for House B and both Republican. One was in 2002, when Vern Tilton (36.5%) narrowly defeated Sherril

Tillotson (33.7%) an Tony Hancock (29.7%). The second, in 2006, when Richard Kirkham (8.6%) defeated Lance Kolbet.

Senator JIM GUTHRIE, R-McCammon

Web: www.jimguthrie.us

Background: Rancher. Owner, small grocery store and service station. Ash Grove Cement, 1979-93.

Political: Board member, Marsh Valley School District, 1995-2001. Elected Commissioner, Bannock County, 2000, 2002. Elected to House, 2010. Elected to Senate, 2012.

Representative KEN ANDRUS, R-Lava Hot Springs

Web: www.kenandrus.com

Background: Rancher, Lava Hot Springs area. Army. Brigham Young University.

Political: Board member, Marsh Valley School District. Elected to House 2004, 2006, 2008, 2010, 2012.

Representative KELLEY PACKER, R-McCammon

Web: kelleypacker.us

Background: Office manager, Idaho Sports and Spine, Pocatello. Bannock County Republican chair, 2010-12. American Intercontinental University.

Political: McCammon City Council, 2003-04. Elected to House 2012.

District 29

District 29 (Bannock County (part)).
District 29 consists of the majority
of the city of Pocatello, a
community of interest in itself, and
is located entirely within Bannock
County. District 29 is compact and
easily distinguished due to its
clearly identifiable boundaries
consisting of interstate highways
and the Bannock County line.
District 29 includes 43,701 people,
a deviation of -2.43% from the
ideal district.

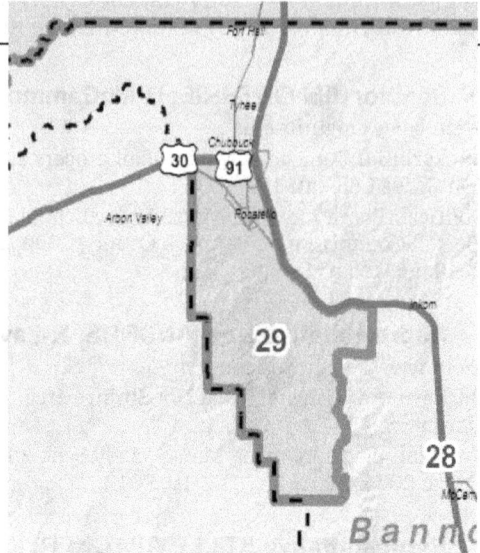

Bannock County's (fading)
reputation as a Democratic
stronghold finds some purchase
in District 29, a close analogue
to the district 30 of the 00s, the third most Democratic district in Idaho. It
includes most of Bannock County's most Democratic precincts, which take
in significant numbers of university employees and students and unionized
manufacturing workers. Excluded was most of Chubbuck, which leans
Republican.

Downtown Pocatello, the central railroad district and Idaho State
University are included in this district, and the older housing around it.
Many of the working-class neighborhoods in the old Alameda area (a
separate city here until the late 50s) are included too. Democratic
candidates still do not have enough votes here to count on easy,
overwhelming wins every time out, but there have been enough for steady
re-elections, as usually was the case through its predecessor central-
Pocatello districts.

In 2012 Democrats did hold on here to these three seats.

The Senate candidacy of Roy Lacey, a well-known community figure
highly active in such disparate areas as the local food back, a clothing store
and Union Pacific Railroad, helped.

Another factor came late in the 2012 campaign season, when in August
that year Nate Murphy, a member of the Pocatello school board, dropped
out of his campaign for a House seat (and quit the school board), saying he
was moving to California for a new job. That might have cost Democrats the
seat, but the nomination went to a community figure with a long-standing
profile, Carolyn Meline. She was a Bannock County commissioner for 22
years, and served on a very long list of state and local boards and
commissions, public and private. In a three-way race (independent Bob
Croker was campaigning actively), she emerged with a narrow win.

The three Democrats here have been centrist caucus members. All three,
like nearly all the other Democrats, voted for the governor's proposed
health insurance exchange in 2012.

Predecessor district 30

ELECTIONS But not always. The main Pocatello district in the 90s (then District 34) had a strong Republican organization, and from its formation in 1992 through 2000 the senator was Republican Evan Frasure, an unusually adept campaign tactician; it also elected Republican Kent Kunz the the House B seat. Then the streak ended. In 2002 Frasure ran for secretary of state (losing the primary), and his Senate seat went to Democrat Edgar Malepeai, a retired teacher. Malepeai had several easy elections after that, though he was held to 54.6% in 2010 against Republican Terry Anderson. He decided to retire in 2012, his place taken by Lacey.

In the last decade the two House seats here also have been held by Democrats. The long-timer was Donna Boe, a former Pocatello city council member first elected to the House in 1996. She opted out in 2010 and was replaced by fellow Democrat Roy Lacey. Lacey's seat, in effect, went to Carolyn Meline in 2012.

The other seat has been held, since 2000, by Democrat Elaine Smith. Her percentages have topped landslide levels only once, however, in 2006, and she had a close call in 2010.

Presdt	Democrat				Republican		
2012	Barack Obama	7,785	43.30%	Mitt Romney	9,547	53.10%

Sen	Democrat				Republican		
2012	Roy Lacey	9,494	53.80%	Greg Romriell	8,142	46.20%
2010	Edgar Malepeai	5,045	54.60%	Terry Andersen	4,195	45.40%
2008	Edgar Malepeai	12,815	100.00%	-	-	-
2006	Edgar Malepeai	9,067	100.00%	-	-	-
2004	Edgar Malepeai	13,384	100.00%	-	-	-
2002	Edgar Malepeai	7,234	64.60%	Dan Rainey	3,959	35.40%

H1	Democrat				Republican		
2012	Carolyn Meline	7,971	45.60%	Dave Bowen	7,178	41.10%
2010	Roy Lacey	5,315	58.20%	Brian Nugent	3,820	41.80%
2008	Donna Boe	12,823	100.00%	-	-	-
2006	Donna Boe	9,056	100.00%	-	-	-
2004	Donna Boe	9,628	60.40%	Keith Frank	6,323	39.60%
2002	Donna Boe	6,816	60.20%	Leslie Romriell	4,506	39.80%

H2	Democrat				Republican		
2012	Elaine Smith	9,470	54.20%	Craig Cooper	7,988	45.80%
2010	Elaine Smith	4,900	53.00%	Dave Bowen	4,344	47.00%
2008	Elaine Smith	8,414	56.90%	Chris Stevens	6,382	43.10%
2006	Elaine Smith	6,495	62.06%	Joshua Thompson	3,644	34.82%
2004	Elaine Smith	8,375	52.70%	Paul Yochum	6,955	43.80%
2002	Elaine Smith	5,947	53.30%	Farhana Hibbert	4,850	43.40%

PRIMARIES The only two contested primaries here in the last decade came in 2012, both among Republicans in this mostly Democratic district.

For the Senate, Greg Romriell (59.7%) beat Terry Anderson. And for House A, Dave Bowen (74.1%) beat Brian Nugent.

Senator ROY LACEY, D-Pocatello

Web: www.roylacey.com
Background: Vice president/operations, Idaho Food Bank. Former owner, Roy's Western Wear. Union Pacific Railroad (25 years). Idaho State University.
Political: Elected to House 2010. Elected to Senate, 2012.

Representative CAROLYN MELINE, D-Pocatello

Web: www.facebook.com/pages/Carolyn-Meline-for-Idaho-Legislature/431944973524201
Background: Retired. State Board of Corrections. Colorado Women's College.
Political: Bannock County Commission. Elected to House, 2012.

Representative ELAINE SMITH, D-Pocatello

Web: www.elainesmith4house.com
Background: Retired. Idaho State University.
Political: Elected to House, 2000, 2002, 2004, 2006, 2008, 2010, 2012.

District 30

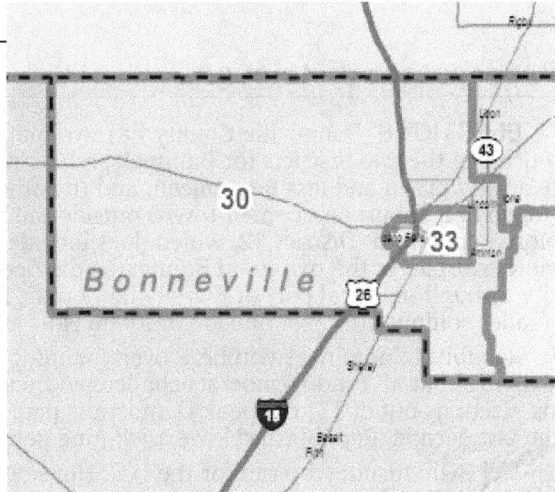

District 30 (Bonneville County (part)). Bonneville County has a large enough population that two complete legislative districts may be contained within the county; however, it is not large enough to form three inclusive legislative districts. Therefore, the Commission finds that Bonneville County must be split in order to comply with the one person one vote requirement. District 30 is contained entirely within Bonneville County and includes local communities of interest that share the area's agricultural emphasis. Further, the district includes the majority of the cities of Lincoln and Ammon, communities of interest in themselves. District 30 contains 46,525 people, a deviation of +3.88% from the ideal district.

District 30, a close counterpart to the district 32 of the 00s, surrounds the central-Idaho Falls District 33 (which retains the same number), one of two island districts in the state. As in the last decade, the more rural and suburban district in the area is the more Republican, while the district focused on the center city (33) is more competitive.

The senator, Dean Mortimer, has been mentioned as a possible candidate for higher office – prospectively, in the role of an anti-establishment contender such as Russ Fulcher is playing in 2014. He was one of the staunchest backers of the "Luna laws," three measures passed in the 2011 session making major changes in Idaho school laws. (All were thrown out by voters the next year.) Mortimer said in debate that "We cannot live with the system we have one more year, in my opinion." He is in a position to make his views felt on school matters; he is vice-chair of the Senate's education committee, and a member of the budget committee.

The House members here are, by some measures, toward the centers of their caucuses: As one measure, Mortimer voted against the governor's health insurance exchange proposal, while both House members supported it. Jeff Thompson has the unusual distinction of having ousted an incumbent Democrat (there having been in recent years few incumbent Democrats to beat) named Jerry Shiveley, who had served one term. Thompson was mentioned as an Idaho Falls mayoral prospect in 2013, but didn't run.

Freshman Wendy Horman has considerable background in education, having been president and member on the Bonneville School Board (for 10 years) and president of the state school boards association; and she serves on the education committee. She also was a member of the Gang of 16, Republican freshmen supporting the insurance exchange proposal.

Predecessor district 32

ELECTIONS Bonneville County has two main districts, and they are much like the two districts for Bannock and Twin Falls counties: One is relatively urban and less Republican, and the other includes mostly territory (much of it suburban or small-town) outside the main city, and is much more Republican. District 32, which does include some of Idaho Falls, is the more exurban of the two main Bonneville districts. It runs out west of the city through the rural part of Bonneville County, and includes some of the smaller communities just outside of Idaho Falls as well.

Republican nominees win here overwhelmingly, when they are challenged at all (and Democrats challenged them in the last decade only six elections out of 15; the peak Democratic percentage was 34.90%). In the last decade, Republicans' lowest winning percentage was 65.1%.

Mel Richardson, who ran for the U.S. House in 1986 and was elected to the Idaho House from this area two years later, was a political mainstay (primarily in the Senate) for a long time until he retired in 2006. successor was Dean Mortimer, so far unopposed in either primary or general.

The House A seat has been held since its 2002 creation by Janice McGeachin, an Idaho Falls business owner who won the seat unopposed in primary or general in her 2002 race, and has faced only light challenges in the general.

House B was held for a while by former state Senator Ann Rydalch, then for one term by Mortimer; in 2008 it went to Erik Simpson of Idaho Falls. Simpson opted out of the legislature after two terms, opening the post-redistricting seat.

Presdt	Democrat			Republican		
2012	Barack Obama	3,755	19.06%	Mitt Romney	15,545	78.92%

Sen	Democrat			Republican		
2012	-	-	-	**Dean Mortimer**	16,309	100.00%
2010	-	-	-	Dean Mortimer	13,482	100.00%
2008	-	-	-	Dean Mortimer	18,025	100.00%
2006	Tom Holm	4,772	30.79%	Mel Richardson	10,729	69.21%
2004	Tom Holm	4,603	24.10%	Mel Richardson	13,649	71.60%
2002	Tom Holm	3,701	27.30%	Mel Richardson	9,367	69.20%

H1	Democrat			Republican		
2012	-	-	-	**Jeff Thompson**	14,533	83.40%
2010	-	-	-	Janice McGeachin	13,121	100.00%
2008	Scott Cannon	5,579	27.00%	Janice McGeachin	15,090	73.00%
2006	Scott Cannon	4,390	28.81%	Janice McGeachin	10,848	71.19%
2004	-	-	-	Janice McGeachin	14,654	100.00%
2002	-	-	-	Janice McGeachin	11,612	100.00%

H2	Democrat			Republican		
2012	-	-	-	**Wendy Horman**	14,517	83.80%

2010	-			- Erik Simpson	12,748	100.00%
2008	-			- Erik Simpson	17,384	100.00%
2006	-			- Dean Mortimer	13,279	100.00%
2004	-			- Ann Rydalch	15,091	100.00%
2002	Jan Brown	4,698	34.90%	Ann Rydlach	8,781	65.10%

PRIMARIES Seven contests, all Republican.

The one Senate primary was a challenge to Senator Mel Richardson in 2002; he won easily (71.9%) over Willis Welker.

In 2012 at seat A, Jeff Thompson was contested but easily won (86.8%) over Trimelda Concepcion McDaniels.

Of the five primaries in House B, four involved former state Senator Ann Rydalch – she won two and lost two. In 2002, Rydalch won (62%) over Jonathan Haines and in 2004 she beat (56.72%) broadcaster Mike Adams. But in 2006 she was defeated (44.6%) by Dean Mortimer (55.4%) for the House seat, and when Mortimer moved to the Senate in the next election, she lost a comeback bid to Erik Simpson (59.2%). When Simpson opened out in 2012, three Republicans filed, with Wendy Horman (46.5%) defeating Stan Bell and Greg Crockett.

Senator DEAN MORTIMER, R-Idaho Falls

Web: www.deanmortimer.org/wordpress/
Background: Founder, First Federal Corporation (mortgage). Construction loan officer, mortgage banking. Ricks College. Utah State University.
Political: Elected to House 2006. Elected to Senate, 2008, 2010.

Representative JEFF THOMPSON, R-Idaho Falls

Web: thompsonforidaho.wordpress.com
Background: Consultant (Idaho National Laboratory). Human resources. Liberty University (Lynchburg, Virginia). Idaho State University.
Political: Elected to House, 2008, 2010, 2012.

Representative WENDY HORMAN, R-Idaho Falls

Web: wendyhorman.org
Background: Dixie State College, Brigham Young University-Idaho.
Political: Bonneville School District board member. Elected to House, 2012.

District 31

District 31 (Bingham County). District 31 includes the entirety of Bingham County, which is large enough to constitute an entire legislative district. District 31 has 45,607 people, a deviation of 1.83% from the ideal district.

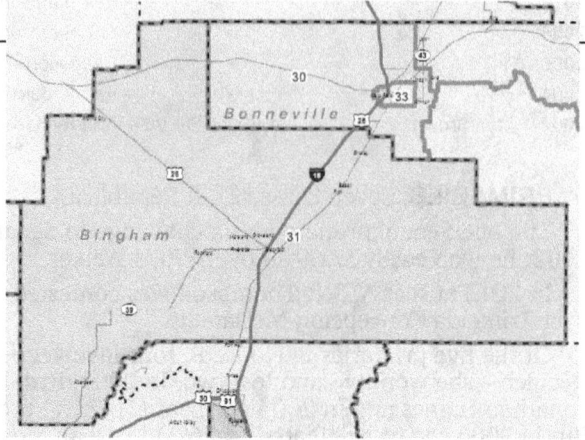

Blackfoot, the main city in District 31 – a close counterpart for the old District 28 of the 00s – is not entirely Republican territory. It has state facilities (including a state hospital) and Idaho's largest Indian reservation, Fort Hall, is located only a few miles south. Much of the Fort Hall Indian Reservation is in Bingham County, and the Fort Hall precinct is one of the Democratic anywhere in the state.

But the occasional Democratic votes there and in Blackfoot are overwhelmed by the Republican margins everywhere else in the county. Bingham is irrigation farming and food processing country, and its economy rises or falls on that basis.

The new District 31 is almost the same as the old 28, except and this one includes all of Bingham County; the old one included all but the Aberdeen and Springfield area in the southwest corner. That does not change it greatly but edges it a bit more in the Republican direction.

The senator, Steven Bair, has ordinarily been toward the center of his caucus, and hasn't been closely challenged in elections.

The two House members, Neil Anderson and Julie Van Orden, are freshmen. Van Orden, who had been chair of the Snake River School Board, was a member of the Gang of 16 backing the governor's health insurance exchange in the 2013 session; all three members of the delegation voted in favor of the measure.

Predecessor district 28

ELECTIONS The best-known legislator from here in the 70s was Allan Larsen, a House speaker who ran for governor in 1978. He later returned to the legislature, retiring in 1996. That second retirement prompted a serious contest, one of the few in general elections in recent years, between former Democratic legislator Israel Merrill and a lesser-known agri-businessman, Dennis Lake. In the Republican tide, Lake narrowly won with 53.5%. He has not faced so close a call since, though his three contests with Democrat Beverly Beach in the last decade all held him to sub-landslide levels (another indicator of that still-alive Democratic base at Blackfoot). Lake became a key legislator in recent years as chair of the House tax committee; he announced his retirement for 2012.

Unusually for this area, all three seats featured Democratic candidates (there was just one in 2010, none in 2008). The results showed, however, the difficulties they faced: The best-performing of the three, Cherie Clawson, received 35.6% of the vote. The peak Democratic vote in the last decade was in a 2004 race between Lake and Democrat Beverly Beach (the second of three matches in a row between then), when Beach received 44.7%.

Presdt	Democrat			Republican		
2012	Barack Obama	3,822	21.71%	Mitt Romney	13,440	76.35%

Sen	Democrat			Republican		
2012	Cherie Clawson	6,104	35.60%	Steven Bair	11,048	64.40%
2010	-	-	-	Steven Bair	9,416	100.00%
2008	-	-	-	Steven Bair	11,524	100.00%
2006	John Hulse	4,512	38.16%	Steven Bair	7,312	61.84%
2004	John Hulse	4,920	32.30%	Stan Williams	10,322	67.70%
2002	-	-	-	Stan Williams	9,971	100.00%

H1	Democrat			Republican		
2012	Barbara Ann Clark	4,681	27.40%	Neil Anderson	12,414	72.60%
2010	Marlene Shurtz	3,411	31.30%	Dennis Lake	7,487	68.70%
2008	-	-	-	Dennis Lake	11,379	100.00%
2006	Beverly Beach	5,298	44.61%	Dennis Lake	6,578	55.39%
2004	Beverly Beach	6,838	44.70%	Dennis Lake	8,472	55.30%
2002	Beverly Beach	4,613	41.00%	Dennis Lake	6,651	59.00%

H2	Democrat			Republican		
2012	Jeannie James	4,148	24.20%	Julie Van Orden	12,989	75.80%
2010	-	-	-	Jim Marriott	9,410	100.00%
2008	-	-	-	Jim Marriott	10,900	100.00%
2006	Jane Lamprecht	4,351	36.84%	Jim Marriott	7,459	63.16%
2004	-	-	-	Joseph Cannon	13,301	100.00%
2002	Delbert Farmer	3,097	27.40%	Joseph Cannon	8,198	72.60%

PRIMARIES All the recent primaries here have been Republican.

The one Senate contest occurred when Stan Williams opted out in 2006, and Steven Bair (62.6%) beat Paul Clark for the nomination. Of the four House B contests, Joseph Cannon won two, in 2002 (52.2%, over Becky Lim and Ronald Reese) and 2004 (58.39%, over Steven Adams). When Cannon opted out in 2006, Jim Marriott won (46.2%) over Reese (35.4%) and Kirk Sheppard (18.4%). In 2012, Marriott lost to Julie Van Orden (62.4%), one of only two House members to fall in the 2012 primary.

In the A seat, opened with Dennis Lake's retirement, four Republicans filed. The tight contest was won by Neil Anderson (39.8%) over Robert Butler, Mike Duff and David Moore.

Senator STEVE BAIR, R-Blackfoot

Web: senatorbair.com
Background: Farmer, investor. Precinct committeeman. Ricks College.
Political: Elected to Senate 2006, 2008, 2010.

Representative NEIL ANDERSON, R-Blackfoot

Web: andersonforthehouse.org
Background: Retired. Agribusiness, financial advisor. U.S. West area operations manager. Blackfoot Chamber of Commerce, president. Idaho State University, Ricks College.
Political: Elected to House, 2012.

Representative JULIE VANORDEN, R-Pingree

Web: julievanorden.com
Background: Co-owner, Garth VanOrden Farms. Co-owner, Wada Farms Potatoes Inc. College of Southern Idaho, Idaho State University Technical School.
Political: Elected to House, 2012.

District 32

District 32 (Bonneville County (part), Bear Lake County, Caribou County, Franklin County, Oneida and Teton County (part)). District 32 is another example of how the Idaho's unique geography and the sparseness population distribution in certain areas necessitate the creation of large districts. District 32 includes the entirety of Bear Lake, Caribou, Franklin, Oneida, and Teton Counties, which still lack population sufficient to constitute a district within acceptable limits of deviation. Therefore a portion of Bonneville County had to be combined with these counties. Together these counties do not have sufficient population to create an entire legislative district and must be combined with portions of other counties in order to meet the one person one vote requirement. Therefore, these counties are combined with the remainder of Bonneville County which is contiguous. This district is evidence of the great difficulty in creating legislative districts in a state the size and shape of Idaho with its diverse landscape and comparatively sparse population density. The Commission recognizes that this district is large and not ideal; however, it is necessary to meet the one person one vote requirement and preserve county boundaries whenever possible. It is particularly revealing that this district comprised of a massive geographical area is still population light, which clearly reflects the disparity between population and county land size evident throughout Idaho. The requirement of Idaho Code sec. 72-1506 (9) (Roads), was waived by the Commission by a 6-0 vote. District 32 includes 44,502 people, a deviation of -0.64% from the ideal district.

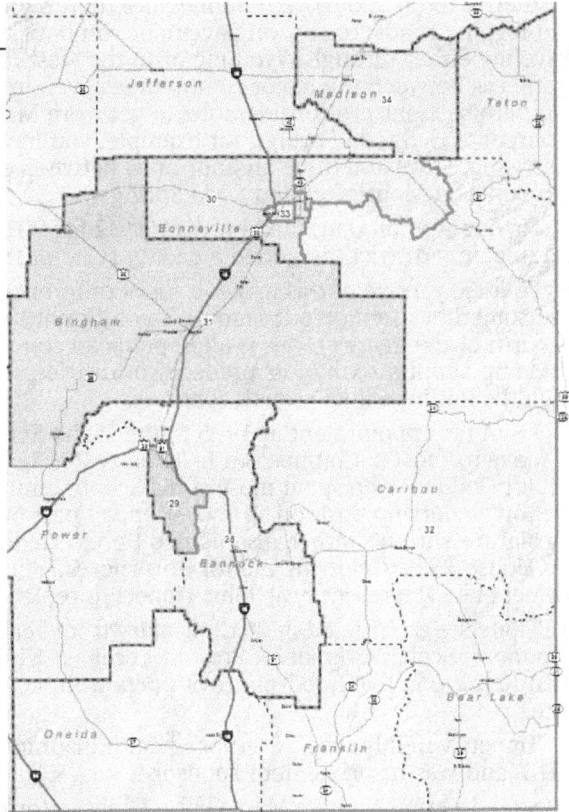

The district 31 of the 00s probably was the most disliked – by the local constituency, and political activists – of any district in Idaho, and an understanding look at a map will show why. On the surface, these counties and communities on Idaho's southeastern edge have a useful unity. (And they do have quite a few social, environmental and economic similarities.) But this is mountain country hard to traverse. Between the southern part of the district (Oneida, Franklin, Bear Lake and Caribou counties) and the northern (Teton and eastern Bonneville) there's only national forest country and logging roads; to stay on pavement you have to leave the district traveling either through Wyoming or to the west through Bannock County. Distances between the major communities even in the northern and southern sections are considerable; to get from Malad to Preston to Montpelier to Spoda Springs, for example, you have to climb mountains on twisty highways and drive an hour or so between each city. (Well, a little less between Montpelier and Soda Springs.)

Having said all that, the new district 32 for 2012 not only retained the old ungainly district but added a county (Oneida) to it.

Politically, none of this makes a lot of difference. Except for competitive and sometimes Democratic-leaning Teton County, which makes up less than a fourth of the district), this is all Republican country. But note: Teton only made up about a sixth of its predecessor district, so in time its influence could be felt here if its growth continues.

From his appointment in 1995 to the Idaho Senate until his resignation to move to the Tax Commission in January 2011, the senator here was Robert Geddes, who spent most of his Senate tenure as president pro tem, the top leadership position. (He overlapped part of that time at the legislature with his father, also named Robert Geddes, who was serving in the House.) The following month Governor C.L. "Butch" Otter named former state Representative John Tippets to replace him.

Tippets was targeted in 2012 primary from Tea Party-allied activists; his opponent, Scott Workman of Preston, received $1,000 from a PAC led by then-Representative Bob Nonimi. Tippets won, however, with 57.1% of the vote.

Tippets voted for the governor's health insurance exchange proposal in 2013, and was its prime floor sponsor.

So did Representative Marc Gibbs. Gibbs, a former member of the Fish & Game Commission and a former president of the Bear River Water Users Association, has been active on resource issues.

The other representative here, Tom Loertscher of Bone, did not, not a surprise for a legislator often regarded as one of the most conservative in the Idaho House. He did surprise a number of people by talking positively about expanding Medicaid in the state, something Governor Otter and many other Republicans have resisted. Loertscher is one of the most senior legislators, first elected to the House in 1986, and before that serving on the Bonneville County commission.

Predecessor district 31

ELECTIONS Politically, this is Republican territory. Teton County has swung more Democratic over the years, even voting for Barack Obama for president in 2010, but its population is small. The electoral weight lies with the southern counties, and most of the legislators have come from there.

Robert Geddes was the leading figure here during most of the last decade. Entering the Idaho Senate (he was appointed in 1995) shortly before his father left a long run in the House, Geddes moved into leadership and was president pro tem about a decade – longer than anyone in Idaho history. He stepped down at the start of the 2011 session, and left the

Senate shortly after to become chair of the state Tax Commission. His newly-appointed replacement, John Tippets, a manager at the Agrium plant near Soda Springs, was not exactly a newcomer: He was a state representative from 1988 to 2000, in the then-southeast corner district.

The real long-timer here is Tom Loertscher, a businessman from rural Bonneville County (east of Idaho Falls) at a spot on the map called Bone. First elected to the House in 1986, he had little trouble with re-election until reapportionment caught up with him in 2002. He lost an initial primary for one of the House seats here, but tried again and won in 2004.

The other House seat, not challenged by a Democrat since 2002, was held for some years by former Franklin County commissioner Larry Bradford, and since 2008 by farmer Marc Gibbs of Grace.

Presdt	Democrat			Republican		
2012	Barack Obama	3,467	17.05%	Mitt Romney	16,490	81.10%

Sen	Democrat			Republican		
2012	-	-	-	John Tippets	16,969	100.00%
2010	-	-	-	Robert Geddes	12,336	100.00%
2008	-	-	-	Robert Geddes	16,225	100.00%
2006	-	-	-	Robert Geddes	12,454	100.00%
2004	-	-	-	Robert Geddes	15,594	100.00%
2002	Galen Woelk	3,114	24.00%	Robert Geddes	9,866	100.00%
H1	Democrat			Republican		
2012	Bob Fitzgerald	4,058	20.90%	Marc Gibbs	15,328	79.10%
2010	-	-	-	Marc Gibbs	12,238	100.00%
2008	-	-	-	Marc Gibbs	15,474	100.00%
2006	-	-	-	Larry Bradford	12,141	100.00%
2004	-	-	-	Larry Bradford	14,736	100.00%
2002	Kirk Olson	3,901	30.10%	Larry Bradford	9,042	69.90%
H2	Democrat			Republican		
2012	Ralph Mossman	5,147	26.30%	Tom Loertscher	14,416	73.70%
2010	Ralph Mossman	4,597	31.60%	Tom Loertscher	9,965	68.40%
2008	-	-	-	Tom Loertscher	15,421	98.20%
2006	-	-	-	Tom Loertscher	12,170	100.00%
2004	-	-	-	Tom Loertscher	14,393	100.00%
2002	Marden Phelps	5,065	39.10%	Eulalie Langford	7,874	60.90%

PRIMARIES Lots of primaries here, all Republican.

In 2012, John Tippets got the first primary challenge for a Senate seat here in many years in 2012, but won with 57.1% over Scott Workman.

In House A, Larry Bradford was challenged but narrowly won in 2002 (51% over Representative Tom Loertscher) and more strongly in 2006 (61.1% over Clair Cheirrett). When Bradford left in 2008, a three-way contest developed, won by Marc Gibbs (46.7%) over Neal Larson (37.1%) and Rex Steele (16.2%).

In seat B, Eulalie Langford in 2002 narrowly defeated (38.6%) legislator Cameron Wheeler (38.1%), by 35 votes, with Clifton Davis coming in third

(23.4%). In 2004 Loertscher, having lost in House A, tried B, and narrowly (50.73%) beat Langford. She tried a comeback against Loertscher in 2006, but fell short (Loertscher, 56.3%). Peculiarly, Loertscher drew a four-way primary in 2008, and won (44.4%) but fell well short of a majority against Al Harrison (23.8%), Elliott Larsen (19.1%) and Nancy Nead (12.6%). In post-redistricting 2012 Loertscher was challenged again, but won 54.4% over Kelton Larsen and Franklyn Vilt.

In House A, there was (uncommonly) a Democratic primary, and a close one at that, between Bob Fitzgerald (who won, 50.8%, by 10 votes) and Rich Bergman.

Senator JOHN TIPPETTS, R-Bennington

Web:

Background: Public affairs manager, Agrium. Brigham Young University. Utah State University.

Political: Elected to House, 1988, 1990, 1992, 1994, 1996, 1998. Appointed to Senate, February 2011. Appointed to Senate, February 2011. Elected to Senate, 2012.

Representative MARC GIBBS, R-Grace

Web: www.votegibbs.com

Background: Farmer (Gibbs Farms LLC). Former member, Idaho Fish & Game Commission. Member, Bear River Commission. Utah State University.

Political: Elected to House, 2008, 2010, 2012.

Representative TOM LOERTSCHER, R-Bone

Web: reptom.com

Background: Farmer, rancher. U.S. Army Reserve. University of Utah.

Political: Elected commissioner, Bonneville County, 1978, 1980. Defeated for Bonneville Commission, 1984. Elected to House 1986, 1988, 1990, 1992, 1994, 1996, 1998, 2000. Unsuccessful run for House, 2002. Elected to House 2004, 2006, 2008, 2010, 2012.

District 33

District 33 (Bonneville County (part)). The majority of the city of Idaho Falls is included in District 33 which is contained entirely within Bonneville County. Idaho Falls is a community of interest requiring statutory protection and the district is compact with easily identifiable boundaries. District 33 has 45,964 people, a deviation of +2.63% from the ideal district.

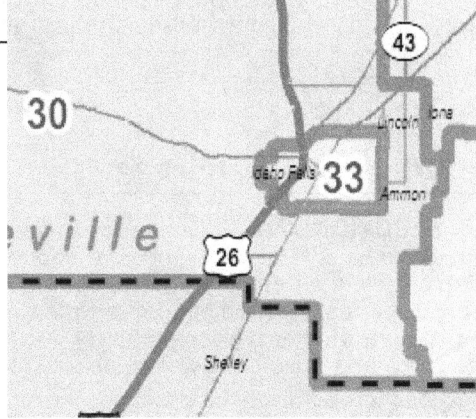

The central Idaho Falls district was numbered 33 in the 00s and retained the number for the 10s. As a partisan matter, it should be similar: Competitive with a Republican lean; but the lean is very clearly Republican. While this was in 2008 the site of the only Democratic legislative win in the Idaho Falls area in decades, that event hasn't been replicated.

Idaho Falls is more complex internally than it is often perceived from outside. The Church of Jesus Christ of Latter-Day Saints is very important here; the city's top landmark still is the LDS temple situated on the banks of the Snake River. But as in Pocatello, the Mormon population is not overwhelmingly dominant, and other components of town, especially the large work force associated with the Idaho National Laboratory, play a role too.

The senator here, Bart Davis, is among the senior senators, holding the post since 1998; he has been Senate majority leader nearly as long. That ought to suggest Davis as a Senate Republican caucus centrist, but local party activists have developed what seems almost like a suspicious attitude toward him. In 2011 the Bonneville Republican organization reprimanded Davis for opposing a state nullification proposal, and there was talk of a "no confidence" vote after Davis supported the governor's health insurance exchange proposal in 2013. The libertarian Idaho Freedom Foundation ranked him low in 2013, eighth from last (-77 points), third from last among Republicans.

One of the more remarkable personal stories about an Idaho politician in 2013 concerned Davis, his wife and the aftermath of the shooting of his son in March 2003 at a party in Boise. The shooter was convicted of manslaughter. In December 2013 he was up for parole, and the Davises said they would not oppose his release; Davis was quoted as saying of the killer's family, "We saw their hearts ache. With time, we prayed with them. With a little more time, we prayed for their son. Our loss is real, but now there is comfort."

One of the House members here, Linden Bateman, has a legislative history reaching back to 1976, but after an abrupt resignation a decade later he did not return until 2010. A teacher by profession, Bateman got some national attention for his effort to support cursive handwriting teaching in school.

143

Both Bateman and the freshman representative here, Janet Trujillo, voted against the governor's health insurance exchange proposal.

Predecessor district 33

ELECTIONS The idea that urban areas were more likely (than rural areas) to elect Democrats got some support in 2006 when long-time teacher Jerry Shively, a Democrat, narrowly won a House seat in central Idaho Falls. It was the first election of a Bonneville County Democrat since Ron Lechelt in 1976. It did not last long. Shively lost (also narrowly) his bid for re-election, and (also closely) a comeback attempt in 2010.

That 2006 Shively election was the only Democratic win here in the last decade. But note that general election winners here have been held to less than 55% or less six times here in the last decade, so that one win was still no fluke.

District 33 is the least solidly Republican legislative district in eastern Idaho north of Pocatello. (Democrat John McGimpsey, running three times in the decade for the other House seat, pulled respectable percentages each time), but it remains mostly Republican.

Its senator, Republican attorney Bart Davis (and for quite a while Senate majority leader), had serious contests in both primary and general for his first run in 1998, but his general election numbers gradually have risen since then. He has had primary challenges through the years, and while his last two (both against Kenneth Walton) yielded large Davis wins, they may not be done yet.

Three-term Representative Russ Mathews left in 2010 to run for the U.S. House (losing in the primary), but left behind an intriguing primary that pitted against each other two former legislators: former Senator Dane Watkins and former Representative (1976-86) Linden Bateman. Bateman prevailed, with 66.8%, and in the general as well.

Presdt	Democrat			Republican		
2012	Barack Obama	5,429	30.56%	Mitt Romney	11,789	66.37%

Sen	Democrat			Republican		
2012	-	-		- Bart Davis	13,809	100.00%
2010	Neil Williams	3,411	33.50%	Bart Davis	6,764	66.50%
2008	Neil Williams	5,136	35.20%	Bart Davis	9,456	64.80%
2006	Neil Williams	4,655	39.99%	Bart Davis	6,985	60.01%
2004	-	-		- Bart Davis	12,380	100.00%
2002	Ellie Hampton	4,831	40.80%	Bart Davis	7,004	59.20%
H1	Democrat			Republican		
2012	Mary E. Haley	5,521	32.30%	Janet Tujillo	10,392	60.90%
2010	Jerry Shively	4,881	47.40%	Jeff Thompson	5,411	52.60%
2008	Jerry Shively	7,195	49.10%	Jeff Thompson	7,465	50.90%
2006	Jerry Shively	6,036	51.25%	Jack Barraclough	5,742	48.75%

	Democrat			Republican		
2004	Pete Welliver	5,294	35.70%	Jack Barraclough	9,537	64.30%
2002	Parrish Worrell	4,665	39.40%	Jack Barraclough	7,182	59.20%
H2	**Democrat**			**Republican**		
2012	**Jim De Angelis**	**6,164**	**36.60%**	**Linden Bateman**	**10,690**	**63.40%**
2010	John McGimpsey	4,174	40.90%	Linden Bateman	6,036	59.10%
2008	John McGimpsey	6,605	45.40%	Russ Mathews	7,952	54.60%
2006	John McGimpsey	5,420	46.63%	Russ Mathews	6,203	53.37%
2004	-	-	-	Russ Mathews	11,416	100.00%
2002	Maureen McFadden	4,774	39.90%	Lee Gagner	5,434	45.50%

PRIMARIES Republican contests only in 33 in the last decade. Senator Bart Davis was primaried four times in the last dozen years. In the first three, he won landslides each time against the same man, Kenneth Walton, in two-man races: 2002 (69.75%), 2006 (70.6%) and 2008 (74.7%) – and progressively larger wins at that. In 2012 he was challenged by Brian Schad, and won with exactly the same percentage as in 2008.

In House A, incumbent Jack Barraclough was primaried in 2002 and 2006 but won each time (59.8% over Kent Higgins and 72.2% over Peter Welliver, respectively). When Barraclough left in 2012, a primary contest resulted in a win of Janet Trujillo (52.0%) over Ronald Lechelt. In House B, incumbent Lee Gagner in 2002 barely fended off (50.8%, a margin of 61 votes) a challenge from Russ Mathews; in 2004, by a margin of just six votes, Mathews won (50.11%) in a rematch. When Mathews left to run for Congress in 2010, two former legislators, Linden Bateman and Dane Watkins, competed for the B seat; Bateman easily won (66.8%). He won again in the 2012 primary, with 75.6% over David Lyon.

Senator BART DAVIS, R-Idaho Falls

Web: www.senatordavis.com
Background: Attorney (business and commercial law). Brigham Young University. University of Idaho.
Political: Elected to Senate 1998, 2000, 2002, 2004, 2006, 2008, 2010, 2012.

Representative JANET TRUJILLO, R-Idaho Falls

Web: jt4rep.com
Background: Certified property tax appraiser. Jordan Technical College; Salt Lake Community College.
Political: Elected to House, 2012.

Representative LINDEN BATEMAN, R-Idaho Falls

Web: www.lindenbateman.blogspot.com
Background: Semi-retired, teacher. Student teacher supervisor, Idaho State University, Brigham Young University-Idaho. Brigham Young University.
Political: Elected to House, 1976, 1978, 1980, 1982, 1984, 1986, 2010, 2012.

District 34

District 34 (Madison County, Bonneville County (part)). Madison County is kept whole within District 34 but it does not contain sufficient population to form an entire legislative district. In order to meet the one person one vote requirement, the Commission included the northern portion of Bonneville County. Although Bonneville County had to be split to comply with Article III, § 5, the communities of Ucon and Iona were maintained. This district is directly connected by Highways 20 and 26 creating commercial corridors and commonality of interests. District 34 has 44,970 people, a deviation of +0.44% from the ideal district.

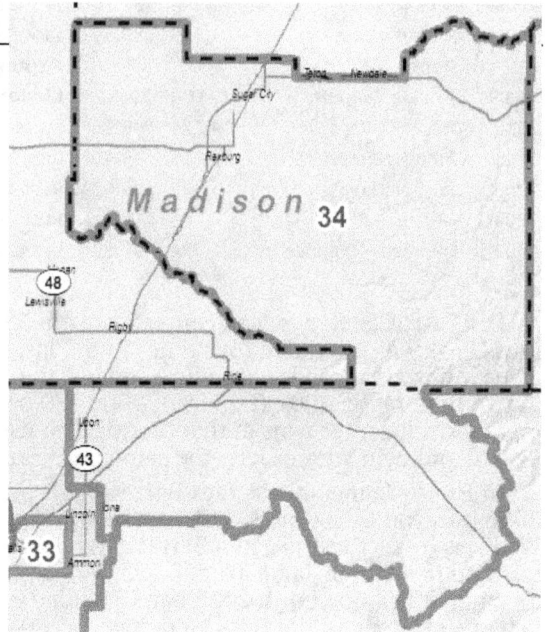

The core of district 34 in the 00s was Madison County, all of which was located in it. And Madison, a fast-growing county owing mainly to the growth of Brigham Young University-Idaho at Rexburg, remains intact and the heart of the new 34 as well. The main difference is that while the old district reached north to Fremont County to pick up additional needed population, the new district reaches south into Bonneville County, northeast of Idaho Falls. As a partisan matter, the difference is unlikely to matter; all of these areas are very strongly Republican.

That much is evident from the statistics – or the absence of them. In the last decade not a single Democrat has run for any of these seats, and primary contests haven't been especially common here either.

The president pro tem of the Senate, Brent Hill, an accountant at Rexburg, has been senator here since he was appointed in 2001, and aroused no significant opposition. Nor has the other long-timer, farmer and Representative Dell Raybould.

Hill has been an active legislator but a low-key personality, to the point that his wife was quoted in a March 2011 profile in the *Idaho Statesman* that he would never have run for the office if he had not initially been appointed to it. His first contest was for the office of pro tem, in December 2010; he defeated Meridian Senator Russ Fulcher for the top job. Hill drew some criticism for his handling of the case of Senator John McGee, a member of leadership who accumulated a series of public problems before finally resigning; the criticism suggested that Hill's cool and conciliatory nature may have let the problems drag on.

He took some heat from other quarters for his support of the governor's health insurance exchange proposal, which cleared the Senate with a strong majority. The libertarian Idaho Freedom Foundation ranked him relatively low on its 2013 index (the health insurance exchange may have been a major factor in that), sixth from last among all legislative Republicans.

Raybould is best known for his work on water-related issues.

He and freshman Representative Douglas Hancey both voted for the governor's health insurance exchange proposal.

Predecessor district 34

ELECTIONS Fitting that Fremont and Madison were so long united in a legislative district, since they were for some time (until 1913) one county – Fremont County. They are quite different though much alike near their border areas: Heavy on irrigated farming and food processing. Madison County has one other very important element as well, Brigham Young University-Idaho (formerly Ricks College), which has grown to a size comparable to Idaho's three state universities. Unlike the communities around those institutions, however, the BYU-I community is strongly Republican. The few dots of Democratic support (there are a few, mainly in northern Fremont) are overwhelmed by the Republican bases in this district.

So Republican is it that there has been no Democratic general election challenge in the last decade, in which exactly three people have held these three seats. There have been a few primary contests, all involving Seat A. A five-way battle in 2002 involving three former legislators (Lynn Loosli, Max Mortensen and Diana Richman) and two newcomers, future statewide candidate Rex Rammell and college administrator Mack Shirley, yielded a surprise win by Shirley. Rammell challenged him in 2004, but Shirley won with 64.3%; and he won with 62.7% in a 2010 challenge. But those have been the only primary contests in the last decade.

Presdt	Democrat			Republican		
2012	Barack Obama	1,240	6.92%	Mitt Romney	16,485	92.00%

Sen	Democrat			Republican		
2012	-	-	-	Brent Hill	16,039	100.00%
2010	-	-	-	Brent Hill	10,083	100.00%
2008	-	-	-	Brent Hill	16,724	100.00%
2006	-	-	-	Brent Hill	10,076	93.33%
2004	-	-	-	Brent Hill	15,282	100.00%
2002	-	-	-	Brent Hill	9,864	100.00%

H1	Democrat			Republican		
2012	Lary Larson	3,420	20.30%	Douglas Hancey	13,424	79.70%
2010	-	-	-	Mack Shirley	10,082	100.00%
2008	-	-	-	Mack Shirley	14,732	84.10%
2006	-	-	-	Mack Shirley	10,815	100.00%

2004	-		-	- Mack Shirley	14,567	91.10%
2002	-		-	- Mack Shirley	9,697	100.00%
H2	**Democrat**			**Republican**		
2012	-		-	**- Dell Raybould**	**15,708**	**100.00%**
2010	-		-	- Dell Raybould	9,892	100.00%
2008	-		-	- Dell Raybould	16,301	100.00%
2006	-		-	- Dell Raybould	10,492	100.00%
2004	-		-	- Dell Raybould	13,501	86.40%
2002	-		-	- Dell Raybould	9,557	100.00%

PRIMARIES Before 2012 House A drew all the primary action here. In 2002, running for a heavily remapped seat, five candidates competed, including three with legislative experience and another who would later run for governor. The winner was the fifth, Mack Shirley (38.8%), over Diana Richman (19.9%), Lynn Loosli (16.9%), Rex Rammell (14.6%) and Max Mortensen (9.8%). In 2004, Shirley was rematched against one of them, Rammell, but won in a landslide (64.28%). Shirley was in a third primary in 2010, against Dan Roberts, but again easily won (63.7%). In 2012, Shirley opted out and three Republicans filed. Douglas Hancey (46.2%) easily defeated Bill Hunter and Harold Jones.

In 2012 Dell Raybould drew a rare primary challenge, and from two candidates. He defeated (58.6%) Dan Roberts and John Baird.

Senator BRENT HILL, R-Rexburg

Web: www.senatorhill.com

Background: Accountant (CPA), certified financial planner. Ricks College. Utah State University.

Political: Elected to Senate, 2000, 2002, 2004, 2006, 2008, 2010, 2012. Elected Senate president pro tem, 2011, 2012.

Representative DOUGLAS HANCEY, R-Rexburg

Web:

Background: Retired, Ford Motor Company dealer. Brigham Young University.

Political: Elected to House, 2012.

Representative DELL RAYBOULD, R-Rexburg

Web: dellraybould.com

Background: Farmer (Raybould Brothers Farm), co-founder, Sun-Glo of Idaho. Former chair, Idaho Potato Commission. Former chair, Committee of Nine. Ricks College.

Political: Elected to House, 2000, 2002, 2004, 2006, 2008, 2010, 2012.

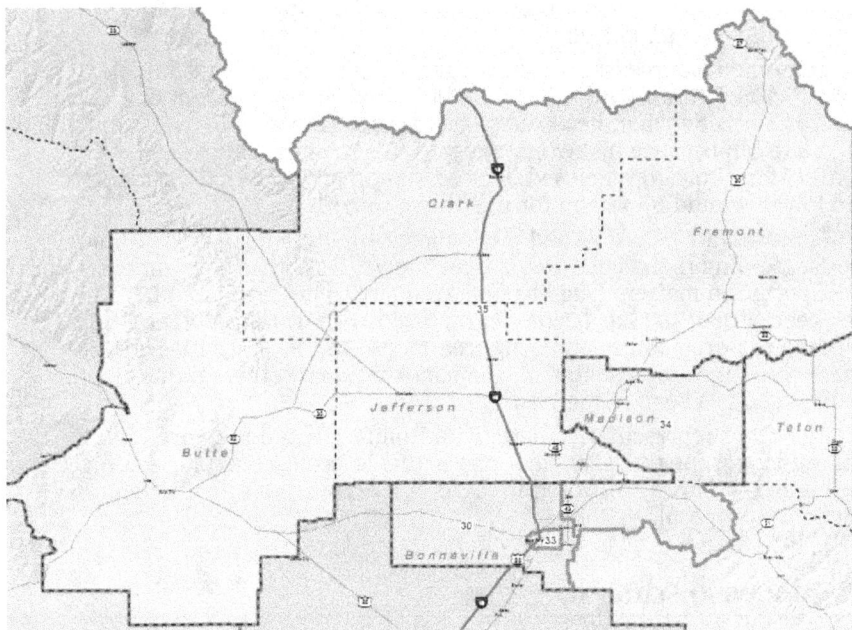

District 35

District 35 (Butte County, Clark County, Jefferson County, and Fremont County). District 35 is contiguous, bounded by Idaho's borders with Montana and Wyoming, and made up of all of Butte, Clark, Jefferson and Fremont counties. Individually, the population of these counties is insufficient to meet the one person one vote requirement and therefore they must be combined. This is another large geographic district that must come together to create a population adequate to satisfy the one person one vote requirement. As vast as the area is, it does share a common interest in natural resources, farming, ranching, and recreation. District 35 contains 43,255 people a deviation of -3.42% from the ideal district.

District 35 was in the 00s, and in the 90s (and most of the time in the years before that since the first reapportionment in 1966) Idaho's geographically largest legislative district. With the 2012 redistricting, and the removal of Lemhi and Custer counties from its territory (these were joined with southwestern counties in the new district 8) district 35 is the largest no more, though still sizable by any reasonable measure, running from Yellowstone National Park in the northeast to the Craters of the Moon National Monument in the southwest – a drive of three hours or so. The largest city in this vast area, Rigby (just north of Idaho Falls), has fewer than 4,000 people: This is rural territory. Very Republican.

The senator, Jeff Siddoway, is a sheep rancher and a member of one of the most prominent families in the region. He also has served as a Fish & Game commissioner, and he has been most visible on resource-related issues. He has been a leading advocate of killing wolves introduced into Idaho; describing his Senate Bill 1305 in 2012, he said "You can basically go after them [wolves] by any means available," Siddoway said. "And when I say 'get 'em' I mean kill 'em."

On some resource issues critics have questioned whether Siddoway had a conflict of interest with his private business. He shot back at one point in the 2012 session when he asked to be excused from an abortion ultrasound mandate bill because his two unmarried daughters could represent a conflict for him. After a closed door session involving Senate leaders, Siddoway wound up voting for the bill.

Representative JoAn Wood is the most senior member of the Idaho House, serving there since 1982. Over the years she has been most active in transportation matters (she has operated a trucking firm). But her range has been broad; she has becoming involved with working for, and finding funding for, drug courts and drug treatment. An unusual situation: Though she is the senior representative, she is not presently a committee chair, though she has been in the past.

The other representative here, Paul Romrell, was a Fremont County commissioner for six years, and long active in hospital administration. He, Wood and Siddoway all voted in favor of the governor's health insurance exchange proposal.

Predecessor district 35

ELECTIONS As was the case even before redistricting, the people here are widely spread out. A lot of it is federal land, and some of the key working stations of the Idaho National Laboratory. The people who live here, scattered in small towns and rural places, work at a variety of things: Timber, mining, recreation and tourism, ranching, and odds and ends.

Presdt	Democrat			Republican		
2012	Barack Obama	2,437	12.96%	Mitt Romney	16,038	85.32%
Sen	Democrat			Republican		
2012	-	-	-	Jeff Siddoway	16,745	100.00%
2010	-	-	-	Jeff Siddoway	12,571	100.00%
2008	Luke Prange	4,189	22.20%	Jeff Siddoway	14,655	77.80%
2006	Luke Prange	4,327	30.59%	Jeff Siddoway	9,818	69.41%
2004	Jerry Browne	3,969	23.20%	Don Burtenshaw	13,155	76.80%
2002	Jerry Browne	3,233	23.80%	Don Burtenshaw	10,370	76.20%
H1	Democrat			Republican		
2012	Jerry Browne	3,579	19.60%	JoAn Wood	14,671	80.40%
2010	-	-	-	JoAn Wood	12,420	100.00%
2008	Calvin Leman	4,027	21.40%	JoAn Wood	14,777	78.60%
2006	-	-	-	JoAn Wood	12,041	100.00%
2004	-	-	-	JoAn Wood	14,603	100.00%
2002	Lenard Van Eps	3,359	24.80%	JoAn Wood		
H2	Democrat			Republican		
2012	Kelly Keele	4,114	22.70%	Paul Romrell	13,994	77.30%
2010	-	-	-	Lenore Barrett	12,200	100.00%

Year						
2008	-		-	- Lenore Barrett	16,160	100.00%
2006	Jon Winegarner	3,888	27.91%	Lenore Barrett	10,041	72.09%
2004	-		-	- Lenore Barrett	14,114	98.80%
2002	-		-	- Lenore Barrett	11,687	100.00%

PRIMARIES Only Republican primary contests here. Senator Don Burtenshaw was primaried in 2002 by Richard Ward, but easily won (74.6%). When he opted out in 2006, a three-way contest developed, won by Jeff Siddoway (48.3%) over Leon D. Clark (27.8%) and George Ellsworth (23.9%). Veteran House A incumbent JoAn Wood has been challenged twice in the new millennium, in 2002, by Jacques Marcotte, winning easily (72.8%); but held to a modest 44.4% in 2012 over Joshua Anderson and Dale Mortimer.

The other veteran House member here, Lenore Hardy Barrett, was challenged more often and to more effect. When she was redistricted out (to district 8, where she was re-elected), four Republicans filed to replace her. Paul Romrell won with 50% over the vote, defeating Karey Hanks, Jon Shelley and Pat Ridley.

Senator JEFF SIDDOWAY, R-Terreton
Web:
Background: Ranching (Juniper Mountain Ranch, sheep, elk, bison). Former, Fish & Game Commission. University of Idaho.
Political: Elected to Senate, 2006, 2008, 2010.

Representative JOAN WOOD, R-Rigby
Web: www.facebook.com/woodforidaho
Background: Partner, farm/ranch.
Political: Elected to House 1982, 1984, 1986, 1988, 1990, 1992, 1994, 1996, 1998, 2000, 2002, 2004, 2006, 2008, 2010. Senior member of the Idaho House.

Representative PAUL ROMRELL, R-St. Anthony
Web: paulromrell.com
Background: Retired. Administrator, Fremont General Hospital. Ricks College.
Political: Coroner, Fremont County (40 years). Fremont County commission. Elected to House, 2012.

Judiciary

All appellate justices (Supreme Court) and judges (Court of Appeals) serve six-year terms. Candidates appear first on the ballot in the primary election, and if one receivbed an outright majority, is declared elected. If no one wins a majority, the top two progress to the general election.

The following election charts all reflect primary elections; only once in the last 20 years has more than two candidates filed and resulted in a general runoff (in 1996, when Wayne Kidwell was ultimately elected over Mike Wetherell).

Supreme Court seats are listed by number (as referenced in the Idaho Blue Books), although voters do not see the designations: Candidates are elected "to succeed" the name of the incumbent.

District judges in the seven districts serve four-year terms.

Supreme Court

FIRST – Daniel Eismann

A native of Owyhee County who lived before the Supreme Court there and in Canyon County, Daniel Eismann had a private law practice for a decade before coming a magistrate judge at Owyhee County, and was in 1995 appointed a 4th district judge in Ada County.

In joining the Supreme Court, Eismann broke a very long streak in Idaho judicial history. While in the first decades of Idaho history justices periodically were unseated at election, the last of those was Ben Dunlap in 1944 (defeated by Bert Miller). In 2000 Eismann filed a challenge against incumbent Justice Cathy Silak (who had survived a challenge four years earlier) and defeated her. That election still marks the only election defeat of an incumbent Idaho Supreme Court justice since 1944. He was unopposed for re-election in 2010.

Eismann served as chief justice from 2007 to 2011.

2012	Daniel Eismann	141,688	100.00%	-		-	-
2006	Daniel Eismann	118,134	100.00%	-		-	-
2000	Cathy Silak	77,658	41.40%	Daniel Eismann	110,063	58.60%
1994	Cathy Silak	90,445	57.70%	Wayne Kidwell	66,358	42.30%

SECOND – Joel Horton

Many justices are identified, pre-court, with one region of the state; Joel Horton spent time in several. Born in Nampa, he took his law degree at the University of Idaho at Moscow, practiced law in Lewiston, served as a deputy prosecutor at Twin Falls County and then a similar job in Ada County before being appointed a magistrate, and then a district judge, there. He was appointed September 2007 to the Idaho Supreme Court, replacing Linda Copple Trout, who had resigned.

2008	Joel Horton	75,691	50.10%	John Bradbury	75,438	49.90%
2002	Linda Copple Trout	98,660	62.10%	Starr Kelso	60,290	37.90%
1996	Linda Copple Trout	99,577	100.00%	-	-	0.00%

THIRD – Jim Jones

Most Idaho Supreme Court justices reach those posts by appointment, not election. The only two recent exceptions followed each other in the third seat. In 1998 veteran Byron Johnson said he would serve out his term but not seek another, leaving the filling of it – as contemplated in the constitution – to the voters. A vigorous three-way contest ensued, leading to the only November runoff of an Idaho Supreme Court seat since at least the 40s. It was won by former Idaho Attorney General Wayne Kidwell. Kidwell, who had also been a legislator and a prosecutor at Ada and Boise counties, in turn served one term and decided to do as Johnson had, leave his succession up to the voters. This time, however, the voters got little choice. Just one candidate filed for the open seat: Another former attorney general (1982-90), Jim Jones, a private practice attorney who also had run for the U.S. House (in 1978 and 1980) and Senate (in 1990). Jones was also unopposed for re-election in 2010.

2010	Jim Jones	145,584	100.00%	-	-	-
2004	Jim Jones	110,310	100.00%	-	-	-
1998	Wayne Kidwell	59,602	47.30%	Mike Wetherell	37,820	30.00%
				Lowell Castleton	28,558	22.70%

FOURTH – Warren Jones

Most Idaho Supreme Court justices have background as a lower court judge before their arrival at the high court most of the rest have served in or run for other political office. Warren Jones did neither (though he did clerk for a chief justice, Joseph McFadden); but he practiced wide-ranging law for 37 years with the Eberle Berlin firm in Boise. Appointed in July 2007, he was elected unopposed to the court the next year.

2008	Warren Jones	125,396	100.00%	-	-	-
2002	Gerald Schroeder	128,920	100.00%	-	-	-
1996	Gerald Schroeder	103,746	100.00%	-	-	-

FIFTH – Roger S. Burdick

The Snake River Basin Adjudication is the largest-scope legal case in Idaho history; five district court judges have been directly in charge of it, and Roger Burdick (a 5th district judge from 1993 to 2003) was the third of them, giving him direct experience with a case that still generates periodic appeals to the high court.

Burdick was appointed in August 2003, following Jesse Walters, who had served on the Supreme Court about six years and the Court of Appeals from its creation in 1982 for about 15 years. In 2011 he was named chief justice.

2010	Roger Burdick	99,788	58.40%	John Bradbury	71,160	41.60%
2004	Roger Burdick	109,213	100.00%	-	-	-
1998	Jesse Walters	103,590	100.00%	-	-	-

Court of Appeals

The four (until 2009 three) judges on the court of appeals are elected to six year terms, like their counterparts on the Supreme Court. But to date, there is this difference: There have been no election contests. Every member of the Court of Appeals has reached those post by appointment, not election; and none of the appointees have been challenged. The three longer-running seats have have had three occupants each.

■ Chief Judge **David Gratton** – Appointed 2009. Up for election 2018.

Darrell Perry, appointed to the Court of Appeals in 1993 (previously a magistrate in the 2nd district), was elected unopposed three times (1994, 2000, 2006) to the court but decided in 2009 to retire. The position went to Boise attorney David Gratton, a partner in the Evans Keane law firm.

■ **Karen Lansing** – Appointed 1993. Up for election 2016.

A private practice attorney (Hawley Troxell Ennis Hawley) who had also been an assistant Boise city attorney, Karen Lansing is the longest-serving Court of Appeals judge. She has been elected three times (2010, 2004, 1998) unopposed.

■ **Sergio Gutierrez** – Appointed 2004. Up for election 2014.

A 3rd district judge from 1993-2002 and a private practice attorney before that, Sergio Gutierrez was appointed to the Court of Appeals in 2002. He has been elected to the post twice (unopposed) since.

■ **John Melanson** – Appointed 2009. Up for election 2018.

John Melanson was the 5th district judge appointed to take over the Snake River Basin Adjudication in 2003 when fellow Judge Roger Burdick was named to the Idaho Supreme Court. In 2009 he became the second SRBA judge named to an Idaho appellate court.

Counties

County commission positions 1 and 3 were elected in 2006; number 2 was elected in 2004.

Positions 1 and 2 were elected in 2008.

Positions 2 and 3 were elected in 2010.

Positions 1 and 3 were elected in 2012.

Positions 1 and 2 will be up for election in 2014.

Sheriffs and prosecutors also were up for election in 2012. Some other positions were up for elected as well, in the case of office holders departing mid-term far enough in advance of the election.

Minority refers to those included in Census reports as other than "white persons not hispanic."

ADA

AREA Communities: Boise, Meridian, Eagle, Garden City, Kuna, Star. 1,060 sq. mi.

POPULATION 392,365 (1st) Increase 00s: 30.4%. Minority: 13.5%. Hispanic: 7.1%.

Save for a blip – no more than that – during the Great Depression, Ada County overall has been steadfast Republican for more than a century. It has not voted for a Democrat for president in well over half a century, not even when the state (narrowly) went for Lyndon Johnson in 1964. The consistency has been stunning for a county with such substantial population growth. In 1960, Ada held 93,460 people, and in 2000 more than thrice as many, more than 300,000. But consistently through that time, the Republican votes for president have tended to be 50% or more higher than the votes for Democrats, and Republicans have throughout that time won most local (legislative + county) offices.

This has cut both ways, however. Although Republican numbers threatened to leave Democratic in the dust a couple of times, Democrats generally have continued to climb in tandem. Evidently, there were in 2004 more Democrats in Ada County than there were Republicans in 1980. The catch for them, of course, is that there are also many more Republicans in 2004 in the county than there were a quarter-century earlier.

Like most counties (especially urban counties), however, Ada is not monolithic, and in one sector actually developed a Democratic core unlike any it had previously. Prior to the mid-70s, no specific part of the county, not even any substantial sector of the city, was reliably Democratic; the closest sectors may have been parts of the older Bench and some areas near what was becoming Boise State University. The city's North End was old-line Republican. But in the 70s, with state Democratic administrations in power and BSU growing rapidly, the North End and the East End began attracting government workers, university employees, activists and others as it had not previously. When in 1976 a Democrat (Ron Twilegar) won a state Senate seat in that area, things changed. That seat has remained Democratic ever since, becoming ever more safely Democratic, and by the late 90s both House seats in that area had become solidly Democratic as well. By 2004, that district had become as unwinnable for Republicans as a number of other Ada districts had for Democrats.

Three other legislative districts bordering on 19 had by 2004 become genuinely competitive: District 16 to its northwest, including the Collister area, Garden City and south to the mall; District 17, the central Boise bench (which long had approached competitive status though electing just one Democrat to the legislature in four decades prior to 2002); and District 18, in southeast Boise. In 2004 each of them elected a Democrat as state senator. In the case of District 16, the most competitive of the three, a Democratic representative was re-elected, and the one Republican (a newcomer) was held to 51.3%. In District 17, a Democrat in 2004 came within nine votes of defeating an incumbent Republican state representative. In District 18, Democrats won two legislative seats back in the 80s, but not since, though they often have held Republicans there to the mid-50's; in 2004, a Democrat did win the Senate seat there against a conservative religious Republican. (These three districts between them in fact held almost all the good news Democrats in the state could muster in 2004.)

Collectively, these four districts hold most of the population of Boise, and (collectively) they tilt Democratic, which means the city of Boise itself is highly competitive; its 2003 election of Democrat David Bieter (on a nonpartisan ballot) should not come as a shock. But as one travels more than four or five miles from Boise's downtown, the less likely one will find a Democratic-leaning precinct; by seven or eight miles out, they are nonexistent. And the one-third, roughly, of Ada County not in Boise is solidly Republican – Democrats seldom obtain much more than a third of the vote in these areas; anything approaching 40% is above average. These, in other words, are the other four of Ada County's eight legislative districts. Republican strength is overwhelming in each of them, and no Democrat has come very close to winning in any of them in many years – though they something did come closer in the 70s and 80s than in the 90s, or since.

That raises a question: Have Republicans been disproportionately been migrating to those areas outside the Boise center, while Democrats have been disproportionately migrating into that core? Something along those lines seems to have been happening. Ada County politics has been sifting out regionally, with Democrats becoming increasingly competitive in the center of the city, while Republicans have become increasingly untouchable outside that area. This appears to be a trend gradually ongoing for the last quarter-century or so.

PRECINCTS (141 – before a re-division of precincts early in 2012) Politically, Ada County has it all – many very Republican and very Democratic precincts, along with many along the spectrum. As in most places, the most Republican precincts (125, 1, 124, 126) are among the most rural and remote and least developed, and outside any of the cities.

Note that the precincts were heavily reorganized and renumbered in 2012.

An overview by city:

■ **Boise.** The north end of Boise is the most populous clearly Democratic region in Idaho. On our list of the most Democratic precincts in Idaho in 2010, nine of the dozen most Democratic (that would be precincts 40, 59, 39, 37, 36, 77, 60, 35 and 72, all roughly between the downtown area and the foothills) precincts are in this area. In these precincts, Republican Mike Crapo lost for the Senate, often by 2-1, and the margins against Governor C.L. "Butch" Otter were even larger.

As the precincts continue out to the northwest, west and southwest from there, however, the deep blue turns purple and, toward the west side of Boise, turns red. In the western precincts of the bench, for example, the parties are clearly competitive. By the time you hit the north-south Cole Road on the west side of Boise, Republican dominance has become clear, and in scattered precincts (31, 32, 66 among others) is as strong as the Democratic in the North End.

■ **Meridian.** Idaho's third-largest city, taken as a whole, is strongly Republican. But if it's all red, the redness does vary. Precincts 63 and 78, the center of old Meridian, are about as Republican as the county overall. Generally, the newer developments and precincts are more strongly Republican, and some of the older outlying developments edge a little closer to competitive (though they never get there, or especially close).

■ **Eagle.** Many of the most Republican precincts in Ada are in or near Eagle. Generally, the Republican margins are softer in the most central (and older) parts of town (such as precincts 6 and 7) and greater in the newer, outlying areas to the north and south. But the difference is often whether a Republican candidate wins by 68% or 73%. None of Eagle is competitive.

■ **Garden City.** Precinct 23k, which includes most of old Garden City along Chinden Boulevard, long has been politically marginal and remains so; in 2010, it voted for the top-ballot Republican winners but by slender margins. Most of the rest of Garden runs a little more Republican than that, but less than the county as a whole.

■ **Kuna.** Solidly Republican in all precincts, by landslide levels. Strongest in precinct 123 to the south, headed out to the Birds of Prey.

■ **Star.** At the far northwest of the county, the governor's home is Ada's most Republican city (as well as its newest); its precincts, 1 and 126, are among the most Republican in Idaho.

PRESIDENTIAL Ada County has not voted for a Democrat for president since 1936, and only once before that, in 1896. Its closest call in recent decades was in 2008, when Obama received a strong vote from the city of Boise but a counter even stronger from the rest of the county.

	Dem	%	Rep	%	Total
2012	77,137	42.72%	97,554	54.03%	180,546
2008	82,236	45.84%	93,328	52.02%	179,402
2004	58,523	37.76%	94,641	61.06%	155,002
2000	40,650	33.06%	75,050	61.03%	122,964
1996	43,040	36.55%	61,811	52.50%	117,743
1992	31,941	28.99%	49,000	44.48%	110,166
1988	30,525	34.95%	54,951	62.92%	87,334

GOVERNOR As solidly Republican as Ada County has long been in presidential contests, it has proven more flexible in governor's races. During the New Deal era it voted periodically for Democrats for governor. In the 24-year run of Democratic governorships of Cecil Andrus and John Evans, Ada supported those Democrats each time. It flipped again in 2002 and 2006, but returned to a strong Republican showing in 2010.

	Dem	%	Rep	%	Total
2010	46,777	38.59%	63,871	52.70%	121,206
2006	62,632	51.99%	55,272	45.88%	120,479
2002	52,360	49.67%	51,258	48.62%	105,424
1998	29,743	32.15%	60,189	65.06%	92,509
1994	43,233	44.58%	51,018	52.61%	96,974
1990	55,177	75.39%	18,012	24.61%	73,189

COUNTY Ada County's courthouse nearly always has been solidly red, the exceptions being very occasional wins by Democrats for county commission seats. The county's overall Republican tilt has come into play in all but a few cases. The most recent example was Democrat Paul Woods, narrowly elected in a surprise (stealth?) race in 2006, but ousted by a slightly larger margin in another surprising race just two years later.

Department heads have rarely been seriously challenged in recent decades, though primary contests have emerged when an official retires.

Com1	Democrat				Republican		
2012	**Larry Rincover**	**60,560**	**35.90%**		**Jim Tibbs**	**108,040**	**64.10%**
2008	Paul Woods	79,732	48.18%		Sharon Ullman	85,761	51.82%
2006	Paul Woods	48,912	43.00%		Steven Kimball	47,667	41.90%
2002	Jerry Carter	46,989	46.60%		Judy Peavey-Derr	53,839	53.40%
Com2	**Democrat**				**Republican**		
2010	Larry Rincover	42,088	36.70%		Rick Yzaguirre	72,686	63.30%
2008	David Langhorst	76,024	46.07%		Rick Yzaguirre	89,006	53.93%
2004	Michael Wilson	71,582	48.97%		Rick Yzaguirre	74,599	51.03%
2002	Michael Rudd	38,726	38.50%		Rick Yzaguirre	61,855	61.50%
Com3	**Democrat**				**Republican**		
2012	**Thomas Howell**	**58,311**	**35.40%**		**Dave Case**	**88,509**	**53.70%**
2010	-	0	0.00%		Vern Bisterfeldt	92,484	100.00%
2006	Chris Grant	46,096	40.38%		Fred Tilman	64,947	56.80%
2004	-	0	0.00%		Fred Tilman	109,900	100.00%

Clerk	Democrat		Republican	
2010	-	0.00%	Chris Rich	100.00%
2006	Chris Grant	40.38%	Dave Navarro	59.62%
Treasurer	**Democrat**		**Republican**	
2010	-	0.00%	Vicky McIntyre	100.00%
2006	-	0.00%	Cecil Ingram	100.00%
Assessor	**Democrat**		**Republican**	
2010	-	0.00%	Robert McQuade	100.00%
2006	-	0.00%	Robert McQuade	100.00%
Coroner	**Democrat**		**Republican**	
2010	-	0.00%	Erwin Sonnenberg	100.00%
2006	-	0.00%	Erwin Sonnenberg	100.00%
Sheriff	**Democrat**		**Republican**	
2012	**-**		**- Gary Raney**	**74.30%**
2008	-	0.00%	Gary Raney	100.00%
2004	Bruce Honey	33.80%	Gary Raney	66.20%
Pros Atty	**Democrat**		**Republican**	
2012	**Ron Twilegar**	**39.70%**	**Greg Bower**	**60.30%**
2008	-	0.00%	Greg Bower	100.00%
2004	-	0.00%	Greg Bower	100.00%

*defeated a Libertarian candidate

ADAMS

AREA Communities: Council, New Meadows, Mesa, Fruitvale. 1,370 sq. mi.

POPULATION 3,976 (40th). Increase 00s: 14.4%. Minority: 5.2%. Hispanic: 2.4%.

Adams County has remained steady-state Republican for decades. Its population has remained stable over the years; it was 2,978 in 1960, and 3,476 some 40 years later. Up to the mid-60s, the county was home to a number of conservative Democrats – traditional Democrats, Wallace Democrats – but in the realignments of that decade many shifted over to the Republicans. Well-regarded local Democrats have won courthouse elections, but that's personality, not partisanship; and their numbers have declined over the years.

The two Council precincts has tended to be the most competitive, but then not by much – it often means the Republican margin is just 30-1. In the small Bear precinct in 2000, Bush beat Gore 25-1; Kerry improved on that (22-4).

Adams County, split among four river basins (Snake, Weiser, Payette and Salmon) and by hills and mountains into a surprising number of settlements and towns (none with a population even approaching 1,000), is what it always has been: a true slice of rural Idaho.

There is a tentativeness to civilization here, a sense underlined by the March 1995 closure in Council of the Boise Cascade sawmill that employed almost 60 people. That accounts for a large chunk of the population and economy of the city of Council (population about 800), and local businesses were concerned through the year about the impact that closure might high.

But that comparative remoteness, small population and slowness, and easiness of life also breed a toughness and self-reliance.

The idea of Council as a center of one's world seems befitting considering its early history. The town was named for and located on the site of large inter-tribal meetings of the Shoshoni, Nez Perce and others. And at Packer John's Cabin, just east of present-day New Meadows, Idaho Democrats held their first convention in 1863.

PRECINCTS (6) All of the precincts are Republican, the standout being thinly-populated and remote Bear. (It typically produces a couple of dozen or so Republican votes for a given office, and three to five for the Democrat.) The Little Salmon River precinct north of New Meadows is now the most competitive, a change over the last generation maybe generated by the new rural and vacation housing developed in the area. Council's two precincts are in the middle.

PRESIDENTIAL Adams is a solidly Republican county overall, and it has been Republican on the presidential level since 1964, typically by large margins.

	Dem	%	Rep	%	Total
2012	577	28.01%	1,413	68.59%	2,060
2008	728	31.38%	1,517	65.39%	2,320
2004	555	26.90%	1,468	71.16%	2,063
2000	336	17.70%	1,476	77.77%	1,898

GOVERNOR Adams last voted Democratic for governor in the 1990 Andrus landslide (though it had not backed him in 1986). Before that, its votes swung back and forth between the parties in governor's races.

	Dem	%	Rep	%	Total
2010	384	22.93%	1,137	67.88%	1,675
2006	635	38.05%	994	59.56%	1,669
2002	547	34.17%	1,009	63.02%	1,601

COUNTY Adams traditionally has had a courthouse split deeply between the parties. It is much less so now, though the treasurer and prosecutor are Democrats (the latter a flip from the Republican side).

Com1	Democrat			Republican		
2012	-		-	- **Joe Holmes**	**1,567**	**100.00%**
2008	-	0	0.00%	Joe Holmes	1,806	100.00%
2006	-	0	0.00%	Joe Holmes	1,354	100.00%
2002	-	0	0.00%	Judy Ellis	1,248	100.00%
Com2	**Democrat**			**Republican**		
2010	-	0	0.00%	Mike Paradis	1,409	100.00%
2008	-	0	0.00%	Mike Paradis	1,846	99.84%
2004	-	0	0.00%	Mike Paradis	1,647	100.00%
2002	Alan York	498	31.70%	Mike Paradis	1,075	68.30%
Com3	**Democrat**			**Republican**		
2012	-		-	- **Bill Brown**	**1,431**	**100.00%**
2010	-	0	0.00%	Bill Brown	1,269	100.00%
2006	-	0	0.00%	Bill Brown	1,185	100.00%
2004	-	0	0.00%	Bill Brown	1,412	100.00%

Clerk	Democrat		Republican	
2010	-	0.00%	Sherry Ward	100.00%
2006	-	0.00%	Sherry Ward	100.00%
2002	-	0.00%	Mike Fisk	100.00%
Treasurer	**Democrat**		**Republican**	
2010	-	0.00%	Connie Kesler	100.00%
2006	-	0.00%	Connie Kesler	100.00%
2002	Lora Barnett	21.50%	Connie Kesler	78.50%
Assessor	**Democrat**		**Republican**	
2012	-		- **Stacey Swift Dreyer**	**69.40%**
2010	Karen Hatfield	61.50%	Robin James	38.50%
2006	Karen Hatfield	100.00%	-	0.00%
2002	Karen Hatfield	100.00%	-	0.00%

Coroner	Democrat		Republican	
2010	-	0.00%	Susan Warner	100.00%
2006	-	0.00%	Susan Warner	100.00%
2002	-	0.00%	Susan Warner	100.00%
Sheriff	**Democrat**		**Republican**	
2012	-	-	**Ryan Zollman**	**49.80%**
2008	-	0.00%	Rich Green*	51.20%
2004	-	0.00%	Rich Green	100.00%
Pros Atty	**Democrat**		**Republican**	
2012	-	-	**Michael Ray Robinson**	**93.30%**
2008	Myron Dan Gabbert	100.00%	-	0.00%
2004	-	0.00%	Myron Dan Gabbert	100.00%

*Green had lost in the primary to Republican George Stokesberry. He won in the general over Stokesberry, who had the Republican nomination.

BANNOCK

AREA Communities: Pocatello, Chubbuck, McCammon, Lava Hot Springs, Inkom, Downey, Arimo, Swan Valley. 1,148 sq. mi.

POPULATION
82,839 (5th).
Increase 00s: 9.6%.
Minority: 13.6%.
Hispanic: 13.6%.

Long regarded as eastern Idaho's Democratic bastion, Bannock County has become increasingly difficult to describe politically. In many respects it is deeply competitive, but almost anything political one says about it has to come with an asterisk attached.

The myth of the Bannock Democratic machine should have been exposed long ago, as far back as the 60s. Not since 1964, in the Johnson national landslide, has a Democratic presidential candidate won Bannock County, and in most counties that sort of record is simply the prelude to Republican takeovers downticket. Some of that has happened here. Republicans have won Bannock in U.S. Senate races since 1992, for the U.S. House most of the time since then as well. In 2004, veteran Bannock state Senator Lin Whitworth ran for the U.S. House against Republican incumbent Mike Simpson; despite his local popularity, he lost Bannock 19,795 to 14,868. Traditionally, the courthouse was solidly or almost solidly Democratic, but Republicans made inroads there in the 90s, at one point taking over all three commission seats. They have done well in many legislative races as well.

Some of the reasons are clear enough. The core of Democratic strength traditionally lay in Pocatello's labor unions; as in many other places, they declined in size (and clout) steadily over the last generation. One of the major union locations, the big Union Pacific railroad center, drastically scaled down

Unlike some other counties, however, Democrats have not been swept from the field. Labor, while not what it once was, remains a substantial force. A decade-long influx of students from the formerly two-year Ricks College at Rexburg – as a group, conservative, Mormon and Republican – to Idaho State University ended with the new millennium at Ricks became the four-year Brigham Young University-Idaho. And the rapid growth of the international high-tech firm AMI Systems threw a moderating influence into the community as well. Beyond all that, veteran local Democrats (Donna Boe, Roger Chase, Richard Stallings, Edgar Malepei, Larry Ghan and others) remained active over the years and built their organization.

The end result is a county usually voting Republican on the top of the ticket with strong, close competition at the legislative, county and city levels.

Bannock long has been split geographically by party, and the urban-rural split is abundant. Pocatello as a whole as of the new millennium is Democratic; the Ricks influx gave Republicans some extra advantage in the 90s, but that has diminished. Parts of Pocatello, however, are highly competitive or (notably in some of the old Alameda district, and in the newer Highlands area to the northeast near Chubbuck) trend Republican. Pocatello is most of the county; but the rest of the county is strongly Republican. "Down county" – the area from Inkom south, through McCammon and Lava Hot Springs and Arimo – is Republican territory, and local activists have spoken of splitting off to join with one of the more Republican counties neighboring. North of Pocatello, growing suburban Chubbuck has some of the Eagle/Meridian effect, as many people see themselves as being outside the central city; this area is both strongly Mormon and very Republican. Republican 2-1 margins are not unusual either in Chubbuck or downcounty.

PRECINCTS (60) Bannock County political people commonly think of the county in three pieces: Pocatello city, which is mainly Democratic; "down county" (south of Pocatello), which is mostly Republican; and Chubbuck to Pocatello's north, which also is mostly Republican. That remains a useful way to approach the county. Its most Republican precincts are Swan Lake and Arimo to the south, both delivering landslides to top-line Republicans (Swan Lake was 78% for Otter in 2010). The most-Republican third of the 60 precincts here also included McCammon, Lava Hot Springs, Pebble Creek and Downey from downcounty, and seven of the 11 Chubbuck precincts. The most Democratic precincts, on the other end, are located in central city, especially around Idaho State University and in some of the older (sometimes still union) neighborhoods inside town. Eight of these voted against Crapo, and 23 against Otter.

PRESIDENTIAL On the presidential level, Bannock is no more Democratic than a lot of traditionally Republican Idaho counties. It has not voted for a Democrat for president since Johnson in 1964, and has not come close in more recent years.

	Dem	%	Rep	%	Total
2012	13,214	37.48%	21,010	59.59%	35,260
2008	14,792	42.14%	19,356	55.14%	35,105
2004	12,903	37.03%	21,479	61.65%	34,843
2000	10,892	35.45%	18,223	59.31%	30,725

GOVERNOR Bannock has often supported Democrats for governor (could this have to do in part with a difference between presidential and off-year voting cohorts?). Democrats have won for governor in Bannock in every election from 1966 (Andrus' first) to present but for two: In 1998 (where the Democratic nominee was former Pocatello legislator Robert Huntley) and 2010..

	Dem	%	Rep	%	Total
2010	10,613	45.06%	11,308	48.01%	23,555
2006	13,287	56.78%	10,912	46.63%	23,400
2002	13,070	52.30%	11,416	45.68%	24,989

COUNTY Bannock has been gradually trending Republican at the courthouse – at least at the commissioner level.

Com1	Democrat			Republican		
2012	**Elmer Martinez**	**15,616**	**45.40%**	**Karl Anderson**	**18,811**	**54.60%**
2008	Karen Cordell	15,778	46.00%	Karl Anderson	18,522	54.00%
2006	Lin Whitworth	13,294	53.33%	Sue Parker	11,635	46.67%
2002	Carol Gunter	11,389	46.60%	Jim Guthrie	13,032	53.40%
Com2	**Democrat**			**Republican**		
2010	-	0	0.00%	Steve Hadley	17,912	100.00%
2008	K.T. Anderson	16,463	48.09%	Steve Hadley	17,772	51.91%
2004	LaRae Millward	14,596	43.12%	Steve Hadley	17,327	51.18%
2002	Tom Liddil	11,755	48.50%	Steve Hadley	12,482	51.50%
Com3	**Democrat**			**Republican**		
2012	**Marla Vik**	**14,257**	**41.70%**	**Howard Manwaring**	**17,239**	**50.40%**
2010	Larry Ghan	9,368	40.70%	Howard Manwaring	13,637	59.30%
2006	Larry Ghan	13,727	55.05%	Craig Cooper	11,210	44.95%
2004	Larry Ghan	17,372	50.94%	Craig Cooper	16,731	49.06%

Clerk	Democrat		Republican	
2010	Dale Hatch	50.40%	Robert Ballard	49.60%
2006	Dale Hatch	55.77%	Alren Wittrock	44.22%
2002	Larry Ghan	59.00%	Eric Hymas	41.00%
Treasurer	**Democrat**		**Republican**	
2010	Radene Barker	58.90%	Paul Des Fosses	41.10%
2006	Radene Barker	55.30%	J.O. Cotant	44.70%
2002	Genie Alexander	52.80%	Jody Hepworth	49.20%
Assessor	**Democrat**		**Republican**	
2010	Geoffrey Ranere	44.10%	David Packer	55.90%
2006	Jo Lynn Anderson	53.37%	Evan Frasure	46.63%
2002	Diane Bilyeu	100.00%	-	0.00%
Coroner	**Democrat**		**Republican**	
2010	Kim Quick	100.00%	-	0.00%
2006	Kim Quick	100.00%	-	0.00%
2002	Jim Allen	63.20%	Jason Myers	36.80%
Sheriff	**Democrat**		**Republican**	
2012	**Lorin Nielsen**	**100.00%**	**-**	**-**
2008	Lorin Nielsen	60.31%	Paul Romriell	39.69%
2004	Lorin Nielsen	56.09%	Bret Schei	43.91%
Pros Atty	**Democrat**		**Republican**	
2012	**Kent Reynolds**	**15,735**	**Stephen Herzog**	**53.80%**
2008	Mark Heidemann	100.00%	-	0.00%
2004	Mark Heidemann	50.31%	Craig Parrish	49.69%

BEAR LAKE

AREA Communities: Montpelier, Paris, Bloomington, St. Charles, Ovid, Dingle, Georgetown. 1,050 sq. mi.

POPULATION 5,986 (36th). Increase 00s: -6.6%. Minority: 5.3%. Hispanic: 3.6%.

Bear Lake has struggled to maintain its rural economy, and from its 1960 population of 7,418 declined over the next 40 years to 6,411. Few people have moved in; what should have emerged as a recreation economy has remained mostly stagnant.

Traditionally, the largest city here, Montpelier, is the most competitive politically. But that means only that Democrats aren't stomped quite so totally; the comparison is to precincts like Bennington, where George W. Bush beat John Kerry by 147-9.

Cecil Andrus and (up to 1974) Frank Church did well in Bear Lake, actually winning the country in some of their better years, and doing better than in some other Mormon/conservative eastern counties. But no up-ticket Democrat has won here since 1990. A few local courthouse Democrats have been elected on the basis of personal familiarity or family ties.

PRECINCTS (14) All of these precincts are landslide Republican territory, in recent cycles none close to competitive. (As late as the 80s one or two Montpelier precincts were competitive in top of ticket races.) The lakeside areas of Fish Haven and St. Charles are the least heavily Republican, and the Montpelier precincts after that.

PRESIDENTIAL Bear Lake went through a somewhat competitive period in the 70s, but not on the presidential level. It has not voted for a Democrat for president since 1964, though occasionally in years prior to that. Its Republican margins in recent years have been massive.

	Dem	%	Rep	%	Total
2012	302	10.70%	1,413	68.59%	2,822
2008	502	17.06%	2,377	80.77%	2,943
2004	494	16.25%	2,506	82.43%	3,040
2000	517	17.88%	2,296	79.39%	2,892

GOVERNOR Bear Lake had a soft spot for Democrat Cecil Andrus, voting for him in his two landslide wins for governor in 1990 and 1974, and in 1970 as well (though not in 1986 or 1966). Otherwise, it has been solidly Republican for governor for many decades, with 2-1 margins being typical.

	Dem	%	Rep	%	Total
2010	592	26.70%	1,484	66.94%	2,217
2006	621	28.13%	1,505	68.16%	2,208

| 2002 | | | 734 | 30.17% | | 1,663 | 68.35% | | 2,433 |

COUNTY Occasionally over the years, a well-connected local figure who happened have a "D" behind his or her name might win a courthouse office, notably if the incumbent had some kind of political issue. But such instances seem to have become less and less commonplace in recent decades. Contested races of any sort, for that matter, have become unusual.

Com1	Democrat				Republican		
2012	Kevin Jacobson	832	29.00%		Bradley Jensen	2,040	71.00%
2008	-	0	0.00%		Montain Kunz	2,503	100.00%
2006	-	0	0.00%		Montain Kunz	1,370	62.08%
2002	-	0	0.00%		Conrad Michaelson	2,053	100.00%
Com2	Democrat				Republican		
2010	-	0	0.00%		DeMar Romrell	2,042	100.00%
2008	-	0	0.00%		DeMar Romrell	2,612	100.00%
2004	-	0	0.00%		Dwight Cochran	1,808	100.00%
2002	-	0	0.00%		Dwight Cochran	1,815	77.00%
Com3	Democrat				Republican		
2012	-	-			Vaughn Rasmussen	2,542	100.00%
2010	-	0	0.00%		Vaughn Rasmussen	1,965	100.00%
2006	-	0	0.00%		Vaughn Rasmussen	1,980	100.00%
2004	-	0	0.00%		Vaughn Rasmussen	2,614	100.00%

Clerk	Democrat		Republican	
2010	-	0.00%	Kerry Haddock	100.00%
2006	-	0.00%	Kerry Haddock	100.00%
Treasurer	Democrat		Republican	
2010	Leslie Tueller	19.70%	Tricia Poulsen	80.30%
2006	Rodney Wallentine	100.00%	-	0.00%
Assessor	Democrat		Republican	
2010	-	0.00%	Lynn Lewis	100.00%
2006	-	0.00%	Lynn Lewis	100.00%
Coroner	Democrat		Republican	
2010	-	0.00%	David Matthews	100.00%
2006	-	0.00%	Leonard Matthews	100.00%
Sheriff	Democrat		Republican	
2012	-	-	Brent Bunn	100.00%
2008	Rex Skinner	47.58%	Brent Bunn	52.24%
2004	-	0.00%	Brent Bunn	100.00%
Pros Atty	Democrat		Republican	
2012	-	-	Roger Jones*	44.30%
2008	-	0.00%	Roger Jones	100.00%
2004	Steven Wuthrich	31.10%	Ardee Helm	68.90%

*In 2012, prosecutor Roger Jones was defeated by a write-in candidate, Steven Wuthrich, who received 1,500 votes (55.7%).

BENEWAH

AREA Communities: St.
Maries, Plummer, Tensed,
Parkline. 787 sq. mi.

POPULATION 9,285
(30th). Increase 00s:
1.2%. Minority: 14.7%.
Hispanic: 2.5%.

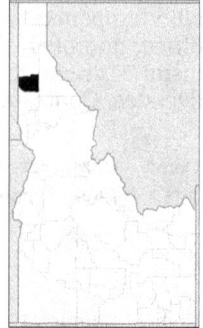

Benewah is another struggling rural county, most of
its population off on remote and little-traveled highways,
its population of 6,036 in 1960 increasing only to 9,171
four decades later. But its character has changed. For
decades Benewah was a timber county, and a generally
prosperous one, with a timber-industry labor base
steering local politics. All that has changed in several
directions. Timber has not gone away but is a far smaller component of the
labor base than it was, and generally confined now to the eastern side of
the county, notably around St. Maries. The big new addition to the mix is
the economic engine of the Coeur d'Alene Tribe, located on the west side of
the county; their casino business complex (located just north of the county
line) is a big factor here. The diminished timber labor force, less of it
unionized and more of it voting Republican, is countered to some extent by
the Democrats at the tribal facilities.

Benewah has become reliably Republican on top of the ticket; for major
offices, it has voted Republican exclusively since 1992. On the legislative
and county front, the picture is more mixed. The courthouse has some long-
time Democrats who are both conservative and so well established in the
community that they are immovable; the courthouse could yet move toward
more Republicans over time, however, as they eventually retire. Once
mostly supportive of Democrats in legislative races, the county in the new
millennium has become mostly supportive of Republicans, crossing over
only occasionally. Partisan standing seems a little more fluid here than in
much of Idaho. This was one of Ross Perot's best counties in 1992; he took
31.5% of the vote. And after Bill Clinton (deeply unpopular here) left the
White House, Democratic votes in 2002 and 2004 took a rachet upward
compared to 2000.

PRECINCTS (11) Apart from local Democrats (mainly for county
office), these are all very Republican precincts now. You might expect
Plummer, which is a Coeur d'Alene tribal center and has a large Latino
population as well, to trend more Democratic, but it hasn't much in recent
races; it votes much like St. Maries now does, Republican. The most-
Republican precinct is relatively remote St. Joe, taking in people along the
"shadowy" St. Joe River and the old Milwaukee railroad line.

PRESIDENTIAL Benewah's move toward Republicans was
foreshadowed by its votes for president in recent decades. It last voted
Democratic for president in 1992, though only by 47 votes and largely
because about 1,200 normally Republican votes went instead to Ross Perot.
Benewah also voted Democratic in 1976, and before that 1964. But in

recent cycles it has been reliably Republican on the upper ranges of the ballot.

	Dem	%	Rep	%	Total
2012	1,164	29.97%	2,596	66.84%	3,884
2008	1,407	33.79%	2,646	63.54%	4,164
2004	1,148	28.37%	2,823	69.76%	4,047
2000	895	24.45%	2,606	71.20%	3,660

GOVERNOR For many years through 1990 Benewah was a solidly Democratic vote for governor. It has not supported a Democrat for the office since then, however.

	Dem	%	Rep	%	Total
2010	773	25.64%	1,969	65.31%	3,015
2006	1,125	37.76%	1,631	54.75%	2,979
2002	1,227	37.84%	1,919	59.17%	3,243

COUNTY Political tends to be personal in Benewah, and it doesn't change rapidly. Democratic commissioners Jack Buell and Bud McCall have held those jobs a very long time, back to the days when Benewah was dominated by Democrats. The courthouse in fact still has more Democrats than Republicans and, because they are often well-established figures locally, they often aren't challenged by Republicans at all. At least for the time being.

Com1	Democrat			Republican		
2012	**Jack Buell**	**2,925**	**100.00%**	-	**-**	**-**
2008	Jack Buell	3,068	100.00%	-	0	0.00%
2006	Jack Buell	2,230	100.00%	-	0	0.00%
2002	Jack Buell	2,269	69.30%	Stan Pugh	1,007	30.70%
Com2	Democrat			Republican		
2010	Christina Crawford	892	30.00%	Philip Lampert	2,080	70.00%
2008	Terry Doupe	2,931	100.00%	-	0	0.00%
2004	Terry Doupe	1,988	50.27%	Russell Lowry	1,254	31.71%
2002	Dave Johnson	2,078	66.40%	Phil Sergent	1,050	33.60%
Com3	Democrat			Republican		
2012	**Bud McCall**	**2,426**	**64.20%**	**Thomas Howard**	**1,351**	**35.80%**
2010	Bud McCall	2,346	100.00%	-	0	0.00%
2006	Bud McCall	2,250	100.00%	-	0	0.00%
2004	Bud McCall	3,172	100.00%	-	0	0.00%

Clerk	Democrat		Republican	
2010	Michele Reynolds	100.00%	-	0.00%
2006	Michele Reynolds	100.00%	-	0.00%
2002	Kay Sather	100.00%	-	0.00%
Treasurer	Democrat		Republican	
2010	Sara Renner	53.10%	Maria Sergent	46.90%
2006	Sara Renner	100.00%	-	0.00%

	Democrat		Republican	
2002	Janice Weinmann	100.00%	-	0.00%
Assessor	**Democrat**		**Republican**	
2010	Teresa Jeffrey	43.90%	Donna Spier	56.10%
2006	Teresa Jeffrey	100.00%	-	0.00%
2002	Teresa Jeffrey	52.50%	Kathy Tweedy	47.50%
Coroner	**Democrat**		**Republican**	
2010	Ronald Hodge	100.00%	-	0.00%
2006	Ronald Hodge	100.00%	-	0.00%
2002	Ronald Hodge	100.00%	-	0.00%
Sheriff	**Democrat**		**Republican**	
2012	**Rick O'Donnell**	**39.40%**	**Dave Resser**	**55.90%**
2008	Robert Kirts	53.66%	Robert Loe	46.34%
2004	Robert Kirts	52.85%	Robert Loe	46.34%
Pros Atty	**Democrat**		**Republican**	
2012	**Douglas Payne***	**100.00%**		
2008	Douglas Payne	100.00%	-	0.00%
2004	Douglas Payne	100.00%	-	0.00%

*In 2012, Douglas Payne was on the ballot as an independent, though he previously had run as a Democrat.

BINGHAM

AREA Communities:
Blackfoot, Shelley,
Aberdeen, Firth, Springfield,
Fort Hall, Moreland, Atomic
City, Basalt. 2,183 sq. mi.

POPULATION 45,607
(7th). Increase 00s:
9.3%. Minority: 25.1%.
Hispanic: 17.2%.

Much more to ponder here than the recent surface readings. Specifically: How did Bingham move from nearly competitive to one-party so swiftly in the mid-90s? Once Democrat Larry EchoHawk's run for governor – he won Bingham County in 1994 – the bottom fell out for Democrats. Since then, no major-office Democrat (even Richard Stallings, who once won here routinely) has won as many as 5,000 votes, while Republican totals have not fallen below 7,600 and routinely pass the 8,500 mark, and up to 12,000 (George W. Bush in 2004, which improved his 2000 mark by 2K+ votes).

But this is a recent phenomenon.

On the presidential level, Republicans have had a clean run of wins here going back more than half a century, and that no Democratic presidential candidate has cracked 5,000 votes since Johnson in 1964 (and even he narrowly lost). But up to 1994, Bingham was very much a competitive county where in-state Democrats were concerned. Cecil Andrus won all four of his gubernatorial runs here, and Frank Church fared well too. Beyond that, though, take a look at the very close races Democrats have run in Bingham (not all of them close statewide): Senate 1990 and 1986, governor 1982. (Governor 1978 was an oddity because favorite son Allan Larsen was on the ballot.) But the voting through this period was variable by race; if a party fielded a relatively weak campaign, Bingham would let them know it. On either side. And on the legislative and county level, both parties were well represented through the 60s and 70s.

And then the Democratic votes dried up. Through the 80s and early 90s, a strong Democratic campaign could figure on pulling 6,500 to 7,500 votes in Bingham, not always enough to win but enough to be competitive. After EchoHawk, 2,000 to 3,000 of those votes stopped coming, not just for the marginal Democratic races but for the substantial ones with substantial candidates as well. On the Republican side, the GOP vote increased a bit – maybe by about 1,000 votes – but no more than that. But the combination in Bingham was devastating. In the last decade, campaigns went from competitive to routine 3-1 Republican wins.

The reasons are not obvious. The county's population has remained largely stable; there have been no major migrational changes. Throughout recent decades, Bingham has been a food processing and farming county, oriented around potatoes, and little has changed. Ballots case and total votes for president, among other measures, have remained about the same.

One possibility is that, increasingly, more voters started taking their cues from the national and presidential campaigns, and started voting more straight party-line, rather than differentiating by race. In 2002, for example,

171

almost all of the Democratic candidates up and down the ballot fell within a few hundred votes of 3,500.

PRECINCTS (27) It almost sounds like a trick question or statement: One of very Republican Bingham's precincts is the fourth most Democratic precinct in Idaho. That is its most unusual: Fort Hall, the location of the headquarters town of the reservation and home to most of the reservation's tribal members. It long has voted Democratic, and continues to. In relative terms, the city of Blackfoot's six precincts are the next most Democratic, but that means they're occasionally competitive, and more often just a little less overwhelmingly Republican than the rest of the county. The more rural farm precincts and smaller cities are all heavily Republican, with the Springfield and Sterling area statistically most strongly so.

PRESIDENTIAL At the presidential level, Bingham is very solidly Republican, a red county for a very long time; Harry Truman in 1948 was the last Democratic nominee to win its vote.

	Dem	%	Rep	%	Total
2012	3,822	21.71%	13,440	76.35%	17,603
2008	4,424	25.79%	12,230	71.29%	17,155
2004	3,605	21.76%	12,734	76.88%	16,564
2000	3,310	22.99%	10,628	73.82%	14,397

GOVERNOR Bingham has been a little more flexible toward Democratic gubernatorial candidates, voting for Andrus in 1990, 1974 and 1970, and Larry EchoHawk (with his strong ties to the Fort Hall Reservation) in 1994. The general rule, however, has been strong Republican support in Bingham.

	Dem	%	Rep	%	Total
2010	4,202	35.30%	6,786	57.00%	11,905
2006	4,801	40.55%	7,387	62.38%	11,841
2002	4,389	35.66%	7,659	62.23%	12,307

COUNTY In decades past, county elections in Bingham were often closely competitive, but not in the new millennium. The office of coroner, oddly, is the only office contested on general election ballots in the last decade, though there have been a few primary contests.

Com1	Democrat			Republican		
2012	-		-	- Mark Bair	**13,971**	**93.00%**
2008	-	0	0.00%	Cleone Jolley	12,613	100.00%
2006	-	0	0.00%	Cleone Jolley	11,037	100.00%
2002	-	0	0.00%	Cleone Jolley	10,700	100.00%
Com2	**Democrat**			**Republican**		
2010	-	0	0.00%	Whitney Manwaring	10,079	100.00%
2008	-	0	0.00%	Donavan Harrington	10,758	80.24%
2004	-	0	0.00%	Wayne Brower	14,189	100.00%
2002	-	0	0.00%	Wayne Brower	10,672	100.00%

Com3	Democrat			Republican		
2012	-		-	- Ladd Carter	14,526	100.00%
2010	-	0	0.00%	Ladd Carter	10,068	100.00%
2006	-	0	0.00%	Errol Covington	10,980	100.00%
2004	-	0	0.00%	Errol Covington	13,709	100.00%

Clerk	Democrat		Republican	
2010	-	0.00%	Sara Staub	100.00%
2006	-	0.00%	Sara Staub	100.00%
2002	-	0.00%	Sara Staub	100.00%
Treasurer	Democrat		Republican	
2010	-	0.00%	Janice Lawes	100.00%
2006	-	0.00%	Janice Lawes	100.00%
2002	-	0.00%	Janice Lawes	100.00%
Assessor	Democrat		Republican	
2010	-	0.00%	Ronald Simmons	100.00%
2006	-	0.00%	Ronald Simmons	100.00%
2002	-	0.00%	Ronald Simmons	100.00%
Coroner	Democrat		Republican	
2010	Glen Capson	23.60%	Mike Gardner	76.40%
2006	-	0.00%	Kyle Lindsay	100.00%
2002	Ren Hill	30.20%	Kyle Lindsay	69.80%
Sheriff	Democrat		Republican	
2012	-	-	Craig Rowland	100.00%
2008	-	0.00%	Dave Johnson*	50.84%
2004	-	0.00%	Dave Johnson	100.00%
Pros Atty	Democrat		Republican	
2012	-	-	Cleve Colson	100.00%
2008	-	0.00%	Scott Andrew	100.00%
2004	-	0.00%	Scott Andrew	100.00%

*Defeating two other candidates, an independent and a write-in.

BLAINE

AREA Communities: Hailey, Ketchum, Bellevue, Carey. 2,655 sq. mi.

POPULATION 21,236 (17th). Increase 00s: 12.6%. Minority: 22.0%. Hispanic: 20.0%.

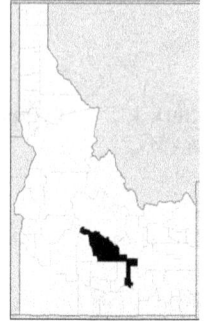

Blaine, now Idaho's most Democratic county, stands out so distinctly that former Senator Larry Craig joked about it not being part of his representational territory. But it is not and never has been a solidly Democratic county in the same sense that two dozen or more counties in Idaho are solidly Republican. In 2004 and 2000 it was the only Idaho county to vote for the Democratic nominee for president, and in 1996 just one of four. (That, together with the votes for state legislature, is enough to qualify it as "most Democratic.") But the numbers do not make Blaine a good counterpart to, say, Madison or Franklin counties on the Republican side. In 2004, John Kerry failed to hit the 60% landslide mark George W. Bush hit in so many Idaho counties, and in 2000 Al Gore on with the commanding percentage of 51.5%. Republicans won in U.S. Senate races in 1998 and 2004; in 2002 the Democrat was favorite son Alan Blinken.

There is also the matter of the courthouse, where Democrats have only recently established a general dominance. Even then: In 2004 the county re-elected a Republican sheriff, and in 2002 a county treasurer (unopposed). Compare that to the many counties with complete Republican sweeps at the courthouse.

Competitive politics are not new to Blaine. It voted for Kennedy and Johnson in 1960 and 1964, and periodically elected Democrats to the legislature years before John Peavey launched the more recent organization after his party conversion in the mid-80s.

There is this to be said for it: Over the long haul, Blaine clearly has been trending Democratic. In a kind of mirror image of some other traditionally competitive counties (Bingham, for example), Blaine voters increasingly seem to be following the lead of their presidential votes – Democrat from 1992 on – and voting straight ticket.

The numbers of Democratic voters compared to Republicans remained relatively static until the 80s, but since have taken off. The presidential vote in 2004 set new mars for both parties. The local Republicans exceeded their previous best vote total by 10%; but the Democrats exceeded theirs by a third. If they can keep it up, Blaine, while not hitherto entirely out of reach for Republicans, could rapidly become so.

Change in Blaine has not been hard to explain. Pre-1940, it was a traditional ranching, timber and mining county, not greatly different from Custer. That changed with the arrival of Sun Valley, and the development of a mass recreation and resort culture, a very different kind of politics set in. The growth has been massive, averaging around 50% increase in population per decade since 1970. This is a rare exception in Idaho to the general rule that immigrants have brought generally conservative politics with them. The parts of the county which have been least changed by that culture – such as around Carey – have remained competitive or in some cases Republican.

PRECINCTS (15) Yale precinct, which includes the remote southeast dogleg of Blaine County and no actual communities at all, was the 14th most Republican precinct in Idaho in 2010, and for decades has ranked among the highest. But it is an outlier. There are two other Republican precincts left here (Carey and Gannett-Picabo, both in the southeast), and the rest in the Wood River Valley are all strongly Democratic. Hailey and Ketchum (especially Hailey 1 and 2, and NW and SW Ketchum) are both among the most Democratic spots in the state, among the few communities to reject Crapo and Otter both in 2010, and not by close margins. The city and precinct of Sun Valley, ironically, is actually more competitive.

PRESIDENTIAL Up to 1992, Blaine's pattern was Idaho normal: Republican in the elections from 1968 to 1988, Democratic in the 1964 landslide. But starting in 1992, it went Democratic, and has stayed blue ever since. The margins were modest through 2000, but by 2008 had moved into landslide territory.

	Dem	%	Rep	%	Total
2012	5,992	58.78%	3,939	38.64%	10,194
2008	6,947	65.72%	3,439	32.53%	10,571
2004	5,992	59.06%	4,034	39.76%	10,146
2000	3,748	47.87%	3,528	45.06%	7,829

GOVERNOR The road to Democratic voting for presidents was paved by Democratic votes for governors. That began with the Democratic (Andrus) landslide of 1974, but has continued solidly ever since. That held even in elections like 1998, when the Democrat lost statewide in a landslide.

	Dem	%	Rep	%	Total
2010	3,843	57.92%	2,516	37.92%	6,635
2006	5,123	77.47%	2,061	31.17%	6,613
2002	3,403	54.22%	2,693	42.91%	6,276

COUNTY Blaine has long had a partisan mix at the courthouse, and periodic competitive races. In the last decade, its commission has moved to a wholly Democratic cast, and the Republican who twice ran for one of the seats lost in landslides each time. Among department heads, Republicans have had somewhat better luck, though the trend toward a Democratic courthouse overall seems in place.

Com1	Democrat			Republican		
2012	**Larry Schoen**	**7,758**	**100.00%**	-	-	-
2008	Larry Schoen	6,355	63.34%	Dale Ewerson	3,678	36.66%
2006	Larry Schoen	4,432	61.69%	Dale Ewerson	2,752	38.31%
2002	Dennis Wright	4,858	100.00%	-	0	0.00%
Com2	Democrat			Republican		

2010	Tom Bowman	5,032	100.00%	-	0	0.00%
2008	Tom Bowman	8,224	100.00%	-	0	0.00%
2004	Tom Bowman	7,480	100.00%	-	0	0.00%
2002	Mary Ann Mix	4,830	100.00%	-	0	0.00%
Com3	**Democrat**			**Republican**		
2012	**Angenie McCleary**	**6,829**	**75.10%**	-	**-**	**-**
2010	Angenie McCleary	4,497	75.20%	-	0	0.00%
2006	Sarah Michael	4,472	64.31%	-	0	0.00%
2004	Sarah Michael	7,203	100.00%	-	0	0.00%

Clerk	**Democrat**		**Republican**	
2010	JoLynn Drage	100.00%	-	0.00%
2006	JoLynn Drage	100.00%	-	0.00%
2002	Marsha Reimann	100.00%	-	0.00%
Treasurer	**Democrat**		**Republican**	
2010	-	0.00%	Vicki Dick	100.00%
2006	-	0.00%	Vicki Dick	100.00%
2002	-	0.00%	Vicki Dick	100.00%
Assessor	**Democrat**		**Republican**	
2010	Valdi Pace	100.00%	-	0.00%
2006	Valdi Pace	100.00%	-	0.00%
2002	Valdi Pace	68.50%	Walter Cochran	31.50%
Coroner	**Democrat**		**Republican**	
2010	Russell Mikel	100.00%	-	0.00%
2006	Russell Mikel	100.00%	-	0.00%
2002	Russell Mikel	100.00%	-	0.00%
Sheriff	**Democrat**		**Republican**	
2014	-		**- Gene Ramsey**	**51.90%**
2008	-	0.00%	Walt Femling*	64.50%
2004	Jeff Gunter	45.25%	Walt Femling	54.75%
Pros Atty	**Democrat**		**Republican**	
2008	Jim Thomas	100.00%	-	0.00%
2004	Jim Thomas	100.00%	-	0.00%

*Defeated independent Steve England.

BOISE

AREA Communities: Horseshoe Bend, Idaho City, Placerville, Crouch. 1,908 sq. mi.

POPULATION 7,028 (34th). Increase 00s: 5.4%. Minority: 6.8%. Hispanic: 3.5%.

Rural Boise County, next door to Ada and increasingly popular as a rural housing region, has increased its population about six fold since 1960. That increase has resulted in higher balloting numbers for both parties, but not evenly. The Democrats have more than doubled their typical vote totals from 1960 to 2004, but that has put them at a steadily greater disadvantage, since the Republican numbers have been growing much faster: In the same four decades, Republican vote totals have increased more than five-fold – 500%. So, from Nixon's 456 votes in 1960, Bush received 2,501 in 2004.

How has that translated? In the 60s, a generally strong-running Democrat could expect to received more than 400 votes, often 450 or so, and that was occasionally enough to win. (Johnson won for president here in 1964, the last Democrat to do so.) In the 70s that number might rise to 600 or so, but that was now routinely less than Republican would get. By 2000, the top Democratic contenders were still held below 1,000 votes, while the Republican base had continued to expand, and Republican candidates could get 2,000 or more. Democrats have lost the population race here.

PRECINCTS (6) All the Boise County precincts are Republican. The Idaho City precinct leaned Democratic for many decades, but now leans Republican and is the closest to competitive of the six. Garden Valley, Horseshoe Bend and Lowman are substantially more Republican.

PRESIDENTIAL Typical among Republican-leaning counties in Idaho, Boise has not voted for a Democrat for president since 1964.

	Dem	*%*	*Rep*	*%*	*Total*
2012	1,053	30.57%	2,284	66.30%	3,445
2008	1,240	32.87%	2,433	64.48%	3,773
2004	970	27.50%	2,501	70.91%	3,527
2000	745	24.63%	2,019	66.74%	3,025

GOVERNOR Republicans have had the run since 1990, when Boise joined the Andrus landslide. But notice the peculiar numbers in the last few cycles. The Republican numbers have been rising steadily, along with the population. Democratic numbers nearly held fro 2002 to 2006, but collapsed in 2010.

	Dem	*%*	*Rep*	*%*	*Total*
2010	717	25.95%	1,756	63.55%	2,763

| 2006 | 1,132 | 41.21% | 1,626 | 59.19% | 2,747 |
| 2002 | 1,184 | 44.36% | 1,394 | 52.23% | 2,669 |

COUNTY Boise County usually has had two or three Democrats in its courthouse – they have not been completely unrepresented. Those numbers have gradually diminished, however, since the early 90s. The trend has been toward ever-wider Republican margins over time, in a county that gently leaned Republican even in 1960.

Com1	Democrat			Republican		
2012	-	-	-	**Barbara Balding**	**2,637**	**100.00%**
2008	-	0	0.00%	Terry Day	2,993	100.00%
2006	-	0	0.00%	Terry Day	2,455	100.00%
2002	-	0	0.00%	Roger Jackson	2,023	100.00%
Com2	Democrat			Republican		
2010	-	0	0.00%	Jamie Anderson	2,154	97.20%
2008	Greg Simione	1,379	38.66%	Jamie Anderson	2,188	61.34%
2004	-	0	0.00%	Fred Lawson	2,411	100.00%
2002	-	0	0.00%	Fred Lawson	1,475	60.40%
Com3	Democrat			Republican		
2012	-	-	-	**Vicki Wilkins**	**2,639**	**100.00%**
2010	-	0	0.00%	Robert Fry	2,219	100.00%
2006	-	0	0.00%	Linda Zimmer	2,272	93.27%
2004	-	0	0.00%	Paul Stutzman	2,188	79.05%

Clerk	Democrat		Republican	
2010	-	0.00%	Mary Prisco	100.00%
2006	-	0.00%	Constance Swearingen*	53.98%
Treasurer	Democrat		Republican	
2010	-	0.00%	April Hutchings	100.00%
2006	-	0.00%	Barbara Balding	100.00%
Assessor	Democrat		Republican	
2010	-	0.00%	Brent Adamson	100.00%
2006	Linda Blough	46.56%	Brent Adamson	53.44%
Coroner	Democrat		Republican	
2010	-	0.00%	Pamela Garlock	100.00%
2006	-	0.00%	Pamela Garlock	100.00%
Sheriff	Democrat		Republican	
2012	-	-	**Ben Roeber**	**100.00%**
2008	-	0.00%	Ben Roeber	100.00%
2004	-	0.00%	Drew Bodie**	42.75%
Pros Atty	Democrat		Republican	
2012	-	-	**Ian W. Gee**	**100.00%**
2008	Ron Twilegar	100.00%	-	0.00%
2004	-	0.00%	Theresa Gardunia	100.00%

*Defeated independent Kerri Pattee Krosch.
** Plurality win; defeated an independent and a write-in.

BONNER

AREA Communities: Sandpoint, Priest River, Clark Fork, Hope, Ponderay, East Hope, Oldtown, Sagle, Dover. 1,918 sq. mi.

POPULATION 40,877 (8th). Increase 00s: 11%. Minority: 5.6%. Hispanic: 2.2%.

Bonner is one of those formerly Democratic north Idaho counties which has gone over to Republican domination – though reality here is a little more complex. This is one of the most politically dynamic counties in Idaho, and one of the most difficult to pigeon-hole.

It has grown substantially – more than doubled in size from 1960 to the millennium – but not steadily; in the 60s Bonner actually lost population. It grew by more than half in the 70s, however; slowed to a walk in the 80s; then ramped up in the 90s again, adding nearly half again its population. Before all this, in the 50s and prior to, Bonner was a Democratic-leaning county which elected Republicans with some regularity. On the presidential level, it generally voted Republican – though it did go for Kennedy in 1960, Johnson in 1964 and Clinton in 1992 – but below that it was much more mixed. Its courthouse had almost always been a mixed bag; if it consistently registered as mixed, that is not because of stability, because voters routinely have tossed out incumbents in favor of the other party – and that has continued to the present day. If in some respects there's a circusy aspect to it, there is also this: People in the county respond directly to what their local elected officials do, and do hold them accountable.

On the legislative and state levels (less so – rarely – on the congressional), Democrats long enjoyed a slight edge here through the 80s, suggesting that the big influx in the 70s did not dramatically change the partisan balance the way it did in Kootenai or Ada. The 90s influx, however, seems another matter. The long Democratic grip on the legislative seats here vanished in the 90s, and the Democratic vote for major offices – not just president – stagnated. Both sides shot to new highs in the 2004 voting, but the Republican depth was much greater: The once-clear Democratic edge had vanished, and Republicans could now typically expect to lead Democrats with about 50% more of the vote (often around 60-40).

PRECINCTS (35) The central Sandpoint precinct (25) is Democratic, though not by a large margin. A half-dozen others – Washington (at Sandpoint), Hope, Priest Lake, Humbird, Baldy – mostly on the water, can be considered marginal though usually Republican-leaning. The rest, from Oldtown on the west to Clark Fork on the east, are definably Republican, in a number of cases (including those two) a transition from a generation ago. Regionally, the area of Bonner south of Lake Pend Oreille probably is the most Republican part of the county.

PRESIDENTIAL Republican as noted, though it crossed over in 1992 (the Perot factor was doubtless important); it last went Democratic before that in 1964.

	Dem	%	Rep	%	Total
2012	6,500	35.07%	11,367	61.32%	18,536
2008	7,840	40.11%	11,145	57.02%	19,547
2004	6,649	37.61%	10,697	60.50%	17,681
2000	4,318	29.90%	8,945	61.95%	14,440

GOVERNOR Democrats running for governor did fairly well in Bonner for many years. Bonner loyally supported favorite son Republican Don Samuelson in 1970 and 1966, but after that stuck with Cecil Andrus and John Evans, and then in 1994 Larry EchoHawk, even amid the general Republican tide of that year. That was the end, though; Bonner has gone Republican for governor since.

	Dem	%	Rep	%	Total
2010	4,297	30.61%	8,742	62.28%	14,036
2006	6,505	46.96%	6,933	50.05%	13,851
2002	4,932	44.89%	5,797	52.76%	10,988

COUNTY The trend at the courthouse has been Republican, but the line in that direction has been jagged, not smooth. Democrats last elected a predominantly Democratic courthouse in 1978. For the quarter-century after that, control of various offices shifted and swung, and hotly contested races were frequent. Then in the mid-90s Republicans began winning with more consistency. (For an instructive example, look at the Commissioner 2 races of Democrat Brian Orr, his party's nominee four times in the last decade.) The Democratic mainstay at this point has been Clerk Marie Scott, who also has had close elections.

Com1	Democrat		%	Republican		%
2012	-	-	-	Joyce Broadsword	11,110	65.20%
2008	Todd Crossett	8,747	47.55%	Cornel Rasor	9,643	52.42%
2006	Todd Crossett	8,476	64.55%	Bud Mueller	4,654	35.45%
2002	Wayne Benner	5,194	48.50%	Marcia Phillips	5,519	51.50%
Com2	Democrat			Republican		
2010	Brian Orr	4,865	35.50%	Mike Nielsen	8,837	64.50%
2008	Brian Orr	7,951	43.54%	Joe Young	10,311	56.46%
2004	Brian Orr	7,521	45.44%	Joe Young	7,882	47.62%
2002	Brian Orr	5,126	47.80%	Larry Allen	4,359	40.70%
Com3	Democrat			Republican		
2012	-	-	-	Cary Kelly	13,493	100.00%
2010	Mel Davis	4,914	36.30%	Lewie Rich	8,631	63.70%
2006	-	0	0.00%	Lewis Rich	5,970	46.52%
2004	Dale Van Stone	6,939	41.90%	Karl Dye	8,120	49.03%

Clerk	Democrat		Republican		
2010	Marie Scott	54.20%	Bud Mueller		45.80%

2006	Marie Scott	51.02%	Kathrynn Feist	45.60%
2002	Marie Scott	48.50%	Kathrynn Feist	45.60%
Treasurer	**Democrat**		**Republican**	
2010	-	0.00%	Cheryl Piehl	100.00%
2006	-	0.00%	Cheryl Piehl	100.00%
2002	Howard Faux	34.80%	Cheryl Piehl	65.20%
Assessor	**Democrat**		**Republican**	
2010	-	0.00%	Jerry Clemons	100.00%
2006	Judie Conlan	41.71%	Jerry Clemons	48.12%
2004	Judie Conlan	51.48%	Steven Carter	48.52%
2002	James Boatwright	54.70%	Tom Sykes	45.30%
Coroner	**Democrat**		**Republican**	
2010	-	0.00%	Kitt Rose	100.00%
2006	-	0.00%	Kitt Rose	100.00%
2002	-	0.00%	Kitt Rose	100.00%
Sheriff	**Democrat**		**Republican**	
2012	-	-	**Daryl Wheeler**	**73.90%**
2008	Larry Hanna	29.24%	Daryl Wheeler	70.76%
2004	Tony Lamanna	38.32%	Elaine Savage	38.53%
Pros Atty	**Democrat**		**Republican**	
2012	-	-	**Louis Marshall**	**48.20%**
2008	-	0.00%	Louis Marshall	100.00%
2004	-	0.00%	Phil Robinson	100.00%

BONNEVILLE

AREA Communities:
Idaho Falls, Ammon,
Iona, Uncon, Irwin, Swan
Valley. 1,897 sq. mi.

POPULATION 104,234
(4th). Increase 00s:
26.3%. Minority: 14.7%.
Hispanic: 11.4%.

You have to go back a long way to track substantial
Democratic support in Bonneville County (whose largest
city, Idaho Falls, had from 1993 to 2005 a Democrat –
on a nonpartisan ballot – as mayor). The pieces of
Democratic support would seem to be there: A large
federal installation, substantial labor union presence,
among other things. But, though other counties outrank for sheer one-
sidedness, Bonneville is clearly Republican. The last Democrat elected to
the legislature from this area was Richard Egbert, a conservative Tetonia
rancher whose tenure in the legislature went back deep into the days when
he represented just Teton County; no Democratic House members have
been elected here since 1976. Bonneville has elected just one Democrat
(Edith Stanger) to the county commission in decades. It has voted all-
Republican for president since the late New Deal era. It almost always
supports Republicans for major office, exceptions including the 1990 Cecil
Andrus run for governor and a couple of Richard Stallings' re-elections to
the U.S. House.

In terms of raw partisan results, the county has been mostly static since
the late 50s and almost completely static since the late 70s, except that the
all-Republican tendency solidified still further in the 90s. Taken in the
aggregative, Republican margins have increased gradually over the last
half-century.

And what about raw numbers? Bonneville's population has increased by
just under 50% in the last four decades, but Republican votes have tended
to rise faster, Democratic votes slower. Indicative: The all-time record for
most votes for a Democratic presidential candidate in Bonneville County –
and he still lost here – was Lyndon Johnson in 1964, with 9,637 votes. No
Democrat has ever cracked 10,000 running for that office; from 1960
onward, no Republican running for president has ever gotten less than that
amount.

PRECINCTS (55) Generally, the most competitive part of Bonneville
County is (as you'd expect) central Idaho Falls, notably in the near-
downtown area around precincts 7 through 15. Bonneville's four least
Republican precincts (12, 8, 9 and 11) are among them. These might be
considered Democratic in some years; in 2010, they could be called only
competitive. With the limited exception of another precinct or two
(debatably, 19 and 21), everything else is solidly Republican. Ammon is
overall more Republican than Idaho Falls. That becomes ever truer the
smaller the community in the county, and the farther from Idaho Falls. The
most Republican precinct is 57 (formerly called Jackknife), the large rural

eastern end of the county, where non-Republicans only occasionally get any votes at all.

PRESIDENTIAL Bonneville isn't much competitive at all, and certainly not at the top of the ticket. It is overwhelmingly Republican there now, and last went for a Democrat in 1948.

	Dem	%	Rep	%	Total
2012	9,903	22.92%	32,276	74.69%	43,213
2008	11,417	27.38%	29,334	70.34%	41,703
2004	8,356	21.50%	30,048	77.30%	38,871
2000	7,235	21.65%	24,988	74.78%	33,415

GOVERNOR With the exceptions of the 1990 and 1974 Cecil Andrus landslide, Bonneville has supported Republicans for governor for many decades.

	Dem	%	Rep	%	Total
2010	11,438	38.84%	16,204	55.03%	29,448
2006	12,447	42.55%	16,900	57.78%	29,250
2002	10,380	36.45%	17,520	61.52%	28,480

COUNTY Democrats have mounted serious challenges to Republicans at the courthouse level in recent decades, but hardly ever have won. The last (and at the time the first in decades) was Edith Stanger, elected to the commission in 1990 (then ran for secretary of state in 1994). No Democrat has cracked 40% of the vote for a county office since.

Com1	Democrat			Republican		
2012	-		-	- **Roger Christensen**	**33,536**	**100.00%**
2008	-	0	0.00%	Roger Christensen	31,841	100.00%
2006	-	0	0.00%	Roger Christensen	24,320	100.00%
2002	Claire Heckathorne	8,200	29.70%	Roger Christensen	19,390	70.30%
Com2	**Democrat**			**Republican**		
2010	-	0	0.00%	Dave Radford	23,594	100.00%
2008	-	0	0.00%	Dave Radford	31,199	100.00%
2004	Ellie Hampton	12,310	33.17%	Dave Radford	24,806	66.83%
2002	Andrea Poppleton	8,581	31.50%	Dave Radford	18,672	68.50%
Com3	**Democrat**			**Republican**		
2012	-		-	- **Lee Staker**	**32,458**	**100.00%**
2010	-	0	0.00%	Lee Staker	23,165	100.00%
2006	-	0	0.00%	Lee Staker	23,783	100.00%
2004	-	0	0.00%	Lee Staker	30,161	100.00%

Clerk	Democrat		Republican	
2010	-	0.00%	Ron Longmore	100.00%
2006	-	0.00%	Ron Longmore	100.00%
2002	John McGimpsey	26.70%	Ron Longmore	73.30%
Treasurer	**Democrat**		**Republican**	

	Democrat			Republican	
2010	-		0.00%	Mark Hansen	100.00%
2006	-		0.00%	Mark Hansen	100.00%
2002	Shirley Gooden		31.80%	Mark Hansen	68.20%
Assessor	**Democrat**			**Republican**	
2010	-		0.00%	Blake Mueller	100.00%
2006	-		0.00%	Blake Mueller	100.00%
2002	Mary Ann Smith		32.20%	Blake Mueller	67.80%
Coroner	**Democrat**			**Republican**	
2010	-		0.00%	Jonathan Walker	100.00%
2006	-		0.00%	Jonathan Walker	100.00%
2002	Madeline Worrell		33.20%	Jonathan Walker	66.80%
Sheriff	**Democrat**			**Republican**	
Jim Tibbs		**108,040**	**64.10%**	**Jim Tibbs**	**108,040**
2008	Luan Cook		27.41%	Paul Wilde	72.57%
2004	-		0.00%	Byron Stommel	100.00%
Pros Atty	**Democrat**			**Republican**	
2012	**-**		**-**	**Bruce Pickett**	**100.00%**
2008	-		0.00%	Dane Watkins	100.00%
2004	-		0.00%	Dane Watkins	100.00%
2002	Victor Bunitsky		36.60%	Dane Watkins	63.40%

BOUNDARY

AREA Communities:
Bonners Ferry, Moyie
Springs, Porthill,
Eastport. 1,277 sq. mi.

POPULATION 10,972
(26th). Increase 00s:
11.2%. Minority: 7.9%.
Hispanic: 3.7%.

The county named for its location next to an
international border – and there are two border
crossings located here – Boundary is a place mainly of
timber and farming. If Bonners Ferry has something of a
transportation emphasis, this is overall a rural county.

Boundary County's case is a little different than some
of the other counties which switched from Democratic to
Republican dominance – as, clearly, it did after 1992. (The strongest
indication is the change from a courthouse dominated by Democrats to one
dominated by Republicans, in just a few cycles.) In a number of other
counties, the change was marked by population increase and Democrats,
while generally holding on to their earlier voting base, failing to bring in
additional Democratic voters (or not enough) while Republicans pick up
most of the newcomers.

That evidently is not the whole story at Boundary. In 1980 Frank Church
set a major-office high for Democrats at 1,982 votes; no major-office
Democrat has come very close to that since (the closest being Cecil Andrus
in 1990 – but even he did not improve much on his 1986 number here, in
contrast to many counties). After 1990 Democratic votes for major offices
seldom rose above 1,100, and after 1994 they rarely reached 1,000. (The
2004 spike for John Kerry, at 1,268 votes, was unusually strong.) This
means the Democratic vote has seen a raw decline.

Republicans have benefited, in addition to that, to – as per usual in
Idaho – picking up most of the votes from newcomers. The Republican
presidential vote has in fact grown slightly faster that the increase in
population overall.

PRECINCTS (7) The Bonners Ferry precinct is the closest to
competitive, but not by much; all of these precincts vote similarly
Republican. Moyie Springs may be marginally the most Republican.

PRESIDENTIAL Like so many other counties that would vote
Democratic in Idaho races, Boundary was solidly Republican on the
presidential, for a long time. It was among those last to vote for a
Democratic president in 1964. The closest call since has been in 1992,
because of the Perot draw-off of Republican votes.

	Dem	*%*	*Rep*	*%*	*Total*
2012	1,225	26.96%	3,138	69.06%	4,544
2008	1,484	31.35%	3,078	65.03%	4,733
2004	1,268	28.96%	3,012	68.80%	4,378
2000	832	21.55%	2,797	72.44%	3,861

GOVERNOR Up through 1990, Boundary was a mostly-reliable Democratic vote for governor (breaking mainly to support Panhandle neighbor Don Samuelson in 1970 and 1966. It has become no less reliably Republican since 1990, however.

	Dem		%	Rep	%	Total
2010		892	25.13%	2,381	67.09%	3,549
2006		1,279	36.73%	1,781	51.15%	3,482
2002		941	33.84%	1,766	63.50%	2,781

COUNTY Before the 90s, the Boundary courthouse was often deeply split between the parties, and before 1980, mostly Democratic-dominated. But especially since 1994, it has become strongly dominated by Republicans.

Com1	Democrat		%	Republican		%
2012	-	-	-	**Lee Pinkerton**	3,469	**100.00%**
2008	Jerry Pavia	1,409	30.46%	Ron Smith	3,216	69.54%
2006	-	0	0.00%	Ron Smith	2,382	100.00%
2002	-	0	0.00%	Ron Smith	1,919	88.20%
Com2	**Democrat**			**Republican**		
2010	Orrin Everhart	1,507	42.80%	Walt Kirby	1,698	48.20%
2008	John O'Connor	1,633	35.29%	Walt Kirby	2,704	58.44%
2004	-	0	0.00%	Walt Kirby	3,245	100.00%
2002	-	0	0.00%	Walt Kirby	2,089	100.00%
Com3	**Democrat**			**Republican**		
2012	-	-	-	**Dan Dinning**	3,479	**100.00%**
2010	-	0	0.00%	Dan Dinning	2,099	60.80%
2006	-	0	0.00%	Dan Dinning	2,368	100.00%
2004	-	-	-	Dan Dinning	3,280	100.00%

Clerk	Democrat	%	Republican	%
2010	-	0.00%	Glenda Poston	100.00%
2006	-	0.00%	Glenda Poston	100.00%
2004	Glenda Poston	61.84%	Dolores Sweet	38.16%
2002	Diane Cartwright	100.00%	-	0.00%
Treasurer	**Democrat**		**Republican**	
2010	-	0.00%	Jenny Fessler	100.00%
2006	John Sanders	24.07%	Jenny Fessler	75.93%
2002	Wilma DeVore	100.00%	-	0.00%
Assessor	**Democrat**		**Republican**	
2010	-	0.00%	David Ryals	80.40%
2006	-	0.00%	David Ryals	100.00%
2002	-	0.00%	David Ryals	100.00%
Coroner	**Democrat**		**Republican**	
2010	Mick Mellett	100.00%	-	0.00%
2006	Mick Mellett	100.00%	-	0.00%

2002	Mick Mellett	100.00% -		0.00%
Sheriff	**Democrat**		**Republican**	
2012	-	-	**Greg Sprungl**	57.00%
2008	-	0.00%	Greg Sprungl	63.84%
2004	Kevin McDonald	27.62%	Greg Sprungl	55.67%
Pros Atty	**Democrat**		**Republican**	
2012	-	-	**Jack Douglas**	**100.00%**
2008	-	0.00%	Jack Douglas	100.00%
2004	-	0.00%	Jack Douglas	100.00%
2002	-	0.00%	Mark Jones	100.00%

BUTTE

AREA Communities: Arco, Butte City, Moore, Howe. 2,237 sq. mi.

POPULATION 2,891 (42nd). Increase 00s: -0.3%. Minority: 7.9%. Hispanic: 3.7%.

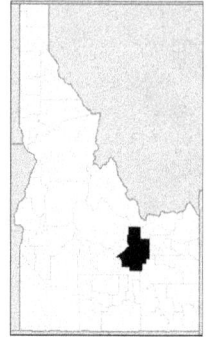

Butte County is one of the places they don't mean when they talk about "fast-growing Idaho" – its population was lower in 2000 than it was in 1960; when its first census was taken 1920, its population was almost exactly (just a shade lower than) where it was in 2000. It exploded a bit (up 28%) in the 50s, ramping up to about 3,500 because of construction at what is now the Idaho National Laboratory; that eased back during the next decade.

But Butte's voting patterns have changed. Small and remote, based mainly through the years (even now) on cattle ranching, Butte had a long tradition of bipartisanship, with moderate/conservative Democrats winning both locally and atop the ticket nearly as often as Republicans. It was a good national presidential bellwether county up to 1976, and even then gave Jimmy Carter a substantial vote, much better than most rural Idaho counties. Into the 80s the two parties closely contested Butte. (Consider 1986, when the four candidates for governor and U.S. Senate, Republicans and Democrats, each received between 768 and 793 votes, and the parties each scored a win in those races.) Into the early 90s the courthouse was bipartisan; there were Democrats around even in the most Republican parts of the 80s. As late as 1992 Democrat Richard Stallings beat Republican Dirk Kempthorne here 793-708.

Then came the 90s. With little change in overall population, Democrats now tended to lose 100 to 200 votes off their earlier norms, while Republicans picked up roughly comparable amounts. The result was that while races were often quite close (between similarly strong candidates and campaigns) in the 80s, were by the late 90s no longer close: 2-1 Republican wins had become commonplace.

PRECINCTS (4) All very Republican at super-landslide levels, with the two Arco precincts slightly less so. The other two, Moore and Howe, take in some very remote areas.

PRESIDENTIAL Since 1964 (and even in 1960 when it went for Kennedy), Butte has been strongly Republican in the presidential contests, often running 3-1 in recent cycles.

	Dem	%	Rep	%	Total
2012	258	20.06%	1,001	77.84%	1,286
2008	318	22.55%	1,056	74.89%	1,410
2004	321	22.83%	1,077	76.60%	1,406
2000	354	24.35%	1,054	72.49%	1,454

GOVERNOR The old-line conservative Democratic background in the county did give Democrats running for governor a shot here, with Andrus wins in 1974 and 1990 (his landslide years) and Evans in 1978 and 1982. Since 1990, Republicans have taken Butte easily.

	Dem	%	Rep	%	Total
2010	306	26.70%	724	63.18%	1,146
2006	402	35.20%	652	57.09%	1,142
2002	469	35.80%	814	62.14%	1,310

COUNTY Following its overall partisan picture, Butte split its courthouse deeply between the parties up to about 1980. Since then (except for the first half of the 90s, when several Democrats managed to win) it has been Republican dominated, and Democrats have only occasionally fielded candidates.

Com1	Democrat			Republican		
2012	-	-	-	**Seth Beal**	**1,105**	**100.00%**
2008	-	0	0.00%	Seth Beal	883	67.00%
2006	John Wanstrom	399	36.94%	Seth Beal	681	63.06%
2002	Steve Keller	545	41.70%	Seth Beal	761	58.30%
Com2	Democrat			Republican		
2010	-	0	0.00%	Kent Cummins	894	100.00%
2008	-	0	0.00%	Kent Cummins	680	48.71%
2004	-	0	0.00%	John Traughber	1,141	99.83%
2002	-	0	0.00%	John Traughber	1,007	80.70%
Com3	Democrat			Republican		
2012	-	-	-	**Brian Harrell**	**1,115**	**100.00%**
2010*	-	0	0.00%	Sandi Drussell	366	32.40%
2006	-	0	0.00%	Mark Stauffer	893	100.00%
2004	-	0	0.00%	Mark Stauffer	1,165	100.00%

*Unusually, the winner was an independent: Brian Harrell came in first (511 votes/45.3%), then Drussell, then Independent Ernie Tate (251/22.3%).

Clerk	Democrat		Republican	
2010	-	0.00%	Trilby McAfee*	56.20%
2006	-	0.00%	Trilby McAfee	100.00%
2002	-	0.00%	Trilby McAfee*	50.30%
Treasurer	Democrat		Republican	
2010	-	0.00%	Lori Beck	100.00%
2006	-	0.00%	Lori Beck	100.00%
2002	-	0.00%	Lori Beck	100.00%
Assessor	Democrat		Republican	
2010	-	0.00%	Laurie Gamett	100.00%
2006	-	0.00%	Laurie Gamett	100.00%
2002	-	0.00%	Laurie Gamett	100.00%
Coroner	Democrat		Republican	
2010**	-	0.00%	-	0.00%

	Democrat		Republican	
2006**	-	0.00%	-	-
2002	-	0.00%	Andy Andersen	100.00%
Sheriff	**Democrat**		**Republican**	
2012	-	-	**Wes Collins**	**100.00%**
2008	-	0.00%	Wes Collins	100.00%
2004	Wes Stewart	15.92%	Wes Collins	84.08%
Pros Atty	**Democrat**		**Republican**	
2012	-	-	**Steve Sephens**	**100.00%**
2008	-	0.00%	Steve Stephens	100.00%
2004	-	0.00%	Lary Sisson	100.00%

* McAfee won over write-ins in 2010 and 2002.
** Independent Chris Merrill won in 2010 and 2006.

CAMAS

AREA Communities: Fairfield, Corrall. 1,077 sq. mi.

POPULATION 1,117 (43rd). Increase 00s: 12.7%. Minority: 9.8%. Hispanic: 6.7%.

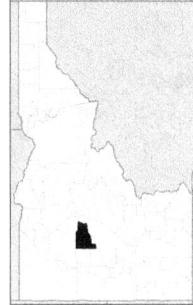

Idaho's second-smallest county, where in local politics personalities can matter. There is only one real community (or incorporated city), Fairfield; the few people who don't live there are widely scattered.

Camas is a small rural county where, as is the normal pattern, Republicans have gained standard super-majority status in the last couple of decades. But there is also this: It often has voted for the Democrats running in the area's legislative district, dominated by neighboring Blaine County.

Camas has become a residential growth area (a small one) for high-priced Blaine, but that has made little difference so far in its politics.

PRECINCTS (2) Virtually no partisan difference between the two precincts, one on the east side, one on the west side of Fairfield.

PRESIDENTIAL Consider the substantial 1960 win here by Democrat John Kennedy, and equally substantial loss here by landsliding Democrat Lyndon Johnson – one of the few counties in the country, surely (and one of only two in Idaho, Custer being the other), with such a pattern. In any event, this has been an easy carry for Republican presidential contenders ever since.

	Dem	%	Rep	%	Total
2012	159	27.51%	402	69.55%	578
2008	187	30.26%	422	68.28%	618
2004	139	23.36%	450	75.63%	595
2000	113	22.42%	359	71.23%	504

GOVERNOR The closeness of Blaine County has made little difference either on gubernatorial races here. Camas did vote for Andrus in his 1990 landslide, but other than that has gone Republican in every gubernatorial contest starting in 1986.

	Dem	%	Rep	%	Total
2010	103	22.79%	305	67.48%	452
2006	153	34.00%	272	60.44%	450
2002	136	33.58%	258	63.70%	405

COUNTY At the courthouse, note the double-tiered Democratic collapse: To clear minority status from 1980 on – Republicans have dominated the courthouse since then – and to being marginalized altogether after 1996.

Com1	Democrat			Republican		
2012	-	-	-	**Barbara McMurdo**	**465**	**100.00%**
2008	-	0	0.00%	Bill Davis	477	100.00%
2006	-	0	0.00%	Bill Davis	363	100.00%
2002	-	0	0.00%	Bill Davis	342	100.00%
Com2	Democrat			Republican		
2010	-	0	0.00%	Janet Croner	359	100.00%
2008	Janet Croner	260	43.33%	Ron Chapman	340	56.67%
2004	-	0	0.00%	Ron Chapman	484	100.00%
2002	-	0	0.00%	Ron Chapman	351	100.00%
Com3	Democrat			Republican		
2012	-	-	-	**Ken Backstrom**	**350**	**62.80%**
2010	-	0	0.00%	Ken Backstrom	319	100.00%
2006	-	0	0.00%	Ken Backstrom	329	100.00%
2004	-	0	0.00%	Ken Backstrom	474	100.00%

Clerk	Democrat		Republican	
2010	-	0.00%	Korri Blodgett	100.00%
2006	-		Rollie Bennett	100.00%
2002	-		Rollie Bennett	100.00%
Treasurer	Democrat		Republican	
2010	-	0.00%	Gayle Bachtell	100.00%
2006	-	0.00%	Gayle Bachtell	100.00%
2002	-	0.00%	Gayle Bachtell	100.00%
Assessor	Democrat		Republican	
2010	Lynn McGuire	100.00%	-	0.00%
2006	-	0.00%	Gene Kuehn	100.00%
2002	-	0.00%	Mickey Dalin	100.00%
Coroner	Democrat		Republican	
2010	-	0.00%	Darla Boggs	100.00%
2006	-	0.00%	Darla Boggs	100.00%
2002	-	0.00%	John Glick	100.00%
Sheriff	Democrat		Republican	
2012	-	-	**David Sanders**	**100.00%**
2008	Monte Cangiamilla	23.15%	David Sanders	76.85%
2004	Monte Cangiamilla	21.09%	David Sanders	78.91%
Pros Atty	Democrat		Republican	
2012	-	-	-	-
2008	Ron Twilegar	100.00%	-	0.00%
2004	-	0.00%	-	0.00%

CANYON

AREA Communities: Nampa, Caldwell, Middleton, Parma, Wilder, Greenleaf, Notus, Melba. 603 sq. mi.

POPULATION 188,923 (2nd). Increase 00s: 43.7%. Minority: 27.7%. Hispanic: 23.9%.

Republican, and (in political terms) it always has been. No changes are variations to report here, right?

Then look at 1978, when Republican James McClure won his race for the Senate, and Governor John Evans for the Democrats. Look at the votes those losers – D and R – got in those races: Almost identical. By this measure, there were almost exactly as many hard-core Republicans and Democrats in Canyon County in 1978. As late as 1990, in the face of another Andrus landslide, the Republican nominee took only a few more votes, fewer than many Democrats were winning in that period.

So, while Canyon's presidential vote has never been in serious contention in the last half-century, other races often ran respectably close here in the 60s and 70s. Republicans began to pull away in the 80s – observe the sharply-defined gap between the parties in the 1986 Senate and governor races – and after 1990 became virtually out of reach. Since 1990, Republicans have been pulling in most cases at least 20,000 votes in Canyon, and in 2004 in the presidential shot all the way up past 40,000, while Democrats have yet to hit Andrus' 1990 peak of 16,246 – they have been stuck, generally, in the 13-14K range, at best.

This growth Republican/static Democrat pattern is common around Idaho. In Canyon County it has special impact since this is, after all, the second largest county in Idaho, and one of the fastest-growing. It's not that the growth in Republican voting has been all that spectacular – from 1960 to 2000 the population increased more than 150% and the Republican vote barely 100% – it's that, despite all that growth, the Democratic vote has increased hardly at all.

Theoretically, Democrats should be able to pick up substantial votes here. Canyon has the second largest city in Idaho, Nampa, home to a private university and a growing state community college and an increasingly urbanized center. And there's a small Democratic base in Caldwell, another top 10 (in population) Idaho city.

PRECINCTS (53) Canyon overall is highly Republican, but in a few places some blue does emerge. Among the dozen or so most competitive precincts (and these still lean slightly Republican in most races), two areas stand out. One is the area of Caldwell around the College of Idaho and some of the Hispanic neighborhoods nearby (4, 5, 6, 7, 10). Another is in central Nampa, not far from the urban downtown area (34, 40, 42, 44). Beyond those areas, nearly all precincts deliver landslide margins to Republicans across not only most of Nampa and Caldwell, but the other communities as well. Most Republican: Grennleaf, and the rural far northern and southern edges of the county.

PRESIDENTIAL Canyon has not voted Democratic for president since Roosevelt in 1936. No Democrat has come close since 1940.

	Dem	%	Rep	%	Total
2012	19,866	30.06%	44,369	67.13%	66,090
2008	20,147	31.36%	42,752	66.54%	64,246
2004	13,415	24.09%	41,599	74.69%	55,692
2000	10,588	24.74%	30,560	71.40%	42,802

GOVERNOR Since the 1930s, Canyon seems to have edge closest to being partisan competitive in the 70s, and it voted for Andrus in 1974 and Evans in 1978. Apart from those races and the 1990 Andrus landslide win, Canyon has been solidly Republican for governor for a very long time.

	Dem	%	Rep	%	Total
2010	10,537	23.72%	29,431	66.25%	44,427
2006	15,237	34.68%	25,897	58.94%	43,940
2002	13,795	37.20%	22,536	60.77%	37,084

COUNTY Canyon's courthouse has been even more completely Republican than Ada's, only rarely in recent decades admitting even a single Democrat at a time (most recently, for sheriff). In the most recent decade, Democrats have fielded few contenders for county offices, and have not reached 40% of the vote in any of those efforts.

Com1	Democrat			Republican		
2012	-		-	- Steve Rule	50,599	100.00%
2008	-	0	0.00%	Steve Rule	50,453	100.00%
2006	-	0	0.00%	Steve Rule	34,448	100.00%
2002	-	0	0.00%	Robert Vasquez	28,762	91.20%
Com2	Democrat			Republican		
2010	Estella Zamora	11,483	26.90%	Kathy Alder	28,147	65.90%
2008	Estella Zamora	20,977	34.96%	Kathy Alder	39,029	65.04%
2004	Dan Romero	18,856	35.65%	Matt Beebe	34,030	64.35%
2002	Dan Romero	13,938	39.50%	Matt Beebe	21,326	60.50%
Com3	Democrat			Republican		
2012	-		-	- Craig Hanson	51,053	100.00%
2010	-	0	0.00%	David Ferdinand	35,130	100.00%
2006	-	0	0.00%	David Ferdinand	34,293	98.94%
2004	-	0	0.00%	David Ferdinand	36,110	72.37%

Clerk	Democrat		Republican	
2010	-	0.00%	Chris Yamamoto	100.00%
2006	-	0.00%	Bill Hurst	100.00%
2002	-	0.00%	Noel Hales	100.00%
Treasurer	Democrat		Republican	

	Democrat		Republican	
2010	-	0.00%	Tracie Lloyd	100.00%
2006	-	0.00%	Tracie Lloyd	100.00%
2002	-	0.00%	Tracie Lloyd	100.00%
Assessor	**Democrat**		**Republican**	
2010	-	0.00%	Gene Kuehn	100.00%
2006	-	0.00%	Gene Kuehn	100.00%
2002	-	0.00%	Gene Keuhn	100.00%
Coroner	**Democrat**		**Republican**	
2010	-	0.00%	Vicki DeGeus-Morris	100.00%
2006	-	0.00%	Vicki DeGeus-Morris	100.00%
2002	-	0.00%	Vicki DeGeus-Morris	100.00%
Sheriff	**Democrat**		**Republican**	
2012	-		**- Kieran Donahue**	**66.30%**
2008	-	0.00%	Chris Smith	100.00%
2004	-	0.00%	Chris Smith*	67.99%
Pros Atty	**Democrat**		**Republican**	
2012	-		**- Bryan Finley Taylor**	**100.00%**
2008	-	0.00%	John Bujak	100.00%
2004	-	0.00%	David Young	100.00%

*Defeated an independent

CARIBOU

AREA Communities: **POPULATION** 6,963
Soda Springs, Grace,   (35th). Increase 00s:
Bancroft, Wayan. 1,799   -4.7%. Minority: 6.9%.
sq. mi.   Hispanic: 4.8%.

Caribou has become a rarity: A place *increasingly* reliant on mining, and now Idaho's leading mining county. It has experienced the ups and downs associated with that industry. The population drop in the early 80s of about 1,600 people – close to a fifth of the population – between 1980 and 1990.

That bleak period seems, in hindsight, to have locked in the Republican advantage in Caribou, though the fundamental change occurred before. Although some Democratic Senate candidates continued to pull votes from 1,050 to 1,200 into the 80s, Democrats have not been really competitive with Republicans since the early 70s. Farther back, the county had a nearly bipartisan cast to it, and both parties were prominent here. But many of those Democrats (like the last Democrat elected to the Legislature from this area, Russell Westerberg) were basically Wallace Democrats, whose migration to the GOP was largely locked in during the late Carter and early Reagan years. And, given the lack of population increase here, this does appear to be a place where considerable conversion took place.

PRECINCTS (10) Soda Springs once was a competitive city, but now its four precincts and the rest of the county are all landslide Republican. The very rural Freedom and Wayan precincts traditionally have been most Republican and still are though other precincts are catching up.

PRESIDENTIAL Caribou has checked in Republican for president consistently since flipping to Johnson in 1964.

	Dem	%	Rep	%	Total
2012	386	12.65%	2,608	85.45%	3,052
2008	553	16.75%	2,656	80.44%	3,302
2004	491	14.96%	2,753	83.91%	3,281
2000	475	15.01%	2,601	82.18%	3,165

GOVERNOR Caribou has broken a Republican pattern for governor in the last half-century only for the Andrus landslides of 1990 and 1974.

	Dem	%	Rep	%	Total
2010	721	31.61%	1,434	62.87%	2,281
2006	765	33.58%	1,637	71.86%	2,278
2002	846	33.49%	1,642	65.00%	2,526

COUNTY A courthouse split between the parties into the 70s (there was some conservative Democratic tradition here) has turned close to uniform Republican from the 80s since.

Com1	Democrat				Republican		
2012	-		-		- Phil Christensen	2,755	100.00%
2008	-		0	0.00%	Phil Christensen	1,902	58.52%
2006	-		0	0.00%	Douglas Hogan	2,179	100.00%
2002	-		0	0.00%	Bart Conlin	2,228	100.00%
Com2	Democrat				Republican		
2010	-		0	0.00%	Earl Somsen	2,083	100.00%
2008	-		0	0.00%	Earl Somsen	2,870	100.00%
2004	-		0	0.00%	Bruce Dredge	2,940	100.00%
2002	-		0	0.00%	Bruce Dredge	2,288	100.00%
Com3	Democrat				Republican		
2012	-		-		- Mark Mathews	2,777	100.00%
2010	-		0	0.00%	Lloyd Rasmussen	2,082	100.00%
2006	-		0	0.00%	Lloyd Rasmussen	2,228	100.00%
2004	-		0	0.00%	Lloyd Rasmussen	2,941	100.00%

Clerk	Democrat		Republican	
2010	-	0.00%	Veda Mascarenas	100.00%
2006	Edie Bush (Izatt)	34.12%	Veda Mascarenas	65.88%
2002	Edie Izatt	60.20%	Chad Christensen	39.80%
Treasurer	Democrat		Republican	
2010	-	0.00%	Diane Crawford	100.00%
2006	-	0.00%	Diane Crawford	100.00%
2002	Diane Meads	100.00%	-	0.00%
Assessor	Democrat		Republican	
2010	-	0.00%	Aaron Cook	100.00%
2006	-	0.00%	Preston Phelps	100.00%
2002	-	0.00%	Preston Phelps	100.00%
Coroner	Democrat		Republican	
2010	-	0.00%	Duayne Sims	100.00%
2006	-	0.00%	Duayne Sims	100.00%
2002	-	0.00%	Duayne Sims	100.00%
Sheriff	Democrat		Republican	
2012	-		- Ric Anderson	100.00%
2008	Michael Haderlie	11.62%	Ric Anderson	61.24%
2004	Ray VanVleet	100.00%	-	0.00%
Pros Atty	Democrat		Republican	
2012	-		- Douglas Wood	100.00%
2008	Jim Aldrich	23.58%	Gregg Haney	76.42%
2004	Jim Aldrich	33.55%	Criss James	66.45%

CASSIA

AREA Communities: Burley, Heyburn, Oakley, Albion, Declo, Malta, Elma. 2,577 sq. mi.

POPULATION 22,952 (14th). Increase 00s: 7.2%. Minority: 6.9%. Hispanic: 4.8%.

Cassia is Republican, and literally always has been; you can go back to the earliest days of Idaho statehood and find hardly any Democrats elected from here. The conservative Democratic tradition that a number of conservative Idaho counties (Custer, Butte, Owyhee, Valley, Adams) have had, has barely ever dented Cassia. A few Democrats have been elected locally over the years, seldom more than one at a time. The last legislative Democrat elected from here (Robert Saxvik) won in 1974, and he lost four years later.

The only change has been in the ever-growing size of the Republican margin, as population expansion has boosted Republican votes, while not changing significantly those for Democratic candidates (except for a notable drop for some in 2010).

PRECINCTS (26) The seven Burley precincts, especially from the middle of the city and facing the Snake River and working outward, are the closest to competitive (though not very close – these are all clearly Republican precincts; but two of the Snake-facing precincts were the only two precincts in the county to oppose Right to Work in the 80s). Albion is the next closest to competitive. The most Republican precincts generally are among the most rural and remote (Almo, Heglar-Yale, View, Sublett).

The rural precincts of Cassia County accounted for an extraordinary number of the most Republican precincts in Idaho. Almo was the third most-Republican precinct in Idaho in 2010 in our analysis; Heglar-Yale ranked sixth; View was eighth; Sublett ninth; Oakley 2 was 12th; Oakley 1 was 18th; Parsons was 19th. More than a third of the 20 most Republican precincts in Idaho, more than any other county in that group, are in Cassia.

PRESIDENTIAL The last Democratic presidential to win in Cassia: Roosevelt in 1940. In recent decades, they've taken only sliver votes.

	Dem	%	Rep	%	Total
2012	1,098	13.08%	7,154	85.21%	8,396
2008	1,332	16.99%	6,309	80.45%	7,842
2004	1,153	14.74%	6,562	83.90%	7,821
2000	1,087	14.99%	5,983	82.49%	7,253

GOVERNOR Think Republican: Only Andrus in his landslide years have won here for Democrats.

	Dem	%	Rep	%	Total
2010	929	16.60%	4,250	75.96%	5,595

| 2006 | | 1,576 | 28.38% | 3,912 | 70.45% | 5,553 |
| 2002 | | 1,479 | 24.70% | 4,377 | 73.08% | 5,989 |

COUNTY The Cassia County courthouse has been all-Republican going way back. No Democrat has served in an elective post there in at least 50 years, and possibly much longer.

Com1	Democrat			Republican		
2012	-		-	- Paul Christensen	7,166	100.00%
2008	-	0	0.00%	Paul Christensen	6,648	100.00%
2006	-	0	0.00%	Paul Christensen	4,817	100.00%
2002	-	0	0.00%	Paul Christensen	5,167	100.00%
Com2	Democrat			Republican		
2010	-	0	0.00%	Robert Kunau	4,889	100.00%
2008	-	0	0.00%	Clay Handy	6,490	100.00%
2004	-	0	0.00%	Clay Handy	6,589	100.00%
2002	-	0	0.00%	Clay Handy	5,132	100.00%
Com3	Democrat			Republican		
2012	-		-	- Dennis Crane	7,140	100.00%
2010	-	0	0.00%	Dennis Crane	4,760	100.00%
2006	-	0	0.00%	Dennis Crane	4,819	100.00%
2004	-	0	0.00%	Dennis Crane	6,587	100.00%

Clerk	Democrat		Republican	
2010	-	0.00%	Joseph Larsen	100.00%
2006	-	0.00%	Larry Mickelsen	100.00%
Treasurer	Democrat		Republican	
2010	-	0.00%	Patty Justesen	100.00%
2006	-	0.00%	Gayle Erekson	100.00%
Assessor	Democrat		Republican	
2010	-	0.00%	Dwight Davis	100.00%
2006	-	0.00%	Martell Holland	100.00%
Coroner	Democrat		Republican	
2010	-	0.00%	Paul Young	100.00%
2006	-	0.00%	Paul Young	100.00%
Sheriff	Democrat		Republican	
2012	-		- Jay Heward	86.90%
2008	-	0.00%	Randy Kidd	85.39%
2004	-	0.00%	James Higens	100.00%
Pros Atty	Democrat		Republican	
2012	-		- Alred Barrus	100.00%
2008	-	0.00%	Alfred Barrus	100.00%
2004	-	0.00%	Alfred Barrus	100.00%

CLARK

AREA Communities: **POPULATION** 982 (44th).
Dubois, Spencer.   Increase 00s: -3.9%. Minority:
1,764 sq. mi.   43.2%. Hispanic: 40.5%.

Idaho's smallest county, one of its most remote from urban centers, Clark had a bipartisan old-time tradition that has faded to near invisibility since Republicans have become dominant in the last couple of decades.

Not much variation here, except that as the population rose by a quarter in 90s and dropped a little in the 00s, the county's raw vote for Democrats actually dropped, while not changing much on the Republican side. That may reflect some dying-out; most of the few Democrats elected to county offices and such here came out of old families (some of them electing generation after generation to the legislation and other offices).

PRECINCTS (3) Scant difference between these three precincts, which ordinarily vote super-landslide Republican. The most Republican, often with margins of 9-1 and more: Precinct 3, the totally rural area west of Dubois, including Small and Medicine Creek.

PRESIDENTIAL Republican since Roosevelt's win in 1932 – one of the longest such streaks of any Idaho county.

	Dem	*%*	*Rep*	*%*	*Total*
2012	66	20.12%	235	71.65%	328
2008	64	17.07%	305	81.33%	375
2004	46	13.03%	302	85.55%	353
2000	63	16.49%	311	81.41%	382

GOVERNOR Clark voted for Andrus in his landslide years and Evans in 1978, but otherwise has been loyally Republican.

	Dem	*%*	*Rep*	*%*	*Total*
2010	91	26.61%	227	66.37%	342
2006	92	26.90%	229	66.96%	342
2002	72	23.53%	226	73.86%	306

COUNTY Historically, Clark split its courthouse between the parties, often electing Democratic rancher and farmers (conservative of course) as commissioners. They put a stop to that by the early 90s.

Com1	Democrat		Republican		
2012	-	-	- **William Fredricksen**	**162**	**54.20%**
2008	Ernest Sill	184	49.33% William Fredericksen	189	50.67%
2006	-	0	0.00% Michael Leonardson	247	100.00%

2002	-	0	0.00%	Michael Leonardson	258	100.00%
Com2	**Democrat**			**Republican**		
2010	Kate Stronlund	114	34.90%	Gregory Shenton	213	65.10%
2008**	Kate Stromlund	41	10.70%	Gregory Shenton	199	51.96%
2004	-	0	0.00%	Gregory Shenton	286	100.00%
2002	-	0	0.00%	Gregory Shenton	272	100.00%
Com3	**Democrat**			**Republican**		
2012	-	-	-	**Tod Shenton**	**274**	**100.00%**
2010*	-	0	0.00%	Allyn May	144	43.40%
2006	-	0	0.00%	Allyn May	171	51.82%
2004	-	0	0.00%	Ted Edwards	283	100.00%

*An independent write-in candidate won here. Todd Shenton (188 votes, 56.6%) won over Republican Allyn May, who had barely beaten a write-in two years before.

**In 2008 commission 2 race, incumbent Repubican Shenton got a serious contest from a write in, Mac Wagoner, who got 143 votes, though not from the Democrat who – although she was on the ballot – got 41.

Clerk	Democrat		Republican	
2012	-		**Velvet Killian**	**100.00%**
2010	-	0.00%	Lisa Black	100.00%
2006	-	0.00%	Lisa Black	100.00%
2002	-	0.00%	Conni Owen	100.00%
Treasurer	**Democrat**		**Republican**	
2012	-		**Annette Zweifel**	**100.00%**
2010	-	0.00%	Velvet Killian	100.00%
2006	-	0.00%	Velvet Killian	100.00%
2002	-	0.00%	Bonnie Burns	100.00%
Assessor	**Democrat**		**Republican**	
2010	-	0.00%	Carrie May	100.00%
2006	Pamela Sincomb	19.29%	Carrie May	80.71%
2004	-	0.00%	Carrie May	100.00%
2002	-	0.00%	Vicki Gunter	100.00%
Coroner	**Democrat**		**Republican**	
2010	Deborah Newton	34.80%	Brenda Laird	65.20%
2006	-	0.00%	Orvin Jorgensen	100.00%
2002	-	0.00%	Orvin Jorgensen	100.00%
Sheriff	**Democrat**		**Republican**	
2012	-		**Bart May**	**100.00%**
2008	-	0.00%	Craig King	100.00%
2004	-	0.00%	Craig King	100.00%
Pros Atty	**Democrat**		**Republican**	
2012	-		**-**	-
2008*	-	0.00%	-	0.00%
2004	-	0.00%	-	0.00%

* Independent Arlynn Horne elected.

CLEARWATER

AREA Communities: Orofino, Pierce, Weippe, Elk River, Greer. 2,488 sq. mi.

POPULATION 8,761 (31st). Increase 00s: -1.9%. Minority: 8.0%. Hispanic: 3.1%.

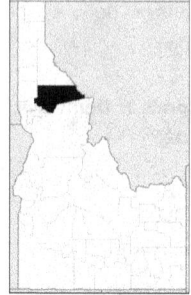

Clearwater has been a true marker county: When it went Republican, as it finally did in the mid-90s, that was a sign that the last Idaho Democratic bailiwicks from the old days were gone. There was the matter of symbolism, too, since this was where Cecil Andrus came to politics.

It's not that Republican never used to win here. Andrus had to work to win his first election to the Idaho Senate in 1960, challenging a veteran Republican senator. Even after that, there were often one or two Republicans at the courthouse, and Clearwater joined in the Nixon and Reagan landslides. But mainly, Clearwater was one of those places most Democratic candidates, those not hopelessly outgunned, could expect to pick up some margin. It went Democratic in the presidential in 1988 and 1992. In the razor close governor's contest in 1982, Clearwater accounted for almost a third of Democrat John Evans' ultimate statewide margin over Phil Batt, beating him more than 2-1 here.

After that, the Democratic strength started slipping, subtly at first, visible now in hindsight. When Andrus returned to run for governor in 1986, he won the county but by less than Evans had four years earlier. It is true that economic reversals reduced Clearwater's population almost 15% in the 80s. But it is also true that, contrasting with much of the state, Andrus' 1990 Republican opponent actually outpolled his 1986 opponent.

Consider also three Senate races, all won statewide by Republicans with similar percentages statewide: McClure-R/Davis-D in 1972, Craig-R/Twilegar-D in 1990, and Craig-R/Minnick-D in 1996. In the first, while losing decisively statewide, Davis beat McClure nearly 2-1 in Clearwater. In the second, while losing big statewide and running next to Andrus on the ballot, Twilegar narrowly lost Clearwater in 1990. By 1996, Minnick, also running against Craig, lost Clearwater decisively.

The turning point clearly seems to be the mid to late 80s into the early 90s, after which Republican dominance was rapidly completed, all the way through a courthouse that had remained mostly Democratic for decades. Environmental issues were likely a factor in this timber production area.

PRECINCTS (15) In a traditionally Democratic county that has moved generally Republican, the small-community (and fairly remote) precinct of Greer has remained solidly Democratic – the 8th most Democratic statewide in 2010. It is in sharp relief compared to the other precincts, all of which lean Republican on top of ticket races. Aside from Greer, the five Orofino precincts vote a little more competitively than the rest of the county, but no longer by much. The remote Fraser and Teakean precincts are the most Republican.

202

PRESIDENTIAL Other than in the Reagan years and the Nixon 1972 landslide, Clearwater was a dependable Democratic county on the presidential level for a long time. In 1992 it barely remained so, owing to a strong vote for Ross Perot, but from 1996 to date has voted solidly Republican for president.

	Dem	%	Rep	%	Total
2012	1,032	27.92%	2,541	68.75%	3,696
2008	1,211	31.00%	2,569	65.77%	3,906
2004	1,117	27.69%	2,839	70.38%	4,034
2000	841	21.83%	2,885	74.88%	3,853

GOVERNOR The partisan switch on the governor level came about the same time. Clearwater voted consistently for Democrats for governor for a long time. In 1946 it supported, narrowly, Republican C.A. Robins for governor, but no other Republican after that until Phil Batt in 1994. And no Democrats since.

	Dem	%	Rep	%	Total
2010	891	30.43%	1,768	60.38%	2,928
2006	1,346	46.56%	1,562	54.03%	2,891
2002	1,423	45.52%	1,635	52.30%	3,126

COUNTY A courthouse that for most of a century had been mostly Democratic flipped, around 2000 and in the elections since, to mostly Republican.

Com1	Democrat			Republican		
2012	Don Ebert	1,749	50.10%	Trever Heighes	1,744	49.90%
2008	Don Ebert	1,942	51.72%	Joy Hall	1,813	48.28%
2006	Don Ebert	2,234	100.00%	-	0	0.00%
2002	Don Ebert	1,766	57.20%	Ric Hood	1,322	42.80%
Com2	Democrat			Republican		
2010	-	0	0.00%	Stan Leach	2,406	100.00%
2008	-	0	0.00%	Stan Leach	3,093	100.00%
2004	-	0	0.00%	Stan Leach	3,315	100.00%
2002	David Ponozzo	1,258	40.60%	Stan Leach	1,840	59.40%
Com3	Democrat			Republican		
2012	John Allen	1,908	54.40%	Carole Galloway	1,598	45.60%
2010	John Allen	1,412	48.70%	Carole Galloway	1,488	51.30%
2006	John Allen	1,676	56.55%	Dennis Williams	1,288	43.45%
2004	Nick Albers	1,750	44.29%	Pete Curfman	2,201	55.71%

Clerk	Democrat		Republican	
2010	-	0.00%	Carrie Bird	100.00%
2006	Robin Christensen	100.00%	-	0.00%
2002	Robin Christensen	64.80%	Dennis Fuller	35.20%
Treasurer	Democrat		Republican	

2010	Dawn Erlewine	56.00%	David King	46.00%
2006	Jeannie Johnson	100.00%	-	0.00%
2002	Jeannie Johnson	68.40%	David King	31.60%
Assessor	**Democrat**		**Republican**	
2010	Mellisa Stewart	100.00%	-	0.00%
2006	Mellisa Stewart	100.00%	-	0.00%
2002	Mellisa Stewart	66.10%	Bill Howard	33.90%
Coroner	**Democrat**		**Republican**	
2010	Steve McGill	49.30%	Will Rambeau	50.70%
2006	Thomas Atkinson	47.85%	Steve McGill	39.38%
2002	-	0.00%	Maurice Masar	100.00%
Sheriff	**Democrat**		**Republican**	
2012	-	-	**Chris Goetz**	**98.80%**
2008	-	0.00%	Chris Goetz	99.39%
2004	Fred Partney	37.60%	Alan Hengen	62.40%
Pros Atty	**Democrat**		**Republican**	
2012	-	-	**Clayne Tyler**	100.00%
2008*	-	0.00%	-	0.00%
2004	John Swayne	100.00%	-	0.00%

*Won by write-in Clayne Tyler, who later ran as a Republican.

CUSTER

AREA Communities: Challis, Mackay, Stanley, Clayton. 4,938 sq. mi.

POPULATION 4,368 (38th). Increase 00s: 0.6%. Minority: 6.0%. Hispanic: 4.0%.

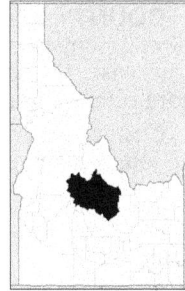

As in some other rural counties in Idaho, was a time when both parties elected people here. That was when there were conservative Democrats. In the years before Custer was joined with other counties under legislative reapportionment, it was represented in the Legislature by a Democratic senator and a Democratic representative, both conservative in the southern mold. For years beyond that, county voters had no problem sending Democrats to the courthouse (albeit never a majority).

The transition was largely locked in by 1970, when Democrat Cecil Andrus was narrowly beating Republican Don Samuelson statewide (in part in opposition to mining in the White Cloud mountains here), he took only 135 votes to Samuelson's 1,164. Four years later Andrus actually won Custer, but only barely, while he roared statewide to a landslide win. Democrats have seldom does much better here since. That lock-in is even clearer on the presidential. There's been a standard Democratic ceiling here of a little over 600 votes, while the Republican raw vote has grown.

PRECINCTS (10) Stanley remains an electoral oddity: For a generation and more a genuinely Democratic precinct (denying Otter in 2010 even 40% of the vote) amidst a vast Republican territory. In Custer, it is very much alone. Mackay, which has a politically varied background, is the closest to competitive among the remaining precincts. Otherwise, the Challis-area and outlying precincts generally deliver results in Republican super-landslide territory.

PRESIDENTIAL Solid, heavy Republican. Democrat John Kennedy's 838 votes (he was the last presidential Democrat to win here) have not been exceeded in the half-century since, nor LBJ's 714, even though he lost Custer.

	Dem	%	Rep	%	Total
2012	530	22.53%	1,744	74.15%	2,352
2008	611	25.98%	1,694	72.02%	2,352
2004	559	23.71%	1,762	74.72%	2,358
2000	416	17.90%	1,794	77.19%	2,324

GOVERNOR Custer did seem to forgive Andrus enough (over the White Clouds) to back him in the 1974 and 1990 landslide, and John Evans in 1978. Otherwise, it has been solidly Republican.

	Dem	%	Rep	%	Total
2010	419	22.51%	1,267	68.08%	1,861

| 2006 | | 602 | 32.61% | | 1,228 | 66.52% | | 1,846 |
| 2002 | | 480 | 27.00% | | 1,248 | 70.19% | | 1,778 |

COUNTY In the 00s, Democrat Lin Hintze has won repeatedly for commission seats, though when challenged by Republicans, only narrowly. Otherwise, the courthouse has been solidly Republican, and hasn't seen more than one or two Democrats at a time since the mid-70s.

Custer got a new prosecutor in January 2012, when Val Siegel took over the job, replacing an interim prosecutor.

Com1	Democrat			Republican		
2012	**-**	**-**	**-**	**Wayne Butts**	**1,645**	**79.50%**
2008	-	0	0.00%	Wayne Butts	1,664	100.00%
2006	-	0	0.00%	Wayne Butts	1,520	100.00%
2002	-	0	0.00%	Wayne Butts	1,484	100.00%
Com2	**Democrat**			**Republican**		
2010	-	0	0.00%	Doyle Lamb	1,599	100.00%
2008	-	0	0.00%	Cliff Hansen	1,415	66.68%
2004	-	0	0.00%	Cliff Hansen	1,750	100.00%
2002	-	0	0.00%	Cliff Hansen	1,103	66.60%
Com3	**Democrat**			**Republican**		
2012	**Lin Hintze**	**1,582**	**100.00%**	**-**	**-**	**-**
2010	Lin Hintze	947	51.70%	Max Bingham	883	48.30%
2006	Lin Hintze	1,490	100.00%	-	0	0.00%
2004	Lin Hintze	1,301	57.90%	Bob Vaden	946	42.10%

Clerk	Democrat		Republican	
2010	-	0.00%	Barbara Tierney	100.00%
2006	-	0.00%	Barbara Breedlove	79.51%
2002	-	0.00%	Ethel Peck	100.00%
Treasurer	**Democrat**		**Republican**	
2010	-	0.00%	Sandy James	100.00%
2006	-	0.00%	Sandy James	100.00%
Assessor	**Democrat**		**Republican**	
2010	-	0.00%	Christine James	100.00%
2006	-	0.00%	Christine James	100.00%
Coroner	**Democrat**		**Republican**	
2010	-	0.00%	Vicki Armbrister	100.00%
2006	-	0.00%	Vicki Armbruster	69.97%
Sheriff	**Democrat**		**Republican**	
2008	Marla Colson	34.18%	Stu Lumpkin	65.82%
2004*	Marla Colson	14.80%	Robert Taylor	39.27%
Pros Atty	**Democrat**		**Republican**	
2008**	-	0.00%	-	0.00%
2004	-	0.00%	James Smirch	100.00%

*Winner was independent Tim Eikens, 45.93%.
** Winner was Independent Shawn Glen, 100%.

ELMORE

AREA Communities:
Mountain Home, Glenns
Ferry, Hammett, Kings Hill.
3,103 sq. mi.

POPULATION 27,038
(12th). Increase 00s:
-7.2%. Minority: 24.9%.
Hispanic: 15.2%.

The impulse toward Democrats is not yet completely evaporated in Elmore County – note the 2002 election of Fred Kennedy to the state Senate, basically on Elmore votes (he served one term and the seat then went to a Republican) – mainly because one of the anchors for it remains in place: Mountain Home Air Force Base. But he has become the rarity, and not just because he served just one term and then retired: This is another county with bipartisan or even Democratic leanings to move ever more solidly into the Republican column.

In the last generation, the number for winning Elmore has been about 3,000 votes, and among major Democratic candidates, that's been hit just a few times – Frank Church 1980, Richard Stallings 1988. Even Cecil Andrus in 1990, while winning the county, fell short of 3,000. Republicans, on the other hand, started hitting 3K in 1972 with Richard Nixon, and their statewide landsliders have often passed 4,000. That trend accelerated in 90s, when the county also saw its first (in recent decades) big population increase, and Republicans were the beneficiaries. A small drop at the base and in the county in the 00s seems not to have changed the calculus.

PRECINCTS (19) Our 2010 precinct analysis ranks Elmore's Chattin Flats precinct (in the very remote far southwest corner of the county, away from any community) as the second-most Republican in the state. (It delivered all 32 votes to Republican Crapo, and all but one to Otter – that one going to independent and former Republican Jana Kemp). Such votes have not been unusual in recent years, though before the mid-90s they were a little less totally lopsided. Pine, in the also-remote area on the opposite side of the county (known mostly as a recreational area), is not too far behind. But most of Elmore, while leaning Republican, has margins a little closer. The small and remote mining community of Atlanta, high in the mountains, is actually competitive between the parties, and the nine Mountain Home precincts pick up from just-beyond competitive to strongly Republican. Glenns Ferry, Kings Hill and other small communities are landslide Republican places.

PRESIDENTIAL Elmore has long been Republican on the presidential level: Since 1964, when it went for Johnson.

	Dem	%	Rep	%	Total
2012	2,513	31.41%	5,227	65.33%	8,001
2008	2,591	30.71%	5,665	67.15%	8,436
2004	1,959	24.31%	6,011	74.59%	8,059
2000	1,840	26.52%	4,891	70.49%	6,939

GOVERNOR For some decades, Elmore could reasonably be considered a swing county in races on the state level – until after the 1990 election, when it began to stick solidly with Republicans.

	Dem	%	Rep	%	Total
2010	1,373	25.45%	3,511	65.08%	5,395
2006	2,177	40.83%	3,282	61.55%	5,332
2002	2,082	39.25%	3,131	59.02%	5,305

COUNTY Before 1980, Elmore usually had a Democratic-majority courthouse, and in the 80s the parties split the offices fairly closely. Both parties still do contest most of the courthouse seats, and Democrats still win sometimes, but the wins have become increasingly concentrated in the last decade on the Republican side.

Com1	Democrat			Republican		
2012	-	-	-	**Bud Corbus**	**4,644**	**60.40%**
2008	Janet Langfitt	2,955	37.25%	Arlie Shaw	4,977	62.75%
2006	Jim Sanders	2,198	39.91%	Arlie Shaw	3,309	60.09%
2002	Mary Eguisquiza-Stanek	2,661	51.20%	Arie Shaw	2,534	48.80%
Com2	Democrat			Republican		
2010	-	0	0.00%	Wesley Wootan	3,393	66.20%
2008	-	0	0.00%	Larry Rose	5,950	88.66%
2004	-	0	0.00%	Larry Rose	6,201	100.00%
2002	-	0	0.00%	Larry Rose	4,282	100.00%
Com3	Democrat			Republican		
2012	**Michael Crawford**	**2,688**	**35.50%**	**Albert Hofer**	**4,893**	**64.50%**
2010	Connie Cruser	2,178	41.40%	Albert Hofer	3,084	58.60%
2006	Connie Cruser	3,344	60.48%	Calvin Ireland	2,185	39.52%
2004	Connie Cruser	4,303	55.52%	Calvin Ireland	3,447	44.48%

Clerk	Democrat		Republican	
2010	-	0.00%	Barbara Steele	100.00%
2006	Merrilee Hiler	44.53%	Marsa Grimmett	55.47%
2002	Gail Best	100.00%	-	0.00%
Treasurer	Democrat		Republican	
2010	Rose Plympton	100.00%	-	0.00%
2006	Rose Plympton	100.00%	-	0.00%
2002	Rose Plympton	100.00%	-	0.00%
Assessor	Democrat		Republican	
2010	-	0.00%	Ronald Fisher	100.00%
2006	Joe Gridley	100.00%	-	0.00%
2002	James Haydon	100.00%	-	0.00%
Coroner	Democrat		Republican	
2010	-	0.00%	Jerry Rost	100.00%
2006	-	0.00%	Jerry Rost	100.00%
2002	-	0.00%	Marla Spence	100.00%

Sheriff	Democrat		Republican	
2012	-	-	**Rick Layher**	100.00%
2008	Robbin Ellis	16.55%	Rick Layher	53.52%
2004	-	0.00%	Rick Layher	78.72%
Pros Atty	**Democrat**		**Republican**	
2012	**Kristina Schindele**	**100.00%**	-	-
2008	Kristina Schindele	100.00%	-	0.00%
2006	Kristina Schindele	100.00%	-	0.00%
2004	-	0.00%	Aaron Bazzoli	100.00%

FRANKLIN

AREA Communities: Preston, Dayton, Franklin, Weston, Oxford. 667 sq. mi.

POPULATION 12,786 (23rd). Increase 00s: -2.3%. Minority: 8.2%. Hispanic: 6.6%.

Home of the first permanent town settlement in Idaho, those early settlers from Utah foretold the tight connection people have with their neighbors to the south. The people here are mostly in the Cache Valley, and their main urban center is Logan, Utah.

Unsurprisingly, Franklin is solid, solid Republican ... though it should be noted, perhaps, that in decades bygone Franklin County voters were willing to cross the ticket now and then. They occasionally elected Democrats to the legislature, back in the 50s and 60s, and backed Cecil Andrus in his two landslides.

Franklin has been a static place: Population in 1950 was very close to the figure in 1990. The 90s did see a spike, which as elsewhere appears to have had the main political effect of padding Republican totals. The most successful Democratic presidential candidate of the last half-century, Lyndon Johnson, who still lost this county decisively, got more than three times as many raw votes here as John Kerry did in 2004.

PRECINCTS (18) Not much variation in this extremely Republican county. The least Republican precinct is Thatcher-Cleveland, a rural area in the northwest of the county abutting Bannock and Caribou counties; but it cannot be considered competitive. All the other precincts here, including Preston's five, are super-landslide Republican. The most Republican of them, rural Banida-Winder, is the 15th most Republican precinct in the state; but others in the smaller Franklin communities aren't far behind.

PRESIDENTIAL Solid Republican ever since a Roosevelt vote in 1944.

	Dem	%	Rep	%	Total
2012	325	5.80%	5,195	92.77%	5,000
2008	600	11.83%	4,246	83.70%	5,073
2004	456	9.02%	4,527	89.57%	5,054
2000	513	12.14%	3,594	85.07%	4,225

GOVERNOR Apart from the two Andrus landslide years, Franklin last voted Democratic for governor for C. Ben Ross in 1934. It's rarely been close since.

	Dem	%	Rep	%	Total
2010	890	23.72%	2,612	69.62%	3,752
2006	899	24.33%	2,859	77.37%	3,695
2002	588	17.98%	2,611	79.82%	3,271

COUNTY The "right" Democrat has occasionally won election to the courthouse here – never more than two at a time, and generally department heads. The most recent, and only one in the 00s, was Assessor Richard Umbel. This is a Republican courthouse.

Com1	Democrat			Republican		
2012	-		-	**- Boyd Burbank**	**4,963**	**50.50%**
2008	-	0	0.00%	Richard Westerberg	4,173	100.00%
2006	-	0	0.00%	Richard Westerberg	2,932	100.00%
2002	Lee Chaney	710	22.10%	Alan S. Carter	2,504	77.90%
Com2	**Democrat**			**Republican**		
2010	-	0	0.00%	Scott Workman	3,346	100.00%
2008	-	0	0.00%	Scott Workman	4,225	100.00%
2004	-	0	0.00%	Dal Von Atkinson	3,502	70.42%
2002	-	0	0.00%	Craig Thomas	2,868	100.00%
Com3	**Democrat**			**Republican**		
2012	-		-	**- Dirk Bowles**	**4,861**	**49.50%**
2010	-	0	0.00%	Dirk Bowles	3,326	100.00%
2006	-	0	0.00%	Dirk Bowles	3,543	100.00%
2004	-	0	0.00%	Bill Palmer	4,474	100.00%

Clerk	Democrat		Republican	
2010	-	0.00%	Shauna Geddes	100.00%
2006	David Lunz	47.18%	Elliott Larsen	52.82%
2002	-	0.00%	Elliott Larsen	100.00%
Treasurer	**Democrat**		**Republican**	
2010	-	0.00%	Jeanette McKay	100.00%
2006	-	0.00%	Jeanette McKay	100.00%
2002	-	0.00%	Jeanette McKay	100.00%
Assessor	**Democrat**		**Republican**	
2010	-	0.00%	Jase Cundick	100.00%
2006	Richard Umbel	64.12%	Bruce Petersen	35.88%
2002	Richard Umbel	100.00%	-	0.00%
Coroner	**Democrat**		**Republican**	
2010	-	0.00%	Douglas Webb	100.00%
2006	-	0.00%	Douglas Webb	100.00%
2002	-	0.00%	Douglas Webb	100.00%
Sheriff	**Democrat**		**Republican**	
2012	**Alan Riggs**	**23.40%**	**David Fryar**	**76.60%**
2008	-	0.00%	Don Beckstead	100.00%
2004	-	0.00%	Don Beckstead	100.00%
Pros Atty	**Democrat**		**Republican**	
2012	-		**- Vic Pearson**	**54.80%**
2008	-	0.00%	Todd Garbett	100.00%
2004	-	0.00%	Todd Garbett	100.00%

FREMONT

AREA Communities: St. Anthony, Ashton, Parker, Island Park, Teton, Newdale. 1,894 sq. mi.

POPULATION 13,242 (22nd). Increase 00s: 12.0%. Minority: 14.9%. Hispanic: 12.8%.

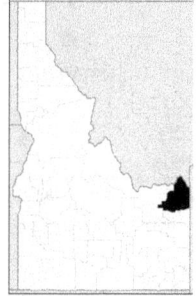

Southern Fremont is much like most of eastern Idaho in its farm and food processing economy and Mormon culture, but the northern half of it is more varied, more organized around recreation (it includes a slice of Yellowstone National Park). One city, Island Park, even was formed (more than half a century ago) specifically with the aim of providing gambling outlets. The southern half, however, dominates in population and politics.

Still, Fremont adheres to a familiar rural eastern Idaho pattern, with stagnating or even slightly declining Democratic stats in the 90s as Republican numbers continue an inexorable climb. A stronger growth period in the 90s just built that up, a little.

PRECINCTS (16) St. Anthony, the county seat and largest city, is the closest to competitive here, though it typically turns in low-landslide numbers for Republicans. From there, it turns into high-landslide numbers. The small outlying communities such as Drummond, Newdale, Parker, Chester and Egin are the most overwhelmingly Republican.

PRESIDENTIAL Republican from 1968 to now.

	Dem	%	Rep	%	Total
2012	810	13.96%	4,907	84.57%	5,802
2008	1,065	18.11%	4,700	79.93%	5,880
2004	741	12.84%	4,965	86.06%	5,769
2000	699	13.83%	4,242	83.90%	5,056

GOVERNOR Apart from the Andrus landslides (1974 and 1990), Fremont has voted Republican for governor for a very long time. The last previous was Arnold Williams in 1946.

	Dem	%	Rep	%	Total
2010	1,137	28.26%	2,645	65.73%	4,024
2006	1,221	30.53%	3,007	75.18%	4,000
2002	1,110	28.00%	2,749	69.35%	3,964

COUNTY Fremont's courthouse usually has been majority Republican, but for decades had two or three Democrats as well.

The last of them, Treasurer Patricia McCoy, switched (over primary opposition) from Democratic to Republican between her 2006 and 2010 elections.

Com1	Democrat				Republican		
2012	-		-		**- William Baxter**	**5,251**	**100.00%**
2008	-	0	0.00%	Skip Hurt		4,649	100.00%
2006	-	0	0.00%	Skip Hurt		3,141	73.30%
2002	-	0	0.00%	G Smith		3,485	100.00%
Com2	**Democrat**				**Republican**		
2010	-	0	0.00%	Le Roy Miller		3,428	100.00%
2008	-	0	0.00%	Le Roy Miller		5,089	100.00%
2004	-	0	0.00%	Donald Trupp		5,145	100.00%
2002	-	0	0.00%	G Davis		2,603	100.00%
Com3	**Democrat**				**Republican**		
2012	-		-		**- Jordon Stoddard**	**5,174**	**100.00%**
2010	-	0	0.00%	Jordon Stoddard		3,425	100.00%
2006	-	0	0.00%	Paul Romrell		3,691	100.00%
2004	-	0	0.00%	Paul Romrell		5,158	100.00%

Clerk	Democrat		Republican	
2010	-	0.00%	Abbie Mace	100.00%
2006	-	0.00%	Abbie Mace	100.00%
2002	-	0.00%	Abbie Mace	100.00%
Treasurer	**Democrat**		**Republican**	
2010	-	0.00%	Patricia McCoy	100.00%
2006	Patricia McCoy	100.00%	-	0.00%
2002	Patricia McCoy	100.00%	-	0.00%
Assessor	**Democrat**		**Republican**	
2010	-	0.00%	Kathy Thompson	100.00%
2006	-	0.00%	Kathy Thompson	81.98%
2002	-	0.00%	Ivel Burrell	100.00%
Coroner	**Democrat**		**Republican**	
2010	-	0.00%	Bonnie Burlage	100.00%
2006	-	0.00%	Dennis Birch	100.00%
2002	-	0.00%	P Romrell	100.00%
Sheriff	**Democrat**		**Republican**	
2012	-		**- Len Humphries**	**100.00%**
2008	-	0.00%	Len Humphries	49.23%
2004	-	0.00%	Ralph Davis	58.40%
Pros Atty	**Democrat**		**Republican**	
2012	-		**- Karl Lewies**	**100.00%**
2008	-	0.00%	Joette Lookabaugh	100.00%
2004	-	0.00%	Karl Lewies	100.00%

GEM

AREA Communities:
Emmett, Sweet, Letha.
564 sq. mi.

POPULATION 16,719
(19th). Increase 00s:
10.1%. Minority: 10.9%.
Hispanic: 8%.

Yet another rural county which was periodically competitive years back, but the Republican numbers have run away in the 90s. Here as elsewhere, Democratic numbers in the 00s would have looked per for the course back in the 60s, while Republican numbers from that era have doubled.

Gem is unusual among the rural counties in having a traditional Democratic base: The big timber mill at Emmett. Even so, Democrats were never much more that competitive here, though they were so in the 60s and into the 80s. As mill employed declined and ultimately ended in the 90s, the remaining rural base – farm, primarily, and some food processing – gained some importance. There is also, since the late 90s, some infusion of rural oriented bedroom community population (Boise commuters) which theoretically should behave like similar populations at Eagle, Kuna or Meridian – and apparently do.

PRECINCTS (14) All precincts here are landslide level Republican. At the low end of that: The central Emmett precincts (especially Central and South Emmett). The most Republican precinct is the lightly-populated northern tip at Ola (the 38th most Republican precinct in Idaho).

PRESIDENTIAL The normal Idaho Republican pattern: All GOP presidential candidates, ever since but not including Barry Goldwater, won won here, usually overwhelmingly.

	Dem	%	Rep	%	Total
2012	1,957	26.13%	5,311	70.91%	7,490
2008	2,166	27.26%	5,585	70.28%	7,947
2004	1,628	22.82%	5,416	75.92%	7,134
2000	1,346	22.61%	4,376	73.51%	5,953

GOVERNOR Again, not unusually, Gem voters made an exception for Andrus (landslide years only) and Evans in 1978, otherwise sticking with Republicans for governor in recent decades.

	Dem	%	Rep	%	Total
2010	1,073	19.45%	3,901	70.70%	5,518
2006	2,041	37.33%	3,450	63.09%	5,468
2002	2,182	41.02%	3,014	56.65%	5,320

COUNTY Occasional Democrats were elected to the courthouse in the 70s and 80s. In the 00s, only one ran, once, and then barely pulled a third of the vote.

Com1	Democrat			Republican		
2012	-		-	**- Carlos Bilbao**	**4,674**	**64.60%**
2008	-	0	0.00%	Sharon Pratt-Church	5,669	86.26%
2006	-	0	0.00%	Sharon Pratt-Church	4,438	100.00%
2002	-	0	0.00%	Sharon Pratt-Church	3,777	100.00%
Com2	**Democrat**			**Republican**		
2010	-	0	0.00%	Lan Smith	4,417	100.00%
2008	-	0	0.00%	Lan Smith	4,560	66.26%
2004	B Pultz	2,361	34.65%	Lan Smith	4,452	65.35%
2002	-	0	0.00%	Ed Mansfield	2,750	61.20%
Com3	**Democrat**			**Republican**		
2012	-		-	**- Mark Rekow**	**5,236**	**73.30%**
2010	-	0	0.00%	Michele Sherrer	4,465	100.00%
2006	-	0	0.00%	Michele Sherrer	4,411	100.00%
2004	-	0	0.00%	Michele Sherrer	5,489	100.00%

Clerk	Democrat		Republican	
2010	-	0.00%	Shelly Gannon	100.00%
2006	-	0.00%	Shelly Atkinson	100.00%
2002	-	0.00%	Susan Howard	100.00%
Treasurer	**Democrat**		**Republican**	
2010	-	0.00%	Connie Goins	100.00%
2006	-	0.00%	Connie Goins	100.00%
2002	-	0.00%	Marilyn Frasier-Knighton	100.00%
Assessor	**Democrat**		**Republican**	
2012	-		**- Rick Johnston**	**100.00%**
2010	-	0.00%	Greg Hines	100.00%
2006	-	0.00%	Greg Hines	100.00%
Coroner	**Democrat**		**Republican**	
2010	-	0.00%	John Buck	100.00%
2006	-	0.00%	John Buck	100.00%
Sheriff	**Democrat**		**Republican**	
2012	-		**- Chuck Rolland**	**75.60%**
2008	-	0.00%	Chuck Rolland	53.33%
2004	-	0.00%	C Short	89.82%
Pros Atty	**Democrat**		**Republican**	
2012	-		**- Richard Linville**	**100.00%**
2008	-	0.00%	Richard Linville	100.00%
2004	-	0.00%	T Fleming	100.00%

GOODING

AREA Communities: Gooding, Hagerman, Wendell, Bliss. 733 sq. mi.

POPULATION 15,464 (21st). Increase 00s: 9.2%. Minority: 30.4%. Hispanic: 28.1%.

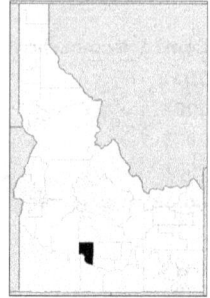

Gooding is classic south-central Idaho, its northern reaches dryland plains and cattle fields (nowadays, massive CAFOs), and its southern areas scenic Hqgerman and the Thousand Springs. It is typically Republican, too. There is some Democratic background in Gooding, but to find it you have to search out the conservative Democrats of the 40s, 50s and early 60s; after that, their ranks thinned. Vern Ravenscroft is the emblematic figure: A conservative Democrat representing this area through most of the 60s, he turned Republican in the 70s and became a leader of that party (chairman at one point), very much in its mainstream in his Sagebrush Rebel mode.

If Gooding still initially seems more bipartisan than some other rural counties, that comes from its long-standing yoke in a single legislative district with larger Blaine County; the Democratic legislators representing this area have been Blaine's choice primarily, though they have won some increasing numbers of votes in Gooding.

PRECINCTS (8) Gooding city's two precincts lean Republican but can be competitive in some cases. The other precincts, especially the very Republican two Wendell precincts, are very reliably landslide Republican.

PRESIDENTIAL Gooding did not join in the 1964 Johnson vote, or that of any other Democrat for a very long time; the last was Roosevelt in 1936.

	Dem	%	Rep	%	Total
2012	1,287	25.15%	3,696	72.22%	5,118
2008	1,489	27.62%	3,765	69.84%	5,391
2004	1,278	24.00%	3,973	74.61%	5,325
2000	1,282	25.63%	3,502	70.03%	5,001

GOVERNOR During the years when Democrats held Idaho's governor's office for a long stretch, Gooding would periodically support them: Andrus and Evens got its votes in 1974, 1978, 1982 and 1990. Since then, it has been solidly Republican, though the percentages have sometimes been more competitive than in many other Republican Idaho counties.

	Dem	%	Rep	%	Total
2010	1,024	25.80%	2,544	64.10%	3,969
2006	1,740	44.24%	2,267	57.64%	3,933
2002	1,487	36.14%	2,543	61.81%	4,114

COUNTY Since the mid-70s, there's rarely been more than a single Democrat at the courthouse, and none in the last decade.

Com1	Democrat			Republican		
2012	-		-	- **Helen Edwards**	**4,580**	**100.00%**
2008	Troy Hurd	1,366	25.79%	Helen Edwards	3,931	74.21%
2006	Troy Hurd	1,469	36.02%	Helen Edwards	2,609	63.98%
2002	-	0	0.00%	Thomas Bingham	3,436	100.00%
Com2	**Democrat**			**Republican**		
2010	-	0	0.00%	Tom Faulkner	3,317	100.00%
2008*	-	-	0.00%	David Maestas	1,977	37.27%
2004	-	0	0.00%	Carolyn Elexpuru	4,152	100.00%
2002	-	0	0.00%	Carolyn Elexpuru	3,378	100.00%
Com3	**Democrat**			**Republican**		
2012	-		-	- **Wayne Chandler**	**4,431**	**100.00%**
2010	-	0	0.00%	Terell Williams	3,369	100.00%
2006	-	0	0.00%	Terrell Williams	2,817	73.94%
2004	-	0	0.00%	Bob Morgado	2,477	51.21%

*In 2008 Comm 2, Maestas lost to "independent" Tom Faulkner, who got 3,327/62.73%. Faulkner was a Republican; he won election as such the next cycle.

Clerk	Democrat		Republican	
2010	-	0.00%	Denise Gill	100.00%
2006	-	0.00%	Denise Gill	100.00%
2002	-	0.00%	Helen Edwards	100.00%
Treasurer	**Democrat**		**Republican**	
2010	-	0.00%	Christina Wines	100.00%
2006	-	0.00%	Christina Wines	100.00%
2002	-	0.00%	Fae Christopherson	100.00%
Assessor	**Democrat**		**Republican**	
2010	-	0.00%	Patty Bauscher	100.00%
2006	-	0.00%	Patty Bauscher	100.00%
2002	-	0.00%	Patty Bauscher	100.00%
Coroner	**Democrat**		**Republican**	
2012	-		- **Steve Spence**	**100.00%**
2010	-	0.00%	Gary Loder	100.00%
2006	-	0.00%	Gary Loder	100.00%
Sheriff	**Democrat**		**Republican**	
2012	-		- **Shaun Gough**	**100.00%**
2008	-	0.00%	Shaun Gough	100.00%
2004	-	0.00%	Shaun Gough	100.00%
Pros Atty	**Democrat**		**Republican**	
2012	-		- **Luverne Shull**	**100.00%**
2008	-	0.00%	Calvin Campbell	100.00%
2004	-	0.00%	Calvin Campbell	100.00%

IDAHO

Grangeville, Cottonwood, Riggins, Kooskia, Stites, Ferdinand, Harpster, White Bird. 8,503 sq. mi.

POPULATION
16,267 (20th).
Increase 00s: 4.9%.
Minority: 7.6%.
Hispanic: 2.6%.

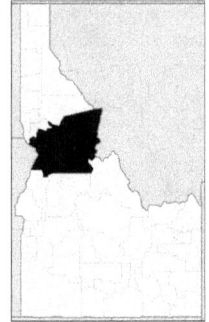

Anchored by Grangeville, this largest – geographically – of Idaho's counties has quite a few pieces. There's the rolling Camas prairie on which Grangeville, Cottonwood and a number of other small farm towns sit. There are the small communities below, on the Clearwater River and its tributaries. There is, to the south, the Salmon River country and its recreation community (still, somehow, not gentrified), Riggins. And there's the great interior to the east, the wilderness and forest land where few people ever have lived.

Natural resources are the economic driver here, farming and timber, though the timber side has been in overall decline for several decades.

This is the quintessential Idaho switchover county: Once (from the 30s up until the mid-70s) timber-Democratic, more recently solidly conservative Republican. And yet the situation shouldn't be overstated. Republicans have been active here for decades; for almost all of the latter half of the twentieth century, they've been a presence at the courthouse. And since James McClure began winning congressional races in the latter half of the 60s (narrowly winning in this county in 1968 over former Democratic Representative Compton White), Idaho County has been trending Republican on the federal level – no Democrat has won here for president since 1964. So Republican strength here goes back to the partisan realignment of the mid-60s.

Little of this has had to do with population increase overall. It may have related to population replacement, as timber and other workers who lost their jobs over this period left, and with environmental issues.

PRECINCTS (27) The only truly competitive and maybe marginally Democratic precinct here in 2010 was Joseph, a lightly-populated rugged area in the northwest of Idaho County, facing both the Salmon and Snake rivers. If that seems odd, the next most competitive is Lowell, the camping spot on Highway 12 east of all other Idaho communities on that road. Also a little less Republican than most: Kooskia and Kamiah, possibly in part reflecting the Nez Perce tribal influence there. The Grangeville precincts, once a little more Democratic than most of Idaho County, now are scattered around the county's voting norm, which is landslide Republican or close to it. Most Republican of these precincts is Fenn, on the Camas Prairie; it went 75% for Otter in 2010. Slate Creek and White Bird are nearly as Republican.

PRESIDENTIAL As noted: Republican on the presidential level since 1964, with once-modest margins growing into super-landslides.

	Dem	%	Rep	%	Total
2012	1,708	21.79%	5,921	75.55%	7,837
2008	2,017	24.57%	5,895	71.80%	8,210
2004	1,689	21.21%	6,017	75.54%	7,965
2000	1,187	16.16%	5,806	79.06%	7,344

GOVERNOR Idaho continued to back Democratic legislators and governors for a while after leaving the party on the federal level. But it went Republican in Andrus' narrow 1986 re-election; after joining in his landslide in 1990, it has voted for Republicans since.

	Dem	%	Rep	%	Total
2010	1,505	22.96%	4,324	65.95%	6,556
2006	2,251	34.98%	3,892	60.48%	6,435
2002	2,075	31.84%	4,252	65.24%	6,517

COUNTY The Republican shift seemed to translate last to the courthouse level, where by the late 90s Republicans became dominant. Early in the next decade, around 2002 and 2004, local Democrats saw a resurgence at the courthouse level, but lost ground again toward the end of the decade.

Com1	Democrat			Republican		
2012	-		-	- Skip Brandt	5,372	100.00%
2008	-	0	0.00%	Skip Brandt	6,151	100.00%
2006	Richard Adams	2,794	48.28%	John Schurbon	3,186	51.72%
2002	-	0	0.00%	Alice Mattson	3,750	60.50%
Com2	Democrat			Republican		
2010	-	0	0.00%	James Rockwell	4,537	71.50%
2008	Shelly Dumas	2,005	25.64%	James Rockwell	5,815	74.36%
2004	Randy Doman	2,890	37.12%	Twila Hornbeck	2,712	34.83%
2002	-	0	0.00%	Pat Holmanberg	4,717	100.00%
Com3	Democrat			Republican		
2012	Jim Rehder	3,680	47.80%	Jim Chmelik	4,023	52.20%
2010	Jim Rehder	2,898	43.90%	Jim Chmelik	3,700	56.10%
2006	Jim Rehder	3,193	50.58%	Jim Chmelik	3,120	49.42%
2004	Jim Rehder	4,100	52.99%	Jim Chmelik	3,638	47.01%

Clerk	Democrat		Republican	
2010	-	0.00%	Kathy Ackerman	100.00%
2006	-		Rose Gehring	100.00%
2002	-		Rose Gehring	77.90%
Treasurer	Democrat		Republican	
2010*	-	0.00%	-	0.00%
2006	Sharon Cox	100.00%	-	0.00%
2002	Sharon Cox	100.00%	-	0.00%
Assessor	Democrat		Republican	
2010	-	0.00%	James Zehner	100.00%

2006	Ron Fuke	42.09%	James Zehner	57.91%
2002	Jim Beckman	69.80%	Willard Dewar	30.20%
Coroner	**Democrat**		**Republican**	
2010	-	0.00%	Steve Frei	100.00%
2006	Phil Foster	23.39%	Steve Frei	76.61%
2002	-	0.00%	Steve Frei	100.00%
Sheriff	**Democrat**		**Republican**	
2012	**-**	**-**	**Doug Giddings**	**100.00%**
2008	Carlos Martinez	39.26%	Doug Giddings	54.28%
2004	Wayne Sedam	15.08%	Larry Dasenbrock	69.57%
Pros Atty	**Democrat**		**Republican**	
2012	**-**	**-**	**Kirk MacGregor**	**100.00%**
2008	-	0.00%	Kirk MacGregor	100.00%
2004	-	0.00%	Kirk MacGregor	100.00%

*Sharon Cox, who had been elected treasurer unopposed as a Democrat in 2002 and 2006, was re-elected unopposed as an independent in 2010.

JEFFERSON

AREA Communities: Rigby, Menan, Roberts, Ririe, Lewisville, Mud Lake, Terreton. 1,106 sq. mi.

POPULATION 26,140 (13th). Increase 00s: 36.5%. Minority: 12.3%. Hispanic: 10.1%.

No major changes here in one of Idaho's most solidly Republican counties, a combination of farming and bedroom community for Idaho Falls, though the county's population grew in the 90s and faster in the 00s. There is the usual pattern of races that were more closely contested in the early 60s than later – and up to the early 70s, Jefferson did elect Democrats to the legislature from time to time, even for a few years having an all-Democratic delegation. Any such close competition ended, though, in the period of the Wallace splitoff, the McGovern candidacy and the great realignment of the mid-60s. Those set the stage for disproportionate Republican majorities that have lasted since.

The county courthouse has seen some negative headlines in recent years. In December 2013, Prosecutor Robin Dunn was asked to repay about $18,000 in legal fees to the county, the allegation being that he was paid improperly; articles in the Idaho Falls *Post Register* suggested the county commission was involved in the case. The case is pending.

PRECINCTS (18) Solid Republican throughout. Three of the Rigby precincts are the closest to competitive, but even they usually cast landslides for Republican candidates. The *most* Republican in Jefferson: small, relatively remote, rural and agricultural plains precincts Hamer, Monteview, Terreton and (more hilly) Annis.

PRESIDENTIAL The last Democratic win for president here: Roosevelt in 1944. The county was created in 1913 was its first presidential vote was for Woodrow Wilson in 1916. GOP supermajorities are the rule here now.

	Dem	%	Rep	%	Total
2012	1,303	11.45%	9,895	86.94%	11,381
2008	1,641	15.72%	8,540	81.79%	10,441
2004	1,084	12.17%	7,703	86.49%	8,906
2000	1,100	14.09%	6,480	82.98%	7,809

GOVERNOR The Andrus landslides swept Jefferson along, but since the 60s strong Republican votes have been the norm here. (Jefferson has a colorful competitive history in the 40s and 50s, though.)

	Dem	%	Rep	%	Total
2010	1,923	25.54%	5,024	66.74%	7,528
2006	1,880	25.15%	5,220	69.82%	7,476
2002	1,661	24.85%	4,902	73.33%	6,685

COUNTY Jefferson has seldom allowed more than one or two Democrats in the courthouse at the same time. In the last decade, there've been none – and no Democrats ran for any county office in all that time.

Com1	Democrat			Republican		
2012	**-**		**-**	**- Brian Farnsworth**	**9,974**	**100.00%**
2008	-	0	0.00%	Debbie Karren	9,248	100.00%
2006	-		-	Brett Olaveson	6,531	100.00%
2002	-	0	0.00%	Brett Olaveson	6,092	100.00%
Com2	Democrat			Republican		
2010	-	0	0.00%	Tad Hegsted	6,377	100.00%
2008	-	0	0.00%	Tad Hegsted	8,961	100.00%
2004	-	0	0.00%	Tad Hegsted	7,667	100.00%
2002	-	0	0.00%	Darwin Casper	5,946	100.00%
Com3	Democrat			Republican		
2012	**-**		**-**	**- Jerald Raymond**	**9,797**	**100.00%**
2010	-	0	0.00%	Jerald Raymond	6,580	100.00%
2006	-	0	0.00%	Ron Baxter	6,470	100.00%
2004	-	0	0.00%	Ron Baxter	7,700	100.00%

Clerk	Democrat		Republican	
2010	-	0.00%	Christine Boulter	99.10%
2006	-	0.00%	Christine Boulter	100.00%
2002	-	0.00%	Christine Boulter	100.00%
Treasurer	Democrat		Republican	
2010	-	0.00%	Kristine Lund	100.00%
2006	-	0.00%	Kristine Lund	100.00%
2002	-	0.00%	Kristine Lund	100.00%
Assessor	Democrat		Republican	
2010	-	0.00%	Cody Taylor	100.00%
2006	-	0.00%	Joyce Briggs	100.00%
Coroner	Democrat		Republican	
2010	-	0.00%	LaVar Summers	100.00%
2006	-	0.00%	LaVar Summers	100.00%
Sheriff	Democrat		Republican	
2012	**-**		**- Blair Olsen**	**69.20%**
2008	-	0.00%	Blair Olsen	100.00%
2004	-	0.00%	Blair Olsen	100.00%
Pros Atty	Democrat		Republican	
2012	**-**		**- Robin Dunn**	**100.00%**
2008	-	0.00%	Robin Dunn	100.00%
2004	-	0.00%	Robin Dunn	100.00%

JEROME

AREA Communities: Jerome, Hazelton, Eden. 605 sq. mi.

POPULATION 1,871.
Increase 00s: -2.3%.
Minority: 33.1%. Hispanic: 31.0%.

Across the Snake River from Twin Falls, Jerome County is focused on food processing (it has several large plants), irrigated agriculture and CAFOs – contained animal feeding operations. Its business has been growing but its population has been static.

Not much change here politically, other than the familiar pattern of relatively close numbers up until the early 70s, and then a Republican pulling away from a static or slightly diminishing Democratic number. The county's population increase of about 50% during this time helps account for the Republican increase; apparently few Democrats moved in.

PRECINCTS (11) Republican landslides are the norm throughout Jerome. Those wins are slightly smaller in the close-in Jerome precincts (Northwest and Southeast). Canyonside and Hazelton cast the most sweeping Republican votes.

PRESIDENTIAL Jerome, along with Cassia, may be the most solidly Republican of the Magic Valley counties. It beat Cassia by voting consistently Republican for president from 1940 to present (Cassia was 1944 the present).

	Dem	%	Rep	%	Total
2012	1,699	25.43%	4,804	71.91%	6,681
2008	1,794	26.20%	4,897	71.52%	6,847
2004	1,344	20.43%	5,177	78.68%	6,580
2000	1,360	22.78%	4,418	74.00%	5,970

GOVERNOR Like many other counties, Jerome did go along with the Democrats for a time in the 70s (1974, 1978) and in the Andrus 1990 landslide. It has not come close since.

	Dem	%	Rep	%	Total
2010	1,129	24.14%	3,138	67.11%	4,676
2006	1,849	39.82%	2,876	61.94%	4,643
2002	1,427	31.16%	3,065	66.94%	4,579

COUNTY Predictably, not many Democrats have been elected in recent decades to the courthouse – hardly any at all in the last half-century. None at all in the 00s, a period when only one Democrat in one race ran for county office here.

Com1	Democrat			Republican		
2012	-	-	-	**Cathy Roemer**	**5,794**	**100.00%**
2008	-	0	0.00%	Cathy Roemer	5,677	100.00%
2006	Samuel Harris	1,686	37.57%	Diana Obenauer	2,802	62.43%
2002	-	0	0.00%	Veronica Lierman	3,853	100.00%
Com2	**Democrat**			**Republican**		
2010	-	0	0.00%	Charles Howell	4,057	100.00%
2008	-	0	0.00%	Charles Howell	5,721	100.00%
2004	-	0	0.00%	Charles Howell	5,518	100.00%
2002	-	0	0.00%	Alvin Chojnacky	3,918	100.00%
Com3	**Democrat**			**Republican**		
2012	-	-	-	**Roger Morley**	**5,755**	**100.00%**
2010	-	0	0.00%	Roger Morley	4,069	100.00%
2006	-	0	0.00%	Joe Davidson	3,647	100.00%
2004	-	0	0.00%	Joe Davison	5,194	100.00%

Clerk	Democrat		Republican	
2010	-	0.00%	Michelle Emerson	100.00%
2006	-	0.00%	Michelle Emerson	100.00%
2002	-	0.00%	Cheryl Watts	100.00%
Treasurer	**Democrat**		**Republican**	
2010	-	0.00%	Mary Childers	100.00%
2006	-	0.00%	Mary Childers	100.00%
2002	-	0.00%	Mary Childers	100.00%
Assessor	**Democrat**		**Republican**	
2010	-	0.00%	Rick Haberman	100.00%
2006	-	0.00%	Rick Haberman	100.00%
2002	-	0.00%	Bonnie Tolman	100.00%
Coroner	**Democrat**		**Republican**	
2010	-	0.00%	Gerald Brant	100.00%
2006	-	0.00%	Gerald Ostler	100.00%
2002	-	0.00%	Gerald Ostler	100.00%
Sheriff	**Democrat**		**Republican**	
2012	-		-	**Douglas McFall**	**77.80%**
2008	-	0.00%	Douglas McFall	61.11%
2004	-	0.00%	Jim Weaver*	50.06%
Pros Atty	**Democrat**		**Republican**	
2012	-		-	**John Horgan**	**100.00%**
2008	-	0.00%	John Horgan	100.00%
2004	-	0.00%	Jon Nicholson	100.00%

*In this unusual contest, Weaver beat two previous sheriffs (George Silver and Wayne Childer).

KOOTENAI

AREA Communities: Coeur
d'Alene, Post Falls, Hayden,
Rathdrum, Dalton Gardens,
Hayden Lake, Harrison, Spirit
Lake, Worley, Hauser, Huetter,
Stateline. 1,310 sq. mi.

POPULATION
138,494 (3rd).
Increase 00s:
27.4%. Minority:
8.0%. Hispanic:
3.8%.

Kootenai was never a hard-core Democratic county –
there were periodic elections of Republicans to the
legislature back in the 40s – but it was a socially
conservative working class place which once could be
called conservative union Democratic, then seized on the Republican
presidential message at the end of the 60s and early 70s. The split, here as
in the south, came after the decisive Johnson win here in 1964 (57.4% to
42.6%), when George Wallace split the Democrats (Wallace got 10% or
1,472 votes; his plus Humphrey would equal 7,679, or a clear win over
Nixon, and not so great a comedown from Johnson). The Wallace votes
then attached to the Republicans – an old story nationally, but especially
stark here.

The other standard issue element of this is that the presidential contest
led the way, in waves. It was with that 1968 election that James McClure,
running for the House, edged past Democrat Compton White, to amass
larger numbers after that, and the trend for that office held when Steve
Symms won Kootenai in 1972, albeit not by much. Still (aside from the
1972 election which had an unusual for the time Republican insurgency,
and didn't last) the Democratic presumption for most offices continued into
the 70s, though their margins slipped as the county's population grew. The
tipping point hit around 1980 when, even as Frank Church won the county,
Republicans scored a string of wins on the legislative and county fronts.
From there, Republican numbers grew, steadily.

This was masked somewhat in the late 80s and early 90s on the local
(legislative and county) level by a split within the Republican Party, as Ron
Rankin led splinter candidacies that gave Democrats enough votes to win a
batch of races. But with hindsight, that was not fated to last, as Republican
numbers kept climbing and Rankin and the local Republicans made up. By
2004, the picture was stark: The Democratic presidential vote here was
17,584, almost exactly where it was in 1996, while the Republican vote
during that time doubled from 18,740 to 36,173. The available Republican
vote seems to be simply a lot higher than the Democratic.

Yet there was one highly interesting development here in 2002 and
2004, one which matched with small-scale Democratic resurgence
elsewhere: A central-city Democratic vote. Through the 80s and 90s, as the
partisan votes split and splintered, the area considered best for Democrats
was the Post Falls area close by the Washington line; in the 90s it elected
several Democrats (usually in splintered-GOP situations). Coeur d'Alene
itself, despite the influence of North Idaho College, had been thought for
some time to be strongly leaning Republican. But in 2002, after having been
wiped out of the delegation for some years, two Democrats returned – both

from the central Coeur d'Alene district – the closest thing the county has to a center city, as opposed to suburban development. One of them held on through the 2008 election, though the district returned to all-GOP in 2010.

PRECINCTS (75) The one remaining Democratic base in Kootenai County, where Democrats have either a majority (58, 56, 59, 55) or are closely competitive (54, 60, 51, 53, 57) are all in one place: central, and older, Coeur d'Alene, from the downtown and lakefront area north and east to I-90. One other precinct to note: 71, which includes the northern part of the Coeur d'Alene Reservation, and is politically competitive (with a Republican lean). Apart from a dozen or so Democratic or competitive precincts in those areas, the rest of the 75 are all clearly Republican, from fairly strong to super-landslide strength.

The most overwhelmingly Republican area in Kootenai is the area north of Hayden to the Bonner County line (precincts 6, 2, 3) on either side of Highway 95 – Athol, and Chilco and the developing areas around them. Nearly as Republican: The hills south of Coeur d'Alene across the lake and the Spokane River (precincts 64, 63, 65, 67) – an area not far from the city but off the beaten traffic lanes and hard to navigate if you don't know it well. Those register the highest Republican percentages, but almost everywhere else in the county registers high.

PRESIDENTIAL Mostly Republican up to 1930, most Democratic from then to the mid-60s, including the 1964 Johnson landslide. When the Wallace Democrats joined the Republicans, Kootenai flipped again, and has been solidly Republican in the presidentials since.

	Dem	*%*	*Rep*	*%*	*Total*
2012	18,851	31.51%	39,381	65.82%	59,828
2008	22,120	35.72%	38,387	61.98%	61,932
2004	17,584	32.21%	36,173	66.26%	54,596
2000	13,488	30.97%	28,162	64.67%	43,547

GOVERNOR Below the federal level, Kootenai remained highly competitive through the 80s, and Democrats won gubernatorial races here more than they lost through 1990. Since that landslide year, they have not come close.

	Dem	*%*	*Rep*	*%*	*Total*
2010	11,246	26.59%	28,381	67.10%	42,297
2006	16,246	38.88%	20,154	48.24%	41,780
2002	12,547	39.01%	18,967	58.98%	32,160

COUNTY The courthouse has been Republican dominated, with a period of some Democratic resurgence in the late 80s, since about 1980. During the 00s Democrats retained one of the nine offices – Dan English as county clerk. But he was defeated in 2010, turning the courthouse all-GOP.

Com1	Democrat			Republican		
2012	-		-	- Todd Tondee	44,459	93.80%
2008	Bruce Noble	19,466	33.52%	Todd Tondee	33,046	56.90%

Year	Democrat			Republican		
2006	-	0	0.00%	Todd Tondee	23,036	67.50%
2002	Paula Laws	10,388	33.20%	Gus Johnson	18,978	60.60%
Com2	**Democrat**			**Republican**		
2010	-	0	0.00%	Jai Nelson	30,899	86.70%
2008	Stephen Caires	18,149	31.16%	Rick Currie	31,079	53.36%
2004	-	0	0.00%	Rick Currie	41,387	100.00%
2002	-	0	0.00%	Rick Currie	17,243	56.40%
Com3	**Democrat**			**Republican**		
2012	-	-	-	**Dan Green**	**45,128**	**97.30%**
2010	-	0	0.00%	Dan Green	34,021	100.00%
2006	-	0	0.00%	Rich Piazza	28,862	100.00%
2004	-	0	0.00%	Katie Brodie	41,559	100.00%

	Democrat		Republican	
Clerk	**Democrat**		**Republican**	
2010	Dan English	39.50%	Cliff Hayes	60.50%
2006	Dan English	100.00%	-	0.00%
2002	Dan English	53.30%	Tina Jacobson	42.30%
Treasurer	**Democrat**		**Republican**	
2010	-	0.00%	Tom Malzahn	100.00%
2006	Dan Duffey	34.68%	Tom Malzahn	100.00%
2002	-	0.00%	Tom Malzahn	81.80%
Assessor	**Democrat**		**Republican**	
2010	-	0.00%	Mike McDowell	100.00%
2006	-	0.00%	Mike McDowell	100.00%
2002	-	0.00%	Mike McDowell	100.00%
Coroner	**Democrat**		**Republican**	
2010	Jody Hissong	34.00%	Debbie Wilkey	66.00%
2006	-	0.00%	Robert West	100.00%
2002	-	0.00%	Robert West	78.70%
Sheriff	**Democrat**		**Republican**	
2012	-	-	**Ben Wolfinger**	**72.50%**
2008	-	0.00%	Rocky Watson	75.03%
2004	-	0.00%	Rocky Watson	76.37%
Pros Atty	**Democrat**		**Republican**	
2012	-	-	**Barry McHugh**	**100.00%**
2008	-	0.00%	Barry McHugh	100.00%
2004	-	0.00%	Bill Douglas	100.00%

LATAH

AREA Communities: Moscow, Troy, Potlatch, Harvard, Bovill, Genesee, Deary, Kendrick, Onaway, Juliaetta, Viola. 1,077 sq. mi.

POPULATION 37,244 (11th). Increase 00s: 6.6%. Minority: 9.4%. Hispanic: 3.6%.

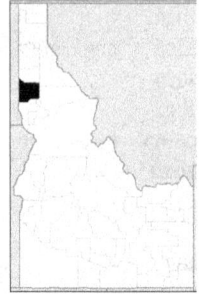

Once considered something of a Republican holdout in a Democratic northern Idaho, the situation has flipped: Competitive, not locked down by either party, available to either side, but increasingly Democratic-leaning.

Latah has an unusual voting history in the region. In hardly any other cases do the available votes for both parties for president match up in the early 60s and the 00s the way they do here, both parties nearly doubling their vote in the county, both winning presidentials. Latah, competitive in the 60s, remains competitive in a similar fashion in the new millennium. Hardly any counties have had such deeply split legislative delegations and courthouses in so many cycles, year in year out – even while office holders found they had to scramble to hang on. In electoral structure, it may be the least changed county in Idaho, one of the least changed in the northwest.

It has increased in population by more than 50%, as many changed counties have. But its nature hasn't changed greatly. Much of the expansion has come at the University of Idaho, and the university-area precincts have trended Democratic; the Moscow precincts generally have been Democratic. There's been scarcely any conventional suburban development to speak of, and that's where much of the growth in Republican numbers has arisen from in other places.

PRECINCTS (33) The remote Farmington precinct, rolling wheat country near the Benewah County and Washington state lines and very much off the much-traveled roads, is the fifth most Republican precinct in Idaho. (18 of its 20 votes for governor in 2010 went for Otter, and one of the others went for the libertarian.)

Farmington is an outlier here. The biggest impact in Latah comes from Moscow's 18 precincts, more than half the total. And 11 of those precincts in recent elections have been clearly Democratic in lean (very strong in Moscow 15, 16, 6, 13, 10, 14, 11 and 18, those in or near downtown and the University of Idaho) and all the rest are at least competitive. Atop that, several of the smaller communities (Bovill, Troy, Kendrick, Potlatch) often are competitive as well. Farmington aside, the true Republican precincts in Latah are Linden, Princeton, Harvard, Cora, Deary, Genesee and Viola.

PRESIDENTIAL How about this for a track record: Since the mid-40s, Latah has voted for the winner in every presidential contest but three: It voted for Republicans Nixon in 1960 and Ford in 1976 and Democrat Dukakis in 1988, all prefiguring later party swings. In 2008 it was once of three Idaho counties voting for Democrat Obama.

	Dem	%	Rep	%	Total
2012	8,306	49.56%	7,589	45.28%	16,759
2008	9,195	51.91%	7,988	45.09%	17,714
2004	8,430	48.04%	8,686	49.50%	17,547
2000	5,661	37.45%	8,161	53.99%	15,116

GOVERNOR Latah is more Democratic when it comes to voting for governor, than just about anywhere else – and just about any other Idaho county. It voted Republican for the office in 1998 (when Democrat Robert Huntley lost in a landslide), but that was the first time it had done so since supporting Republican Robert Smylie in 1958. That Democratic gubernatorial streak is surpassed only by Shoshone County.

	Dem	%	Rep	%	Total
2010	5,857	47.31%	5,696	46.01%	12,381
2006	7,155	58.41%	4,461	36.42%	12,249
2002	6,456	55.26%	4,963	42.48%	11,683

COUNTY As you might expect, courthouse races here often have been competitive, and both counties have elected plenty of county officials. In the 00s, Democrats have held a small edge, but Republicans have consistently held several offices as well.

Com1	Democrat			Republican		
2012	**Steve Cooke**	**7,388**	**46.30%**	**Richard Walser**	**8,559**	**53.70%**
2008	Jennifer Barrett	10,052	60.95%	Carl Hulquist	6,440	39.05%
2006	Jennifer Barrett	6,421	55.00%	Donald Ball	5,253	45.00%
2002	John Arno	4,953	44.00%	Paul Kimmell	6,309	56.00%
Com2	Democrat			Republican		
2010	Tom Stroschein	6,311	52.50%	Bill Goesling	5,710	47.50%
2008	Tom Stroschein	13,552	100.00%	-	0	0.00%
2004	Tom Stroschein	9,385	57.32%	Jeff Harkins	6,987	42.68%
2002	Tom Stroschein	6,261	55.90%	Mel Wilks	3,877	34.60%
Com3	Democrat			Republican		
2012	**-**	**-**		**David McGraw**	**12,064**	**100.00%**
2010	Robin Ohlgren	5,090	42.28%	David McGraw	6,104	50.70%
2006	Linda Pike	5,792	49.23%	Jack Nelson	5,972	50.77%
2004	Linda Pike	7,542	46.07%	Jack Nelson	8,829	53.93%

Clerk	Democrat			Republican		
2010	-		0.00%	Susan Petersen		100.00%
2006	-		0.00%	Susan Petersen		67.37%
2002	-		0.00%	Susan Petersen		100.00%
Treasurer	Democrat			Republican		
2010	-		0.00%	Lois Reed		100.00%
2008	-		0.00%	Connie Ferguson		100.00%
2006	Khaliela Wright		44.02%	Les Proctor		55.98%

2002	-	0.00%	Les Proctor	100.00%
Assessor	**Democrat**		**Republican**	
2010	Patrick Vaughn	52.40%	Jerry Coleman	47.60%
2006	Patrick Vaughn	50.47%	Connie Ferguson	49.53%
2002	Steve Fiscus	100.00%	-	0.00%
Coroner	**Democrat**		**Republican**	
2010	Catherine Mabbutt	100.00%	-	0.00%
2006	Catherine Mabbutt	53.86%	David Hutton	46.14%
2002*	-	0.00%	-	0.00%
Sheriff	**Democrat**		**Republican**	
2012	**Keith Wilson**	**47.20%**	**Wayne Rausch**	**52.80%**
2008	Keith Wilson	44.37%	Wayne Rausch	55.63%
2004	Jeffrey Crouch	40.01%	Wayne Rausch	55.63%
Pros Atty	**Democrat**		**Republican**	
2012	**Bill Thompson**	**100.00%**	-	-
2008	Bill Thompson	63.32%	Brian Thie	36.68%
2004	Bill Thompson	100.00%	-	0.00%

* Independent Dan Schmidt (in 2010 elected as a Democrat to the Idaho Senate) was elected unopposed.

230

LEMHI

AREA Communities: Salmon, Leadore, Lemhi, North Fork, Carmen, Shoup. 4,571 sq. mi.

POPULATION 7,936 (32nd). Increase 00s: 1.7%. Minority: 5.0%. Hispanic: 2.3%.

What's startling with some of the most Republican counties – now – in Idaho is how bipartisan they once were. That does not translate to broadly ideological: Those long-ago Democrats who could win votes here were as conservative, or more so, as the Republicans they ran against. The few times since that Democrats have won some votes in Lemhi County – as they did for commission seats here for a time in the 90s – ideology does not seem to have been a factor; rather, other elements (such as a bitter dispute involving the local hospital in this case) seem to be primarily relevant.

Its remoteness – this county could make a good case as being the most remote from major communities of any in the state – may be a factor. Lemhi has not been especially fast-growing, but most of the remote-seeking people who have arrived have translated into Republican votes, as the Democratic has remained static or dropped slightly from 1960.

PRECINCTS (9) All solidly Republican – all of the precincts here are ordinarily Republican on landslide levels. The strongest may be the notably remote Pahsimeroi (along the same-named river).

PRESIDENTIAL Lemhi last voted for a Democrat (Roosevelt) for president in 1940; not even the LBJ landslide brought these voters across.

	Dem	%	Rep	%	Total
2012	960	23.36	3,029	73.70%	4,110
2008	1,061	25.85%	2,938	71.57%	4,105
2004	915	22.58%	3,079	75.97%	4,053
2000	660	18.25%	2,859	79.07%	3,616

GOVERNOR With one striking exception (Democrat Evans in 1978), Lemhi last voted Democratic for governor in 1962. (The Democratic nominee's pro-gambling stance may have been a factor that year.)

	Dem	%	Rep	%	Total
2010	729	21.61%	2,272	67.36%	3,373
2006	1,162	34.80%	1,928	57.74%	3,339
2002	873	24.93%	2,533	72.33%	3,502

COUNTY Lemhi is more apt to elect an independent to county office (as has happened occasionally in the last generation) than a Democrat. No Democrats ran for the courthouse here in the 00s.

Com1	Democrat				Republican		
2012	**Luke Prange**	**1,265**	**32.50%**		**Robert Cope**	**2,626**	**67.50%**
2008	-	0	0.00%		Robert Cope	3,258	100.00%
2006*	-	0	0.00%		-	0	0.00%
2002*	-	0	0.00%		-	0	0.00%
Com2	Democrat				Republican		
2010	Cindy Phelps	1,042	31.20%		Richard Snyder	2,293	68.80%
2008	-	0	0.00%		Richard Snyder	3,264	100.00%
2004	-	0	0.00%		Richard Snyder	3,142	100.00%
2002	-	0	0.00%		Richard Snyder	2,777	100.00%
Com3	Democrat				Republican		
2012	-	-			**John Jakovac**	**3,493**	**100.00%**
2010	-	0	0.00%		John Jakovac	2,397	73.10%
2006	-	0	0.00%		Brett Barsalou	2,554	100.00%
2004	-	0	0.00%		Joe Proksch	2,907	100.00%

*Robert Cope was listed as an independent on the 2002 and 2006 ballots, and he was unopposed each time. He later listed himself as Republican.

Clerk	Democrat		Republican	
2010	-	0.00%	Terri Morton	100.00%
2006	-	0.00%	Terri Morton	100.00%
2002	-	0.00%	Terri Morton	100.00%
Treasurer	Democrat		Republican	
2010	-	0.00%	Mary Heiser	100.00%
2006	-	0.00%	Mary Heiser	100.00%
2002	-	0.00%	Mary Heiser	100.00%
Assessor	Democrat		Republican	
2010	-	0.00%	Jenny Rosin	100.00%
2006	-	0.00%	R.J. Smith	100.00%
2002	-	0.00%	R.J. Smith	51.30%
Coroner	Democrat		Republican	
2010	-	0.00%	Mike Mitchell	76.30%
2006	-	0.00%	Mike Mitchell	100.00%
2002	-	0.00%	Mike Mitchell	72.10%
Sheriff	Democrat		Republican	
2012	-	-	**Lynn Bowerman**	**80.70%**
2008	-	0.00%	Sam Slavin	100.00%
2004	-	0.00%	Sam Slavin	43.43%
Pros Atty	Democrat		Republican	
2012	-	-	**Paul Bruce Withers**	**100.00%**
2008	-	0.00%	Paul Bruce Withers	100.00%
2004	-	0.00%	Paul Bruce Withers	100.00%

LEWIS

AREA Communities: Kamiah, Craigmont, Nezperce, Winchester. 480 sq. mi.

POPULATION 1,871.
Increase 00s: -2.3%.
Minority: 11.1%.
Hispanic: 3.3%.

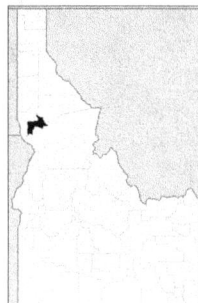

Hilly but not really mountainous Lewis county, dedicated to farming and ranching (with a substantial Nez Perce tribal center as well), was traditionally a solidly Democratic county. As in so much of Idaho, that has changed – mostly.

The Republican pattern is almost complete here, but not quite. Democrats still fared competitively or better in Lewis up to around 1990, but after that the county started a steady pattern of Republican votes for major offices, and then at the legislative level. At the courthouse, however, Democrats still are hanging on, and they're only occasionally challenged by Republicans.

PRECINCTS (8) Lewis may still vote for Democrats down-ticket, but at the top it is now solidly Republican; in 2010, only the small Reubens precinct was even close to competitive. Winchester and East Kamiah were the most Republicans parts of the county as of 2010.

PRESIDENTIAL The Lewis default on the presidential level used to be: Democratic except in case of a Republican landslide (it backed Nixon in 1972 and Reagan in 1980 and 1984). After 1992, however, it flipped Republican on the top of the ticket, and has stayed there since.

	Dem	%	Rep	%	Total
2012	396	24.54%	1,173	72.68%	1,614
2008	479	26.55%	1,275	70.68%	1,804
2004	440	24.18%	1,359	74.67%	1,820
2000	335	19.94%	1,295	77.08%	1,680

GOVERNOR Lewis was for decades a reliable Democratic county in gubernatorial races. That lasted through the 1990 Andrus landslide, but in 1994 went Republican. It has stayed there in governor's races.

	Dem	%	Rep	%	Total
2010	358	27.41%	827	63.32%	1,306
2006	578	44.77%	773	59.88%	1,291
2002	618	44.30%	754	54.05%	1,395

COUNTY Republicans now have a secure majority on the county commission, but they have not wiped out Democrats in the rest of the courthouse, as in so many counties. Four of the other six offices, in fact, were not challenged by Republicans at all in the 00s.

Com1	Democrat			Republican		
2012	**Charles Doty**	**458**	**29.00%**	**Greg Johnson**	**1,119**	**71.00%**
2008	Charles Doty	1,285	100.00%	-	0	0.00%
2006	Charles Doty	1,046	100.00%	-	0	0.00%
2002	Charles Doty	1,118	100.00%	-	0	0.00%
Com2	**Democrat**			**Republican**		
2010	-	0	0.00%	Carroll Keith	1,139	100.00%
2008	-	0	0.00%	Carroll Keith	1,162	62.64%
2004	Bill Baldus	503	27.71%	Carroll Keith	834	45.95%
2002	Joe Leitch	798	58.50%	George Thompson	566	41.50%
Com3	**Democrat**			**Republican**		
2012	**-**	**-**	**-**	**Don Davis**	**1,403**	**100.00%**
2010	-	0	0.00%	Don Davis	1,145	100.00%
2006	-	0	0.00%	Don Davis	836	67.47%
2004	-	0	0.00%	Leann Trautman	1,422	100.00%

Clerk	Democrat		Republican	
2010	Cathy Larson	100.00%	-	0.00%
2006	Cathy Larson	100.00%	-	0.00%
2002	Cathy Larson	100.00%	-	0.00%
Treasurer	**Democrat**		**Republican**	
2010	Pauline Malone	100.00%	-	0.00%
2006	Pauline Malone	100.00%	-	0.00%
2002	Pauline Malone	100.00%	-	0.00%
Assessor	**Democrat**		**Republican**	
2012	**Shelley Brian**	**100.00%**		
2010	Leslie Snyder	100.00%	-	0.00%
2006	Leslie Snyder	100.00%	-	0.00%
2002	Leslie Snyder	100.00%	-	0.00%
Coroner	**Democrat**		**Republican**	
2010	Robert Pratt	100.00%	-	0.00%
2006	Robert Pratt	100.00%	-	0.00%
2002	Robert Pratt	54.80%	Gordon Hawkins	45.20%
Sheriff	**Democrat**		**Republican**	
2012	**-**	**-**	**Brian Brokopp**	**64.50%**
2008	Brian Brokopp	43.93%	Joe Albright	32.28%
2004	Brian Brokopp	32.99%	Phil Steen	34.40%
Pros Atty	**Democrat**		**Republican**	
2012**	**-**	**-**	**-**	**-**
2008*	-	0.00%	-	0.00%
2004*	-	0.00%	-	0.00%

*Independent Kimron Torgerson elected in these two races, unopposed.
**Independent Zachary Pall was elected in 2012, unopposed.

LINCOLN

AREA Communities: Shoshone, Dietrich, Richfield, Kimama. 1,206 sq. mi.

POPULATION 5,208 (37th). Increase 00s: 28.8%. Minority: 30.7%. Hispanic: 28.3%.

But for the fact that rural and ranching Lincoln is tossed into the same legislative district as Blaine County, the top of the partisan chart, in the late 80s and since, would look pretty much all red – its legislative delegation is Democratic because of Blaine, though Lincoln voters have more or less gotten used to them. Most of the county still is organized around the rural economy, and to some extent transportation (remnants of the rail operation, and a regional highway office at Shoshone).

Lincoln's population has not changed greatly, spiking a bit in the late 90s and again in the 00s since with spillover growth from the Wood River Valley. Doesn't seem to have helped the local Democrats, though.

PRECINCTS (6) The two central Shoshone precincts (1 and 2) are the most competitive, but still lean Republican. The others lean very strongly. The most rural, Kimama, is the most Republican. The fastest-growing, Dietrich, is the next most Republican.

PRESIDENTIAL Consistently Republican; last voted for a Democrat in 1948 (Truman).

	Dem	%	Rep	%	Total
2012	469	28.22%	1,141	68.65%	1,662
2008	545	29.14%	1,232	65.88%	1,870
2004	466	24.85%	1,388	74.03%	1,875
2000	437	27.92%	1,049	67.03%	1,565

GOVERNOR Aside from votes for Andrus and Evans, Lincoln has been steadily Republican – borderline landslide in recent cycles.

	Dem	%	Rep	%	Total
2010	354	27.87%	773	60.87%	1,270
2006	599	47.50%	769	60.98%	1,261
2002	508	37.74%	807	59.96%	1,346

COUNTY Only occasionally does a Democrat slip through to county office (most recently, Commissioner Marsha Hiatt). The department heads, all Republicans, have been uncontested by Democrats in the 00s.

Com1	Democrat			Republican		
2012	-		-	- Cresley McConnell	888	54.40%

	Democrat			Republican		
2008*	-	0	0.00%	Joy Loesche	835	49.20%
2006	-	0	0.00%	Joy Loesche	695	51.98%
2002	-	0	0.00%	Rusty Parker	1,059	100.00%
Com2	**Democrat**			**Republican**		
2010	Marsha Hiatt	943	100.00%	-	0	0.00%
2008	Marsha Hiatt	1,077	60.30%	Wendell Johnson	709	39.70%
2004	-	0	0.00%	Lawrence Calkins	1,455	100.00%
2002	-	0	0.00%	Lawrence Calkins	1,092	100.00%
Com3	**Democrat**			**Republican**		
2012	**-**	**-**	**-**	**Roy Hubert**	**1,297**	**100.00%**
2010	-	0	0.00%	Jerry Nance	1,031	100.00%
2006	Jerry Heimerdinger	563	39.59%	Jerry Nance	655	46.06%
2004	-	0	0.00%	Jerry Nance	1,503	100.00%

*In 2008 commission 1, Loesche narrowly lost to independent Charles Ritter. In 2006, she had beaten him by a similar percentage.

Clerk	**Democrat**		**Republican**	
2010	-	0.00%	Suzanne McConnell	100.00%
2006	-	0.00%	Liz Kimer	100.00%
2002	-	0.00%	Liz Kimer	100.00%
Treasurer	**Democrat**		**Republican**	
2010	-	0.00%	Cathy Gilbert	100.00%
2006	-	0.00%	Cathy Gilbert	100.00%
2002	-	0.00%	Cathy Quiroga	100.00%
Assessor	**Democrat**		**Republican**	
2010	-	0.00%	Linda Jones	74.00%
2006	-	0.00%	Linda Jones	100.00%
2002	-	0.00%	Wendell Johnson	72.70%
Coroner	**Democrat**		**Republican**	
2010	-	0.00%	Keith Davis	100.00%
2006	-	0.00%	Keith Davis	100.00%
2002	-	0.00%	Keith Davis	100.00%
Sheriff	**Democrat**		**Republican**	
2012	**-**	**-**	**Kevin Ellis**	**87.20%**
2008	-	0.00%	Kevin Ellis*	48.84%
2004	-	0.00%	Kent McBride	100.00%
Pros Atty	**Democrat**		**Republican**	
2012	**-**	**-**	**Scott Paul**	**100.00%**
2008	-	0.00%	Scott Paul	100.00%
2004	-	0.00%	Scott Paul	100.00%

*Ellis won over an independent, a Constitition party candidate and a write-in.

MADISON

AREA Communities: Rexburg, Sugar City. 473 sq. mi.

POPULATION 37,536 (10th). Increase 00s: 36.7%. Minority: 8.8%. Hispanic: 5.9%.

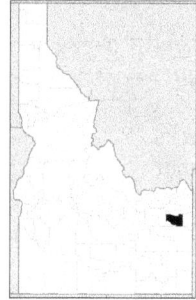

Madison once bipartisan? Well, in local and legislative races anyway. But the real trend here is in the presidential: The Republican vote for president quadrupled between 1960 and 2004, while the Democratic fell by half. All of that occurred while the county roughly tripled in size, and – with the growth of Brigham Young University-Idaho – continues to grow. The Democrats date back to a period of some strength in the 50s and 60s and to high regard for Ray Rigby and others less active for years.

Democrats from out of town are rejected out of hand. The last to win here, and not by much, were Andrus for governor and Stallings for the U.S. House in 1990; but it took Stallings years to win over this county even though he had taught at Ricks and was a Rexburg resident, and it turned against him later. This is a tough crowd if you're not Republican.

PRECINCTS (20) In this very Republican county, the least Republican precincts (and they still landslide to the GOP) are a string of counties with a population base in central Rexburg (14, 16, 8, 5, 9, 7) and with the Sugar-Salem precinct (6). The more rural and outlying precincts (17, 19, 1, 3) are also the most strongly Republican. But: Precinct 13, in southern Rexburg near BYU-Idaho, was the fourth most Republican precinct in Idaho in 2010.

PRESIDENTIAL Madison is another of those counties that sends you back well over half a century (to 1948) to find a Democratic vote for president. It now generates some of Idaho's very highest county percentages for Republican presidential nominees.

	Dem	%	Rep	%	Total
2012	832	5.77%	13,445	93.29%	14,412
2008	1,627	12.46%	11,131	85.25%	13,057
2004	826	7.10%	10,693	91.89%	11,637
2000	816	9.14%	7,941	88.92%	8,930

GOVERNOR Madison is not far from that track in governor's races. In the last half-century only Andrus in 1974 and 1990 pulled its vote.

	Dem	%	Rep	%	Total
2010	2,594	33.63%	4,739	61.44%	7,713
2006	2,118	27.61%	5,554	72.41%	7,670
2002	1,771	24.67%	5,280	73.56%	7,178

COUNTY Democrats used to supply as many as two or three county officials out of the nine, up to the mid-70s. In the last decade, they've rarely run for the jobs at all.

Com1	Democrat			Republican		
2012	**-**		**-**	**Kimber Ricks**	**12,720**	**100.00%**
2008	-	0	0.00%	Kimber Ricks	11,638	100.00%
2006	-	0	0.00%	Kimber Ricks	7,221	100.00%
2002	-	0	0.00%	Roger Muir	6,416	100.00%
Com2	Democrat			Republican		
2010	-	0	0.00%	Jon Weber	5,683	78.80%
2008	-	0	0.00%	Jon Weber	11,501	100.00%
2004	-	0	0.00%	Ralph Robinson	10,198	100.00%
2002	-	0	0.00%	Reed Sommer	6,469	100.00%
Com3	Democrat			Republican		
2012	**-**		**-**	**Todd Smith**	**12,692**	**100.00%**
2010	-	0	0.00%	Todd Smith	6,700	100.00%
2006	-	0	0.00%	Robert Hansen	7,142	100.00%
2004	-	0	0.00%	Brooke Passey	10,080	100.00%

Clerk	Democrat		Republican	
2010	Bill Moss	28.60%	Kim Hinckley-Muir	71.40%
2006	-	0.00%	Marilyn Rasmussen	100.00%
2002	-	0.00%	Marilyn Rasmussen	100.00%
Treasurer	Democrat		Republican	
2010	-	0.00%	Sherry Arnold	100.00%
2006	-	0.00%	Sherry Arnold	100.00%
2002	-	0.00%	Sherry Arnold	100.00%
Assessor	Democrat		Republican	
2010	-	0.00%	Brent Saurey	100.00%
2006	-	0.00%	Brent Saurey	87.09%
2002	-	0.00%	Leeanne Archibald	75.90%
Coroner	Democrat		Republican	
2010	-	0.00%	Rick Davis	100.00%
2006	-	0.00%	Rick Davis	100.00%
2002	-	0.00%	Rick Davis	100.00%
Sheriff	Democrat		Republican	
2012	**-**		**Roy Klingler**	**74.00%**
2008	-	0.00%	Roy Klingler	100.00%
2004	-	0.00%	Roy Klingler	100.00%
Pros Atty	Democrat		Republican	
2012	**-**		**Sid Brown**	**100.00%**
2008	-	0.00%	Sid Brown	100.00%
2004	-	0.00%	Sid Brown	100.00%

MINIDOKA

AREA Communities: Rupert, Paul, Acequia, Minidoka, Kimima. 762 sq. mi.

POPULATION 20,069 (18th). Increase 00s: -0.5%. Minority: 34.8%. Hispanic: 32.4%.

The substantial Hispanic and food processing factory communities, in Rupert and the others nearby, suggest at least a theoretical base for Democrats in Minidoka. So far, that prospect remains mostly theoretical.

Since about 1980 especially, Republicans have consistently won almost everything in sight. Another gentle decline of Democratic numbers alongside a somewhat stronger rise in Republican numbers. But who has been moving in?

PRECINCTS (12) All of Minidoka is landslide Republican – all precincts. The lighter producers among them are four of the Rupert precincts (1, 3, 4 and 5). The most Republican precincts here are the more rural Emerson and Pioneer precincts.

PRESIDENTIAL Republican for a very long time, ever since it went for Roosevelt in 1940.

	Dem	%	Rep	%	Total
2012	1,390	19.93%	5,442	78.04%	6,973
2008	1,630	23.66%	5,087	73.83%	6,890
2004	1,331	18.49%	5,797	80.51%	7,200
2000	1,344	20.80%	4,907	75.95%	6,461

GOVERNOR Minidoka joined in some of the Andrus and Evans Democratic wins (1970, 1974, 1978, 1990), but otherwise has been reliably Republican for governor.

	Dem	%	Rep	%	Total
2010	1,000	20.67%	3,448	71.27%	4,838
2006	1,688	35.26%	3,217	67.20%	4,787
2002	1,630	30.64%	3,569	67.10%	5,319

COUNTY The courthouse has been solidly Republican for more than a decade. In the 00s, only one Democrat has even run for county office, and then finished with less than a quarter of the vote.

Com1	Democrat			Republican		
2012	-		-	- Bob Moore	5,957	100.00%
2008	-	0	0.00%	Bob Moore	5,780	100.00%
2006	-	0	0.00%	Bob Moore	4,475	100.00%
2002	-	0	0.00%	Marvin Bingham	4,486	100.00%

Com2	Democrat			Republican		
2010	-	0	0.00%	Kent McClellan	4,276	100.00%
2008	-	0	0.00%	Daniel Stapelman	5,634	100.00%
2004	-	0	0.00%	Daniel Stapelman	5,883	100.00%
2002	-	0	0.00%	Daniel Stapelman	4,497	100.00%
Com3	**Democrat**			**Republican**		
2012	**-**	**-**	**-**	**Sheryl Koyle**	**5,849**	**100.00%**
2010	-	0	0.00%	Sheryl Koyle	4,230	100.00%
2006	-	0	0.00%	Lynn Hunsaker	7,142	100.00%
2004	-	0	0.00%	Lynn Hunsaker	5,792	100.00%

Clerk	Democrat		Republican	
2010	-	0.00%	Patty Temple	100.00%
2006	-	0.00%	Duane Smith	100.00%
2002	-	0.00%	Duane Smith	100.00%
Treasurer	**Democrat**		**Republican**	
2010	-	0.00%	Laura Twiss	100.00%
2006	-	0.00%	Laura Twiss	100.00%
2002	-	0.00%	Laura Twiss	100.00%
Assessor	**Democrat**		**Republican**	
2010	-	0.00%	Max Vaughn	100.00%
2006	-	0.00%	Max Vaughn	100.00%
2002	-	0.00%	Max Vaughn	100.00%
Coroner	**Democrat**		**Republican**	
2010	-	0.00%	Lucky Bourn	100.00%
2006	-	0.00%	Joel Heward	100.00%
2002	Joanne Hollebeck	28.30%	Donald Fisher	58.00%
Sheriff	**Democrat**		**Republican**	
2012	**-**	**-**	**Kevin Halverson**	**69.90%**
2008	-	0.00%	Kevin Halverson	100.00%
2004	-	0.00%	Kevin Halverson	48.86%
Pros Atty	**Democrat**		**Republican**	
2012	**-**	**-**	**Lance Stevenson**	**100.00%**
2008	-	0.00%	Lance Stevenson	52.11%
2004	-	0.00%	Jason Walker	100.00%

NEZ PERCE

AREA Communities:
Lewiston, Lapwai, Culdesac,
Peck. 855 sq. mi.

POPULATION 39,265
(9th). Increase 00s:
5%. Minority: 11.3%.
Hispanic: 2.8%.

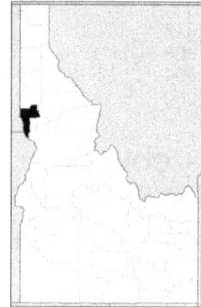

One of Idaho's original population centers – Lewiston was founded as a support and supply depot for the mining operations in the Clearwater Valley – Nez Perce County long had a clear economic base in timber and resources. Some of that remains at the Clearwater plant, but Lewiston's economy now is more diverse, a good thing since the timber economy in northern Idaho isn't what it once was.

Apart from Latah County, Nez Perce is about as close as North Central Idaho still gets to being a Democratic county – and it's no longer realistic to call it a Democratic county. Nez Perce's association with that image is of a different type, more union-based. More properly these days, however, Nez Perce is competitive: Both parties have a solid shot at electing their candidates, and in the new decade Republicans seem to have an edge. The nature of the candidates and their campaigns really does matter here, more than in almost any other Idaho county (Latah aside).

With the odd exception, Nez Perce voted mainly though not wholly for Democrats for many years, from the Depression years up to the early 90s. Then, even while voting Clinton for president in that decade, the county started voting for Republican state officials, legislators and more county officials as well. The late 90s saw a stretch of Republican near-dominance, holding all three local legislative seats and winning most major races. Then in the 00s, Democrats bounced back, partly. At decade's end, the two parties seemed to be in close balance.

What does all this add up to? A competitive stability? A turnaround against the Republicans? A last gasp from the Democrats? The 2012 election may provide some clues. Till then, maybe this: In the center of the city, around the university community, we find the strongest Democratic support. The urban/rural pattern holds.

PRECINCTS (38) The Lewiston precincts are no longer a Democratic redoubt, as they once were. The most Democratic precinct in Nez Perce now is the dominated by that tribe: Lapwai, which in 2010 declined support for both Republicans Crapo and Otter, the only Nez Perce precinct to do so. Only one Lewiston precinct (3) came close, and on top of the ticket only seven or eight other Lewiston precincts were truly competitive (mainly, 11, 2, 4, 9, 1 and 7). These precincts are mostly bunched in central Lewiston. On the flip side, the most Republican precincts in Nez Perce were mostly rural – Leland, Tammany, Rimrock, Gifford.

PRESIDENTIAL Nez Perce was among the last counties to flip from Democratic to Republican for president; it went for Republicans in landslides (Reagan twice, Nixon 1972) but otherwise staying with

Democrats through the Clinton years. But in the 00s it went Republican, and by substantial margins. This is a relatively unusual pattern.

	Dem	%	Rep	%	Total
2012	6,451	38.29%	9,967	59.16%	16,848
2008	7,123	39.97%	10,357	58.11%	17,823
2004	6,476	36.59%	11,009	62.20%	17,700
2000	4,995	31.31%	10,577	66.31%	15,951

GOVERNOR Nez Perce has been a little more Democratic in gubernatorial races. In recent decades it broke from the pattern only to vote for Batt in 1994 and Kempthorne in 1998, and again for Otter in 2010. Before 1994 the line of Democratic support goes back to 1962.

	Dem	%	Rep	%	Total
2010	4,438	35.15%	7,289	57.73%	12,625
2006	6,355	50.81%	5,583	44.64%	12,508
2002	6,523	51.88%	5,867	46.66%	12,573

COUNTY Republicans have been highly competitive at the commission level in recent years, in 2010 winning a commission majority (as they'd had on and off in the preceding decade and a half). Democrats have continued to hold most of the departments.

Com1	Democrat			Republican		
2012	**Kevin Kelly**	**6,052**	**37.50%**	**Bob Tippett**	**10,104**	**62.50%**
2008	JR Van Tassel	8,054	46.26%	Mike Grow	9,358	53.74%
2006	JR Van Tassel	9,545	100.00%	-	0	0.00%
2002	JR Van Tassel	6,656	53.60%	Keith Kinzer	5,227	42.10%
Com2	Democrat			Republican		
2010	Ron Wittman	5,960	48.20%	Douglas Havens	6,401	51.80%
2008	Ron Wittman	13,273	100.00%	-	0	0.00%
2004	Ron Wittman	11,515	70.79%	-	0	0.00%
2002	Ron Wittman	6,563	53.10%	Barbara Davis	5,791	46.90%
Com3	Democrat			Republican		
2012	-	-	-	**Douglas Zenner**	**13,684**	**100.00%**
2010	Pete Gertonson	5,243	42.40%	Douglas Zenner	7,113	57.60%
2006	Dave Stradley	5,063	42.38%	Douglas Zenner	6,883	57.62%
2004	Larry Vincent	8,238	47.90%	Douglas Zenner	8,962	52.10%

Clerk	Democrat			Republican		
2010	Patty Weeks		100.00%	-		0.00%
2006	Patty Weeks		100.00%	-		0.00%
2002	Patty Weeks		57.80%	Carol Reed		42.20%
Treasurer	Democrat			Republican		
2010	Barbara Fry		100.00%	-		0.00%
2006	Barbara Fry		100.00%	-		0.00%
2002	Barbara Fry		100.00%	-		0.00%
Assessor	Democrat			Republican		

		Democrat		Republican	
2010	Daniel Anderson	100.00%	-		0.00%
2006	Daniel Anderson	100.00%	-		0.00%
2002	Daniel Anderson	100.00%	-		0.00%
Coroner	**Democrat**			**Republican**	
2010	Gary Gilliam	100.00%	-		0.00%
2006	Gary Gilliam	100.00%	-		0.00%
2002	Gary Gilliam	51.80%	Larry Ballard		48.20%
Sheriff	**Democrat**			**Republican**	
2012	**Dale Buttrey**	**49.60%**	**Joe Rodriquez**		**50.40%**
2008	Dale Buttrey	52.61%	Steve Jenkins		46.72%
2004	Jim Dorion	51.42%	Randy Kingsbury		48.58%
Pros Atty	**Democrat**			**Republican**	
2012	**Kimron Torgerson**	**37.50%**	**Daniel Pickler**		**62.50%**
2008	-	0.00%	Daniel Spickler		100.00%
2004	-	0.00%	Daniel Spickler		100.00%

ONEIDA

AREA Communities: Malad, Samaria, Holbrook. 1,202 sq. mi.

POPULATION 4,286 (39th). Increase 00s: 3.9%. Minority: 5.0%. Hispanic: 2.9%.

There is an actual Democratic tradition in rural, remote and LDS-dominated Oneida County.

This small-population county has spawned a number of statewide leaders who are mostly Democrats (from 1899 House Speaker David Evans to, more recently, Governor John Evans and state Controller J.D. Williams). For a time in the 70s it was politically a competitive county, and through the 90s kept a number of Democrats at the courthouse, even while voting mostly Republican toward the top of the ballot.

This has changed. Oneida in the 00s became nearly as solidly Republican as any of the other rural eastern Idaho counties.

PRECINCTS (6) All six precincts are super-landslide Republican. The four Malad precincts are on the lower end of that spectrum (and formed the basis of Democratic strength, when that still existed), while Holbrook typically produces Republican wins well above 80%.

PRESIDENTIAL Oneida has not been competitive on the presidential level since New Deal Days, and last voted for a Democrat for president in 1948.

	Dem	%	Rep	%	Total
2012	217	10.39%	1,838	87.98%	2,089
2008	381	17.62%	1,724	79.74%	2,162
2004	304	14.25%	1,789	83.87%	2,133
2000	307	17.15%	1,426	79.66%	1,790

GOVERNOR Oneida voted for favorite son John Evans in 1978 and 1982 (and for him in his 1986 Senate run), and for Andrus in his two landslides. Otherwise, it has been a reliably Republican vote for governor.

	Dem	%	Rep	%	Total
2010	308	18.88%	1,219	74.74%	1,631
2006	448	27.62%	1,030	63.50%	1,622
2002	299	23.29%	955	74.38%	1,284

COUNTY Not so very long ago, as recently as the 90s, Democrats were in a position of parity or better at the courthouse, and held a commission majority. No longer. The last Democratic commissioner departed in 2008, and long-time Democratic Clerk Shirlee Blaisdell was defeated in 2010, making the Oneida courthouse all Republican.

Com1	Democrat			Republican		
2012	**Shellee Smith Daniels**	**1,151**	**55.90%**	**Alden Neal**	**908**	**44.10%**
2008	-	0	0.00%	Cecil Sweeten	1,411	69.78%
2006	Gerald Goodenough	965	62.99%	Blaine Price	567	37.01%
2002	Gerald Goodenough	1,063	100.00%	-	0	0.00%
Com2	Democrat			Republican		
2010	-	0	0.00%	Dale Tubbs	1,410	100.00%
2008	-	0	0.00%	Larry Etherington	1,742	100.00%
2004	-	0	0.00%	Dallan Nalder	1,726	100.00%
2002	-	0	0.00%	Jerry Bush	1,094	100.00%
Com3	Democrat			Republican		
2012	-	-	-	**Max Firth**	**1,865**	**100.00%**
2010	Bob Christopherson	656	40.10%	Max Firth	979	59.90%
2006	Joe Daniels	1,214	100.00%	-	0	0.00%
2004	Joe Daniels	1,171	55.66%	Jim Moss	933	44.34%

Clerk	Democrat		Republican	
2010	Shirlee Blaisdell	45.10%	Lon Colton	54.90%
2006	Shirlee Blaisdell	100.00%	-	0.00%
2002	Shirlee Blaisdell	100.00%	-	0.00%
Treasurer	Democrat		Republican	
2010	-	0.00%	Diane Pett	100.00%
2006	-	0.00%	Diane Pett	100.00%
2002	-	0.00%	Diane Pett	100.00%
Assessor	Democrat		Republican	
2010	-	0.00%	Dixie Hubbard	100.00%
2006	-	0.00%	Dixie Hubbard	100.00%
2002	-	0.00%	Kathryn Hill	100.00%
Coroner	Democrat		Republican	
2010	-	0.00%	Spence Horsley	100.00%
2006	-	0.00%	Spence Horsley	100.00%
2002	Sara Eames	12.90%	Spence Horsley	87.10%
Sheriff	Democrat		Republican	
2012	-	-	**Jeffrey Semrad**	**62.40%**
2008	-	0.00%	Jeffery Semrad	58.89%
2004	-	0.00%	Jeffery Semrad	64.34%
Pros Atty	Democrat		Republican	
2012	-	-	**Dustin Smith**	100.00%
2008	-	0.00%	Dustin Smith	100.00%
2006	-	0.00%	Dustin Smith	100.00%
2004	-	0.00%	Stevin Brooks	100.00%

OWYHEE

AREA Communities: Homedale, Marsing, Grandview, Bruneau, Murphy, Riddle, Silver City, Three Creek. 7,666 sq. mi.

POPULATION 11,526 (25th). Increase 00s: 8.3%. Minority: 31.7%. Hispanic: 25.8%.

Owyhee County still is the closest Idaho has to the old west – wide open spaces (the second largest county geographically) and a low, scattered population, and vast tracts where no one lives at all. Most people live near the Snake River, farming and ranching and working on allied activities, and some are exurbanites who work in the Boise-Nampa area. Politically, these are conservative and overwhelmingly Republican people; little remains of what was once a substantial conservative Democratic core. (The remote exception, to the south on the Nevada line, are the Shoshone-Paiute people on the Dick Valley Reservation, who vote Democratic.)

PRECINCTS (13) All heavily Republican, with one exception – the small rural precinct of Riddle (presumably owing to the influence of the Duck Valley Reservation). Pleasant Valley, the vast and very remote area well south of the Snake River toward the Nevada border, was the single most Republican precinct in Idaho in 2010. It voted 52-1 for Crapo for the Senate and 53-0 for Otter for governor. Also-remote Oreana precinct, the second-most Republican here, ranked 13th statewide. The larger Homedale and Marsing were more diverse in their voting, but not by much.

PRESIDENTIAL Owyhee is among the counties that stayed Republican in 1964, the Johnson national wave notwithstanding. Its Republican presidential streak goes back to 1940, when it went for Roosevelt.

	Dem	%	Rep	%	Total
2012	833	22.37%	2,794	75.03%	3,724
2008	944	23.26%	3,024	74.52%	4,058
2004	685	19.08%	2,859	79.64%	3,590
2000	623	19.63%	2,450	77.21%	3,173

GOVERNOR Owyhee went for Andrus in his landslide, and Evans in 1978, but otherwise has long been a reliable Republican county.

	Dem	%	Rep	%	Total
2010	472	16.38%	2,128	73.86%	2,881
2006	780	27.41%	1,972	69.29%	2,846
2002	785	29.77%	1,771	67.16%	2,637

COUNTY The Owyhee courthouse has periodically had Democratc officeholders, some even well-known (Sheriff Tim Nettleton of the Claude Dallas case for one). But in the 00s the courthouse has been all-GOP.

Com1	Democrat				Republican		
2012	-		**-**	**-**	**Jerry Hoagland**	**3,137**	**100.00%**
2008	Joe Gannuscio	1,041	26.82%	Jerry Hoagland	2,840	73.18%
2006	-	0	0.00%	Jerry Hoagland	2,415	100.00%
2002	-	0	0.00%	Harold Tolmie	2,168	100.00%
Com2	**Democrat**				**Republican**		
2010	Jaymie Mercado	331	13.90%	Kelly Aberasturi	2,045	86.10%
2008	-	0	0.00%	George Hyer	3,368	100.00%
2004	-	0	0.00%	Harold Tolmie	2,941	100.00%
2002	-	0	0.00%	Chris Salove	2,294	100.00%
Com3	**Democrat**				**Republican**		
2012	-		**-**	**-**	**Joe Merrick**	**3,052**	**100.00%**
2010	-	0	0.00%	Joe Merrick	2,429	100.00%
2006	-	0	0.00%	Dick Freund	2,258	100.00%
2004	-	0	0.00%	Dick Reynolds	2,972	100.00%

Clerk	Democrat		Republican	
2010	-	0.00%	Charlotte Sherburn	100.00%
2006	-	0.00%	Charlotte Sherburn	100.00%
2002	-	0.00%	Charlotte Sherburn	100.00%
Treasurer	**Democrat**		**Republican**	
2010	-	0.00%	Brenda Richards	100.00%
2006	-	0.00%	Brenda Richards	100.00%
2002	-	0.00%	Barbara Wright	100.00%
Assessor	**Democrat**		**Republican**	
2010	-	0.00%	Brett Endicott	100.00%
2006	-	0.00%	Brett Endicott	100.00%
2002	-	0.00%	Brett Endicott	100.00%
Coroner	**Democrat**		**Republican**	
2010	-	0.00%	Harvey Grimme	100.00%
2006	-	0.00%	Harvey Grimme	100.00%
2002	-	0.00%	Harvey Grimme	100.00%
Sheriff	**Democrat**		**Republican**	
2012	-	-	**Perry Grant**	**82.20%**
2008	-	0.00%	Daryl Crandall*	59.15%
2004	-	0.00%	Gary Aman	63.93%
Pros Atty	**Democrat**		**Republican**	
2012	-	-	**Douglas Emery**	**100.00%**
2008	-	0.00%	Douglas Emery	100.00%
2004	-	0.00%	Matthew Faulks	100.00%

* Defeated Sheriff Gary Aman, who was a write-in in the general.

PAYETTE

AREA Communities: Payette, Fruitland, New Plymouth. 403 sq. mi.

POPULATION 1,871. Increase 00s: -2.3%. Minority: 28.7%. Hispanic: 14.9%.

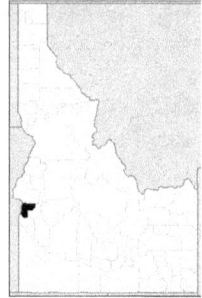

Talk about traditionally Republican – that's Payette, home to two conservative Republican senators (Herman Welker and James McClure – conservatives of rather different temperament) who each represented this county in the state Senate.

As elsewhere, the Republican margins have simply expanded over time, though they were always significant to start with. All of that said, Payette is a little more up for grabs – below the presidential level – than some Republican counties. In those cases of Democratic landslides, Payette would occasionally cross over.

PRECINCTS (3) No precincts short of strong landslide levels here. Little variation, but the most overwhelming Republican votes were in the precincts covering the foothills east of the Payette Valley (precinct 7) and around Sand Hollow (precinct 9).

PRESIDENTIAL Solidly Republican since its last Democratic vote for president in 1936.

	Dem	%	Rep	%	Total
2012	2,271	26.73%	6,004	70.68%	8,495
2008	2,415	28.04%	5,988	69.52%	8,613
2004	1,848	22.59%	6,256	76.48%	8,180
2000	1,643	24.04%	4,961	72.59%	6,834

GOVERNOR Payette last crossed over with the 1990 Andrus landslide (despite a favorite son, Roger Fairchild, as the Republican nominee).

	Dem	%	Rep	%	Total
2010	1,104	18.29%	4,342	71.94%	6,036
2006	1,946	32.54%	3,723	62.25%	5,981
2002	1,930	34.63%	3,530	63.34%	5,573

COUNTY Occasional Democrats were elected to the courthouse from the 60s into the 80s (notably, Sheriff Robert Barowsky). But there were never more than two or three, and none at all in the 00s – in fact, only one Democrat in the 00s even ran for a county office.

Com1	Democrat			Republican		
2012	-	-	-	Rudy Endrikat	7,013	100.00%
2008	Stephen Macklin	2,799	34.36%	Rudy Endrikat	5,346	65.64%

2006	-		0	0.00%	Rudy Endrikat	4,691	100.00%
2002	-		0	0.00%	Rudy Endrikat	3,796	78.80%
Com2	**Democrat**				**Republican**		
2010	-		0	0.00%	Marc Shigeta	5,210	100.00%
2008	-		0	0.00%	Marc Shigeta	7,339	100.00%
2004	-		0	0.00%	Marc Shigeta	6,378	100.00%
2002	-		0	0.00%	Marc Shigeta	4,649	100.00%
Com3	**Democrat**				**Republican**		
2012	**-**		**-**		**- Larry Church**	**7,154**	**100.00%**
2010	-		0	0.00%	Larry Church	5,179	100.00%
2006	-		0	0.00%	Larry Church	4,938	100.00%
2004	-		0	0.00%	Larry Church	4,890	65.27%

Clerk	**Democrat**			**Republican**	
2010	-		0.00%	Betty Dressen	100.00%
2006	-		0.00%	Betty Dressen	100.00%
2002	-		0.00%	Betty Dressen	100.00%
Treasurer	**Democrat**			**Republican**	
2010	-		0.00%	Donna Peterson	100.00%
2006	-		0.00%	Donna Peterson	100.00%
2002	-		0.00%	Donna Peterson	100.00%
Assessor	**Democrat**			**Republican**	
2010	-		0.00%	Sharon Worley	100.00%
2006	-		0.00%	Robert MacKenzie	100.00%
2002	-		0.00%	Robert Mackenzie	100.00%
Coroner	**Democrat**			**Republican**	
2010	-		0.00%	Keith Schuller	100.00%
2006	-		0.00%	Keith Schuller	100.00%
2002	-		0.00%	Keith Schuller	100.00%
Sheriff	**Democrat**			**Republican**	
2012	**-**			**- Chad Huff**	**100.00%**
2008	-		0.00%	Chad Huff	100.00%
2004	-		0.00%	Chad Huff	100.00%
Pros Atty	**Democrat**			**Republican**	
2012	**-**			**- Anne-Marie Kelso**	**100.00%**
2010	-		0.00%	Anne-Marie Kelso	100.00%
2008	-		0.00%	Brian Lee	100.00%
2004	-		0.00%	Brian Lee	100.00%

POWER

AREA Communities: American Falls, Arbon, Rockland. 1,442 sq. mi.

POPULATION 7,817 (33rd). Increase 00s: 3.7%. Minority: 33.9%. Hispanic: 29.8%.

Power County, mainly agricultural but also a bedroom for Pocatello-based factory and food processing work, has grown by about two-thirds since 1960, much of that growth in the precincts adjacent to Bannock County. Quite a few factory employees live there, and some Shoshone-Bannock tribal members too, and these have kept Power County as one of Idaho's most competitive counties, on the courthouse level at least.

Still, the record shows a strong Republican pattern in the 90s and since, prevailing in every presidential since 1964. While an otherwise strong Democrat would ordinarily win Power even up into the early 90s, that has evaporated as Democrats have stagnated and Republicans gradually – more gradually than in some counties – enhanced their numbers.

PRECINCTS (7) Except for the Arbon area (precinct 5), which votes so strongly Republican that it's the 11th most Republican precinct in Idaho, Power's precincts fall into the range of leaning slightly Republican but voting competitively – an unusual county in Idaho. A peculiarity: Precinct 6, in the east county by Pocatello where many of the Simplot (and formerly FMC) plant workers have lived, voted in 2010 more Republican than most of Power County, an apparent shift from a decade and two before.

PRESIDENTIAL Republicans have won solidly since 1964, by margins a little less than most nearby counties.

	Dem	%	Rep	%	Total
2012	982	33.83%	1,870	64.42%	2,903
2008	1,027	36.14%	1,754	61.72%	2,842
2004	829	28.03%	2,105	71.16%	2,958
2000	755	27.95%	1,872	69.31%	2,701

GOVERNOR From the New Deal up through the 1990 Andrus landslide, Power was ordinarily a Democratic county in governor races. From 1998 to present, it has voted solidly Republican.

	Dem	%	Rep	%	Total
2010	811	36.63%	1,268	57.27%	2,214
2006	884	40.16%	1,229	55.84%	2,201
2002	932	40.86%	1,324	58.04%	2,281

COUNTY Power long has had a deeply split courthouse, and unlike many counties that could say that a generation ago, it still does.

Commission majorities swing back and forth over time, and both parties hold department offices.

Com1	Democrat			Republican		
2012	**Ronald Funk**	**2,296**	**100.00%**			
2008	Ronald Funk	2,419	100.00%	-	0	0.00%
2006	Ronald Funk	1,082	50.12%	Ray Zimmerman	1,077	49.88%
2002	Patty Porath	762	33.74%	Ray Zimmerman	1,190	52.64%
Com2	Democrat			Republican		
2010	Vicki Meadows	1,686	100.00%	-	0	0.00%
2008	Vicki Meadows	2,387	100.00%	-	0	0.00%
2004	Vicki Meadows	2,300	100.00%	-	0	0.00%
2002	Vicki Meadows	1,247	55.20%	Valerie Hoybjerg	1,011	44.80%
Com3	Democrat			Republican		
2012	-	-	-	**Delane Anderson**	**2,076**	**74.10%**
2010	-	0	0.00%	Delane Anderson	1,983	100.00%
2006	-	0	0.00%	Ken Estep	1,853	100.00%
2004	-	0	0.00%	Ken Estep	2,321	100.00%

Clerk	Democrat		Republican	
2010	Christine Steinlicht	52.00%	Sharee Sprague	48.00%
2006	Christine Steinlicht	100.00%	-	0.00%
2002	Christine Steinlicht	100.00%	-	0.00%
Treasurer	Democrat		Republican	
2010	Donna Thornton	40.00%	Deanna Curry	60.00%
2006	-	0.00%	Bobbie Mauch	100.00%
2002	-	0.00%	Bobbie Mauch	100.00%
Assessor	Democrat		Republican	
2010	Douglas Glascock	100.00%	-	0.00%
2006	Douglas Glascock	100.00%	-	0.00%
2002	Douglas Glascock	100.00%	-	0.00%
Coroner	Democrat		Republican	
2010	-	0.00%	Mark Gunn Rose	100.00%
2006	-	0.00%	Mark Gunn Rose	100.00%
2002	-	0.00%	Mark Gunn Rose	100.00%
Sheriff	Democrat		Republican	
2012	**Jim Jeffries**	**64.00%**	**Frederick Harms**	**36.00%**
2008	Jim Jeffries	100.00%	-	0.00%
2004	Jim Jeffries	65.89%	James Morse	31.39%
Pros Atty	Democrat		Republican	
2012	**Randall Kline**	**37.00%**	**Ryan Peterson**	**63.00%**
2008	Randall Kline	59.69%	Jan Skeen	40.31%
2004	Paul Laggis	100.00%	-	0.00%

SHOSHONE

AREA Communities: Kellogg, Wallace, Pinehurst, Osburn, Mullan, Smelterville, Kingston, Wardner, Gem, Murray. 2,640 sq. mi.

POPULATION
12,765 (24th).
Increase 00s: -7.3%.
Minority: 6.5%.
Hispanic: 3.0%.

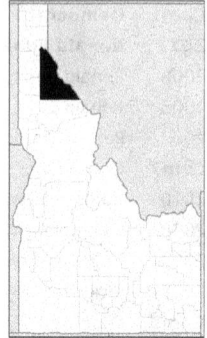

One of the places most remote from most of Idaho, one of the hardest for southern Idahoans to connect with, Shoshone has been one of the slowest to change. Its (still) mining-based Silver Valley, where the bulk of the population lives, retains a feel of remove from the rest of the world.

Traditionally, this is Idaho's most Democratic county, though no longer. The courthouse has remained a Democratic bedrock (so far), to be sure, and the county still periodically votes for Democrats for the legislature (though more and more they lose to Republicans as Shoshone represents less and less of a portion of a legislative district). But Democrats have been losing increasing numbers of upper-ballot races here since the mid-90s, and the stage may be set for more Democratic erosion.

The raw votes have to be evaluated a little differently here, since – owing largely to mining shutdowns – Shoshone lost a third of its population in the 80s. That may have damaged Democrats more than Republicans, because while the Republican numbers now are only a little below their peaks in the 70s, the Democratic numbers are a lot lower.

PRECINCTS (3) At the top of the ticket, Shoshone now leans Republican but keeps the margins mostly competitive – a description that now describes nearly all of its precincts. Just one is flat-out Democratic in the old manner: Mullan, the most remote and closest to the Montana line,which went for Democrats for governor and Senate in 2010 by landslides. Its Republican mirror image was Calder, a small town south of the Silver Valley and more connected to Benewah County, which voted just as strongly Republican. Among the other Silver Valley precincts, Wallace and Wardner remained relatively Democratic, but the valley towns to the west – Pinehurst, Silverton, Kellogg, Kingston, Cataldo – registered higher Republican numbers.

PRESIDENTIAL Shoshone's presidential default for many years was Democratic, though any recent look at Shoshone presidential voting patterns has to factor in its varied presidential patterns over time. It voted for Reagan in 1980 and 1984, Ford in 1976, Nixon in his 1972 landslide and Eisenhower in 1952 and 1956.

Still, it voted for Dukakis (1988) and Clinton (1992, 1996), suggesting that some Democratic resurgence might be underway. But since 2000 it has voted for Republicans (though the margin shrank a little in 2008).

	Dem	%	Rep	%	Total
2012	2,277	44.23%	2,699	52.43%	5,148
2008	2,521	44.49%	2,953	52.12%	5,666
2004	2,331	43.68%	2,922	54.75%	5,337
2000	2,225	41.70%	2,879	53.95%	5,336

GOVERNOR Shoshone has remained a relatively solid county for Democratic gubernatorial candidates, breaking to vote Republican in recent decades only twice, in 1998 for Kempthorne and in 2010 for Otter. Before that it last voted Republican for governor in 1946 (Robins).

	Dem	%	Rep	%	Total
2010	1,343	34.66%	2,186	56.41%	3,875
2006	2,225	58.29%	1,434	37.57%	3,817
2002	2,378	55.50%	1,802	42.05%	4,285

COUNTY The courthouse has remains strongly Democratic; in recent decades, independents have odds about as good as Republicans of winning a spot there (and about as many of them have run).

Com1	Democrat			Republican		
2012	**Jim Best**	**2,529**	**51.20%**	**Joan Block**	**2,414**	**48.80%**
2008	Vince Rinaldi	4,008	100.00%	-	0	0.00%
2006	Vince Rinaldi	3,106	100.00%	-	0	0.00%
2002	Jim Vergobbi	2,148	50.40%	Doug Burmeister	2,110	49.60%
Com2	Democrat			Republican		
2010	Vern Hanson	1,636	42.20%	Larry Yergler	2,243	57.80%
2008	Vern Hanson	3,136	66.94%	-	0	0.00%
2004	Sherry Krulitz	4,218	95.11%	-	0	0.00%
2002	Sherry Krulitz	2,525	59.00%	Terry Smith	1,578	36.90%
Com3	Democrat			Republican		
2012	**Julianne Zook**	**1,788**	**34.90%**	**Leslee Stanley**	**1,868**	**36.50%**
2010	Jon Cartmanessa	1,556	40.20%	Claudia Childress	1,053	27.20%
2006	Jon Cartmanessa	3,007	100.00%	-	0	0.00%
2004*	Mary Decker	1,918	36.43%	Bob Stephens	1,246	23.67%

*Comm 3 in 2004 was won by independent Jon Cartmanessa, with 2101 votes/39.91%; he later took the Democratic label.

Clerk	Democrat		Republican	
2010	Peggy DeLange-White	100.00%	-	0.00%
2006	Peggy DeLange-White	100.00%	-	0.00%
2002	Peggy DeLange-White	58.00%	Sue Hansen	42.00%
Treasurer	Democrat		Republican	
2010	Ellen Sauer	100.00%	-	0.00%
2006	Ellen Sauer	100.00%	-	0.00%
2002	Ellen Sauer	100.00%	-	0.00%
Assessor	Democrat		Republican	
2010	Jerry White	100.00%	-	0.00%
2006	Jerry White	100.00%	-	0.00%

2002	Jerry White	67.40%	Lee Haynes	32.60%
Coroner	**Democrat**		**Republican**	
2010	Lonny Duce	100.00%	-	0.00%
2006	Lonny Duce	100.00%	-	0.00%
2002	Lonny Duce	100.00%	-	0.00%
Sheriff	**Democrat**		**Republican**	
2012	**Mitchell Alexander**	**60.00%**	**Gene Marquez**	**40.00%**
2008*	Gary Yergler	42.08%	-	0.00%
2004	Chuck Reynalds	100.00%	-	0.00%
Pros Atty	**Democrat**		**Republican**	
2012	**Keisha Stutzke**	**66.10%**	**James McMillan**	**33.90%**
2008	Val Siegel	63.33%	-	0.00%
2004	Michael Peacock	59.89%	-	0.00%

*Yergler lost to write-in candidate Mitchell Vince Alexander, who took 57.92%.

TETON

AREA Communities: Driggs, Victor, Tetonia, Felt. 450 sq. mi.

POPULATION 10,170 (28th). Increase 00s: 69.5%. Minority: 18.5%. Hispanic: 16.9%.

Teton is the steelhead of Idaho counties: As other small, rural Republican counties became much more Republican in the 80s, 90s and 00s, Teton turned competitive. Calling it Democratic might be a stretch, but it's a temptation – it was one of three in Idaho to vote for Obama in 2008. Its fast-growing vacation and resort environment has led to a cultural sea change in this lightly-populated valley over the hill from Jackson, Wyoming.

Small and remote as it may be, Teton has become – locally – a place of hotly contested politics, with growth and its implications usually a major subtext of campaigns here.

PRECINCTS (5) This county leaning Democratic has one clearly-distinctive Democratic precinct: 3, the Driggs area, one of the unusual precincts in Idaho to vote against the Republicans for both governor and U.S. senator in 2010. (The absentee precinct went strongly Democratic too.) The other three regular precincts, two in Victor and one in Tetonia, voted in 2010 slightly more Republican than Democratic.

PRESIDENTIAL Teton raised eyebrows when it went Democratic in the 2008 presidential, not least because that's the first time it voted that way since 1948. It reversed that direction in 2012, however.

	Dem	%	Rep	%	Total
2012	1,928	42.58%	2,458	54.34%	4,523
2008	2,302	49.42%	2,263	48.58%	4,658
2004	1,416	38.37%	2,235	60.57%	3,690
2000	720	27.01%	1,745	65.45%	2,666

GOVERNOR Ordinarily Republican in recent decades, Teton did vote for Andrus in his landslides – not unusual among small rural counties – but also Democrat Larry EchoHawk in 1994, and for Democrats in 2006 and 2010 (the latter a crushing statewide Democratic loss).

	Dem	%	Rep	%	Total
2010	1,706	50.40%	1,470	43.43%	3,385
2006	1,653	49.24%	1,286	38.31%	3,357
2002	1,043	44.78%	1,245	53.46%	2,329

COUNTY From the mid-70s to the mid-90s, Teton's courthouse was nearly all Republican. A series of local planning and other issues led to a big party switch in 1996, which was reversed again in 1998, then fought to near draws the next few cycles. Teton has lots of competitive races, in which, in the 00s, Democrats are winning more than not.

Com1	Democrat				Republican		
2012	**Kim Keeley**	**2,227**	**49.40%**		**Sid Kunz**	**2,278**	**50.60%**
2008	Bob Benedict	2,490	54.40%		Kendall Jolley	2,087	45.60%
2006	Alice Stevenson	1,684	54.73%		Ryan Kearsley	1,393	45.27%
2002	Jay Calderwood	1,313	56.90%		Buzz Rasmussen	996	43.10%
Com2	**Democrat**				**Republican**		
2010	Kathy Rinaldi	1,742	51.40%		Tony Goe	1,649	48.60%
2008	Kathy Rinaldi	2,535	55.12%		Mark Trupp	2,064	44.88%
2004	Jeff Carter	1,709	46.24%		Mark Trupp	1,987	53.76%
2002	David Hensel	1,152	49.40%		Mark Trupp	1,178	50.60%
Com3	**Democrat**				**Republican**		
2012	**Sue Muncaster**	**2,087**	**46.40%**		**Kelly C. Park**	**2,407**	**53.60%**
2010	Larry S. Young	1,653	49.00%		Kelly C. Park	1,721	51.00%
2006	Larry S. Young	1,682	53.97%		Ray Breckinridge	1,377	45.01%
2004	Roger Hoopes	1,872	52.76%		Ronald Ramirez	1,676	47.24%

Clerk	Democrat		Republican	
2010	Mary Lou Hansen	54.60%	Rick Beard	45.40%
2006	Mary Lou Hansen	53.97%	Nolan Boyle	46.03%
2002	-	0.00%	Nolan Boyle	100.00%
Treasurer	**Democrat**		**Republican**	
2010	Bonnie Hatch	100.00%	-	0.00%
2006	Bonnie Hatch	86.14%	Darrel Howell	13.86%
2002	Bonnie Hatch	100.00%	-	0.00%
Assessor	**Democrat**		**Republican**	
2010	Bonnie Beard	74.20%	-	0.00%
2006	Bonnie Beard	100.00%	-	0.00%
2002	Denny Thomas	60.60%	Jenny Moulton	39.40%
Coroner	**Democrat**		**Republican**	
2010	-	0.00%	Timothy Melcher	100.00%
2006	-	0.00%	Timothy Melcher	100.00%
2002	-	0.00%	Timothy Melcher	100.00%
Sheriff	**Democrat**		**Republican**	
2012	**Tony Liford**	**50.40%**	**Lindsey Moss**	**49.60%**
2008	Kim Cooke	27.89%	Tony Liford	49.59%
2004	Bob Fitzgerald	19.57%	Ryan Kaufman	56.38%
Pros Atty	**Democrat**		**Republican**	
2012	**Kathy Spitzer**	**100.00%**	-	-
2008	Kathy Spitzer	100.00%	-	0.00%
2004	Laura Lowery	40.64%	Bart Birch	59.36%

TWIN FALLS

AREA Communities: Twin Falls, Buhl, Kimberly, Filer, Murtaugh, Hansen, Castleford, Hollister, Rogerson. 1,957 sq. mi.

POPULATION 77,230 (6th). Increase 00s: 20.1%. Minority: 17.3%. Hispanic: 13.7%.

Twin Falls, the agribusiness, commercial and service centerpiece of the Magic Valley (roughly, from east of Glenns Ferry to east of Rupert), and with the fast-growing College of Southern Idaho the educational center as well, has been in the last couple of decades the growth center of the Magic Valley as well, while many of the smaller communities within an hour's drive have struggled.

And this area is, as you would expect, very solidly Republican – you'd have to twist the numbers in some odd way to come to any other conclusion. A number of Democrats in the 00s have claimed to spot transition in the works, but that's hard to justify on the numbers. Twin has not elected a Democrat to the legislature in more than half a century, and its courthouse has remained either exclusively Republican or nearly so just as long.

It is somewhat permeable. Democrat Richard Stallings did well here in his re-election campaigns, as did Cecil Andrus. And there is one other factor: Central Twin has been developing a little bit of a Democratic core, near the College of Southern Idaho. Still, no one should be fooled: Any Democrat who manages better than a third of the vote here is doing well.

PRECINCTS (47) There are no clearly Democratic precincts in Twin Falls County, but about seven (Twin Falls 16, 20, 8, 6 and 3 and Buhl 5 and 4) were close enough in 2010 and 2008 to be considered competitive. But if Twin Falls County's Republican margins are less spectacular than a number of other southern Idaho counties, they ordinarily are still quite solid. Outside the central and college-area portions of Twin Falls, and to a very limited extent in Buhl, there's no real Democratic base. And all of the other rural parts of the county vote very strongly Republican. The strongest: Hollister, in the lightly-populated southern part of the county.

PRESIDENTIAL A Goldwater county in 1964, Twin has one of Idaho's longest streaks of voting Republican for president – it last voted for a Democrat in 1936 (Roosevelt). Its more recent votes for Republicans have ranged in margins between 2-1 and 3-1.

	Dem	%	Rep	%	Total
2012	7,541	26.80%	19,773	70.26%	28,142
2008	8,621	30.42%	19,032	67.15%	28,344
2004	6,458	24.43%	19,672	74.42%	26,435
2000	5,777	25.74%	15,794	70.38%	22,440

GOVERNOR As noted, Democrat Andrus won favor here in 1990 and 1974, and John Evans in 1978. Those cases aside, Twin last voted Democratic for governor, as for president, in 1936.

	Dem	%	Rep	%	Total
2010	5,650	29.96%	11,511	61.04%	18,858
2006	8,071	43.17%	11,049	59.10%	18,695
2002	6,433	35.88%	11,187	62.40%	17,929

COUNTY The Twin Falls courthouse has been unanimously Republican – or, given a few occasional independents who do sometimes win, Democrat-less – since the mid-70s. Democrats only occasionally challenge for these seats, and in recent decades rarely have cracked 40% of the vote when they do.

Com1	Democrat			Republican		
2012	-		-	- Terry Kramer	23,187	100.00%
2008	-	0	0.00%	Terry Kramer	23,007	100.00%
2006	-	0	0.00%	Terry Kramer	13,744	73.87%
2002	Howard Meiers	6,853	39.20%	Gary Grindstaff	10,623	60.80%
Com2	Democrat			Republican		
2010	Gary Eller	5,105	28.10%	Leon Mills	11,042	60.70%
2008	-	0	0.00%	Tom Mikesell	21,736	100.00%
2004	Bob Powers	10,022	39.05%	Tom Mikesell	15,641	60.95%
2002	Bob Powers	6,707	38.40%	Tom Mikesell	10,771	61.60%
Com3	Democrat			Republican		
2012	-		-	- George Urie	22,833	100.00%
2010	-	0	0.00%	George Urie	15,745	100.00%
2006	Mike Ihler	6,956	36.50%	George Urie	12,099	63.50%
2004	Mike Ihler	8,321	33.25%	William Brockman	16,701	66.75%

Clerk	Democrat		Republican	
2010	-	0.00%	Kristina Glascock	100.00%
2006	-	0.00%	Kristina Glascock	100.00%
2002	Oleta Bybee	31.50%	Robert Fort	68.50%
Treasurer	Democrat		Republican	
2010	-	0.00%	Debbie Kauffman	100.00%
2006	-	0.00%	Debbie Kauffman	100.00%
2002	-	0.00%	Debbie Kauffman	100.00%
Assessor	Democrat		Republican	
2010	-	0.00%	Gerry Bowden	100.00%
2006	-	0.00%	Gerry Bowden	100.00%
2002	Gary Baty	27.10%	Gerry Bowden	100.00%
Coroner	Democrat		Republican	
2010	-	0.00%	Dennis Chambers	100.00%
2006	-	0.00%	Dennis Chambers	100.00%
2002	-	0.00%	Dennis Chambers	100.00%
Sheriff	Democrat		Republican	

	Democrat		Republican	
2012	-		- Tom Carter	**68.60%**
2008	-	0.00%	Tom Carter*	55.87%
2004**	Paul Bach	17.31%	Robin Stubblefield	33.67%
Pros Atty	**Democrat**		**Republican**	
2012	-		- Grant Loebs	**100.00%**
2008	-	0.00%	Grant Loebs	100.00%
2004	-	0.00%	Grant Loebs	100.00%

* Carter defeated three independents including Sheriff Wayne Tousley.
** The winner was independent Wayne Tousley.

VALLEY

AREA Communities: McCall, Cascade, Donnelly, Smiths Ferry, Yellow Pine. 3,733 sq. mi.

POPULATION 9,862 (29th). Increase 00s: 28.9%. Minority: 5.9%. Hispanic: 3.9%.

There's some speculation Valley County, with its skiing and lakes and growing resort development (even amid the financial collapse of the Tamarack development near Donnelly), may become a somewhat larger political counterpart to Teton County – a traditionally conservative Republican place moving toward competition.

You can find some evidence for this. Several Democratic congressional candidates, notably Walt Minnick, did well here in the 00s, as have some Democratic legislative candidates. The 2010 election was strongly Republican here, however, so it's too early to make any clear calls about where Valley is headed.

PRECINCTS (9) Old patterns, some of them anyway, have become inverted in Valley County. For decades, the most Democratic (relatively) precinct in this Republican county was Cascade, home of the courthouse and a timber mill. By 2010, McCall and Donnelly, both with strong second-home and resort development (troubled, in Donnelly's case) had turned Democrat, albeit by small margins. Now, most of the other Long Valley precincts, Cascade included, are simply competitive, and just three smaller and more remote precincts – Yellow Pine, Alpha and West Mountain – remain as strongly Republican. Valley County's precincts underwent perhaps more change in the last decade than those of any other county.

This should be noted: The backcountry here remains very Republican. Yellow Pine was in 2010 the 21st most Republican precinct in Idaho.

PRESIDENTIAL Republican since 1964, and many elections before. Note however the GOP percentage drop from 2004 to 2008.

	Dem	%	Rep	%	Total
2012	2,095	42.59%	2,664	54.16%	4,919
2008	2,405	45.41%	2,772	52.34%	5,296
2004	1,843	38.62%	2,863	60.00%	4,772
2000	1,129	28.45%	2,548	64.21%	3,968

GOVERNOR Valley is not unusual among Republican counties in voting Democratic for governor in Andrus and Evans elections (1974, 1978, 1982, 1990). It is among the smaller number that switched to Democratic in 2006 (Brady), though returning to the GOP fold in 2010.

	Dem	%	Rep	%	Total
2010	1,385	35.87%	2,170	56.20%	3,861
2006	1,934	50.64%	1,889	49.46%	3,819

| 2002 | 1,463 | 43.99% | 1,803 | 54.21% | 3,326 |

COUNTY The courthouse has remained, with few exceptions in the 90s, Republican. No Democratic candidates for departments in the 00s.

Com1	Democrat			Republican		
2012	-		-	**-Elting Hasbrouck**	**3,841**	**100.00%**
2008	-	0	0.00%	Jerry Winkle	3,692	100.00%
2006	-	0	0.00%	Jerry Winkle	2,783	100.00%
2002	-	0	0.00%	Phillip Davis	2,519	100.00%
Com2	**Democrat**			**Republican**		
2010	Travis Hatfield	1,551	41.00%	Gordon Cruickshank	2,230	59.00%
2008	Travis Hatfield	2,402	46.89%	Gordon Cruickshank	2,721	53.11%
2004	-	0	0.00%	Thomas Kerr	3,332	100.00%
2002	-	0	0.00%	Thomas Kerr	2,560	100.00%
Com3	**Democrat**			**Republican**		
2012	-		-	**- Bill Willey**	**3,994**	**100.00%**
2010	Frank Eld	1,827	48.20%	Ray Moore	1,967	51.80%
2006	Frank Eld	2,304	59.57%	Judy Van Komen	1,564	40.43%
2004	Frank Eld	2,543	53.81%	Terry Gestrin	2,183	46.19%

Clerk	Democrat		Republican	
2010	-	0.00%	Archie Banbury	100.00%
2006	-	0.00%	Archie Banbury	100.00%
2002	-	0.00%	Lee Heinrich	100.00%
Treasurer	**Democrat**		**Republican**	
2010	-	0.00%	Glenna Young	100.00%
2006	-	0.00%	Glenna Young	100.00%
2002	-	0.00%	Diana Healy	100.00%
Assessor	**Democrat**		**Republican**	
2010	-	0.00%	June Fullmer	100.00%
2006	-	0.00%	Karen Campbell	100.00%
2002	-	0.00%	Archie Banbury	100.00%
Coroner	**Democrat**		**Republican**	
2010	-	0.00%	Marvin Heikkila	100.00%
2006	-	0.00%	Marvin Heikkila	100.00%
2002	-	0.00%	Marvin Heikkila	100.00%
Sheriff	**Democrat**		**Republican**	
2012	-		**- Patti Bolen**	**100.00%**
2008	-	0.00%	Patti Bolen	100.00%
2004	-	0.00%	Patti Bolen	89.58%
Pros Atty	**Democrat**		**Republican**	
2012	-		**- Jay Kiiha**	**100.00%**
2008	-	0.00%	Matthew Williams	100.00%
2004	-	0.00%	Matthew Williams	100.00%

WASHINGTON

AREA Communities: Weiser, Cambridge, Midvale. 1,474 sq. mi.

POPULATION 10,198 (27th). Increase 00s: 2.2%. Minority: 19.9%. Hispanic: 16.8%.

A farm and food processing county that may now be best known for it's nationally-praised fiddle festival, Washington County has the look of a settled and stable place, though its rural communities, like those in much of Idaho, have struggled in recent decades.

Once truly competitive between the parties, Washington County no longer is, as the once-substantial Democratic vote here has shrunk by about a third. Republicans ordinarily win easily county-wide; the courthouse has seen no electoral cliffhangers for a few years. There are two courthouse Democrats, but little should read into their success; both are newcomers following in the tracks of veterans.

PRECINCTS (11) As in so many counties, there are no truly Democratic or competitive precincts left. Among the Republican precincts, however, four of the five Weiser precincts (2, 3, 4 and 5) are closer to competitive than the rest of the county. (Does the fiddler contest affect that?) The most Republican part of Washington County: Midvale precinct.

PRESIDENTIAL Republican on the presidential level since 1964, its percentages usually run to super-landslides.

	Dem	%	Rep	%	Total
2012	1,104	25.50%	3,128	72.24%	4,330
2008	1,241	27.54%	3,168	70.31%	4,506
2004	1,033	23.70%	3,274	75.11%	4,359
2000	980	24.17%	2,899	71.49%	4,055

GOVERNOR After from backing Andrus and Evans in some elections (1974, 1978, 1982, 1990), Washington had had a clear Republican default. Its support of Republican candidates for governor grew in the 00s, as the Democratic raw vote declined.

	Dem	%	Rep	%	Total
2010	746	21.09%	2,505	70.82%	3,537
2006	1,185	33.67%	2,142	60.87%	3,519
2002	1,043	32.52%	2,112	65.86%	3,207

COUNTY The days of Democrats holding a third or more of the courthouse offices are long gone. Only occasional Democrats even ran in the 00s, and exception in a sheriff's race, none were competitive.

Com1	Democrat				Republican		
2012	**-**		**-**		**- Tom Anderson**	**3,555**	**100.00%**
2008	Marshall Dickerson	1,545	35.19%		Michael Hopkins	2,845	64.81%
2006	-	0	0.00%		Diana Thomas	2,764	100.00%
2002	-	0	0.00%		Diana Thomas	2,760	100.00%
Com2	**Democrat**				**Republican**		
2010	-	0	0.00%		Rick Michael	2,920	100.00%
2008	-	0	0.00%		Rick Michael	3,549	100.00%
2004	-	0	0.00%		Rick Michael	3,498	100.00%
2002	Dan Randleman	1,121	36.00%		Rick Michael	1,996	64.00%
Com3	**Democrat**				**Republican**		
2012	**-**		**-**		**- Kirk Chandler**	**2,906**	**76.20%**
2010	-	0	0.00%		Dave Springer	2,906	100.00%
2006	Esther Smith	800	24.70%		Roy Mink	2,407	74.31%
2004	-	0	0.00%		Roy Mink	3,369	100.00%

Clerk	Democrat		Republican	
2010	-	0.00%	Betty Thomas	100.00%
2006	-	0.00%	Sharon Widner	100.00%
2002	-	0.00%	Sharon Widner	100.00%
Treasurer	**Democrat**		**Republican**	
2010	Wanda Goins	26.30%	Ann Frei	73.70%
2006	-	0.00%	Ann Frei	100.00%
2002	-	0.00%	Ann Frei	100.00%
Assessor	**Democrat**		**Republican**	
2010	-	0.00%	Georgia Plischke	100.00%
2006	-	0.00%	Georgia Plischke	100.00%
2002	-	0.00%	Georgia Plischke	100.00%
Coroner	**Democrat**		**Republican**	
2010	-	0.00%	Bowe von Brethorst	100.00%
2006	Frank Thomas	20.66%	Robert Thomason	79.34%
2002	-	0.00%	Robert Thomason	100.00%
Sheriff	**Democrat**		**Republican**	
2012	**-**		**- Matt Thomas**	**100.00%**
2008*	Scott Crimin	47.05%	Melvin Williams	47.16%
2004	Scott Crimin	35.60%	Melvin Williams	64.40%
Pros Atty	**Democrat**		**Republican**	
2012	**-**		**- Delton Walker**	**100.00**
2008	-	0.00%	Delton Walker	100.00%
2004	-	0.00%	Charles Kroll	100.00%

* Williams won by five votes; an independent had 261 votes.

Cities

This section focuses on recent politics in the 10 largest cities in Idaho – about 5% of the cities in the state, but accounting for most of the urban population in Idaho.

2013 was an eventful election year for them, but it was eventful too for many of Idaho's other cities.

Among them:

Moscow. Challenger Bill Lambert took 58% of the vote over incumbent Mayor Nancy Chaney.

Jerome. Mayor John Shine lost to challenger David Davis, who took 46% of the vote in a four-way contest. No runoff is needed in Jerome.

Chubbuck. The city chose as mayor Kevin England, with 50% of the vote.

Blackfoot. One race undecided as of November 5 was the Blackfoot mayoral, in which neither Paul Loomis nor Dan Cravens, the leaders in the six-candidate contest, was able to reach 50% of the total vote. The runoff election is set for December 3.

Mountain Home. One council member (Richard Urquidi) was re-elected and another (Alaine Isaac) was turned out.

Burley. Merle Smedley was elected as mayor, defeating incumbent Terry Greenman.

Ketchum. Mayor Randy Hall was defeated, decisively, in a surprise result, by challenger Nina Jonas.

Glenns Ferry. Connie Wills was elected the new mayor.

Albion. The two candidates for mayor of the small city south of Burley, Don Bowden and John B. Davis, each received 60 votes. Their contest was decided by the flip of a coin on December 5; Bowden retained his seat.

BOISE

Population 2010: 205,671; 2000: 193,161

Mayor **David Bieter**, elected 2003, up 2015. Council: Lauren Mclean, Ben Quintana, David Eberle, TJ Thomson, Elaine Clegg, Maryanne Jordan.

Boise, Idaho's largest city (for nearly all of the state's history) and its capita, long was a quiet community in its city politics. It became a lot noisier during the dozen years (still a record length) when Richard Eardley was its mayor. A former newscaster, Eardley first joined the city council and in 1974 was elected mayor on a program of upgrading Boise city government and its downtown area. He became a key figure in upgrading much of Boise city government, but also highly controversial for his downtown redevelopment efforts, which centered around building a regional shopping mall in downtown. That effort gained little traction (progress seemed elusive year after year), and in 1986 Eardley stepped down. Advocates for building in a more suburban area took over the city council and mayoralty; his successor as mayor was one of those advocates, future Senator and Governor Dirk Kempthorne.

When Kempthorne was elected to the Senate in 1992, he was replaced by council member Brent Coles, a veteran of the shopping center wars (on the same side as Kempthorne) was appointed as mayor by the council. Coles won election to the seat twice, but in 2002 became embroiled in financial legal issues that placed Coles behind bars, and he resigned in February 2003. With an election just months away, Council member Carolyn Terteling-Payne was appointed by the council to fill the spot until then (she did not run for the post). Several council members left office about then as well.

2003 wound up as pivotal in recent Boise history. The three-way mayoral contest then was highly competitive and set the political direction for Boise ever since. Candidates included Ada County Sheriff Vaughn Killeen and former Ada County Highway District commissioner, and a generally prominent local figure, Chuck Winder. But the race was narrowly won outright (with a majority) in the primary by Democratic state Representative David Bieter.

Bieter was re-elected to the post in 2007 (winning easily over Council member and former police officer Jim Tibbs) and again in 2011 after drawing only low-key opposition. His political strength in town has been substantial, and may indicate a turning point in the city's political leanings. The city's previous three mayors were identified generally as Republicans; Bieter was a Democratic office holder when he was elected.

He has not indicated whether he plans to seek a fourth term.

Bieter has not escaped controversy altogether. In 2010 he proposed an ambitious city streetcar system which soon drew more opposition than support. He strongly backed a big bond issue in 2013 that failed to reach needed support. But he remains a major figure in city politics, and apparently popular.

Most council seats in recent years have not been much more closely contested; most incumbents have been relatively easily re-elected. Contests are sometimes fairly close in the case of open seats (and remember that elections in Boise city, as in all Idaho cities, are non-partisan).

Perhaps the highest-profile of these races in recent years was the Seat 4 race in 2009, when T.J. Thomson, who had been one of the lead Idaho organizers for Democratic presidential candidate Barack Obama, defeated (though not by a large margin) attorney David Litster, who had strong Republican support. That race was widely viewed as running along party lines, and two early conservative candidates dropped out to back Litster.

Despite several controversies including streetcar and other matters, Boise voters gave landslide margins to all the council members on the ballot in 2013.

Mayor	winner			others		
2011	David Bieter	12,640	74.28%	David B. Hall	4,377	25.72%
2007	David Bieter	20,556	64.07%	Jim Tibbs	11,528	35.93%
2003*	David Bieter	22,320	51.87%	Chuck Winder	11,230	26.10%
				Vaughn Killeen	8,168	18.98%
				Max Mohammadi	1,313	3.05%
Cncl 1						
2011	Lauren McLean	13,685	100.00%	-	0	0.00%
2007	Alan Shealy	15,685	55.21%	Steven Kimball	8,841	31.12%
				Frances Wray	3,885	13.67%
Cncl 2						
2013	Ben Quintana	15,261	68.24%	Tyler Smith	7,104	31.76%
2011	Ben Quintana	9,227	56.25%	Michael Cunningham	4,851	29.57%
				L.W. Johnson	2,325	14.17%
2009	Vern Bisterfeldt	13,239	71.36%	Daniel Dunham	3,283	17.70%
				David Honey	2,030	10.94%
2005	Vern Bisterfeldt	24,611	77.56%	Mark Seeley	7,121	22.44%
Cncl 3						
2011	David Eberle	12,539	78.10%	Pappy Honey	3,516	21.90%
2007	David Eberle	18,629	65.78%	Marlene K. Smith	6,267	22.13%
				Redgie Bigham	3,425	12.09%
Cncl 4						
2013	TJ Thomson	12,127	54.35%	Jill G. Humble	5,234	23.46%
				Bill Jarocki	4,951	22.19%
2009	TJ Thomson	10,988	57.37%	David Litster	8,165	42.63%
2005	Jim Tibbs	17,911	55.00%	Jerome Mapp	14,655	45.00%
Cncl 5						
2011	Elaine Clegg	13,310	100.00%	-	0	0.00%
2007	Elaine Clegg	18,795	66.09%	Carol Wingate	9,645	33.91%
Cncl 6						
2013	Maryanne Jordan	14,092	62.35%	Paul Edmond Fortin	4,680	20.71%
				Bryce Peterson	3,829	16.94%
2009	Maryanne Jordan	11,337	61.08%	Lucas Baumbach	4,098	22.08%
				David Webb	3,126	16.84%
2005	Maryanne Jordan	22,918	70.14%	Brandi Swindell	9,758	29.86%

*primary

NAMPA

Population 2010: 81,557; 2000: 71,713

Mayor **Bob Henry**, elected 2013, up 2017. Council: Paul Raymond, Stephen Kren, Pam White, Randy Haverfield.

Once a farm-based food processing town, Nampa has retained much of its long-time industrial base while adding on much else, from high tech development to extended services and businesses. Central Nampa has been growing into a satellite urban area of its own. As fast as it has grown, to the point of abruptly becoming Idaho's second largest city, Nampa has managed to avoid heavy-duty internal city conflict in most of the last few decades.

Mayor Tom Dale was the anchor figure here for some time. A council member from 1995, he won the job of mayor six years later, and won easy re-election in 2005 and 2009.

The senior council member is Stephen Kren, elected 1995; his son served in the Idaho House. Martin Thorne (whose father was a long-time state senator) was elected in 1997. The other two are more recent: Pam White was appointed June 2007, and elected twice since; and Bob Henry was elected in 2011.

Winds of discontent blew in 2013, however. Disagreements over taxes evidently were the prime factor leading that year to Dales's loss in a bid for a fourth term, narrowly defeated by council member Bob Henry.

Mayor	winner			others		
2013	Bob Henry	3,510	44.89%	Tom Dale	3,397	43.45%
				Robert D. Muse	735	9.40%
				Melissa Robinson	177	2.26%
2009	Tom Dale	5,640	70.04%	Gene Blamires	1,355	17.84%
				Jim Dorsey	735	9.13%
				Melissa Robinson	227	2.82%
2005	Tom Dale					
Cncl 1						
2013	Paul Raymond	4,078	55.58%	Victor Rodriguez	3,267	44.48%
2009	Martin Thorne	3,931	51.85%	Bob Henry	3,602	48.15%
Cncl 2						
2011	Stephen Kren	2,441	54.98%	Lance McGrath	1,999	45.02%
2007	Stephen Kren					
Cncl 3						
2013	Pam White	3,847	52.02%	K. Lynn Miller	3,548	47.98%
2009	Pam White	5,337	71.62%	Mark Stevens	2,078	27.89%
2007	Pam White			Bob Henry		
Cncl 4						
2011	Bob Henry	2,181	48.98%	Curtis Homer	1,566	35.17%
				Justin Harrison	406	9.12%
2007	Curtis Homer					
Cncl 5						
2013	Randy Haverfield	4,501	62.78%	Lance McGrath	2,669	37.22%

MERIDIAN

Population 2010: 75,092; 2000: 52,240

Mayor **Tammy de Weerd**, elected 2003, up 2015. Council: David Zaremba, Joe Borton, Charles Rountree, Keith Bird, Genesis Milam, Luke Cavener.

Explosion city.

Those living in Ada County in the 70s remember Meridian as a small dairy town, not so different in size or feel from Emmett or Fruitland. In the generation since it has become a big suburban city, the third largest city in Idaho, its economic core being mainly service and retail, its bounds stretching close to the only two larger Idaho cities – Boise to the east and Nampa to the west.

Such explosiveness would seem to make Meridian ready-made for heated internal civic warfare. In general that hasn't happened, maybe because so many people here seem of like mind about their politics. (The Republican vote here for partisan offices is much more uniform than in Boise or even Nampa.

The 2011 mayoral race drew regional interest, however, even though Mayor Tammy deWeerd, seeking a third term after two decisive previous wins, had no obvious political problems. Gun store owner and former state Senator (and former staffer for Representative Bill Sali) Gerry Sweet was her main opponent, and he ran on an approach along the lines of the Tea Party, which had some real strength here. His backers tried to persuade the other two candidates in the race to drop out. They didn't, but it wouldn't have mattered: deWeerd won with an outright majority.

Meridian long had a council consisting of four members, but in advance of the 2013 election the council for the fast-growing city was expanded to six members; the seat 5 position initially was elected for a short two-year term to stagger alongside seat 6. The two new seats generated extra interest in 2013; one city official was quoted as saying, "We've never had 17 people run in a city council election in Meridian." The 2013 contests may have been crowded, but they were not notably acrimonious.

Mayor	winner			others		
2011	Tammy de Weerd	4,359	51.47%	Gerry Sweet	2,257	26.65%
				Jason Monks	1,669	19.71%
				Lisa Paternoster	144	1.70%
2007	Tammy de Weerd	2,609	62.54%	James Hotlzclaw	1,563	37.46%
2003	Tammy de Weerd	2,212	51.72%	Jim Johnson	1,477	34.53%
				Keith Bird	446	10.43%
				Jonathon Howard	142	3.32%
Cncl 1						
2011	David Zaremba	4,812	64.88%	John Shawcroft	2,605	35.12%
2007	David Zaremba	3,370	100.00%	-	-	-
Cncl 2						
2013	Joe Borton	3,019	58.46%	Patrick Malloy	2,145	41.54%
2009	Brad Hoaglun	1,414	100.00%	-	-	-
2005	Joe Borton	632	91.46%	-	-	-
Cncl 3						

Year	Winner	Votes	%	Opponent(s)	Votes	%
2011	Charles Rountree	4,335	55.92%	Patrick Malloy	3,417	44.08%
2007	Charles Rountree	3,374	100.00%	-	-	-
Cncl 4						
2013	Keith Bird	2,673	52.18%	Russell Joki	1,273	24.85%
				Matthew Townsend	1,177	22.97%
2009	Keith Bird	1,163	69.72%	James Holtzclaw	505	30.28%
2005	Keith Bird	588	85.09%	Christopher Cluphf	32	4.63%
Cncl 5						
2013	Genesis Milam	1,635	31.87%	Ty Palmer	1,600	31.18%
				Jeff Hoseley	824	16.06%
				Terry Benson	486	9.47%
				Michael V. Long	340	6.63%
				Drew Wahlin	246	4.79%
Cncl 6						
2013	Luke Cavener	1,301	24.72%	Shaun Wardle	1,256	23.87%
				David Moberly	914	17.37%
				Stephen Warren	819	15.56%
				Steven Yearsley	763	14.50%
				Curtis Munson	209	3.97%

IDAHO FALLS

Population 2010: 56,813; 2000: 52,338

Mayor **Rebecca Casper**, elected 2013, up 2017. Council: Sharon Parry, Dee David Whittier, Thomas Hally, Ed Marohn, Michael Lehto, Barbara Ehardt.

Idaho Falls, the co-leader among cities in Eastern Idaho (with similarly-sized Pocatello), was for many years an agricultural hub, a role it still plays to some extent. In the last few generations it also has become much more, very much an organization city. The Idaho National Laboratory is a dominant presence, as more of its people work in town than out on "the site" miles out to the northeast in the desert; its technical workforce is a factor in town. So in other ways is the Church of Jesus Chris of Latter Day Saints, which built its first Idaho temple, still one of the city's most prominent landmarks, here in 1937.

Politics in Idaho Falls for most of the city's history was quiet, dominated by officeholders (mainly older men) who tended to serve on the council for many years.

Things shook up a bit after a challenger named Joe Groberg in 1989 topped a ballot and won a council seat, Mayor Tom Campbell, who ran as an outsider in 1975 and dominated city hall for some years, opted out in 1993. He was followed a relatively new council member, a moderate (and, it was reputed, a Democrat) named Linda Milam. She would go on to serve as mayor for three terms, declining in 2005 to run for a third term. Her most formidable opponent in those elections was a Bonneville County commissioner, Bill Shurtleff, and when he filed for the job in 2005 he was considered the front-runner. The election instead went to a little-known 18-year police officer (who had Milam's endorsement) named Jared Fuhriman. Fuhriman was re-elected in 2009.

As many headlines may have been made by Council member Larry Lyon, elected to the board in 2003 and became the subject of many headlines. From one 2007 news report in the Idaho Falls *Post Register*: "Idaho Falls City Councilman Larry Lyon has filed a tort claim against the city of Idaho Falls for emotional distress. He alleges that in January a city police officer threatened and intimidated him while trying to cite him for having a dog at large. Lyon is asking for $500,000." Lyon is no longer on the council.

The veteran into 2013 was Ida Hardcastle, in her fifth term (since 1994), but she departed that year, amid a number of changes.

In 2009 the Bonneville Republican organization made clear its desire to have an effect the city elections but without large apparent impact.

Mayor	winner			others		
2013	Rebecca Casper	5,085	53.91%	Sharon D. Parry	2,927	31.03%
				Brian Lapray	954	10.11%
				Timothy Downs	466	4.94%
2009	Jared Fuhriman					
2005	Jared Fuhriman		58.00%	Bill Shurtleff		56.00%
Cncl 1						
2011	Sharon Parry	3,115	100.00%	-	0	0.00%
Cncl 2						

Year	Name	Votes	%	Opponent	Votes	%
2013*	Dee David Whittier	3,622	41.55%	Paul D. Menser	3,062	35.13%
				Jill Peterson	1,591	18.25%
				Alfred Higley	442	5.07%
Cncl 3						
2011	Thomas Hally	1,957	52.83%	Barbara Ehardt	1,747	47.17%
Cncl 4						
2013*	Ed Marohn	3,255	36.93%	Jilene Burger	3,249	36.86%
				Evan Bastow	2,309	26.20%
2009	Ida Hardcastle			Alex Creek		
Cncl 5						
2011	Michael Lehto	3,108	100.00%	-	0	0.00%
Cncl 6						
2013*	Barbara Ehardt	4,146	45.46%	Karen Cornwell	3,793	41.58%
				Ryan Davis	1,181	12.95%

*These numbers reflect general election results. All three council seats in 2013 were submitted to a runoff, since the leaders fell short of 50%; but in all three cases, the general election first-place holder won the runoff.

POCATELLO

Population 2010: 54,255; 2000: 53,372

Mayor **Brian Blad**, elected 2009, up 2017. Council: Jim Johnston, Steve Brown, Eva Nye, Craig Cooper, Michael Orr, Gary Moore.

In Pocatello, an industrial, transport and university community, politics often has carried on a feel different than in most Idaho cities – more, some observers have suggested, like a smaller version of an eastern rust belt city. In places Pocatello looks the part, with its still-large railroad operations (though Union Pacific railroad employment is only a fraction of what it was a generation ago) and significant industrial plants.

In many respects, taken as a whole, it has neither much advanced nor regressed in the last couple of generations. In 1980 its population was 46,036, and it has grown only very gradually in the years since. It has made aggressive moves in economic development, and its downtown has seen vigorous attempts at upgrades, but the city also has had periodic bad economic news in 2013, such as the massive Hoku operation and the long-running Kraft plant.

Its city government has long been fluid, cycling a wide variety of people through its offices of mayor and council. For many years in the 70s and 80s the constant was the unelected city manager, Chuck Moss. In 1985, the city moved from a council-manager to a strong-mayor system, and the stakes for elective office seemed to rise thereafter.

The mayors have cycled through with regularity since. The first elected under the new system, Dick Finlayson, drew seven challengers in his bid for re-election, and in a runoff one of them, little-known university housing manager Peter Angstadt, beat him. Angstadt was able to win re-election, but declined to run again. In a tight three-way contest involving three high-profile community figures, Council member Greg Anderson won in 1997. But in 2001 he was replaced by Roger Chase, a Democratic state representative, who was re-elected in 2005. In 2009, he seemed to be headed for an easy re-election against a little-known opponent in a low-key race, but instead – in a very low-turnout election – lost to Brian Blad, an insulation business owner.

That might have seemed like an opportunity for a rematch, and in 2013 Blad and Chase faced each other on the ballot again. But Chase failed to gain much traction, and Blad walked away with the election.

Mayor	winner			others		
2013	Brian Blad	6,938	66.40%	Roger Chase	2,896	27.72%
				Paul Shepard	439	4.20%
				Sierra Carta	176	1.68%
2009	Brian Blad	3,792	52.60%	Roger W. Chase	3,417	47.40%
2005	Roger Chase	5,508	57.17%	Sharon Nilson	4,127	42.83%
Cncl 1						
2011	Jim Johnston	3,320	52.50%	Brad Huerta	3,004	47.50%
Cncl 2						
2011	Steve Brown	2,667	43.04%	Scott Odekirk	1,766	28.50%
				Mark Balzer	1,763	28.45%

Cncl 3						
2011	Eva Nye	4,200	67.75%	Paul Gagliardi	1,999	32.25%
Cncl 4						
2013	Craig Cooper	3,601	36.07%	Amy W. Manning	3,042	30.47%
				Mark Villano	2,639	26.43%
				Barbara Pancoast	351	3.52%
				Kevin Perry	350	3.51%
2009	Craig Cooper	3,863	55.47%	Robert Richway	3,101	44.53%
2005	Richard Stallings	6,234	65.93%	Jennifer Traylor	2,034	21.51%
Cncl 5						
2013	Michael Orr	5,078	51.51%	Roger Bray	4,780	48.49%
2009	Roger Bray	5,741	100.00%	-	0	0.00%
2005	Roger Bray	3,715	39.88%	Harry Neuhardt	3,707	39.79%
				Edmund Cook	1,894	20.33%
Cncl 6						
2013	Gary Moore	5,224	53.40%	Charlene Young	4,558	46.60%
2009	Gary Moore	4,825	70.29%	Ethan Ciccone	2,039	29.71%
2005	Gary Moore	4,100	43.74%	Marjanna Hulet	3,475	37.07%
				Paul Gregerson	1,798	43.74%

CALDWELL

Population 2010: 46,237; 2000: 34,433

Mayor **Garret Nancolas**, elected 1997, up 2017. Council: Mike Ollard, Dennis Callsen, Rob Hopper, Shannon Ozuna, Jim Blacker, Terrence Biggers.

Caldwell may be Canyon County's seat but it has become very much the county's second city, growing but at a slower pace than its neighbor Nampa. (Its location away the center of the Boise metro area may have been significant.) Its residential sectors have been expanding in the last couple of decades, as its census numbers indicate; but its downtown and business sectors have not, generally, kept pace, and balancing the city's growth has been a challenge for City Hall for years.

But its city government has been stable and generally quiet for many years. Garrett Nancolas is the long-timer among mayors in Idaho's larger cities, elected first in 1997 (57.4% in a three-way contest), and four more times since; his easy-going, non-confrontational demeanor may be one reason for his political success. (Nancolas followed a mayor whose style was much more confrontational.) While mayors in many other cities in the region were hotly challenged in 2013, Nancolas cruised to another landslide win.

Mayor	winner			others		
2013	Garrett Nancolas	1,758	65.21%	Paul Alldredge	938	34.79%
2009	Garrett Nancolas			Helmut Kohler		
2005	Garrett Nancolas					
Cncl 1						
2013	Mike Ollard	2,157	100.00%	-	0	0
2009	Jim Dakan			Victor Sanchez		
Cncl 2						
2013	Dennis Callsen	2,168	100.00%			
2009	Dennis Callsen			Marlene Boucher		
Cncl 3						
2013	Rob Hopper	2,158	98.54%	-	0	0
2009	Rob Hopper			Karen Alldredge		
Cncl 4						
2011	Shannon Ozuna	878	39.80%	Erik Makrush	732	33.18%
				Kent Marmon	596	27.02%
Cncl 5						
2011	Jim Blacker	1,062	48.23%	Rem Fox	732	33.24%
				Jerry Kilbourne	408	18.53%
Cncl 6						
2013	Terrence Biggers	2,108	100.00%	-	0	0
2011	David B. Clark	1,316	63.03%	Jeremy Feucht	772	36.97%

COEUR D'ALENE

Population 2010: 44,137; 2000: 40,059

Mayor **Steve Widmyer,** elected 2013, up in 2017. Council: Ron Edinger, Amy Evans, Dan Gookin, Woody McEvers, Steve Adams, Kiki Miller.

Coeur d'Alene is one of the most beautifully-situated cities in Idaho, perched on the north shore of Lake Coeur d'Alene, with elegant large-scale resort facilities built to take advantage of it. The city has grown smartly in many ways. But it also has been home to some of the most contentious politics of any Idaho muncipality.

While Kootenai County overall is Republican, the city of Coeur d'Alene is politically closely competitive, and people of widely varying politics run and do win in races for the non-partisan city offices. The city's mayors and councils have been a varied group over the decades, sometimes leaning toward environmentalist viewpoints, sometimes veering toward business interests. But in the last decade the battles have moved into a new, ideological, arena. A collection of Republican-aligned groups roughly sympathetic with the Tea Party have become highly active in local government elections, and in some ways the city of Coeur d'Alene has become ground zero for those conflicts.

One of the most dramatic such cases in recent years was the 2009 council election in which challenger Jim Brannon, who had plenty of Republican support, held Seat 2 incumbent Mike Kennedy, who had plenty of Democratic support, to a five-vote win. And the counting on election night, and the recount after that, was mere preface to the year-long legal case that followed.

At this book went to press, the mayor and members of the city council were facing a proposed recall election. That seems emblematic: Politics in the lake city is not dull for long. The elections are often competitive and council and mayoral positions often turn over. The last mayor, Sandi Bloem (the first woman to hold the office here), in 2013 completed her third term, and has been a strong vote-getter; but she is the first three-term mayor in the city's history.

In the spring of 2012 a group of Tea Party-aligned activists under the banner of RecallCDA, complaining specifically about the city's planned renewal of the McEuen Field waterfront area, launched a recall attempt against Mayor Sandi Bloem and three council members, Kennedy, Deanna Goodlander, and Woody McEvers. They needed 4,311 valid signatures for each petition, but fell short (they obtained, respectively, 4,126 for Bloem, 4,073 for Goodlander, 4,077 for Kennedy, and 4,060 for McEvers). While the anti-recall forces cheered, three of those targets, Bloem, Kennedy and Goodlander, opted not to run again for city office in 2013.

That set up a big 2013 fight between the Tea Party forces and the counter force, organized as Balance North Idaho (and with components including both Democrats and Republicans). On election day, BNI emerged as a big winner, with all its endorsees winning, including Steve Widmyer for mayor, and McEvers, Amy Evans and Kiki Miller for council. Evans was even dubbed "Obama girl" by the opposition, but she seemed not to feel any political damage as a result.

That was, at least, the 2013 result. Heated local battles along similar lines are likely to continue for a while in Kootenai County.

Mayor	winner			others		
2013	Steve Widmyer	4,719	56.13%	Mary Souza	3,556	42.30%
2009	Sandi Bloem	3,955	62.09%	Joseph Kunka	2,388	37.49%
2005	Sandi Bloem	4,211	76.16%	Joseph Kunka	1,318	23.84%
Cncl 1						
2011	Ron Edinger	4,459	71.94%	Adam Graves	1,739	28.06%
2007	Ron Edinger	2,626	53.75%	Dan Gookin	2,260	46.25%
Cncl 2						
2013	Amy Evans	4,799	58.08%	Chris Fillios	3,464	41.92%
2009	Mike Kennedy	3,165	50.04%	Jim Brannon	3,160	49.96%
2005	Mike Kennedy	2,726	48.89%	Dan Yake	1,507	27.03%
				Mary Souza	1,343	24.09%
Cncl 3						
2011	Dan Gookin	3,409	54.12%	George Sayler	2,435	38.66%
				Patrick Mitchell	239	3.79%
2007	Al Hassell	2,067	42.81%	Jim Brannon	1,865	38.63%
				Chris Patterson	467	9.67%
				Jerry Weaver	429	8.89%
Cncl 4						
2013	Woody McEvers	4,354	52.79%	Sharon Hebert	3,238	39.26%
				Amber Copeland	656	7.95%
2009	Woody McEvers	3,280	52.91%	Steve Adams	2,919	47.09%
2005	Woody McEvers	3,211	62.53%	Steven Foxx	1,924	37.47%
Cncl 5						
2011	Steve Adams	3,490	56.13%	John Bruning	2,070	33.29%
				Amber Copeland	658	10.58%
2007	John Bruning	2,331	48.45%	Susan Snedaker	1,443	29.99%
				Anita Banta	438	9.10%
				Wayne Frisbie	374	7.77%
				Joseph Kunka	225	4.68%
Cncl 6						
2013	Kiki Miller	4,644	56.32%	Noel Adam	3,219	39.04%
				Gary Herfurth	383	4.64%
2009	Deanna Goodlander	3,146	50.23%	Dan Gookin	3,117	49.77%
2005	Deanna Goodlander	2,897	54.71%	Susan Snedaker	2,398	45.29%

TWIN FALLS

Population 2010: 44,137; 2000: 38,630. Incorporated 1904.

Council: Suzanne Hawkins, Lance Clow, James Munn, Shawn Barigar, Chris Talkington, Gregory Lanting, Don Hall, Rebecca Sojka. Manager **Travis Rothweiler**. 735-7271

The economic, social and political centerpoint for the Magic Valley, Twin Falls has had mostly low-key city politics over the years, a situation maybe enhanced by its long-time use of the city manager as administrator of the city government.

The council does turn over periodically, but familiar names do crop up over the years. Council member Chris Talkington, for example, is a former mayor who has been involved in Twin Falls area politics back into the 80s; defeated in a council rate in 2009, he returned running for another seat in 2011.

	winner			others		
Cncl 1						
2013	Suzanne Hawkins	1,007	66.38%	Marilyn Dedman	271	17.86%
				Kelly Hassani	239	15.75%
2009	Lance Clow		100.00%	-	-	-
Cncl 2						
2011	James Munn	2,914	96.20%	-	0	0.00%
Cncl 3						
2011	Shawn Barigar	1,275	39.30%	Allen Starley	1,010	31.13%
				Trip Craig	959	29.56%
Cncl 4						
2011	Chris Talkington	1,276	39.46%	Suzanne Hawkins	1,164	35.99%
				Wayne Bohrn	527	16.30%
				Jim Schouten	267	8.26%
Cncl 5						
2013	Gregory Lanting	1,281	100.00%	-	-	-
2009	Gregory Lanting	956		Chris Talkington	834	
				Steve Garner	213	
				Jim Schouten	181	
Cncl 6						
2013	Don Hall	1,337	100.00%	-	-	-
2009	Don Hall		100.00%	-	-	-
Cncl 7						
2011	Rebecca Sojka	1,660	51.22%	Neil Christensen	940	29.00%
				Christopher Reid	350	10.80%
				Kevin Cope	291	8.98%

LEWISTON

Population 2010: 31,894; 2000: 31,081. Incorporated 1861.

Council: Michael Collins, Ryan Johnson, Bob Blakey, Jesse Maldonado, James Kleeburg, Clinton Daniel, Ged Randall. Manager **Jim Bennett**. 746-3671

Idaho's first real city, and its first territorial capital (as drivers headed east over the Snake River bridge from Washington are immediately reminded), its growth due to the mining and then timber and farming nearby, a service and goods center enabled by its location at the confluence of the Snake and Clearwater rivers. That confluence remains significant, as the Port of Lewiston is still one of the key business components in town. The large paper mill (formerly Potlatch) also remains one of the economic linchpins.

Traditionally Democratic (though on the conservative side), Lewiston has become politically competitive, voting for Democrats in close races but willing to support Republicans is many that aren't. Its city council has been a post held by people from both parties.

Lewiston long has been one of the few manager-council cities in Idaho, the formal executive being a city manager, with policy direction and oversight from the council.

	winners			others		
2013	Michael Collins	2,245	14.65%	Gordon Gregg	1,773	11.57%
	Ryan Johnson	2,206	14.39%	Kevin Poole	1,738	11.34%
	Bob Blakey	2,112	13.78%	Dennis Ohrtman	1,710	11.16%
	Jesse Maldonado	2,069	13.50%	Walter Phillips	1,472	9.61%
2011	James Kleeburg	1,448	30.89%	Matthew Carlson	857	18.28%
	Clinton Daniel	1,214	25.90%			
	Ged Randall	1,169	24.94%			
2009	Bradley Cannon	3,679	19.10%	James Kluss	1,999	10.38%
	Thyra Stevenson	2,935	15.23%	Douglas Havens	1,953	10.14%
	Kevin Poole	2,923	15.17%	John Mock	1,801	9.35%
	Dennis Ohrtman	2,660	13.81%	Zach Hasenoehrl	1,316	6.83%
2007	John Currin	1,678	22.58%	Daniel King	1,095	14.74%
	James Kleeburg	1,500	20.19%	Frank Ehrmantraut	1,016	13.67%
	Matthew Carlson	1,498	20.16%	A.P. Jones	627	8.44%

POST FALLS

Population 2010: 27,574; 2000: 23,162. Incorporated 1890.

Mayor **Clay Larkin**. Council: Kerri Thoreson, Alan Wolfe, Joe Molloy, Betty Ann Henderson, Skip Hissing, Linda Wilhelm.

Once a small Spokane River timber town, Post Falls now has the strategic position of location on I-90 partway between Coeur d'Alene and Spokane. That residential position (as well as being a useful spot for manufacturing and distribution) has led to explosive growth in the last generation, a population quadrupling since 1980. It has changed politically too, from an ideologically centrist base when it was a smaller community, to a strongly Republican base in the last couple of decades.

In 2013, the same Tea Party-Balance North Idaho conflict that roiled Coeur d'Alene inserted itself into city politics at Post Falls as well. As in Coeur d'Alene, the Balance North Idaho forces won across the board, electing among others the city's new mayor, Ron Jacobson.

Mayor	winner			others		
2013	Ron Jacobson	1,365	60.03%	Kerri Thoreson	909	39.97%
2009	Clay Larkin	1,648	75.25%	Steven Degon	288	13.15%
				Matthew Behringer	254	11.60%
2005	Clay Larkin	1,228	100.00%	-	-	-
Cncl 1						
2011	Kerri Thoreson	1,058	59.40%	Joe Bodman	496	27.85%
				Jim Edgington	227	12.75%
Cncl 2						
2013	Alan Wolfe	735	34.00%	Barry Rubin	542	25.07%
				Joe Bodman	454	21.00%
				Jim Hail	431	19.94%
2009	Ronald Jacobson	1,048	51.07%	Keith Hutcheson	1,004	48.93%
2005	Ronald Jacobson	1,182	100.00%	-	-	-
Cncl 3						
2011	Joe Molloy	1,228	69.81%	Scott Grant	531	30.19%
Cncl 4						
2013	Betty Ann Henderson	982	45.85%	Christi Fleischman	595	27.78%
				Jayson Cornwell	565	26.38%
2009	Betty Ann Henderson	1,200	55.66%	Joe Bodman	956	44.34%
2005	Joe Bodman	559	42.19%	Jackie McAvoy	504	38.04%
				Joe Doellefeld	262	19.77%
Cncl 5						
2011	Skip Hissong	1,061	60.87%	Barry Rubin	682	39.13%
Cncl 6						
2013	Linda Wilhelm	1,885	100.00%	-	-	-
2009	Linda Wilhelm	1,291	61.24%	Bob E. Flowers	817	38.76%

Parties

Major parties

As in other states, the two major parties in Idaho are the Republican and the Democratic; nearly everyone elected to partisan office in Idaho above the county level, for generations, has run under one of those banners, though plenty of independent and minor party candidates also have run. (A few independent and minor party candidates have been elected, from time to time, at the county level.)

Party membership in Idaho long has been an informal thing, but the Idaho Republican Party changed that somewhat with its decision in 2010 to require that only voters registering as Republicans – that is, filing a registration form so declaring – could vote in Republican primary elections. Up to that point, Idaho voters at the primary election could choose the primary ballot of any one party to case votes.

The Secretary of State's web site describes the new rules this way:

- *Only registered Republican voters will be allowed to vote in the Republican Primary.*
- *Members of the Democratic, Republican, Constitution or Libertarian Parties and those who do not affiliate with any party will be permitted to vote the Democratic Ballot if they so choose.*
- *Those not registered with a party may do so on election day.*
- *The poll book and registered voter history will reflect which ballot the elector voted.*

Beginning in 2011, a law went into effect that restricts an elector to voting only in the primary election of the political party for which he or she is registered, unless a party notified the Secretary of State in writing that the political party elects to allow additional voters (unaffiliated voters and/or voters registered with another party) to participate in the party's primary election. (See Idaho Code 34-904A.*)*

On November 2, 2011, the Democratic Party exercised the option to open their primary election to include voters not affiliated with the party.

The Republican Party did not exercise the same option. Voting in the Republican Primary election will be limited to party members only.

Therefore, for the 2012 Primary Election, the only electors who can vote on the Republican Ballot are those who have affiliated, including those who affiliate on election day, with the Republican Party. Members of the Democratic, Republican, Constitution or Libertarian Parties and those who do not affiliate with any party will be permitted to vote the Democratic Ballot if they so choose. An elector can vote only one party ballot however, and the poll book and registered voter history will reflect which ballot the elector voted.

PRECINCTS These were the strongest Republican precincts in Idaho in the 2010 general election, using a calculation in the votes for U.S. Senate, governor and superintendent of public instruction – all races featuring active and competing candidates, but with distinctive dynamics.

The chart shows the total ballots cast and those received by the Republican candidates.

	Precinct	Ballots	Crapo	Otter	Luna	R overall
Owyhee	5 Pleasant Valley	53	52	53	49	99.37%
Elmore	Chattin Flats	32	32	30	30	97.85%
Cassia	109 Almo	75	70	69	59	89.13%
Madison	13 *tied	21	18	16	19	88.57%
Latah	Farmington 20 *	20	18	18	17	88.33%
Cassia	114 Heglar-Yale	66	63	58	53	88.29%
Butte	Howe *	147	133	124	119	87.83%
Cassia	125 View	132	126	117	99	87.63%
Cassia	123 Sublett	35	30	30	28	87.25%
Bonneville	57 *	9	8	6	6	86.90%
Power	5 *	89	81	76	67	85.82%
Cassia	118 Oakley 2	246	220	198	200	85.58%
Owyhee	8 Oreana	83	70	68	72	85.38%
Blaine	9 Yale *	9	9	7	7	85.19%
Franklin	Banida-Winder #6	99	82	75	84	84.91%
Fremont	4 Drummond/ Lamont/Squirrel	101	88	84	81	84.89%
Jefferson	Hamer	187	160	154	156	84.68%
Cassia	117 Oakley 1	197	179	159	148	83.92%
Cassia	119 Parsons	47	44	35	35	83.74%
Idaho	6 Fenn	91	84	65	69	83.40%
Valley	Yellow Pine	48	39	37	37	83.11%
Cassia	113 Grandview	243	221	198	177	82.92%
Jefferson	Monteview	146	126	116	115	82.85%
Benewah	8 St. Joe *	37	32	29	29	82.61%
Oneida	Holbrook 6 *	61	53	48	46	82.55%
Owyhee	10 Bruneau	215	172	159	165	82.16%
Elmore	Pine	59	48	47	46	82.00%
Owyhee	7 Murphy	147	129	114	115	81.91%
Jefferson	Terreton	329	294	254	252	81.88%
Washington	7 Midvale	357	302	291	272	81.82%
Oneida	Curlew 5	83	69	67	55	81.56%
Kootenai	6	765	625	606	600	81.55%
Kootenai	2	531	429	416	426	81.32%
Kootenai	64	276	227	215	214	81.28%
Cassia	120 Pella	190	164	152	137	81.19%
Kootenai	13	246	198	197	188	81.19%
Elmore	Prairie	52	42	37	40	80.91%
Oneida	Malad 4	279	238	224	205	80.89%
Cassia	112 Elba	73	67	50	56	80.86%
Gem	13 Ola *	75	62	63	52	80.83%
Kootenai	63	551	443	424	430	80.76%
Cassia	115 Jackson	121	106	96	87	80.53%
Franklin	Dayton #8	242	198	181	186	80.50%
Madison	17	133	123	95	98	80.41%
Franklin	Treas-Riverdale #14	199	160	153	149	80.34%
Fremont	7 Newdale	137	130	105	92	80.31%
Cassia	121 Springdale	335	296	253	241	80.17%
Ada	125	44	39	32	30	80.16%
Gem	10 Brick	418	356	328	308	80.04%
Owyhee	9 Grand View	259	219	196	198	80.00%

These are the "weakest Republican" precincts in Idaho – not strictly the same as the strongest Democratic because of some variance in minor party votes, but very close.

Ada	40	503	145	82	112	22.98%
Ada	59	1015	328	220	232	26.01%
Ada	39	810	266	162	201	26.39%
Bingham	Fort Hall 20	303	124	48	67	27.05%
Ada	37	856	300	175	212	27.40%
Ada	36	723	235	161	190	27.59%
Ada	77	802	270	177	210	27.89%
Clearwater	7 Greer *	28	7	7	10	29.32%
Ada	60	740	271	194	217	31.47%
Ada	35	347	128	101	103	32.66%
Nez Perce	Lapwai 33	305	137	75	77	32.74%
Ada	72	515	199	149	148	32.96%
Bannock	Pocatello 31	291	119	76	87	33.04%
Blaine	7 Hailey #2	508	190	150	156	33.43%
Blaine	1 NW Ketchum	381	152	96	124	33.59%
Bannock	Pocatello 24	233	102	60	72	34.19%
Blaine	2 SW Ketchum	368	131	112	122	34.25%
Latah	Moscow 15	497	186	146	165	34.38%
Latah	Moscow 16	277	99	84	94	34.76%
Blaine	6 Hailey #1	340	146	93	110	35.13%
Shoshone	2 Mullan	250	81	86	79	35.29%
Latah	Moscow 6	322	125	99	112	35.70%
Bannock	Chubbuck 60	348	154	102	106	36.00%
Blaine	14 Hailey #4	738	309	225	252	36.17%
Latah	Moscow 13	309	125	100	101	36.55%
Bannock	Pocatello 6	261	107	82	89	36.58%
Ada	86	459	193	140	154	36.69%
Ada	85	846	378	255	286	36.88%
Bannock	Pocatello 26	242	109	77	81	37.44%
Bannock	Pocatello 8	226	102	63	83	37.56%
Ada	58	338	135	118	123	37.94%
Latah	Moscow 10	438	185	139	158	37.95%
Ada	38	901	436	280	293	37.98%
Ada	76	792	363	264	251	37.98%
Latah	Moscow 14	367	146	123	129	38.21%
Ada	69	546	249	185	184	38.27%
Bannock	Pocatello 4	403	180	130	142	38.28%
Latah	Moscow 11	422	167	133	163	38.80%
Ada	70	457	208	156	161	39.08%
Ada	41	1119	543	345	400	39.12%
Blaine	5 NE Blaine Co	259	111	79	106	39.20%
Ada	34	570	269	198	197	39.41%
Ada	73	894	445	288	317	39.84%
Bannock	Absentee 30	1348	601	489	492	39.85%
Blaine	8 Hailey #3	519	231	176	200	39.95%
Ada	75	296	140	103	102	40.58%
Teton	Absentee	1257	562	439	488	40.66%
Ada	100	796	378	274	303	40.83%
Ada	33	847	390	303	356	41.96%
Ada	84	594	312	206	217	42.00%

Beyond the majors

Apart from the two major parties, two others are listed on the state's "Political Party Affiliation Declaration Form" – Constitution and Libertarian.

Those parties and others have fielded candidates for Idaho office over the years, though they seldom receive more than about 5% of the vote (except in cases where the Republican or Democratic party fails to file a candidate, in which case minor party votes of 30% or even more are not unusual).

In 2010, the Constitution Party filed for U.S. Senate (Randy Lynn Bergquist, 3.9%) and lieutenant governor (Paul Venable, 5%). The Libertarian Party filed for the 1st District U.S., House seat (Mike Washburn, 1.9%) and governor (Ted Dunlap, 1.3%). Both also filed for a number of legislative and other offices.

In 2008, the Libertarian Party filed for U.S. Senate (Ken Marmon, 1.5%), but that was the only minor party filing for a major Idaho office.

Reading

The basic reference on Idaho government, and much more, is the Idaho Blue Book, published biennially by the Idaho Secretary of State's office. It should be on every Idahoan's book shelf.

Ridenbaugh Press has published a series of books, written by the author of this book, on Idaho government and politics. *Paradox Politics* (1988) was a history of Idaho politics focusing on the half-century before its publication; a second edition with updating notes was published in 2009. For detailed political review, the *Idaho Political Almanacs* of 1990, 1992, 1994 and 1996, and the *Idaho Yearbook/Directory* volumes for 1998, 199, 2000 and 2001 are recommended.

A string of useful memoirs and biographies on Idaho political figures – including Robert Smylie, Cecil Andrus, James McClure, Frank Church, Phil Batt, Pete Cenarrusa, Don Samuelson, and others, have emerged in recent years, and these are all well worth review.

Here is some additional reading on Idaho.

Carl Biachi (editor), *Justice for the Times*, Idaho Law Foundation (1990).

Dennis Colson, *Idaho's Constitition: The Tie That Binds*, University of Idaho Press (1991).

Cort Conley, *Idaho for the Curious*, Backeddy Books (1982).

Ronald Limbaugh, *Rocky Mountain Carpetbaggers*, University of Idaho Press (1982).

J. Anthony Lukas, *Big Trouble*, Simon and Schuster, 1997.

Boyd Martin, *Idaho Voting Trends 1890-1974*, University of Idaho (1974).

Carlos Schwantes, In Mountain Shadows: A History of Idaho, University of Nebraska Press (1991).

Susan Stacy (editor), *Conversations*, Idaho Public Broadcasting (1990).

Randy Stapilus, *It Happened in Idaho*, Globe-Pequot Press (2001, 2010).

Perry Swisher, *The Day Before Idaho*, News Review Publishing, 1995.

James Weatherby and Randy Stapilus, *Governing Idaho: Politics, People and Power*, Caxton Press (2005).

RANDY STAPILUS has been researching and writing about Northwest politics for 40 years for newspapers, broadcast, reference books and online. He has reported about Idaho politics for newspapers in Boise, Pocatello, Nampa, Lewiston, Caldwell, and Coeur d'Alene. His weekly column on Idaho politics runs in daily newspapers around the state. He is editor and publisher at Ridenbaugh Press, and edits the *Idaho Weekly Briefing*. He and his wife Linda live in Carlton, Oregon.

MARTY TRILLHAASE is an Idaho native who graduated from the University of Idaho in 1979 and has been fortunate enough to work as a newspaper writer in every corner of the state, including the *Twin Falls Times-News*, the *Idaho Statesman*, the *Idahonian* (now the *Moscow-Pullman Daily News*) and the *Post Register* of Idaho Falls. At present, he is the editorial page editor at the *Lewiston Tribune*. Trillhaase, his wife Karen and daughter Sara live in Lewiston.

www.ingramcontent.com/pod-product-compliance
Lightning Source LLC
Chambersburg PA
CBHW062048270326
41931CB00013B/2987